magical highs

alvin lee & me

a Sixties

woodstock

memoir

loraine burgon

A catalogue record for this book is available from the British Library.
Cover photo: 1971 In the Woods at Robin Hood Barn, Loraine and Alvin playing air guitar.
Photo credit Ruth Casterton.

contents

contents

**For F, S, J and W.
with peace and love.**

Out beyond ideas of wrongdoing and rightdoing,
There is a field. I'll meet you there.
When the soul lies down in that grass,
The world is too full to talk about.
Ideas, language, even the phrase 'each other'
Doesn't make any sense.

Jalaluddin Rumi

chapter 1
Heidi

Rock'n'roll as we now know it did not exist when I was born on November 10, 1946, in Nottingham, a city in the middle of England. Rock'n'roll was as embryonic as I was before my arrival on a Sunday evening, at 10.30 pm, weighing ten and a half pounds, 10 days later than my due date. Yes, 10s surrounded my birth.

My parents were publicans and the pub they ran in the centre of Nottingham, on Mansfield Road, was called The Rose of England. It was our home and I was born there on the second floor. The Rose was an imposing Victorian Gothic revival building whose architect Watson Fothergill was responsible for many wonderful buildings around Nottingham, some of which were sadly demolished in the Brutalist architectural era of the sixties. The Rose of England avoided the wrecking ball and today is a Grade II listed building with a preservation order.

Alvin Lee, as we would come to know him, did not exist when I was born, though Graham Anthony Barnes was born almost two years earlier, two and a half miles across town on December 19, 1944. It wouldn't be until his teens that he became Alvin Lee, his chosen stage name.

"Why Alvin Lee?" I asked him in 1963, when we were first together.

"It was as close as I could get to Elvis Presley... Alvin Lee!" he replied, adding, with emphasis on the syllables, "El - vis Pres - lee, Al - vin Lee, without being obvious."

Well, all young guys at that time wanted to be Elvis. Not long ago I watched an interview with Bob Dylan on YouTube. "I wanted to be Elvis, everyone did," he said. All The Beatles wanted to be Elvis, and Alvin Lee seemed a perfect choice to me. Later in his life he would claim his membership of The Elvis Fan Club was about guitarist Scotty Moore, not Elvis.

Early pictures of Alvin with his blond quiff, duck's arse hairdo, jeans, bomber jackets, black leather Cuban heeled ankle-boots, just as he looked when we met, show that Elvis was his stylist. It was a great look, nothing like the typical young Nottingham guys in their dark, single-breasted, Italian pinstriped suits, skinny ties with matching imitation hankie (on a piece of cardboard) in their breast pockets and black pointed winkle-pickers. He stood out, walked his own path, relaxed, confident, seemingly clearly focused. He was a charismatic teenager.

It was this Elvis Presley/Scotty Moore dichotomy that Alvin struggled with throughout Ten Years After's huge success, especially after the *Woodstock* movie gave his full-screen, beautiful face, the pop star fame of an Elvis. His heart and soul were in the extraordinary virtuosity he expressed through his guitar, the cherry red Gibson ES 335 he called "Big Red" and played into outer space. Alvin had all the talent, musicality, looks and attributes to find a perfect fit in the times in which he lived. It should have been obvious to everyone from his mid-teens and today it would have been spotted very early. However, rock'n'roll music was a frontier in early stages of exploration, not yet a country with its own territories, government, history or a map to plan your route to lifelong success. Alvin was a British pioneer of this new frontier.

When we met we were both teenagers living with our parents, in Nottingham and, until 1966, when we lived together in London, he was Graham to me. I have photos, postcards and even a cookery book (unused) dedicated to me and signed Graham. We met in November 1963 and were together until September 1973, close to ten years; from living at home with our parents in Nottingham to living in a huge, half-timbered Tudor mansion in the Oxfordshire countryside, 50 acres of which we owned. It's hard to believe it was possible for such a journey to happen. It certainly wasn't a trajectory we expected, imagined or even dared to dream back in Nottingham in 1963.

In March 2013, nearly 50 years later, Alvin passed, suddenly, unexpectedly. It was the worst day of my life. At the moment I was told he had died, I experienced a devastating pain in my chest and guts, as if a hand had reached in and torn out the centre of my soul. It was an immediate physical reaction of such force, such intensity that I was numb. Does it sound ridiculous to say, it never crossed my mind that I would be alive and Alvin would not, not on this earth? He had been at the centre of my life for 50 years, since I was 16 years old. Yes, it was 40 years since we had lived in that Tudor mansion together, but the connection between us was never lost, never completely broken.

In 2014, the year after Alvin's death, I was still struggling with regrets and if onlys and why hadn't I said this or shared that with him. And how could I get through the rest of my life, ameliorating the tragedies and accepting that this was the life we lived, that we were never destined to be in the last reel of the movie together, even though there was a time when I was so certain that we would be?

Nottingham and the start of everything was decades past. I left my home town in 1965, and now lived nearly 200 miles away after living in London and a dozen or more other addresses around the South of England.

Along the main road where I currently live, in Whitstable on the North Kent coast, is a row of shops. There is an excellent bakery and a number of charity shops amidst the small supermarket, greengrocer, butcher, florist, barbers, cobbler, dog groomers, toy shop, hairdresser, small gift shops, funeral parlour, car garage, small gym, and typical English tea-shops and take-away restaurants. It is an unremarkable, suburban shopping street and it's been like this for a hundred years or more. It runs parallel with the road along the sea front, which slopes down to the sea, where 500 beach huts nestle, and seagulls hover and swoop, navigating North Sea winds that are often quite brutal in winter. The housing and a 50-bedroom hotel on that seafront road are all good quality and of mixed vintage. In the UK, living on the coast with a sea view doubles or triples the value of your property. It is a favourite dog walking spot, with five stars on Trip Advisor. I love living so close to the sea and try to walk by it every day, or at least drive along the sea-front road when the rain, sleet, snow or winds make walking impossible. Apart from the close proximity of this amazing, ever-changing sea front, it is quite ordinary.

The nearest charity shop to me is a local RSPCA (Royal Society for the Prevention of Cruelty to Animals) shop, about 100 yards from my home. I think it's a magic shop. In late 2006 I spent three weeks in the USA, travelling through five West Coast states, casually looking without success for a pair of deep-red leather trainers. I returned home and, walking past the door of the RSPCA shop, glanced in and spotted on a shoe rack the perfect, barely-worn pair of deep red leather Reebok trainers I'd been looking for, perfect colour, perfect fit, perfect money. I wore them out and they endeared me to my magic RSPCA shop.

There's more. Sometime in 2012, I had gone for a walk by the sea with the seagulls, and on to the bakers to collect my weekly loaf. Walking back past the RSPCA shop something in the window caught my eye, a jacket, a skirt, a shirt. I don't actually remember but It looked like it might fit, so I took it into the back of the shop where there was a mirror and a little privacy to try on clothes for fit and look. Did I buy it? Did it suit? I have no memory of that but as I was walking back to the front of the shop I spotted the spine of a book.

Now I don't generally buy books or look at them in charity shops, but the spine of this book, quite low down on the shelves, seemed familiar and I took it off the shelf to examine it more closely. It was a copy of a book from my childhood, and the same edition: *Heidi*, by Johanna Spyri, with drawings by Janet & Anne Johnstone, published by The Heirloom Library London. Set in Switzerland, it was the illustrations of Heidi and her friends, brightly coloured, quaint images that I loved as a child: Heidi, in the mountains, with Peter the goatherd and the goats; Heidi with her friend Clara and Grandad Nunky with whom she lived in the mountains in a log cabin; and, most especially, Heidi dressed up to visit grandmamma, in her little red ankle boots, an item of clothing always in my own wardrobe. For a girl growing up in the grey, East Midland industrial city of Nottingham, Heidi was special.

Smiling at the memories, I thumbed through the book and those illustrations. They took me straight down a time tube. Whoever had owned this book had even coloured in a charming black and white picture of Heidi in her peasant girl outfit, standing in a meadow, with gaudy wax crayons, not very neatly, just as I had done.

Well it was very cheap, old and well-used, quite scruffy, so of course I had to buy it. I thought when I got the chance I would read it again and see if the story might reconnect me with young Loraine. So, it came home with me and sat on a bookshelf and was forgotten, barely hovering on the bottom of my to-do list. In March 2013, Alvin died. In May 2013 my mother died, aged 96, after fading away gradually and quite gently. I hope I have inherited her longevity genes.

Christmas 2013 was spent in Switzerland, in the mountains at Wildhaus, with my son, daughter-in-law, two grandsons and extended family members. My daughter-in-law's brother had married into a lovely Swiss family and this Christmas gathering was arranged to celebrate the arrival of their baby son. About 25 of us, Americans, Swiss, English, Scots all enjoyed the mountains, the snow, the sledging, the babies, the cooking of traditional dishes to share. It was a wonderful week, plenty of youngsters, laughter, Christmas silliness and very healing for me after my losses. I had only been to Switzerland once before, to the Montreux Jazz Festival when Ten Years After played there in 1971.

Back home, in the New Year 2014, I decided to read *Heidi* while the joy and memories of the Swiss mountain Christmas, Heidi's world, was still around me. And read it I did, quite enthusiastically to start with and then after a while I realised it was a classic morality tale, centred around the little angelic Heidi. It was perfectly suitable for a girl under 10 years old, but for a woman in her late sixties was unlikely to challenge her political, or critical, awareness. Shame, never mind. I read a few pages in bed, my habit before I nod off. *Heidi* sent me to sleep quite soon but I was determined to finish it. I always do.

In September 2014, my dear friend Troy, whom I had known since 1991 when we were neighbours in a small Sussex village, came to visit with her newly married husband Kevin. Troy and I talked nonstop and, naturally, my recent Swiss Christmas was discussed. This led to *Heidi*. I fetched it from the bookshelf by my bed and as I thumbed through the book a page dropped open between the inside of the jacket and the frontispiece.

On it there was an ink inscription, scrawled, misspelt, crossed out, scrawled again and blobbed: "If This Book shou" (crossed through) and underneath on two lines, "This Book Bolongs (spelling error) to… Loraine Burgon" the n in Burgon dropping away to the right. My mind did something very strange. It seemed to spin, travel into dozens of recesses, then freeze and become blank. This was *my* book, my own book that I had last seen 200 miles away in Nottingham in the pub where I lived before leaving home in 1965. It was totally inexplicable.

Troy was looking at me curiously. It was the first time I had stopped talking.

"What is it?" she asked.

I showed her the hidden page, the page I hadn't stumbled on before when I had looked through it, or been reading it, during the two years it had been in my possession.

"It's my book, it is my book, how can that be? I bought it down the road, how did it get there from Nottingham?"

"Are you sure you haven't had it all these years?" Troy asked, probing my memory, trying to find a logical explanation.

"I'm certain. I've moved so many times, it's been 55 years. I would remember packing and unpacking it. Plus, I didn't take anything like this from my childhood when I left home, only clothes and records."

Kevin had noticed our change of mood and was now becoming curious. He took a stab at another possibility. "Might it have been in your mother's items that you brought here after she died?"

"No." I was definite. "All I brought were family photos and a small amount of costume jewelry. Besides she had always got rid of anything that she didn't have a use for every time she moved. She had moved from the pub, where I had left this book in 1965, sometime in 1975 the year after my father died and she moved a further half dozen more times before she died."

Later, when we had said goodnight and gone off to our beds, still marveling at the odds of me finding this book again, I sat quietly in my room holding my *Heidi* book, casually bought for childhood memories but now the most precious, mysterious object I owned.

Where, how and why finally gave way to the realization that this extraordinary happenstance proved to me that all the steps, places, people, experiences of my life, everything that had led me here to this place and time, were unavoidably meant to be. The realization made me gently weep. I was meant to leave Alvin, my perfect soul mate. It wasn't my biggest stupid mistake.

chapter 2
Found and Lost

Thanks to modern technology and the internet, during the last 10 years of his life, Alvin and I became increasingly close and open with each other again, sharing both memories and present-day interests. The mail account on my Mac was my "Alvin" email. If there was a red notification it was mainly from Alvin and I was always happy to see it there. For several years he scanned slides and sent me photos that he'd taken when we were together, mostly of me and sometimes the two of us, on the road in Europe, Scandinavia and America and in the various homes we shared.

I did the same, scanning and sending my collection of photos from when we were together, and the different homes in which we had lived. His were taken on his 35mm Nikon, extremely good quality. Alvin took photography seriously and told me he wished he'd taken more photos of people instead of places. Many are from our favourite home, Robin Hood Barn, taken with the fisheye lens he bought in Japan in 1972. I only had a compact camera, but some of my favourite photos of the two of us were taken with it.

During those later years we often discussed "the book" that needed to be written. It became an ongoing conversation and I would encourage him to write. Sometimes he said he would "go off and write about something", after we had been reminiscing on the phone. After all, what we had lived through was so fantastic that "someone should write about it".

From 1967 to 1973, under the pseudonym, Vicky Page, I had created and run the Ten Years After Music Lovers Society which involved some writing about touring and compiling the fan club magazine, *The Palantir*. In 1998 I went to art school. Having done little serious writing since, the essays and final dissertation were quite a challenge but fascinating all the same. After graduating in 2001 with a 2:1 BA (Hons) Fine Art degree from the Kent Institute of Art & Design, I could handle 12,000 words and use a computer.

I had joined the modern world, and it dawned on me that I could write the fantastic story that "should be written about".

Life intervened. Over the next seven years I established an art practice and built a small studio where I held a couple of shows. I also visited Alvin and his partner Evi in Spain several times, and saw him on tour in the UK with Edgar Winter. Being with Alvin always rekindled the strong connection that we had forged and maintained since the sixties. We would talk easily and at great length, joke and laugh about the times we shared, often about our psychedelic adventures, oblivious to anyone else there. After a visit I would experience a deep, empty sadness and a strong sense of unfinished business.

In October 2008, my son and his wife left the UK, and moved to San Francisco. I visited them for their first Christmas in the USA. For part of the visit, I took off by Amtrak on a long-desired trip to Marfa, a small but very interesting arts town located on a desert plateau, at 5,000 ft, in the Chihuahua desert of South West Texas. Staying there alone in a small house, with a large notepad and no distractions I started to write. The words came easily.

I'm sure it helped being in America. San Francisco unlocked so many memories of 1968-1973. It was a city Alvin really loved, along with New York, Boston and New Orleans, all cities where a day off would be scheduled when TYA toured the US. We loved to explore San Francisco's record and music stores, book stores and thrift shops for unique clothes. We saw *Barbarella* and *Zabriskie Point* at a cinema in San Francisco. Most of all we loved to walk together down its streets with the beautiful young hippy tribes, flashing peace signs, all smiling unspoken greetings, twinkling and full of hope, believing that love would soon end all wars and bring peace to the world.

"Being in space is like being someplace magic," said Col. Pamela Ann Melroy of the US Air Force, the second female astronaut to command a shuttle mission. I belong to a generation sometimes affectionately referred to as "space cadets", who journeyed to inner space. Some made the odd day trip or orbited the planet only a few times but many metaphorically walked on the moon. The innocence of the sixties was a reality, we were pulled along by an invisible force, believing ourselves free thinkers, originals, individuals. Yes, we were rewriting many social ideas and rules but it was a collective venture. We still wanted to fit in, to be part of a community. It was an era of consciousness expansion, that would spawn the ecological, green and whole earth movements of today. The liberalisation of society, increased tolerance for differences of all kinds, sexual, racial, fiscal. Whether people were physically or mentally challenged? None of this mattered in the great idealism of "turn on, tune in and drop out".

What exactly were we dropping out from? The "straight" world? The world of differences, competition, aggression? The world that had managed, in half a century, to fight World War One and World War Two? And last but not least the Atom Bomb, Hydrogen Bomb and Cold War? We baby boomers grew up expecting annihilation. How could it be otherwise? We were a scared generation, we were expected to be fearful, it was encouraged. Yet we managed to liberate ourselves from fear and embrace a new community idea, Peace and Love. Maybe the fear was a catalyst? Born in 1946, someone once told me I was born in the first year of peace. That made me smile. When I was a child, peace wasn't heard as often as war.

In Marfa, at the start of seriously writing and trawling those old magical highs for "the book", there was New Year's Eve. I stepped outside as the clock struck midnight, gazed up at the clear West Texas desert sky where the Milky Way was dripping over me, and saw my first shooting star of 2009. An auspicious augury. For two years I researched and filed, made notes and organised and typed and constructed a 30-chapter synopsis and completed a half dozen full chapters. I emailed Alvin from Texas and told him that I was in magic Marfa starting to write "the book". I gave it a working title "Rock 'n' roll, Drugs and Sex", which seemed the correct order of importance, though I doubted it would be the final title.

From early 2009, back in the UK I continued writing and transferring ideas onto the computer. My dreams were exceptional, full of the past and Alvin. Waking would bring more memories to write down. My mind was exploding with being allowed the freedom to trawl back to those happy days. We talked on the phone a number of times, and discussed our shared memories. Afterwards he would email to say how many memories were triggered for him too, and thanks for the re-boot. He was concerned how I would write about him, if I would say "mean stuff" or "too personal stuff". I said that our time together was so special and my memories were full of joy. I hoped to be able to let people know what extraordinary times we lived through, what a truly unexpected adventure it had been. My only anxiety was that it would become a hagiography.

From February 2009 Alvin started to send scanned photos of me from his extensive (30,000) slide collection, taken on his Nikon cameras, which was an elaborate task. In return I scanned and sent my photos of him from Nottingham, London and some on tour. I had moved from stills to taking Super 8 movies, and can see the camera bag on my shoulder in many of his pictures of me. We planned that I would pick those up from him at some time, rather than risk them to the Spanish post. He was also using a movie camera, a 16mm Bolex. Somewhere there are extraordinary movies and I hope one day they will be found.

Throughout 2009 our emails with attachments went back and forth with so many surprises for us both. Opening the emails I saw stunning pictures of my young self, alone in my private space. Many had been taken without my knowing, from behind or in profile. They were such tender images, beautifully framed with light falling on me, shot with love. I felt overwhelmed to see these and realise the full depth of his feelings, four decades before.

I emailed lengthy commentaries on the images. He loved the feedback and complimented my artist's eye. Despite the fact that I remained in love with him, and those emotions had now intensified, I wrote to him only as a friend in case Evi would also be reading what I said. To have lost my connection with him again now, had Evi objected, would have been intolerable. On December 5, 2009, he wrote: "Last of the photos I'm afraid, kinda sad, it's been fun," and the following year we started to share links on YouTube, music, arts, photos.

One day Alvin sent me an email with a link. I opened it and recognised his blues guitar but not the melodic tune that emerged. It was 'The Bluest Blues'. I had never heard it and knew that the story of our greatest heartbreak had been turned into something bleakly wonderful. I wept as I read the comments underneath, seeing how hundreds of thousands of people had been moved by it. One woman wrote, "When I go to heaven I want this to be playing." I emailed, telling him how stunning it was and, the next time we spoke on the phone, directly asked him if it was written about me. "You crossed my mind a couple of times," was all he said.

Our last phone call was several hours long and covered such a lot, but never once did he mention his health problems. We parted saying we must talk more often. "Every three months, give me a nudge to call," he said.

During the winter of 2012 I was painting canvases for a show at the Horsebridge Gallery, Whitstable, where I'd exhibited before. The show ran from February 20-26 and was called "Head In The Clouds". On the last day I sat alone looking at a painting called Jonathan L S. The bottom right-hand clouds seemed to show a profile of a man which, as I looked, shifted through into a profile of a sleeping or dead man. It was so clear to me and I could not shake off the transformed image. I went up to the Horsebridge cafe on the first floor and as I came out I was accosted by a man, maybe in his fifties.

"Excuse me," he said. "Were you Alvin Lee's wife?"

This had never ever happened before in all those decades and I was taken aback. "No, we were never married, but I was with him. Would you like to see my paintings?" I asked.

I don't know who he was. We went back downstairs to my show and I deliberately talked about my paintings but not about Alvin. In my head I was confused. It had unnerved me but I wasn't sure why. The show was finished and taken down, sold paintings were wrapped and delivered and a week can go by so quickly. Before the show Alvin and I had been exchanging emails about an acid trip we had taken in the Bronx Zoo in 1970. A comment I made about it had sparked a strange, adverse reaction from him and I wanted to get an email back about it. There is always so much time to do things until the day there isn't.

Back in my part-time, pay-the-bills job as receptionist in a Canterbury Hotel on Wednesday March 6, 2013, an odd text from a friend arrived on my mobile. "So sorry to hear about Alvin, thinking of you." What did it mean? What could have happened to him? I thought, perhaps an accident. I didn't respond.

My hotel manager looked online, on Google. "Nothing there," he said.

He was lying to protect me, people are so kind.

"Go home," he said. I was in a daze but also in denial of the one thing that should have been obvious.

"Yes, I will, thanks Simon."

I never answer my mobile when I drive and it rang a number of times. Goodness, what could have happened? I was convinced it was an accident. His health was nowhere on my mind. A half hour later I was home, alone. I rang my oldest friend, Johnnie Clifton, who had first introduced me to Alvin, on November 5, 1963. It was Johnnie who had been calling my mobile.

"Hey Johnnie, you called me, what's happening?"

Dear, dear Johnnie his voice was low and calm, gentle and deliberate.

"Loraine," he paused, took a breath, "Alvin is dead."

An unseen hand reached into my chest and pulled out my heart and my guts, an appalling wrenching sensation like I had never experienced before. Maybe I screamed, groaned. I don't remember. Just a hollow dark frozen feeling and tears, weeping in disbelief.

"Oh! Johnnie, No! No! No! What happened?"

Johnnie told me Alvin had died in hospital that morning following straightforward heart surgery. I could not take in what he was saying.

We talked for a while more. I said I would call Evi, call the house, try to find out more.

Evi answered. "Oh Loraine, I knew I would forget someone."

She had been calling people all day and was obviously tired, but offered more detail. The heart operation was a routine surgery. It was supposed to give him ten more good years. They decided to go ahead. It was elective surgery. He was anxious the night before and they travelled by train to Madrid for the operation. The surgeon was the top Spanish heart surgeon. He had operated on the King of Spain.

During the operation he had come out and told Evi they had discovered Alvin's heart was worse than they expected. They felt they were losing him. They did get him through the operation, but Alvin died in intensive care after suffering two heart attacks. Those are the details I remember. I offered Evi my sympathies. "Oh! I will be fine," she said. "I have my cats."

I knew then that she was in deep shock and just functioning on automatic. How could it be otherwise?

Alvin had told me many times, over the years, that he had always thought he would have some kind of rock'n'roll death, that he had not expected to live beyond 30, and hadn't wanted to become old. He was not enjoying aging which he described as "a bad joke". He was 68.

There were strange surreal conversations over the next few days, dear friends calling to offer support. Johnnie and I wanted to go to Spain for his funeral but were told it was just his partners, Evi and Suzanne and his daughter, Jasmine, and it would be soon, that weekend sometime and not to go. I was in such a numb state I had no fight in me to insist, though I thought Johnnie and I, his dear old friends, should have been able to say goodbye. I still think that.

I was glad to learn from his obituary that he and Evi were married; I knew in Spain the property laws are draconian. I liked Evi and was pleased that in her grief she would not have to deal with Spanish law. Over the coming weeks and months good people came back into my life, some of whom I'd had no contact with for four decades, musicians and friends, many who had wondered all those years about me. It was very moving. Chris Wright, Alvin's manager, somehow found an email for me and sent his deep sympathies. "You were the first person I thought of when I heard Alvin had died," he wrote. Overwhelmingly my confusion boiled down to a small, sad dark point. How was I still alive and on Earth when Alvin was not?

In May 2013, my 96-year-old mother died of old age, as it says on her death certificate. She left gradually and quite peacefully, losing weight, losing her powers, losing her muscles, her appetite, speech and finally her breath, such a contrast to Alvin's rapid traumatic exit. I had not told her that Alvin died in March. She was still very bright and I couldn't trust how she might respond, that what she would say might give me more unnecessary pain. She had told me quite recently, "I never ever liked Alvin." I didn't need to hear more of her nonsense.

In mid-June I was back in San Francisco with my son and daughter-in-law, and first magical grandson, born 2010. A new baby was due and I was delighted to have been asked to visit and help out with number one grandson, now three years old, while number two baby was born. It was a very healing trip, love really is the answer when we have been broken. Grandson number two arrived two weeks late on July 9, 2013, my brother Harold's 63rd birthday, cementing the links between the generations of people I love.

2013 had produced the very worst and best events. Without Alvin and without my mother I felt orphaned, which as well as bringing grief also brings a subtle awareness of freedom. When my thoughts returned to "the book", I knew for certain I had to complete the task. Only Alvin or I could write it, bring together all the experiences, the adventures. Now he had left me behind to finish the project. Before I thought he would read it and I had always wanted his approval. Now who was I writing for?

In an email from Alvin dated February 6, 2009, when I was in Marfa, Texas, he had cautioned me not to write about childhood and schools. "Unless you are a really good writer the early years and schooldays etc. can be quite uninteresting to other people," he wrote. "Even Stephen Fry has a hard time keeping your attention with his Public-School stories. Just my opinion you understand, but worth thinking about."

That said, I always want to know how and where the adventure began; the place, the times, the culture, the background, the characters, once upon a time.

chapter 3
Nottingham Childhoods

Alvin and I were both born and raised in Nottingham in the UK's East Midlands, albeit in quite different circumstances. Famous as the home of Raleigh cycles, Boots the Chemist and Players cigarettes, it is 130 miles north of London with a population of around 300,000. There was plenty of light factory work which famously attracted young women and after I left the town I was often asked, "Are there really 14 women for every man?" or "Don't all the pretty girls come from Nottingham?" Neither was true, but both were quite positive urban myths that helped to attract working age men to the town.

Growing up in the fifties I had a sense that the working population was proud of Raleigh, Boots and Players, and also the lace and textile manufacturers. This was not only a job to pay the bills, Nottingham was thriving and people who had just lived through the wretchedness of World War II were aspiring to build better lives for their families.

Nottingham was a city proud of its heritage and standing in the country. Did I mention Robin Hood? Perhaps he had something to do with it. He had robbed from the rich and distributed his ill-gotten gains to the poor. Wherever I have travelled all over the world people have heard of Robin Hood, despite the doubtful facts of his actual existence. He didn't really fit in with the general culture and ethos of the city I knew, perhaps his legend had opened a small seam of rebellion that survived the centuries and helped to create a number of famous writers: Lord Byron, D H Lawrence and Alan Sillitoe, all rebels in their own way.

Like most people, my childhood was formed more by my parents and two older brothers than Nottingham itself. I was born in 1946 in the very centre of the town, in the pub run by my mum and dad, where working people, locals and passers-by came to drink and socialise. The Rose Of England was a large old Victorian Gothic Revival building in the ornate, fantasy-style loved by local architect Watson Fothergill, purpose built in 1898 and, since July 12, 1972, a Grade II listed building, which cannot be demolished.   What is a pub? A pub or public house, is a premises whose landlord/landlady is licensed by the local council to sell alcohol. It is a traditional British social centre for the local community to meet, drink and be merry.
It was also our home.

Two of my brothers, Barry, born in 1936, and Graham, in 1938, were considerably older than me, while Harold, who arrived in 1950, was younger, so there was a huge divide between the pre-war and post-war Burgon children. Alvin was also the third child in his family with two elder sisters, Irma and Janice, also born pre-war. I'm not sure the Barnes family has such a gap, since Doris and Sam, his parents, were very liberal.

If you lived through WWII as a child, you would have heard the rantings of Hitler, the stirring patriotic speeches by Churchill, and experienced the city's air raid sirens and bombings. However, for us postwar children, it was the stories we heard, of air raids or of the family members lost, among them my mother's beloved only brother Harold, who did not come home. The shadow of World War II, the Atomic Age and the Cold War created a fear-filled cultural environment in which children grew up. It was a black and white world, where good and, more especially, evil couldn't be hidden from curious young minds. Apocalyptic scenarios were not considered far-fetched. I believe this created an overwhelming desire for change, as evidenced by the relief and enthusiasm with which we would embrace 'Peace & Love', in California in the late sixties.

Alvin and I were still only teenagers, big kids really, just 16 and 18 when we met, and we didn't talk much about our childhoods. That's how it is when you're young, excited about the future. You live in the present. We were both still living at home with our own parents, which created logistical problems for intimacy. That preoccupied us more than what our childhoods had been like, but the truth is we hadn't really left them behind us, not yet.

When we met, Alvin was living in the childhood home where he was born with Doris and Sam Barnes, his mum and dad. It was a warm and welcoming family home, set on a suburban side road, a three-bedroom semi-detached bungalow on an estate, rented from the council.

It was set back from the road on a plot, with a large, pretty, lawned back garden, at the bottom of which Sam had a shed.

For Doris the shed was an eyesore that she endlessly tried to hide behind plants and shrubs, a good-natured source of domestic dispute. Sam would happily spend hours "pottering" and repairing, mostly with a "fag" (cigarette!) dangling on his lip. He was lovely in every way, a relaxed and caring man who adored his family and was content in himself.

Irma told me a story from when she and Janice were young. "One evening, when Sam had come in from work and was sitting at the table waiting for his dinner, Doris came in with his meal on a tray. Somehow, she dropped the tray on the floor, the dinner plate staying perfectly as it had been with all the dinner intact. Janice and I looked at one another and were a little nervous of what would happen next. Sam, however, got up, took his knife and fork and sat crossed legged on the floor and, without a word, proceeded to eat his dinner from the tray on the floor." He was a man ahead of his time. That story tells us so many things about him.

Thanks to Doris, Alvin's home was always open and welcoming to his mates and to me. Alvin's elder sisters, Irma and Janice, had long left home and Doris was using their bedroom as a hairdressing salon, working from home, cutting and perming local ladies of all ages, which added to the hustle and bustle. Open-hearted, fun and relaxed, she would feed you if you were there at mealtimes, including you in everything that took place in her colourful, tidy home.

She adored Alvin, and he adored Doris. They were always very close. She sewed and would make him interesting clothes and no doubt customised his jeans in the late fifties, when shop bought fashion was still well behind the images of "cool" coming out of America. The rich blue, rayon velvet jacket, with zip and embroidered braid front, knitted collar, cuffs and hip band, which he wore in many early images, his firm favourite, was made by Doris. She massaged his back, which gave him problems even in his teens due to the guitar strap slung across it, the weight carried on one shoulder. I daresay this is a common complaint to guitarists. Seamstress and masseur were two of the positions in Alvin's life that I would take over from Doris once we were living together, as well as housekeeper and cook.

Sam and Doris were completely accepting of me. Doris never gave me any sense that I was not the right person for him to be with, nor was she jealous of my relationship with her son. From my experience as a mother of a married son, I know there is a shift that happens, when we see that this boy, whom we raised, loved unconditionally and who loved us intensely, falling for another woman.

The Barnes home and home life, good humour, interesting conversations and, especially, their fondness of music, lack of stress and sense of inclusion was endlessly fascinating to me. Living in a pub was totally different from a typical family life. I might as well have come from the moon.

We were not neglected, we were well fed, clothed, schooled and given great toys and most of what we asked for. What we were not given was a real, family home life in any way resembling what I found at Alvin's. It was wonderfully overwhelming.

A pub as a home is a very stressful environment. The business side, the bars, the entertainment, food, cellars, toilets and everything connected with the needs and pleasures of your customers take precedence over everything else. Our home life and living accommodation was separate, above the pub itself, but meals and the needs of the family had to fit in around the business, which ran relentlessly in the background seven days a week. Likewise, parenting was fitted in while mum and dad, as landlord or landlady, were performers in the hospitality industry, first and foremost.

We kids became emotionally and physically independent very young and, when I was very small I was blessed to have Barry and Graham to take on some of the parenting.

Here's another coincidence. My nurturing and loving older brother Graham, who played such a major part in my childhood, was born on December 19, 1938 – six years to the day before Graham, aka Alvin, was born into his loving and nurturing family on December 19, 1944.

chapter 4
Parental Influences

The more I got to know Graham, the more I realized that the musical family environment created by his family was essential to his life. Sam was not only his father in all the loving and practical aspects, he was truly his first musical mentor. I wish I could tell you when and why Sam had become such a lover and collector of black Mississippi Delta blues and black prison work songs.

In 1963 a radiogram sat in the lounge where Sam's records were played. Both he and Doris would pick up acoustic guitars and, with Graham, play and sing, producing fine harmonies. Sam had a tremendously rich bass voice, great phrasing and a relaxed, soulful delivery. Doris too had a rich voice, harmonising with confidence. They played together for fun, amateurs who loved music with no motivation beyond the joy it brought. They surrounded their growing son with a most unusual musical environment, music that was far removed from the pop music of the day. Janice has told me that she would sing while Sam and Doris played, and they occasionally performed locally as The Barnes Family.

Christmas 1963 was a family gathering at one of his sisters, probably Irma. Janice was there with husband George, a clarinet player in a jazz band, a piano the centre of the evening's fun. This was my first introduction to the Barnes family musical gatherings. Jazz standards as well as blues were played. I loved singing and would have joined in but at just 17 years, I was completely over-awed and simply a rapt audience.

Irma, Graham's eldest sister, told me that once Graham started playing the guitar he played endlessly, and would go over and over the same phrases. She told me, laughing in light of his later success, that at times she would tell him "shut that racket up", so there was some balance there.

Irma was 14 when, on December 19, 1944, she was sent by Doris to run and get the midwife as "the baby is coming". Irma and Janice, then

10, delighted in the big, blond baby boy, born at home into this loving musical world. Janice remembered coming home from school that day and "wondered who this strange baby was, in her mum's bed".

A studio photo of young Sam and Doris, probably in their twenties, shows that it wasn't only their taste in music that was cool. Both are dressed in the holiday style of the day, vests and baggy trousers, Doris' shoulders covered by a short cape collar top, with an edging of black and white stripes, similar to the finishing on the hem of her wide bottom trousers. All topped off with a jaunty angled, white sailor style hat for Doris, and white shoes for Sam who holds a cigarette, the essential cool prop of the day. They smile, looking fabulous and obviously happy and in love, against the painted backdrop of sky, tropical islands and ocean waves.

In all the photos of Graham as an infant, he is aware of the camera, staying still and posing for the images, as we all did in those days. I have looked intently at the few images of young Graham Barnes to try to find a sense of who and how he was, but as with my own young images, they are too static to suggest very much.

In one picture Janice is holding him outside their house. He is obviously a relaxed baby, with a slightly mischievous smile and a glorious head of blond tousled hair. Maybe a year old, he is quite an armful. Janice looks delighted and proud of her baby brother.

My favourite photo was taken when he was three. He is on a stage, with Sam holding the number 24 and looking down calmly to his son, who already comes up to his waist. He is a finalist in a parent and child competition, probably at Butlins, Skegness, where many families from Nottingham took their holidays. It is impossible to tell if he has first place or third place. To his far left is a father with twin curly-haired boys and between them a boy with rather knobbly knees, whose mum leans over, fussing a little.

Though I suspect the twins won first prize, Graham is stunning, blond, upright, long soft limbs and perfect proportions. A lady in a Butlin's redcoat blazer, who smiles towards him, holds his relaxed left arm and hand. His right hand is flat against his hip, resting on his baggy wool swim trunks, with a small hoop logo embroidered on them. Because we know that he will become a virtuoso guitarist it is difficult not to look at his hand, displayed as it is, and marvel at what lies ahead. The picture is by a professional photographer, Graham stares back at him with serious calm composure. It is the only picture I have seen of Sam Barnes without a cigarette.

Sam was a quantity surveyor and a builder and in a picture on a beach, five-year-old Graham shows a magnificent fortified sandcastle, with flying buttresses, turrets, towers, minarets topped by flag poles, ramps and openings, all surrounded by a wall and grand entrance. He wears a shirt, shorts and warm jacket, so not a sunny day at the beach, but his wide smile shows that father and son are having a great time.

Because his older sisters were in their later teens, falling in love and would soon be leaving home to start their own families, Graham became almost like an only child. In interviews he often said that when he was young he didn't really remember his sisters or feel close to them. My two elder brothers were similarly in their late teens and involved in their own lives by the time I turned six. To be a girl with two older brothers or a boy with two older sisters initiates a relaxed involvement with the opposite sex. They are not a mystery to you, they are your siblings and I have always felt that men were my brothers. This would lead to some misunderstandings but it was very helpful on the rock'n'roll road with an all-male band and road crew.

Graham was the last child Sam and Doris would have, the baby of the family. I was also the third child, the much-desired girl who arrived after two boys, but I was not the baby of the family. My younger brother, Harold Stuart, was born when I was three and a half. My mum would refer to him as "my baby" even when he was a grown-up. She would also tell the rest of us that we were still her babies and claim we never cried. She said she would have liked a dozen children and wanted to adopt but was unable to because she lived in a pub. These claims were extravagant and best taken with a pinch of salt since they were quite disconnected from our reality.

Where Graham Barnes' early childhood was stable, mine was totally the opposite. After my birth at The Rose of England in November 1946, until I left home in May 1965, we moved three times, always into live-in businesses. By 1948 we were living in a grocers' shop on Grassington Road, the only time we were not in pubs. Years later, after my dad had died, my mother told me that it was because of his drinking, but when I spoke to a cousin after my mother's death in 2013, a different story emerged. Evidently there was a family feud between my father and his three brothers, and the license for the Rose, which they had tried to take from my parents.

My father's mother, grandma Burgon, became the licensee after grandfather Burgon had "run away with a very young woman". He divorced grandma, and would go on to have a second marriage and a further three children. My parents ran the pub with grandma after grandad ran away. When my father was away with the RAF during the war, my mother ran the pub with grandma Burgon. Tragically, grandma was incapacitated during a routine operation for a prolapsed womb. Given a spinal anesthetic, a new procedure in those days, she suffered a massive stroke. This left her paralysed to such an extent that she never walked or talked again, but survived bedridden for a further 15 years. My father was given compassionate leave from the RAF but in the meantime his brothers tried to take on the license for the Rose. One of them informed the brewery that dad had been buying black market alcohol, quite typical in war shortages, and he went to court and lost his license.

This was the real reason why we had left the Rose and took on the greengrocers' shop. It was also why – thanks to the outrage of my grandfather's adulterous exodus and the betrayal by my father's brothers – we were left with no knowledge or contact with grandfather or my uncles. This tragic story that unfolded during the war years was kept hidden from me and Stuart. There was an unspoken atmosphere, which no doubt impacted on us little ones. I do recall life being hard work for them, especially at the greengrocers.

My father, Hector, born in June 1909, was the son of a publican, a strong character and a perfect pub landlord, in control of everything, fearless and hilariously funny. I have never in my entire life met anyone else who could tell jokes, long "shaggy dog stories" that would have you falling about laughing. His humour kept us all going at the greengrocers, "The Shop" as it became known. "I have to get up in the morning, at five o'clock, to go to the market and fetch stinking rotten cauliflowers," we repeated with mirth. My fondest and only warm family memory is from this time. On Sunday evenings, when I was three, I would be bathed, dressed in pajamas and put to bed. Mum, teenagers Barry and Graham, and dad would come into my room, sitting around and on the bed, and tell stories about the comings and goings in their lives.

It was like something from *The Dandy* and *The Beano*, favourite comics of the day. There were stories about "old Ma White", who lived next door, and the boys banging her door knocker and running away, or putting stink bombs through her letterbox. Later on, I heard that dad had a criminal record on account of old Ma White. Mum had hung-out a line of white washing down the garden, close to the adjoining fence. Old Ma White had lit a bonfire in her garden, the smoke from which wafted onto our washing. Dad went out with a bucket of water intent on putting out her fire but she had other ideas and stood between dad and the bonfire.

He slung the water over her as well as the fire. She took him to court, he was fined and also had to pay for a new dress.

Soon enough we would move to The Albany, a huge detached pub, with its own music hall and an upstairs smart bar, the Rainbow Room. Better for us not to be so close to neighbours. We moved there in 1951 with Stuart a toddler, I was four and a half and already at school and having my hair permed. Barry was 14 and brother Graham 12, two mischievous teenagers. It was spacious, with three floors, way too much room even for a family of six. Mum put washing lines in the top rooms and one had a full-sized billiard table, on which I once fell asleep. There was one bedroom, which for a short while was occupied by Uncle Fred, in need of a bed. Another room had a model airport built by my flying mad brothers, hung all round with aircraft kit models. Being taken to air displays became a particularly thrilling part of my young life, sitting on sunny hillsides as jet planes whizzed past at ear-shattering decibels no doubt helped program me for my later love of loud rock music.

The Albany had huge extractor fans. In those days everyone smoked in pubs and the Players cigarette factory was only a few hundred yards away. Big sliding levers behind the bar controlled these fans. Barry would sit me on the bar while they "flew the building", a lever each, gradually increasing the throttle as high and loud as they dared. This was done when the pub was shut in the afternoon, mum and dad occupied with errands, Stuart sleeping and me in their unsafe hands. They were very tolerant with me, and found parts for me in their games. When they were cowboys I was the Indian, to be tied up. When they joined the Air Training Corps I was "drilled" in how to stand to attention, stand at ease and present arms with a toy rifle.

Amongst this very male, highly charged atmosphere my mother, Audrey, was *uber* feminine, immaculately groomed and efficient whether serving behind the bar or getting meals for her family. She had married young, at 18, and made a pact with my 26-year-old father that they would never fight, like their own parents. My two elder brothers were born before she was 20 and, unexpectedly, her own mother died in her forties from an abscess on the liver. When WWII began, my father joined the Royal Air Force and was posted abroad, leaving her to cope with two small boys and run the Rose with grandma Burgon.

Audrey was born in December 1916 and at the age of just 14 was already "courting" my father, who was seven years her senior. What would be shocking today was, in 1930, a popular match. Her mother thought Hector was wonderful. That same year Audrey's uncle, Alderman Arthur Pollard, became Lord Mayor of Nottingham. His niece was called on to attend some functions and dinners in the very grand, newly built, Council House in the Old Market Square.

My mother's beloved only brother, Sonny (Harold), joined the army, spent three and half years in the African desert and was killed in 1945 in Burma, where his troop was diverted to assist on their way home to England. When my father came home from WWII, the emotional roller coaster of her previous ten years created an atmosphere of unspoken and unresolved pain. I remember her doing my hair as I sat in front of a mirror, and I saw she was crying as she wound curls around her fingers. "Today would have been Sonny's birthday," she said. I was too young to understand but I knew she was really hurting from the memory.

It is clear that my birth eight and ten years after my two older brothers gave her a new focus, an opportunity to groom me to become an eligible young lady. Maybe she hoped I would have the life she had wanted for herself. I would marry the richest local man I could attract and produce a healthy brood of grandchildren.

Her role model for me was Shirley Temple and while she didn't want me to be a performer she thought elocution, acting, piano, ballet and poetry classes would add to my allure, and certainly curls were de rigueur by any means available. My straight blond hair was no deterrent. From the age of three I was taken to the hairdresser for my hair to be permed, a long, stinky and elaborate procedure, involving noxious chemicals and tight curlers. Eventually, after being permed and neutralized, a huge, hood hairdryer was lowered over my hair-netted head, big cotton wool pads covered my ears and hot air was blown around my head. I was given a heavy, rubberised contraption with a dial and told which way to turn the nob if it got too hot. Sitting under the whirring dryer, I remember being transfixed by music that seemed to be playing in my head, repeating itself over and over. There is a name for it, Auditory Paredolia, the brain's tendency to form patterns from sound, my first hallucination.

Every night, yes, really every night, my mother would sit me on the kitchen table and, as she happily told people, put "100 pipe cleaners in my hair", to create 100 tight curls. The white, fluffy, cotton covered type, meant for pushing through the stems of pipes, with pointed wire sticking out each end, which would poke into my head during the night. If any broke loose during my sleep, leaving a straggly bit of hair, the curling tongs (heated in the flames of the cooker hobs) were used to singe and tame that unruly curl. The smell of burnt hair was very familiar to my young nose.

A ribbon tied in a bow on top of my head and two hair slides, either side to keep the bow in place, set my head up for that day. There is a school photo of me when I was about nine. Somehow, I had escaped the pipe-cleaners and the morning grooming so it's clear mum was unaware it was a school photo day. My hair is wild, I look as if I have survived a hurricane and the grin on my face is totally jubilant. It was certain that I would become a rebel.

At the age of three, I was sent to a fee-paying, private school, University House School for Young Ladies, founded in 1868. We were dressed in gingham dresses, cardigans and straw hats in the summer and gymslips, shirts, ties and blazers in the winter, our legs always bare, with ankle socks and Clarks leather sandals or lace up shoes. For gym we wore grey knickers and vests. All of those improvement classes for young ladies – the elocution, acting, poetry speaking, piano and ballet – were available alongside academic courses.

I was taken to Speech and Drama festivals, put on stages to recite poems, alone or as a duo with my schoolfriend Jackie. Her father had a moustache that he waxed to a point at each end. When he took us swimming I was fascinated by his moustache, now wet, hanging down to two vertical droopy waxed points. No one in my family had any facial hair. Hector would not have approved.

With my school I went to open-air festivals with maypole dancing, weaving lovely coloured patterns, which I liked, and Scottish Country dancing, elaborate line routines such as 'Strip the Willow' and 'The Gay Gordons'. My school reports described me as keen, lively, talkative, intelligent, enjoying life, though I lacked concentration, which I imagine is often the case with lively, bright children placed in dull, stuffy environments. In my imagination I was already living in a curious fantasy world, where I might be a prima ballerina or a great actress, over-stimulated as I was by my ever-active home life and my noisy, talented brothers.

chapter 5
The Albany

The Albany's music hall was a big space with a stage at one end and a piano to one side for accompanying variety acts. I was too young to watch the evening entertainment, but we loved to use the space in the afternoons when the pub was shut. Stuart was now three, the perfect age to learn simple parts in piano duets, and we spent hours banging out tunes or dancing and singing on the stage. With a little imagination and long strands of coloured crepe paper, the structural pillars in the room became maypoles.

Like Graham Barnes, there was plenty of music in my life, classical from ballet classes and piano lessons, and in the pub the pop of the day, Perry Como, Mel Tormé and Doris Day drifting up from the public sound system. I loved an unusual, up-tempo Hawaiian song called 'She Wore Red Feathers And A Hula Hula Skirt' which I sang and danced to in the afternoons in the empty music hall. Guy Mitchell's lyrics were a mystery: "She lived on coconuts and fish from the sea" just as we were coming to the end of the food rationing from WWII. What was a hula hula skirt?

In 1951 my dad threw a Christmas party for local children at The Albany. The music room was laid out with benches, and trestle tables topped with sandwiches, jellies and pop, a real feast for those kids still on rationing. In one of my favourite photos dad stands smiling, surrounded by happy looking kids while adults peer through the windows, and in another young Stuart in a Kiss Me Quick hat is passed through the air from dad to Graham to a highchair to eat jelly. But the best shows me standing by my dad, singing into a large microphone, while young boys watch with open mouths. The song was 'Rudolph the Red Nosed Reindeer', my voice amplified through the PA speakers. I was hoping that mum, upstairs in the kitchen serving up the party fare, could hear. It was a memorable day.

When King George VI died In February 1952, his daughter, Princess Elizabeth, only 25, became Queen Elizabeth II, and like so many others we bought a television set to watch her Coronation on June 2. It was housed in a huge wooden case, with doors concealing a tiny, four-inch screen that showed the first moving images I ever saw. It seemed utterly magical, and despite being black and white we saw colour in our imaginations, the golden fairy-tale coach and all her glittering jewels and ladies-in-waiting holding up her long train. The new Queen's two young children, dressed in their Prince and Princess finery, peered down from a balcony. I was six, a similar age, and knew only about fairy stories.

The most magical moment in the whole affair was when young Elizabeth's heavy robes and coronet were solemnly removed and, bare-headed, she was taken and hidden under a silken canopy to be "anointed with oil from a golden spoon". Everything else seemed straightforward but this anointing was magic, as if she stopped being human and became a Queen.

Part of me was always in search of the extraordinary, the transcendent. In the Scripture classes at school, phrases like "through a glass darkly, tinkling cymbals, speaking with the tongues of angels, without love I am nothing" resonated with me. They all pointed to something intriguing, something unavailable in everyday life.

I was given a toy model of the golden Coronation coach and horses, which fitted in well with my Disney Cinderella, Prince Charming and Fairy Godmother, all mechanical, wound up to gently spin round and round, weaving noisy clockwork dreams. One day a customer gave mum a small, real flower posy. Dressed in a white lace curtain and with the posy, I spent the day imagining myself a bride.

In July 1955 we were all taken out to the front of our school on Waverley street, and stood in lines along the pavements. Given small, paper, Union Jack flags, we were told when to wave them, as Queen Elizabeth II would go swooshing by in her limousine... whoosh! Did I catch a glimpse of her through the window? I don't remember, but at eight years old, it was exciting to be part of a crowd of youngsters waving flags and whooping "Hurrah! hurrah!" She was visiting the Birkin Lace Company, in Nottingham, while touring her newly acquired Kingdom.

Sewing was an early passion; from age five darning holes in dad's woolen socks I quickly progressed through stuffed felt animals to making my own clothes by the age of eleven. It seemed easy to understand paper patterns and I would challenge myself with harder designs, and was soon able to reproduce a Channel suit, fully lined, by then. I was patient with each detail, the inside was as perfect as the outside.

Mum told me grandma Bowler was an expert seamstress. Maybe we inherit creative skills. She died ten years before I was born. Like me, both my grandmothers were Scorpios, which mum would often refer to. To her we were prone to self-destruction and strange interests, not too encouraging to a growing child. The sixties would change those negatives for me.

Once a year as part of May Slaney's elocution classes, we went by coach on an excursion to the Royal Shakespeare Memorial Theatre by the River Avon at Stratford. I had been put on stages for some years now, reciting poetry, acting in small plays, appearing at speech festivals with the spotlight on me. This was in another league, sitting in the dark in this splendid theatre by the river, and watching brilliant actors telling Shakespearian stories. *A Midsummer Night's Dream* featured the extraordinary Charles Laughton, in one of his last performances, as Bottom. Young handsome charismatic Albert Finney commanded the stage as Lysander. Robert Hardy was Oberon and Mary Ure was Titania, King and Queen of the Fairies.

We saw *All's Well That Ends Well* in 1955, *Love's Labour's Lost* in 1956, and *As you Like It* in 1957, all with astonishing sets and costumes with casts drawn from the Shakespeare company's young acting talents of the day. In the interval we would stand on the balcony by the River Avon, as white swans swam past, my treat a coffee ice cream in a silver dish with a small silver spoon. It seemed very sophisticated, my ritual on every visit.

Overall, life at The Albany was the most magical part of my childhood. Barry and Graham were still at home and full of fun, and young Stuart tagged along, up for piano duets, hide and seek and any adventurous play idea I came up with. With mum and dad full-on running the pub, we were left to our own devices a lot. On one rare family outing, in the dark on the Forest, the vast open park near the Albany, I was on dad's shoulders as we traipsed through the night, gradually gathering more and more people until many hundreds of us arrived together at a tower erected above a large free-standing tank filled with water.

A man climbed the steps on the tower, while the crowd whooped and yelled encouragement to him. At the top he held his arms aloft to great applause. Then flames erupted as fire engulfed the water tank, glowing orange red in the blackness. Was there a drum roll? There should have been. He dove off the platform into the flaming tank, breaking through the flames, which his splashdown seemed to extinguish. Out he leapt to even louder applause. It was amazing. I had seen and been in plays on the stage myself, but this was real, this was dangerous, this was truly exciting. I wonder if Graham Barnes and his family were there that night. I never thought to ask him.

chapter 6
The Newcastle

My brother Barry loved jazz. The Modern Jazz Quartet, Dave Brubeck and Gerry Mulligan all filled the house. As teenagers he and Graham grew their hair longer and wilder, and they listened to *The Goon Show,* a forerunner of *Monty Python's Flying Circus*, in slight rebellion. At eighteen, Barry was conscripted into National Service and, naturally enough, he chose the RAF. After he de-mobbed he settled into pursuing his life's ambition to become a pilot.

Graham, two years behind, turned eighteen just after conscription ended and wasn't called up. He surprised my mum by falling in love at 16, marrying Valerie at 20, and thereafter settling down to a happy family life.

My younger brother, Stuart, aka Harold, and I developed a close and complicated relationship through our childhood, teens and twenties. Music became a love we shared and after I left Nottingham, I influenced him and involved him in some crucial episodes of my life.

Any time there was a local air display I would be taken along by my big brothers. I have some very happy memories of being perched on sunny hillsides with jet planes whizzing past me at great speed. One year in particular we drove to Farnborough to the big air display there. The jets were so loud and they must have been hurting my ears, I started to ask my brothers, "How loud will this plane be?" Perhaps the thunderous roar of the jets and the thrill of the speed helped to prepare me for large, live rock concerts.

Being the only girl with three brothers was no hardship, it was bliss, especially as hormones started to affect my thinking and behavior. Barry and Graham had some beautiful friends, handsome young men, fit, healthy and, like my brothers, full of fun. In the summer holidays, always long with us being at private schools, we all went swimming outdoors to lidos in and around Nottingham. Bulwell was the closest and out-of-town was Papplewick, a fresh water lido that was extremely cold. We would spend all day at the lido, sunshine or rain, all through the summer holidays.

I'm sure that the contact I had with all these emerging Adonai helped boost my increasing hormone levels. I remember sitting on their knees when I was only about nine years old and being accepted by these young men. Little did they know that it was their physicality that I was enjoying. I had crushes on several of them.

Growing up with brothers, feeling so safe and secure and cared for by them, gave me a very healthy attitude towards the opposite sex. I saw them as friends, not a mystery, and I felt comfortable in their company. Even when I was younger and cast as the Indian in games of cowboys and Indians, which might have meant me being tied up, it was great fun. They were never mean to me, at least not that I remember.

Meanwhile, Graham Barnes was growing up with two older, talented, glamorous sisters and definitely found it easy to relate to women. That works both ways and men who become sex symbols, as he inadvertently did, attract women because they are easy and comfortable around them. When he walked into a crowd of female fans, he was relaxed, flirty and fun, and would put them at their ease. Although he never deliberately sought their attention, he certainly enjoyed it.

Throughout my life, I have always felt very comfortable around men, and generally very safe around them. I'm perfectly happy to talk to "strange men", on trains, planes, in shops, socially, but it's sometimes disappointing when my attention has been misread. Where I am seeing them as brothers, other human beings, their interest has obviously been different, and that generally takes me by surprise. In fact, from when I first began to develop curves and morphed into a beautiful, busty blonde, for decades men only ever talked to me with one thing in mind.

I got quite used to it, but it limited my conversation and I looked forward to the day when I could talk in the same way as with women. In my late forties and fifties, my sexuality ceased to be the main attraction and I could talk with men as I did to my brothers. I don't suppose that men in general have any idea what it's like to have someone talk or listen to you, while drooling slightly at your close proximity and with scant interest in the content of the conversation. From the female side, I can tell you it becomes quite obvious, and it is very unattractive, unless the attraction is truly mutual. My relationships with other women became much more complicated, maybe because I didn't have any sisters, or maybe because I had a gorgeous, and very desirable, boyfriend, who they all seemed to fancy.

We moved from The Albany and its magical spaces to The Newcastle Arms. Over the door were the ancestral arms of the Duke of Newcastle, who founded The Park in central Nottingham, a private estate for aspiring Victorians. The Newcastle was even further out from the centre of the city, between a number of housing estates in its own plot with a car park and garden. It was smaller than The Albany, with only two floors, the second our main accommodation, and no music hall. It was a no-nonsense drinking pub, a meeting place for locals, with a large open lounge and upholstered seating. There was a small stage with an upright piano with a TV on the top, for football and snooker. The lounge charged a penny a pint more than the vaults for its mild and bitter "real" ales.

The vaults was for the working men, and many were miners from the local colliery, who would stop off after a hard day's work before going home to their wives for tea. The miners had no pit showers and would arrive covered in coal dust, in jackets, overalls, flat caps and scarves. Now nine, I was fascinated by these men with coal-black faces, white lines radiating around eyes that had been screwed up all day working at the coalface. The wooden seats, tables and tiled floor were easy to wash. On Saturday evenings, scrubbed up and out with their wives, they would pay the extra penny a pint for the soft furnishings of the lounge.

At The Albany, under Shipstones Brewery, hogsheads of mild ale and smaller barrels of bitter were delivered by horse-drawn drays. The horses were large, magnificent white Shires with gleaming brass regalia. We kids would look on in wonder, especially when they stood still as barrels were unloaded. Meanwhile, they unloaded their own steaming mounds of horse shit. After they left this was gathered on shovels by local gardeners to spread on their plants and vegetables, organic recycling. At The Newcastle, Shire horses gave way to Home Ales Brewery wagons, the barrels held in place by bars around the outside, a great climbing frame for Stuart and me. I was especially fond of inventing acrobatic moves around these bars.

To this day I remember all the procedures for delivering the barrels and the strong, hard-working draymen. One on the wagon, rolling and loading the barrel onto the delivery ramp, one at the bottom to stop it. Next the chains and clamps attached to either side were fixed to the rope through the big pulley over the beer cellar opening. The barrels were then winched down to the cellar, a tremendous weight, leather gloved hands and sacking held around the rope for friction to control the whole exercise.

At the bottom, the full barrel was unloaded and an empty barrel put onto the pulley to be winched up and rolled back onto the lorry. The smell of beer, sacking, oil and testosterone, no doubt made it more exciting. The draymen were always very tolerant of us kids and, to be fair, we kept out of their way as we played on the lorry and barrels.

Fred Bentley, our coal man, delivered sacks of coal by horse and cart around to the other side of the building, where removing a grate gave direct access to the boiler room. The coal sacks were opened and the black coal tipped straight onto a pile to supply the huge boiler that gave hot water to the building and central heating to the pub. In the living accommodation, there was plenty of hot water but no central heating. Often in winter we would wake up to frost patterns decorating the windows. As a teenager I was often cold and would sit almost on top of the little Gas Miser in the lounge, which resulted in mottled legs.

Life in a pub is different, extraordinary and actually quite exotic, with lots of freedom for us kids while the grown-ups were all kept very busy. My dad always said The Newcastle was the busiest pub the brewery had, packed every night and busy at lunchtimes too. My childhood was totally unlike that of most families who lived in a house with one or both parents going out to work. When you live above the business you are all expected to help out, to work according to your age, ability and strength. We all earned our pocket money, and since the relentless pub hours formed the routine of our lives, it was hectic and there was no time or place for rebellion or reflection.

Lying alone in bed was the only time when this intense life gave way to a little peace, and I would drift into altered states of mind, pondering the meaning a life before sleep arrived. Beneath me I could still hear the pub, murmurs of conversation, laughter, perhaps a piano player, or gramophone records and every few seconds the ring of the cash register opening up to receive people's hard-earned money in exchange for community and escapism. A public house is a home and a business, operating to sell the drugs, alcohol and tobacco, under license, and at that time there were strict opening hours. Today the hours are looser and the pubs can be open all day. From my own experience, I don't know how today's landladies and landlords cope.

We moved there when I was eight and two years later my whole class of 12 girls was taken one day to a large school in the city to sit the 11+ exam. I knew nothing about it, no one had discussed it, but we were already used to sitting exams in every subject three times a year at the end of each term.

Although my parents paid for me to go to University House School, they never ever asked me anything about my school.

Mum and dad had both left school at 14 and showed no interest in our education. I would bring home my school reports in a large envelope at the end of term and they were put, unopened, into a drawer in the kitchen. Then, on the first day of the next term, I would ask one of them to sign the report, which they duly did, not having read it or commented on it at all. My entire school studies were mine to do or not to do and no one in the family engaged in my achievements or failures. The 11+ was a significant exam as passing it meant you could go to Grammar School, which my mother didn't aspire for me at all. I was safely tucked away from the world in my nice young lady school, and all was well. One thing I remember of this exam was the question, "How many legs has a three-legged stool", which I found very offensive. "They must think we are stupid," I thought. Well, lo and behold, I passed the 11+, the only one in my class to do so, and the only member of my family too.

Mum and dad must have been very confused by this, but my-soon-to-be sister-in- law, Valerie, had gone to The Manning, an all-girls Grammar School about four miles from home and she recommended it highly. My fate was sealed and my horizons suddenly expanded. I have no memory of any fuss or congratulations at school, perhaps they didn't want the younger ones getting ideas. My parents gave me a Kodak camera, which went with me to London on a school trip, the last trip of my junior schooling.

We went to Westminster Abbey, the scene of the Coronation, the outside of the Houses of Parliament and Big Ben next door, then down the Mall to Buckingham Palace where we saw a guardsman in his sentry box, and with my camera I took a roll of black and whites. London seemed a huge, grand place compared with Nottingham and Stratford-on-Avon. Back at school there are photos of my class mates and my teacher, Miss Crowley. Looking at them it's obvious I already had an eye for composition and interesting images, without heads or feet cut off. That camera served me well for years.

Unfortunately, the Manning was not right for my adolescent academic education. My sewing, music and drawing were an ill fit. One thousand girls, Nottingham's finest, bright, future scientists, was what the headmistress Miss Leighton, hoped for. The artistic ones were seen as time wasters, lazy girls and the art teacher was a misery. Her name was Mrs Barnes!

chapter 7
Big Bill Broonzy

The Newcastle was two miles due north of Toston Drive where young Graham Anthony Barnes was in his tenth year, still living happily in the house where he was born. In 1955 he would have taken his 11+. I don't know if he passed but he went to Margaret Glen Bott Bilateral School, a less than 10-minute walk from his home. The school was an intentional experiment in combining Grammar and Secondary school pupils as a precursor to the Comprehensives and to replace the divisive testing and streaming of children at 11 years. That practice certainly limited the horizons of those that did not pass, leaving them feeling unnecessarily inferior at an age before their natural gifts could emerge.

It was a modern building set in acres of grounds that were part of Wollaton Hall's extensive parkland, and was obviously the pride and joy of the local council. Graham Barnes started at Glen Bott the first year it was opened, on September 8, 1955. According to entries on their Facebook page, Miss Lovett was the headmistress, and there was a compulsory uniform that included caps and blazers with striped braiding. To the best of my knowledge there are no photos of Graham in his uniform. I do know that as an adult he hated formal dress of any kind. Apparently, he was quite often sent home for turning up in inappropriate rock'n'roll clothing as he went through his teens. He left school at 15, the earliest legal leaving age in 1960.

Various entries online describe Glen Bott as a happy, pleasant place, with dedicated, enthusiastic staff, who were strict but fair. Typically, in post-war Britain, with a desperate shortage of teachers, qualification standards were lower than today, with fewer academics who made a career in teaching. Some male teachers had been soldiers, worked in the mines, on building sites or in the police, with others who had gone to teacher training college after the war. They believed in rules and discipline, backed up with the cane and pupils were spoken to in ways that would probably be considered abusive today.

In an interview decades later Alvin said: "Many teachers in school were busy concentrating on making students obey and pulling their own weight rather than bringing out the positive in people."

One girl who was in his class published a dramatic account online: "I shared a class with Graham Barnes and remember one of his main claims to fame in those years was walking around the outside of the school on the first-floor window frames. He was caned for his efforts at assembly, which he bore with a grin on his face."

Corporal punishment was still handed out liberally in British schools, right into the seventies, so it was not unusual for Graham to have been caned. However, being caned on the stage, at the morning assembly of the whole school and grinning throughout certainly suggests he was a focused, defiant young man. He never talked to me about that incident, or his schooling, except to say he hated it and as I hated mine. We agreed it was rubbish and not worth discussing.

It's unlikely his obsession with music would have gone down well. "The music teacher's idea of a music class was to write down the lyrics of hymns, for us to copy," he said. In interviews he always spoke of school as something to be endured, never as something he enjoyed. Because he had been caught out misbehaving, he was always under suspicion for any trouble that happened.

He seems to have stayed at the back of the classroom, with a home-made guitar neck, and spent his days practicing chords under the desk. It's doubtful he would have been enthused by the new sports facilities as he was never interested in contact sports and referred to Saturday TV's excessive sport coverage as "national kill-yourself day". Once in Vancouver, on a TYA tour, we were taken up the mountains to a ski resort. Everyone, including their manager Chris Wright had a go at skiing, while Alvin and I spent our time filming the band falling over. I have no idea what became of the film.

Two local school friends, Chris Gaulton and David Wright, told me that they and Graham would meet up in The Spinney, a small area of woodland near their homes. "One afternoon, we were there with a proper bow and some arrows. He challenged us to shoot arrows at him whilst he dodged amongst the trees and used his leather satchel as protection if the arrows got close. We didn't want to do it but he was insistent and very light hearted about it, probably enjoying the buzz. Agile and quick, he was never in real danger. He was a dare devil."

Creative people are often clear at a young age about exactly what they want to do, obsessed with perfecting their skills and finding little to engage them in the rest of their schooling. Graham started his musical journey playing the clarinet. His vocalist sister Janice's husband-to-be, George, played clarinet in a local jazz dance band and this would have influenced his choice. There were acoustic guitars at Toston Drive, which Sam and Doris both played. Doris told me the advent of skiffle, and Lonnie Donegan, its principal exponent, turned Graham's attention towards the guitar. John Lennon was the same.

Donegan played banjo in Chris Barber's jazz band and it was Chris who brought Big Bill Broonzy, Sonny Terry & Brownie McGhee and Muddy Waters to Britain for tours in the late fifties. Through their open-minded love of music and fearless cultural exploration, these two band mates, Donegan and Barber, were the catalysts for much of the music of sixties Britain.

Sam Barnes, with his great love of the blues, went to see those original black bluesmen on tour at the Trent Bridge Inn, a pub by the river in Nottingham. Late that evening Sam and Doris persuaded him to come back to Toston Drive and woke up their 12-year -old son to meet him. Alvin told me he was a bit grumpy at being woken from a deep sleep but when he went into the lounge to find the much larger-than-life Broonzy playing guitar and singing the blues he was amazed. He sat on the floor at Big Bill's feet and, despite having grown up hearing Sam's blues records, found this real-life encounter a mesmerising epiphany. Their home was transformed by an exotic American energy, a performer of great talent and soul. Broonzy was a beautiful six-foot tall charismatic black man, a musical god in his living room, and he never forgot this experience.

Rock'n'roll was also crossing the Atlantic. In 1957 I had the five best-selling records: 'Jailhouse Rock' and 'All Shook Up' by Elvis, 'Diana' by Paul Anka, 'Great Balls of Fire' by Jerry Lee Lewis and 'At The Hop' by Danny & The Juniors. By the autumn, at the start of my first year at The Manning, rock'n'roll had taken over my life. This was the year Sam and Doris sent away by mail order to buy Graham his first electric guitar, a Guyatone made by one of the earliest Japanese manufacturers.

He told me it was the most thrilling day of his life. He came racing home from school and tore open the delivery box to reveal the guitar in its velvet lined case. He thought it was beautiful. "He was over the moon and so happy," said Doris. "We could see that this was his instrument without a doubt. He practiced every single minute he could and got on like crazy with it, so quickly.

It was then I knew the talent was there, and nothing could stop him." He was 12 years old and a year later was playing in a band. Maybe it was during this year, when he turned 13, that he invented Alvin Lee, his stage name equivalent to Elvis Presley.

Young guitarists today have decades of rock guitarists to listen to, to copy, to learn their licks but that was not how it was for the budding Alvin Lee. There were no British rock guitarists, but Scotty Moore, Elvis's guitarist, and Chuck Berry, were influences that could be heard throughout Alvin's life. His life-long friend, Johnnie Clifton, showed Graham how to play Chuck Berry's riffs.

Johnnie watched Graham play at All Soul's Church Hall in Radford, and spoke to him when he came off stage. Johnnie also played guitar and, having mastered Chuck Berry, connected with him to demonstrate the basic fingerings for Berry's hits. "He soaked up whatever I showed him, he was really inquisitive, eager to learn," said Johnnie. For a while, Johnnie played guitar in Alan Upton & The Jailbreakers, with young Graham, at that venue. Talking about Ivan Jay & The Jaycats, the forerunner to The Jaybirds, Johnnie said: "Ivan wore a lavender jacket, had bleached blond hair, but couldn't sing in tune!" I love those early sixties band names.

Escaping from the pub one evening, I first met Johnnie Clifton at "Basford Wakes" on Billy Bacon's field, a local fairground. On fairground rides like the Dodgems and Waltzers, rock'n'roll was played very loud, further heightening the experience of being spun around and around and up and down, all the thrill of the fair. We both loved rock'n'roll and were mates, part of a local gang from then on, and we've remained lifelong friends to the present day.

In the kitchen at The Newcastle, we had a huge, valve-powered radio, with a Perspex front labeled with global radio stations, and large knobs to tune us into the world. Radio Luxembourg was our favourite, though the signal faded in and out, crackling and swooshing through the airwaves. Founded in 1933, it was one of the earliest commercial radio stations broadcasting to the UK, putting out rock'n'roll to capture the youth market. My brothers, whose touch was as delicate as a safe breaker, were expert at finely tuning the big knob to Radio Luxembourg.

Pop singles were still 78 rpm 10" or 12" shellac records. The record player in the pub featured mostly Doris Day, Perry Como and Bing Crosby, music suitable for playing in the background without encouraging dancing. There were also some popular classics, my favourite a 33rpm LP of Tchaikovsky's *Swan Lake*, to which I danced ballet-style in the afternoons when the pub was shut. I sang Mario Lanza's 'Drinking Song' at the top of my lungs.

Lonnie Donegan's skiffle records found their way into the pub via Graham and Barry, the big 78s with bright pink, PYE NIXA logo labels. Even the labels looked modern and exciting. In July 1957, Donegan's. 'Gamblin' Man'/'Putting On The Style' was No 1 in the UK charts, while 'Cumberland Gap' and 'Jack O'Diamonds' were also hits in 1957.

When small 45rpm singles arrived, my record collecting also included Buddy Holly & The Crickets, The Everly Brothers, Little Richard, Gene Vincent and Duane Eddy. All had top ten singles, in 1957. Uplifting music, great harmonies, well-crafted songs, easy memorable lyrics to sing-a-long with and, dance around the pub to. And then there was Elvis.

For me, Elvis went beyond music into something way more erotic as my hormone levels confused daily life. I turned 11 in November and hormones were already affecting my music taste, and Elvis was responsible for much of what we thought love would be. He more than hinted at sex. In 'Love Me', from 1956, his groan halfway through probably caused more hormonal activity in young women than any other sound ever recorded. That was it, all the sex education we required, the only love map we needed. Two miles due south from my bedroom my future rock'n'roll partner, my own personal Elvis, was annoying his sisters endlessly by practicing guitar, fantasising his future and already playing in his first band.

I had become the proud owner of my own state-of-the-art record player with its own built-in speaker. Finished in grey and red leatherette with a multi-record auto changer, it was an all-in-one portable machine called a Dansette, a dream machine, a dancing machine, a time travel machine. Load up a half dozen 45s onto the auto changer, click the plastic slider to auto and wait with anticipation while with various clicks and clunks, the record dropped onto the rubber anti-slip mat. The stylus arm lifted from its housing and made an elegant arc to set the stylus down into the record groove, the record's background hiss and crackle raising the expectation.

The record that truly changed my life was 'Great Balls Of Fire' by Jerry Lee Lewis, bought on the day of release – November 11, 1957 – as a 45rpm vinyl single on the London Records Label. When Jerry Lee brought his 13-year-old bride (also his cousin) to the UK in May of the following year there was a roar of protest which didn't help his career. It was the raunchiest record I had bought, but I didn't know that on any conscious level, I just knew it was very exciting and thrilling. I had no idea what "goodness, gracious, great balls of fire" might be referring to; honestly, I didn't think it was sexual. But it made me feel as if there was something incredible going on somewhere in the world, something much more than I had so far experienced and it made me feel really good.

Whatever this energy was I wanted more of it, I wanted to find it and I wanted to share it.

I took this 7" black vinyl record across the road to my friend of a similar age, Peter. His father was the local butcher and Peter lived above the shop in Nuthall Road. Peter had a small record player in his living room. "Play this record, Peter, listen to it." I could barely contain my excitement.

Jerry Lee's piano hits an ascending four-chord progression, "Listen to the piano, wow!" The solo rocks along, left hand rolling through a bass boogie-woogie riff as his right hand hammered the keys with repetitive intensity. "Put it on again." I was so excited.

I held his attention and his eyes throughout the track and tried to convey to him how this record rocked me. I saw that he got it, and we grinned broadly to each other. Later in the next decade I would experience some of the best British rock musicians working this same alchemy, turning their fellow musicians on to some new music they had discovered, among them some obscure artists. Sharing the connection and the energy through the basic non-verbal language of music. The rhythm, the dynamic, the musical structures, the lyrics and the sheer beauty and energy of heartfelt, soul shaking, music making.

chapter 8
Jiving

My eleventh year was the most pivotal with major changes, though I only remember it as fun and exciting, taking it all in my stride. The effect of mum's over-controlling regime had been to make me focus on myself, longing to grow up and become independent. In the spring I visited London for the first time on the day trip with University House School (for young ladies). I was leaving my safe and exclusive private junior school, with 12 pupils in a class, and was now destined to start at a new all-girls school, Manning Grammar School, the educational and aspirational home for a 1,000 of Nottingham's brightest girls. There were 35 pupils in a class, drawn from all walks of life by virtue of their 11+ exam result.

Our headmistress, Miss Leighton, was very ambitious for us girls; not just to be pretty, accomplished young ladies but to be career women and, especially, scientists. That was admirable enough for those who were academic but ludicrous for the artists, the creatives, who were considered time-wasters and lazy. We were left with the dour, unimaginative Mrs Barnes, our art teacher, and spent many hours drawing or painting a branch, flower or still life, an object in the middle of the table we sat around. Many decades later I realised that since she was teaching art – considered a worthless subject – Mrs Barnes was probably not the most respected teacher in the staff room. No wonder she was such an uninspiring misery. Famous artists were never mentioned or discussed and an outing to an art gallery was never on the agenda.

Socially it was amazing and fascinating to be thrown into the "real" world, warts and all, with girls from all backgrounds and different religions. What united our gang was rock'n'roll and 1957 was especially memorable. As well as Jerry Lee, there was Eddie Cochran, Gene Vincent, The Everly Brothers and Buddy Holly & The Crickets. In my class Vicky became a great pal for the next five years, and we became excellent jive partners, soon to discover Nottingham dance halls. It was an amazing time for music, our hormones delivering all the physical changes, music teaching our bodies how to move and lyrics telling us what to expect from falling in love.

I saw Cliff Richard, our version of Elvis, at the Nottingham Odeon just after my thirteenth birthday, on November 26, 1959, my first "live gig" and screamed so hard I lost my voice for a week. The following year, on March 20, I went by myself, by bus and train, to see Bobby Darin and Duane Eddy at the de Montfort Hall in Leicester, forty miles away. Bobby Darin wasn't very rock'n'roll, but after my experience with Cliff's show I was moved to scream just once, when he sang 'Diana'. No one else was screaming and Darin, seated at the piano, looked in my direction at the end of the song, and said, "Thank you lady!" Duane Eddy and his twangy guitar was far more exciting and definitely rock'n'roll.

Brother Barry was called up for his National Service in 1958. Mum didn't want him to leave home but it was compulsory. With his lifelong love of airplanes, Barry joined the Air Force and because he'd been privately educated was encouraged by mum to apply to Cranwell, where officers were trained. Barry, however, wanted to join with all the other young Nottingham men and serve with the regulars.

I don't know why he choose that path or if he was pleased he did but he didn't fly, as he wanted, and was given a ground job stationed in Singapore for two years. He learnt to play drums and brought his white Trixon kit home when he returned in 1960. He set it up in his bedroom, along with a portable record deck, and played along to Dave Brubeck, Gerry Mulligan and The Modern Jazz Quartet. He taught me how to play, using brushes, and gave me an education in jazz, listening to solos, opening my ears to following the ebb and flow of solo pianos and saxophones.

Periodically Barry would ask mum, in front of me, "Have you had a talk with Loraine yet?" It was a question she never actually answered. I knew it referred to sex, already a hot topic among my friends, and it was quite fun to watch this awkward exchange. "Not necessary," I wanted to say. One evening she sat on my bed and said: "Virginity is like a lock and only one man has the key." Perhaps we were both embarrassed. I didn't say anything and she left, maybe feeling she had done her job, as Barry had suggested.

Our relationship had become increasing complicated since I discovered mum was having an affair with a neighbor. Though I hadn't confronted her about it, the knowledge was extremely confusing to me and for a while I hated her with all the passion a teenager can summon. This was an intense relationship for her that would carry on for several decades, and later, as an adult, I became more tolerant of her infidelity. At the time it altered my idealistic view of marriage, a disillusionment that was never resolved.

All of my life and interests lay outside my home and I realised that how I behaved was my responsibility. My reputation depended on my own choices, and no-one else. On the bus home after a night's jiving, I knew I would be late and dad would shout at me. "However much he shouts, it won't take away the fun and good times," I thought, and this gave me a calm detachment. After all, he was never violent, would only ever shout and we knew that after a while he would have shouted enough and forget all about it. Dear Vicky would arrive home late to find her dad sitting in an armchair with every clock in the house arrayed around him. "What time do you call this, young lady?" That classic dad's question must have tempted her with some witty response. Vicky was very bright and full of fun. We spent as much time laughing as dancing.

The times we were living in were still very innocent and our official sex education at school, as at home, was non-existent. The only nudes we saw were in classical art or in the naturist magazine called *Health And Efficiency*, which got around the censors by airbrushing genitals. Couples enjoying naked tennis were just as hairless and featureless as the classical statues. In my own family, I had never seen the men naked, and my mother shaved herself from head to toe daily.

As ludicrous as this may seem, it is 100% true. When I began to grow pubic hair, I was utterly confused because my mother, whom I had seen undressed, had no hair on her body at all. I didn't know she shaved it all off. I had never seen my father naked. When we were little he would get into the bath with us, wearing navy wool swimming trunks. I had never seen my elder brothers naked. Young Stuart, whom I did see undressed as we had always bathed together, was three years younger, pre-pubescent with no body hair.

From this evidence, or lack of it, I began to think that growing pubic hair and other changes "down there" might mean I was turning into a man, since adult men were the only bodies I had never seen. This may sound very far-fetched, but it was 1959. How was I going to find out if I was "normal", always the principal adolescent concern? Ask any member of my immediate family? Goodness me, that was out of the question, so I devised a plan. There was a young man I knew who was maybe five years older than me. If I had sex with him then I would have an answer one way or another.

So that was what I did. I knew him quite well and would dance with him.

He asked me out to the pictures, and one day we went to his house when his parents were out and after some snogging and general groping it became obvious to him that I was willing to go "all the way". I bled a bit and he mopped me up. I was delighted I wasn't turning into a man, as he expressed no shock at what he found. For me it was almost an out-of-body experience, since I was much more focused on his reaction than enjoying myself. Mission accomplished. Later that day, I do remember wondering whether anyone would notice and say I looked different but no one did and that took care of my virginity, which meant one less thing to have teenage angst about. I didn't tell my unknowing lover that I had been a virgin nor my real motive. Such a wise head on young shoulders, it was my secret and now it isn't anymore. It's assumed that if teenagers are not told about sex they won't be interested, but ignorance is far more confusing and certainly not bliss.

I started 'falling in love' very early in life, my first crush Stewart Buckley at age four, though his red Raleigh tricycle probably had something to do with it. After painfully falling for boys who were not interested in me in my teens, I noticed there were some boys who were interested in me, and that cured my teenage dilemma. I cultivated a sensational beehive hair-do that would have put Brenda Lee to shame, and experimented with make-up. I developed a terrific vampire look, black eyes and white lips. By now I was making my own clothes, tight skirts, or full circle skirts with rock'n'roll net underskirts and very high-heeled winkle-picker shoes, much to my mother's horror. We had no conversations about my metamorphosis though she issued admonitions. "What do you think you look like?", "You'll never live to see 21 looking like that", "If you get into trouble your father will kill us"; all this from a woman I knew to be adulterous who projected her respectability from behind the bar, the glamorous landlady.

Most Sunday afternoons me and young Stuart were expected to go out, in the car, with mum and dad to a local stately home. Mum's great passion was to walk around some large historical pile, filled with antiques, portraits and the expensive knick-knacks of the former aristocrats, all the while expressing envy and admiration. Naturally it became the height of tedium for my teenage self. One Sunday I made the beehive, the white make-up, the black vampire eyes with an extra heavy hand, adding a tight sweater and skirt and the five-inch pointed winkle-pickers, which made me much taller than my 5'2" nemesis. "You're not coming out looking like that are you?" Somehow, I was suddenly calm and icily focused, looking her in the eye. The umbilical cord snapped. "Fuck off!" Nothing more was said. She turned and went out to join dad and young Stuart in the car.

I was 14 and finally free of her fantasies. It felt fantastic.

I was out jiving at least five nights a week. In Nottingham there were excellent dance halls that had been built for ballroom dancing in the big band era. The wooden sprung floors were brilliantly bouncy. The Palais, Colemans, The Rainbow Rooms, and The Locarno (aka The Vic), all played solid chart-topping rock'n'roll records loudly through big PA systems. The DJs didn't talk, they just played rock records back to back, and every hour a few slow smooch records, back to back, to slow the pace down and let the lovers cuddle closer. We called it the creep.

Bright coloured lights on mirror balls were turned up high so we could see the dancers' jive techniques. Then the lighting was turned down low for creeping so we couldn't see who was smooching. At The Vic on Bank Holiday Mondays, they would run 12-hour sessions, from midday until midnight and every hour on the hour they spun Bill Haley's 'Rock Around The Clock'. We all danced and sang along. Maybe each city invented its own specific jive.

Nottingham's jive was intense and all the moves, the arm work, the spins, were strictly with the beat. When I watched music TV shows with jiving audiences, nothing ever seemed to match our stylised version. We all knew the steps, the forms, the spins and it was easy to swop dance partners after a while and enjoy neat little nuances the boys had developed. Alan Fowler, who was short, my height 5'6", had great fast fancy footwork, tremendous tight punchy energy, especially for really fast jiving. Brian Stanley was nearer six foot, much smoother, sexier in his holds and moved with a Fred Astaire elegance and graceful timing.

Dancing with girlfriends like Vicky was also about technique, one of us taking the male part, swopping roles, developing and practising new moves. We all recognised we were amongst the best dancers, but this was never discussed, it just was. We gravitated to each other because of our jiving abilities, my first real personal high. Boys were only noticed if they were good dancers. I wasn't looking for a boyfriend who might cramp my freedom to choose. It was a great dancing high we were after.

All these Nottingham boys wore similar clothes: dark navy "Italian", pinstriped suits, tight trousers, fitted single breasted jackets with narrow lapels, white shirts, mostly red ties and a matching red hanky in their breast pocket. These "hankies" were actually a strip of fabric fastened to a piece of cardboard. Black leather winkle-picker shoes, black or maybe red socks, the clothes topped off with shortish, hairstyles slicked back with Brylcreem, smooth shaven with Old Spice the predominant aftershave.

Working-class lads who had miraculously found a music and dance style that gave them a release from a hard day's work. This was no arty, beatnik crowd from the Nottingham School of Art. Those middle-class kids were into trad jazz and did a strange, jerky, skippy form of jiving that seemed to me disconnected from the real rock'n'roll energy.

In the rock dance halls, there was also a darker energy, as those hard-working boys were handy with their fists and it was not uncommon to see fights, scuffles, head butting. We would move away from any trouble and find a safe space to carry on dancing. This random violence was obviously distracting but I was enjoying the dancing too much to become a spectator. My aversion to the violence of my home town would grow during my teenage years, but at first it just seemed normal. Luckily there was no alcohol at The Vic, which meant the lads had to go out to pubs to drink. This probably kept the violence levels in check.

Hot dogs, coca cola and coffee fuelled our 12-hour sessions. At 13 I'd started to smoke, encouraged by older girls one day in the local park. It was disgusting and made me feel sick but I persevered, thinking it made me look grown up. In the mornings I would sneak a packet of 10 fags out of the pub, and share them with my gang of girls in the breaks and at lunchtime. Technically it was stealing but as I was never given pocket money – I had to do pub work to earn it – I felt I deserved the bonus. My photobooth pics – our version of selfies – show me faking debauchery in my young teen days at The Locarno, posing with fags and mates and finding it all hilarious.

One evening a lad appeared at The Vic with such a compelling look, a stranger, exotic. He was over six feet tall wearing a pale green tweed suit, the jacket double breasted, with slender trousers, obviously a one-off tailored suit. With a white shirt, matching tie and hanky set and brown suede winkle-picker shoes, his outfit was topped off with a short ginger bob (no Brylcreem) over a freckled face with a turned-up nose and a huge grin. In this place at this time this should not have worked at all, but it did because Rod Duncombe was an exceptional dancer, confident, smooth, dynamic, accomplished and literally head and shoulders over most lads on the dance floor. Rod's family had moved to Nottingham from Luton, 20 miles north of London, which made him almost a Londoner and therefore extremely exotic.

It's strange the coincidences that stick in your memory. I had started to read all of Ian Fleming's James Bond books. In Dr No, he is saved from being shot dead at point blank range because his heart was on the wrong side of his body. Rod Duncombe's mother also had her heart on the right of her chest, something present in about one in five million people.

Rod became my jive partner and boyfriend for half a year, lots of smooching and groping, never going "all the way", mostly locked together on the sofa in our lounge.

Stuart worked out that if he stayed in there staring at the TV Rod would give him half a crown to go away. In the kitchen, we would practice our dance moves, our throws and footwork, where I would hold onto the sink to help my balance whilst attempting new somersaults. Before he left I would make him a tomato sandwich, a huge sacrifice as I hated raw tomatoes, the texture, the smell everything about them. He relished them and since we were now in training for jive competitions it seemed a reasonable request.

I only remember us being in one competition. It was thrilling to be jiving with a packed dance hall crowd watching on, and just a handful of other couples. The music was loud and the spotlights followed us. I had made sure to wear something that didn't over-expose me as I was thrown through the air, over shoulders, between Rod's legs. Net petticoats, stockings, suspenders and five-inch heels on my pointed shoes brought my 5'6" frame closer to Rod's 6'3" to make our moves compatible and exciting. A few years later Alvin told me that he was a judge for that competition and he remembered me from there. All I remember is we came second.

chapter 9
The Atomites

Whilst I was learning to jive to rock'n'roll, my own bid for freedom, Graham pre- Alvin, just two miles away, was learning to play rock 'n roll, a life-long pursuit of freedom for him. Two years older than me, by the time he was 13 he was playing rhythm guitar with Vince Marshall & The Square Caps, on the Guyatone, his first guitar, but there are no photos. By 14 he was lead guitarist in Alan Upton & The Jailbreakers. Johnnie Clifton remembers seeing him play at the All Souls Church Hall, Radford. "The stage had curtains and after they finished Alvin emerged," he recalled. They got talking. Johnnie had a guitar and showed him Chuck Berry riffs, which he had not yet mastered. An important musical connection began that night and lasted all of Alvin's life. Johnnie was playing with Faran Christie & The Sapphires but his religious mum, was not happy, one night his grandma dragged him offstage. Johnnie briefly played guitar with Alvin in one of his early bands.

My favourite photo of young Graham, the budding-dreaming-guitarist, shows him sitting on a small back garden wall at Toston Drive, with his second electric guitar, a Burns Vibra-Artist. This was Burns' first solid guitar produced from 1960-1962, with a short scale neck and complex controls. Certainly "the more knobs the better" was the criteria at that time. In the photo the guitar is dark, it would have been a deep cherry red, not brown. He was already dreaming rock'n'roll in colour. At 15, he looks skinny, young and innocent, holding in his lap an extraordinary musical future, certainly beyond his wildest dreams. In later years he would pose many times with "Big Red", the Gibson ES 335, the archetypal thrusting, grimacing, rock guitar superstar a million miles away from this dreaming, vulnerable youth.

Alan Upton & The Jailbreakers, Vince Marshall & The Square Caps – these and dozens of other Nottingham bands from the early sixties encapsulate the unprecedented energy, excitement of the times and a sense of musical community. My dancing partner, Brian Stanley (Stan), played bass with Shane Wyman & The Senators. "When Shane our singer took ill, Alvin stood in for him for about four gigs," he told me. "Despite having to repeat the songs several times, we still went down well."

Even in his teens Alvin was known and respected among local musicians. His very first band gig, at age 13, was at the Palace Cinema, Sandiacre, playing a short set between the B-movie and the A-movie, the Brigitte Bardot film *And God Created Woman*. Two films were a standard night out, and B-movies would decades later be the subject of Gill Scott-Heron's 'We're All playing In A B-movie', about living under Ronald Reagan's Presidency. Reagan was famously a B-movie Star.

The fact that Alvin remembered it was a Bardot movie is interesting. She remained his female archetype fantasy women, his first erotic crush, blond, pouting, busty, long-limbed. Bardot's look not only entered the sexual psyche of the times for young men, she became the role model for hundreds of thousands of young women, even to the present day. Marianne Faithfull, Ursula Andress, Jane Fonda, Julie Christie, Claudia Schaeffer and Kate Moss are just a few whose image owes itself to gamine Bardot, her long tousled blond hair and pout. Her look suggested joy, sexual freedom and adventure, which seemed equal to the male pin-ups of the day. As a natural blond, she was certainly my unconscious inspiration for letting my own hair down from its rigid beehive, freeing it to grow as it would, long, blond and straight.

James Dean's *Rebel Without A Cause* was a movie Alvin often referred to when talking about his youthful behaviour, describing himself as a "rebel without a clue". Certainly, Dean's look, blue jeans, T-shirts, casual bomber jackets, slicked back hair, a subdued version of Elvis' quiff some things young Graham adopted. On his way to becoming Alvin Lee, he toyed with the name Alvin Dean. It showed up in a Nottingham newspaper article about The Jaybirds when he was 18.

Surely the best named band of his early career was The Atomites. The Atom bomb was casting an ominous dark cloud over fifties Britain. Even young rock'n'roll addicted teenagers who didn't watch much TV news, read newspapers or discuss politics found it impossible to totally escape this dark reality.

Between the movies, cinemas would show Pathe newsreels that featured black and white films of nuclear weapon testing. The USA's favourite test site was Bikini Atoll in the South Pacific. There was an all-out-arms-race with the USSR for top dog, the stated aim to have nuclear deterrents to keep us all safe.

From 1953 until 1992, almost 40 years, Britain had a four-minute early warning system wherein sirens would have screamed countrywide to let us know that Russia had launched nuclear missiles. As teenagers we would joke about what we could do in our last four minutes, the usual answer indulge in sexual ecstasy. In 1957 the Campaign for Nuclear Disarmament, CND, was formed along with their famous logo, which would become the global peace sign, a decal of which found its way onto the upper horn of Alvin's "Big Red" Gibson in 1969, in time for the Woodstock festival.

The Atomites has a great fifties science fiction ring to it, and sci-fi was a lifelong interest to Alvin. This was the band in which, aged 15, he played alongside 16-year-old bassist Leo Lyons. As a team they would become the central focus of, first, The Jaycats, then The Jaybirds and finally Ten Years After. Personnel changed over the early years, but Alvin and Leo, both born under the fire sign Sagittarius, had a strong connection. Early on it drove and inspired them and, eventually, it would infuriate and separate them. Neither had brothers and after Alvin died Leo admitted that they were like brothers.

Again, there are no photos of The Atomites. With drummer Pete Evans, The Atomites were short lived. Along with newly recruited lead singer Ivan Jay, they morphed into Ivan Jay & The Jaymen, who further morphed into Ivan Jay & The Jaycats. Between 1960 and 1962, with Pete Evans on drums and Roy Cooper on rhythm guitar, they settled into a rock'n'roll covers band. In a photo from 1960, they wear light-coloured, shiny satin matching suits and white winkle picker shoes, with fabulous slicked back rock'n'roll quiffs. Even Leo has bleached blond hair. The Jaycats looked like a glitzy version of The Shadows. Ivan Jay, in black trousers and lavender jacket, also bleached his hair blond, which Doris Barnes dyed blue on top and pink on the sides. He stands centre stage with mike stand akimbo. Johnnie Clifton remembers Ivan's lavender jacket and claims he wasn't much of a singer. "He sang out of tune," he says.

Later in his life Alvin was happily nostalgic about his early musical steps and especially about Ivan Jay. "I was hanging round with Ivan when I discovered sex and rock'n'roll," he says. "He used to have girls chasing him down the street and I was impressed."

Ivan had a passion for fast cars, which he would also pass on to his protege. Later he moved to Santee, California where he had a successful career driving stock cars under the NASCAR banner at the Cajon Motor Speedway. Alvin at the wheel loved "take it to the edge" driving. It was best to relax and enjoy the ride.

When I was first with him, he had a Berkeley kit car, and liked to impress me by performing a skid turn, without warning, in the Nottingham University grounds. The narrow, winding, university campus road was ideal for pushing the little Berkeley to its limits, to slip and slide around bends, late at night when no one else was around. I think he had the nerve, focus and concentration to have become a racing car driver. He would talk about Juan Fangio, the Argentinian racing driver, and other "skin of the teeth" merchants with true admiration.

chapter 10
First Romances

By the age of 14 I was pretty, busty and blond, hormones controlling my body and emotional life. I was disgusted at the effect I seemed to have on middle-aged men while working at night behind the bar in our pub, uncomfortable with my curves and the attention they inspired. I remember overhearing a customer telling my dad, with lascivious delight, "Your Loraine is growing up." I felt a shudder of shame, as if it was somehow my fault for developing into a young woman when it was something totally out of my control.

Although I was unhappy with the way my body looked – my nose, lips and thighs were all too big – I loved the way it felt, the sensuality and the rush from experimenting with snogging and petting with boys my own age. I was sexually uninhibited and enthusiastic, maybe because there had been very little tender, physical contact as a child in my family.

Despite the lack of formal sex education, I was aware that not getting pregnant was my responsibility. I needed to control these boys and allow only limited exploration rights. The pill had not yet arrived to liberate us from the fear of unwanted pregnancies. If we became pregnant, there was little support, only our families who were unlikely to be sympathetic. During one of her rants about my looks and clothes mum had warned me, "If you get into trouble, your dad will kill both of us!"

A friend did "fall" pregnant on the very first time she let a boy go "all the way". None of us ever knew. She was skinny and somehow continued to come to school throughout her entire pregnancy, all the while keeping it hidden. At a party several months after the birth, she got drunk and poured out her story to me. She had ignored what was happening to her, never went to a doctor, even kept it from her mum and dad. On the day she woke with stomach pains and her waters broke, she went to her mother and said,

"Mum, I'm having a baby."

"When?" asked her mum.

"Today," she replied.

There was no time for admonishment, only for action. Rushed to hospital, all went incredibly well and a healthy baby arrived that day. There was no question that the illegitimate offspring of their teenage daughter would remain with her middle-class family. The baby was adopted and my friend was back at school two weeks later, her slimmed down appearance explained by the removal of an appendix, which convinced everyone. On reflection, it seems our emotional needs were ignored. Cultural and moral rules were paramount. The night she was drunk, weeping and pouring out her heart to me, non-judgmental support was all I could offer, that and to keep her secret and never to ask about it again. Babies were not a part of the life we were enjoying.

My mother's fears about the kind of people I would befriend in my 1,000-pupil girl's grammar school, drawn from all backgrounds but united only by a reasonable level of intelligence, were realistic from her point of view. My safe, fee-paying junior school for young ladies, all drawn from the daughters of the wealthy and the influential, had slipped through her fingers along with her hold on my future life. We had plenty of pointless confrontations along the same clichéd lines as tens of thousands of other teenage daughters and their fearful mothers.

What she did not know was that around my ninth year she had lost my respect one day outside in the garden of The Newcastle. There was a wall, taller than me, and I had climbed on a chair to look over it. On the other side was a double row of lock-up garages and some children, shoeless, were playing in the waste ground between them, their squeals and laughter attracting my attention. I was still at my private junior school, togged out in my expensive uniform and perfect Clark's shiny leather sandals. It was my first glimpse of poverty. Maybe mum came out to hang some washing. Young children don't mince words.

"Mum, there are children over the wall who have no shoes, why?"

"Their parents are lazy, some of their fathers are in prison."

"Why doesn't someone buy them shoes?"

"If they did, their parents would sell them to buy beer. They are not good people, you can't help them."

Some conversations when you are young are truly pivotal and this one was for me. My parents ran a pub. They sold the beer to these people. The beer that was the reason these children's feet were bare. The beer they bought enabled me to have a private school education and wear good quality clothes and Clarks shiny shoes. What we now call a lightbulb moment occurred in my young mind. Nothing more was said but my respect for her views, her world, her ideas and her ideals evaporated. My empathy was fully with the barefoot children. I've always said this was the moment I became a socialist and began to develop a real interest in other people's lives.

The only lessons in school that held my attention were biology classes, how the body worked, all the internal systems, digestion, circulation, excretion, genitals. The five senses, the eyes, the nose, the mouth, the ears, the three little inner ear bones, the malleus, the incus and the stapes have stayed with me forever. The skeleton, the joints, the skin (the largest organ of the body) and the brain, the spine, the central nervous system. The body was incredible to me, my hormones were putting me through an emotional roller coaster ride. Something about learning the mechanics of it all grounded me.

Then there was Latin and a memory that is mixed with guilt and remorse. For only one year we had a Latin teacher, Miss Nutter, pitched against 35 hormone-riddled 14-year old girls; about 5'5", late 40s with a mad, Harpo Marx head of hair, plain features, no make-up, heavy spectacles which stayed in place only after much nose twitching. Her fitted sweater was tucked into a pleated wool skirt, and her large bosom drooped to her waist, where it was contained by a brown leather buckled belt. On her feet were large, flat, brown leather sandals over woolen socks. What cruel act of fate had contrived to bring her to us, like a lamb to the slaughter?

Teenage girls are merciless and teachers need to establish authority. Alas, Miss Nutter failed on both counts. As time went on we failed to even acknowledge her as she came into the room. We carried on chattering away to each other, as she waved her arms and attempted to call us to order. I have a memory of her fainting and us placing her outside the classroom door, on a chair, in the corridor and going back inside, completely ignoring her needs. Miss Nutter was absent from school and then left. It was rumoured she had a nervous breakdown.

In December 1961, just after my fifteenth birthday, I began my first serious relationship. Terry, 18 months my senior, was an excellent dancer, also at grammar school, High Pavement. This was the year of my own O-levels and Terry was sent by the angels to help me at least get some qualifications from my five years at The Manning. He encouraged me to swat and pointed me in the right direction of shortcuts to study. Then there was the coincidence.

He turned up with a book of previous geography O-level papers, picked one for me to do and went over it thoroughly when I'd given it my best effort. Lo and behold, the following week we went into the geography mock O-level exam room, sat down and turned over the paper. Yes, it was the very same one that I had already done, that Terry had hand-picked. Poker-faced but with a happy beating heart, a relaxed two hours followed. I managed five O-levels that year, with Terry as my private coach.

This lovely boyfriend turned out to be an excellent lover, my first real one. One day when we were making love, I started to feel as though I might faint, and focused myself to stop the sensation. The female orgasm had never been discussed in biology, or among my friends, or anywhere. As far as I knew it was something that happened only to men. Yes, we were that naive and ill-informed back in the early sixties. It was 1966 before I experienced my first orgasm. If you don't know something is missing, you don't miss it, so it was never a problem for me.

In November for my sixteenth birthday, Terry gave me a book of Shakespeare's sonnets, inscribed as "Something to remember me by". I wondered why. One Saturday morning, visiting him at his house, he was still in bed and for the first time I climbed into the warm bed with him and snuggled up. How fantastic these rights of passage are, these first times. We didn't make love. His mum was in the kitchen below Terry's bedroom.

A little later, downstairs, she stopped and looked me in the face. "You have worldly eyes," she said, a comment that stayed with me. It seemed so strange and rude at the time. We'd been together for 14 months when Terry proposed to me. This perfectly lovely young man told me he was going to college to become a teacher but a claustrophobic vision of me as a middle-class teacher's wife in Nottingham woke me up. HIs mum was right. There was a world calling me, an adventure beyond my wildest dreams.

Schooldays ended in the summer of 1962. Vicky and I took a holiday together, without adults, going by train to Bournemouth, 200 miles from home. Both November born, we were 15 years old, two of the youngest in our year at school. My only memories of our week at Cedra Court in Boscombe are going to the beach, paddling in the sea and spending a fruitless ten minutes trying to light a cigarette on light bulbs in the room. The legal age for smoking and sex was 16, and on this first trip away from our homes we had packed cigarettes but forgotten the matches. However, I had brought my camera and we posed for each other. On the beach I look kind of lumpen and podgy, very unsure of my rather overdeveloped breasts. Vicky, who was athletic and slender, looks stylish and elegant, how I had hoped to look one day. Recently Vicky found those photos and, looking at them, realised it was because of my breasts that boys chased me. I hadn't noticed that I was chased. Perceptions in friendships are highly personal.

I was working regularly in the pub in the evenings and, with hindsight, suspect I was becoming something of an attraction. It was a busy pub and the work was constant, serving queues of customers, pulling pints, pouring spirits and "glamorous" drinks to wives on their nights out, a Babycham or a snowball made with Dutch Advocaat topped up with lemonade and a glace cherry on a stick with a paper umbrella, opened and propped over the lip of the glass. No wine was served in pubs in those days. Teetotalers drank lemonade. Most customers smoked and despite extractor fans, the air was pretty unhealthy. Living at home free, my meals and laundry done for me, paid the same rates as other bar staff, life was fairly comfortable but going nowhere.

With no clear idea what to do when I grew up, I harboured a secret desire to go to art school. No-one, least of all the art teacher Mrs Barnes, had suggested I had any talent. My academic record had slipped from being in the top three, at age ten, to being in the bottom three by age 15. In June 1962 on my last day leaving the Manning Grammar School building, I clearly remember thinking, "I never want to learn anything again for the rest of my life."

Despite this vow, I was persuaded to go to The People's College in Nottingham part time to try again for my English Literature O-level. It was a revelation. We were respected and treated as adults. The English teacher, Mr Clark, set great essays and I found my love of writing. It was a morning class and, as had been my habit at school, I was invariably late. Mr Clark could see my pending arrival through the building's large plate glass windows, hurrying down the road. He would time my arrival at the classroom and open the door for me to fly into the room. One day he leaned against the door to stop me opening it, as I pushed he opened it, so I fell in. I remember apologising yet again. "To err is human, to forgive divine," he said. Mr Clark was cool and I thank him for healing my dislike of learning establishments.

My sixteenth year, 1963, was filled with rock'n'roll music. The Beatles had arrived and teenage girls were hysterical. My pop star crushes had been Elvis Presley, Eddie Cochran, Cliff Richard, Billy Fury, who I noticed also wrote his own songs. George Harrison was my favourite Beatle. I bought all their singles and albums and was turned on by his broad Liverpool accent. "You over thur with the fur hur."

At the Labour Exchange, where jobs were to be found, I was given a few interviews for factory work, which I didn't get and didn't want. I had deliberately turned down the chance to study typing and shorthand as I didn't want to become a secretary, something I have often regretted since the advent of home computing. My options were limited. An unremarkable man behind a desk suggested I try for an office job at the government owned East Midlands Gas Board, as a filing clerk in the accounts department. They took me on and I worked there, in a grey room of grey filing cabinets and grey desks among grey people. Boxes of dockets for gas repairs were my domain, thin paper sheets, from triplicated pads, the bottom copies left with the customers, the middle ones with the Gas Board shops. The top copies were our domain, filed numerically, into grey boxes, which when full were removed for storage somewhere else that was grey.

Here was a job for life in a nationally owned industry. When someone died we would all receive promotion, eventually retiring with a good pension. The only excitement occurred one evening while walking to the bus stop with several older ladies when a man walked alongside me and made a strange slapping sound. Passing us, he turned around suddenly to block our path, opened his raincoat and revealed a small erect penis. In silence we split up and walked past him on either side, never changing our pace. We informed the police and for several days were accompanied to the bus stop by a policewoman, in uniform. The sound he made with his hands on his penis stayed with me for several months, a disgusting reminder of the slapping flasher.

For a couple of years, Vicky, myself and other school friends went to a local horse-riding school, hacking – as they call it – on Saturday afternoons. It was great fun and the old boy who owned the riding school loved helping pretty young girls up onto the horses, his hands not always in appropriate places.

Some took the riding more seriously and we all had a go at jumping. Being around horses was great fun and very memorable. Grooming, the aromatic smells and softness of their coats was a most magical experience. Nearly 60 years later their names stay with me: Conker, a bay gelding who was lovely to ride, especially in a canter; Stella, a large skewbald bay with white markings, a heavy gentle plodder; and Simon, a smaller black gelding who held his head straight out in front, in line with his body. Surprisingly, he was a great horse to take over small jumps, despite looking as if his head would hit them first.

Barbara, a friend I made at the stables, was from quite a well-to-do family and, along with my horse riding, was approved of by mum. I suspect she was starting to believe that I was growing up and my rock 'n roll days were behind me. In reality Barbara was by far the most adventurous of my teenage friends. She hung around with a crowd of the young of the well-to-do, with their sports cars and comfortable sized family homes. At weekends, with parents away on holiday, there was always an empty house in which to party and I shudder to think of the devastation we visited on these lovely homes. Mainly it was drinking and dancing and a few sexual encounters.

I was foot loose and fancy free but soon noticed that alcohol was not for me. I spent too much time with my head over toilet bowls in tastefully designed bathrooms, throwing up.

I could manage a half pint or a small whisky and would go into hotel bars like the splendid Black Boy, another Watson Fothergill building like my birthplace. The American Bar, the meeting place for the sports car gang, was where my friend Johnnie Clifton also hung out. I have a very dim recollection of seeing Alvin at a table having a drink with Johnnie, my first memory of seeing him. I was talking with others and despite his obviously interesting looks, he seemed quiet and somehow remote, outside of the crowd. I wasn't a bold enough to go over to Johnnie and say hello but I was intrigued.

In summer 1963 I returned to Cedra Court in Boscombe, this time with Barbara and she encouraged us to venture further afield into Bournemouth. On the beach we were chatted up by two young guys in their early twenties, with a white hard-topped MGA sports car, so round and smooth It reminded me of a hard-boiled egg. Black haired Angus, the car's owner, said he was the son of a Canadian manufacturing millionaire living in Newcastle. I didn't believe him for a minute, though it turned out to be true.

His blond friend Henning, also the son of a manufacturer, was visiting from Germany. Angus made a beeline for me and Henning for Barbara. Young and on holiday, we laughed, ate, laughed more and generally had a good time for a few days. We said our goodbyes, exchanged addresses, said we would write and thought that was that. Angus did write and rang, and drove to Nottingham when taking Henning to the airport and met my mum and dad. He invited me to his family's grand country home, and despite me being only 16 my mother couldn't get me on the train fast enough. Her goals of wealth, security and sensible splendour were revived and she was quietly ecstatic.

Sandhoe Hall, Hexham, was a grand Victorian country house in several acres and long views over the surrounding Northumbrian countryside. It was a lot to take in. Angus had his own apartment in this large family pile, and when we arrived from the station no one was about, so we enjoyed his luxurious double bed. It was fun, he was very turned on by me and that was also fun. Being away from home in a house where the family was quite accepting of their son bringing a young lady to spend the night in his bed was very new and heady stuff. Tidying ourselves up, Angus told me we were going out to join his family at a County Fair. It had been raining and was muddy, not suitable for the city girl's high heels. I borrowed a pair of his sister's wellington boots from a long line of similar boots by the back door, hoping I didn't look too ridiculous.

The County Fair seemed very dull, the tedium numbed by vast amounts of alcohol. His father was sweet and attentive for a few minutes and his mother said little, wafting past on her way to meet groups of friends. His sister was friendly but in truth, I was young and my life was dull by their standards. We were worlds apart. Angus didn't care. He thought I was wonderful. Later I met Argos, their prize Polish Arab Stallion, a beautiful creature, a captive in this rich man's world, valued for his excellent offspring. Would that have been my fate here? A breeding mare for a rich man's son?

Angus continued to woo me into the autumn, sending me gifts and flowers and letters. For November 10, my seventeenth birthday, he invited me to London for a weekend to stay in the family's Mayfair apartment. I was flattered by his persistence but I have no memory of missing him or yearning for him, in the way that teenage girls do, though I did think of him as my boyfriend. A weekend in London for a birthday treat, to be taken out and shown the city, how wonderful, how exciting.

On November 5, Johnnie Clifton introduced me to a slightly drunk young man on the steps outside of the Rainbow Rooms, our midweek rock 'n' roll jiving venue. He asked me for a kiss, which I gave him with a smile. I already knew who he was. I had glimpsed him briefly in The American Bar at the Black Boy hotel. He was a local musician with a mysterious, slightly dangerous reputation. Later he offered me a lift home and that evening my future was sealed with more kisses, not with a teacher in Nottingham or a millionaire's son in Newcastle but with a future rock star. I had no idea where my heart was leading me.

His name was Graham Barnes but the world would come to know him as Alvin Lee.

chapter 11
Go Go Go
Little Queenie

"It definitely wasn't love at first sight, nor even lust," I wrote in the late seventies. "Not that he wasn't a handsome young man, he most certainly was. Six-foot tall, lean, blond hair cut short and swept back from a clear, wide forehead. His eyes were green-grey, misty with a positive twinkle, though on this occasion pinkish around the edges due to alcohol, which was also causing him to grin somewhat foolishly and sway unnervingly, like a snake attempting to hyponotise its prey. The nose was perfect. I believe the word is Greek, straight and finely chiseled, the nostrils slightly flared. Set between two fine high cheekbones and above a beautifully shaped mouth, the lips not too full but certainly not thin, the teeth, which flashed at me through a constant grin, white and straight. The jaw was square and strong, not overly so but in exact balance with the rest of his face. The total image was classic Greek."

I daresay I was grinning back at him, disarmed and taken by surprise by his direct request. It was a short and tender kiss, a real connection, a brief meeting of lips despite or perhaps because of him being a little drunk. We grinned at each other, something was said, and I left those two on the wide steps of the Rainbow Rooms to continue up the remaining steps into the music and the dancing.

A DJ was playing rock'n'roll records in a modern hall on the front of the stage, long curtains closing off the stage behind. Low lighting lit a polished wooden dance floor, with a carpeted standing area by a bar to one side. I joined my friends and in the twinkling lights from the glitter ball, we jived and smiled and laughed. From the corner of my eye I saw Johnnie and Alvin arrive. I was being watched. Alvin was not a dancer but later in the evening, he came over. "Do you have a lift home?" he whispered in my ear. Smiling, I accepted his offer and he left me to dance until I was ready to leave. I was excited, nervous. I saw him smiling at me again from the sidelines. My heart was beating faster, and not just from the dancing.

I had heard rumours about Alvin, that "maybe he took drugs" because a friend had seen him "collapse in his dressing room after a show" and that he "had lived with a girlfriend". This was pretty outrageous in 1963 in Nottingham, where most teenagers, including me, drank alcohol and smoked cigarettes, but were pretty moderate in our habits except at weekend parties. So, I was a little nervous but already drawn to his disarming directness and exotic look. He stood out among the Italian pin-striped suits. His casual, suede-fronted, knitted jacket, blue jeans and black Cuban heeled boots gave him an air of confidence and intrigue.

I wish I could remember us leaving the dance hall, walking together, talking, not talking, finding The Jaybirds' Commer van, painted cream and decorated with red birds and "The Jaybirds" painted in large red letters. I do remember him struggling to engage the gears, which caused me to wonder if that was because of his drinking. He assured me it was only a mechanical fault. By this time, I didn't care. I was both confused and entranced.

We parked in the side street outside The Newcastle and kissed and kissed. Our feelings were overwhelming, our connection obvious and complete. "It's in his kiss," sang Betty Everett in 'The Shoop Shoop Song', a huge hit in March 1964.

When I met him, Alvin Lee was only his stage name. He was Graham Anthony Barnes, 18 years old, and living at home with his parents, Sam and Doris, a few miles from my own home. His friends and family all called him Graham, not Gray or any nickname. For me he only became Alvin when we started living together in London in September 1966. So, he was Graham off-stage and Alvin on stage with The Jaybirds. Although I'd heard of them I had never seen them play.

It's many decades ago now but I'm surprised I don't recall the first time I saw The Jaybirds and saw Alvin play. It was definitely in the first week we met, as we were immediately inseparable. We just wanted to be together whenever possible. We just couldn't stop kissing. I have a treasured black and white photo of us, standing, locked together kissing, taken by the official Locarno photographer, the second evening we were together. People are sitting watching us but we are lost to the world, lost in each other and never noticed the picture being taken.

We had met on Tuesday, November 5, and looming in the not too distant future was my birthday weekend in London with Angus. Would I still go? It was pretty obvious that something extraordinary was happening between Graham and me. In hindsight it might seem as if I ought to be thrilled to have as my boyfriend this exceptional musician but in truth he was simply a local lad in a local band and in 1963 in Nottingham, that was no big deal.

So, on November 9 I caught the train to London. In my bag was the kissing photo and another of The Jaybirds, a handout publicity postcard. When Angus met me in his white MGA and drove us to his family's apartment in Mayfair, I knew I was no longer available. Did I tell him there was someone else, or did I just wriggle out of a confrontation by saying my feelings had cooled? The latter I think. Did we go out to eat? We must have and I know we spent the night in bed together and that I put Graham's photos under my pillow. Physically, I kept him at arms-length though I'm sure we spent the next day, my seventeenth birthday, doing stuff in London and he accepted the situation. My mother would not be happy, that was certain, but on the train back to Nottingham that evening I was in no doubt at all. When I arrived back at The Newcastle, The Jaybirds' van was pulled up outside. On the passenger seat sat a large white teddy bear – we were only teenagers after all – a birthday present from the handsome young man who kissed perfectly.

It was two weeks before we actually made love, which became something of a standing joke over the years. "She made me wait two weeks," he liked to say. I wanted it to be special, in a bedroom somewhere warm and cozy, not in a Commer van smelling of oil, diesel and Easy Start, navigating the gear stick and the steering wheel. There was no chance at my home, so it happened on a Saturday afternoon at his Toston Drive bungalow when Sam and Doris were out. We made love in his bedroom on his single bed. I remember it to this day. I was right to wait. I was neither disappointed, nor was I a disappointment.

By his bed he had an intercom, which he would buzz to ask Doris to bring him a cup of tea in the morning. Doris ran a hairdressing salon at Toston Drive, catering for local ladies and she probably didn't want her teenage son wandering around half dressed. On one occasion, though not the first time, we were in the house alone making love in his room when over the intercom we heard the kitchen door open and Sam and Doris come in chatting. We dressed quickly, climbed out of his bedroom window, crouched below window height and went around the bungalow and came in the front door, whistling.

Sam and Doris were cool enough not to say a word. As liberal as his folks were, we would never have asked to spend the night together.

In July 1964 we went on holiday for a few days, to Sheringham, on the Norfolk Coast, in his Berkeley sports car. We found a bed & breakfast and booked into two rooms. I remember sitting in the living room, with the no nonsense, middle-aged landlady, giving our addresses, paying and asking for two single rooms. We would not have dared to ask for a double. We spent the night snuggled tight in one single bed, but made sure to be back in two rooms each morning. By today's standards all of that sneaking about looking for opportunities for bliss may seem ridiculous but I think it added excitement.

We look really young in the black and white photos from that holiday. I snapped Graham and he snapped me, back in the days before selfies, too shy to ask a stranger to snap us together. On the drive back the bonnet of the fiberglass Berkeley flew open into the windscreen a couple of times when we went fast, so we stopped and fastened it back again. The soft top was down, and it rained heavily, a quick intense summer storm. It had been sunny and dry for days and the rain released that delightful smell called petrichor, an earthy musty whiff of wetness. All my senses were heightened by our time alone, lazing on the beach, snuggling at night. It had been wonderful, easy, we were relaxed together, gentle and calm, no friction. Graham Barnes was a thoughtful and kind young man. I loved him very much and he loved me.

What did I think of Alvin Lee, his stage personality, The Jaybirds and their music? I loved dancing, jiving all evening was my thrill but the local bands were usually not worth dancing to. We would sit through the bands and dance in the intervals, when they took a rest and the current hit records were put on. The Jaybirds, however, were an exception, a brilliant three-piece.

Alvin handled vocals and played guitar, his "Big Red" Gibson ES 335 which was already an extension of his mind, body and hands. Leo Lyons pounded his Fender Jazz bass and Dave Quickmire was a natural and technically smart rock'n'roll drummer. Leo was never a backline bassist, though the head-to-head sparring with Alvin that created a tremendous dynamic in Ten Years After was still to come. Leo and Alvin both had microphones but Leo sang/shouted only one song 'Mashed Potato, Yeah!', a hit for Billy Thorpe & The Aztecs, and didn't even contribute backing vocals. Between some numbers, however, Alvin and Leo would chat about their day, about anything, about nothing, having a laugh. It was quite surreal but they were so at home on stage together that the audience just accepted it.

In 2017, I did an interview for Radio Nottingham about Alvin and the early days with Alan Clifford who asked me, "Were your friends jealous of my handsome young musician?" It was something I had never considered. As I wrote before, playing in a local band, however brilliantly, was no big deal, more of a novelty than a springboard to an international career. They had twice tried their luck in London with little success. Did I feel special, or like I had caught a great prize? No, I was simply in love with him.

Alvin's experiences with Ivan Jay as his mentor in the red-light areas of Hamburg had given him sexual confidence and this was obvious on stage. He loved to look at the pretty girls, stage front, while they twinkled back at him. Who could blame him? Sometimes their boyfriends would not be so appreciative. One crowded night I watched as he was pulled off the low stage by a guy who'd obviously had enough of his girlfriend twinkling at Alvin. However, Alvin, like all the young guys I knew in Nottingham, could "handle" himself. He thumped the guy and laid him out. It was messy and scrappy, like all instant fights. He clambered back onto the stage, dusted himself down, checked "Big Red" and started into the next Chuck Berry cover. No doubt the adrenaline upped the tempo.

I was certainly very happy to have found a boyfriend who played music I could dance to, a band who were as good and exciting as the records of the day. After a few months, however, Alvin was wasn't too happy when I danced with other boys while he was on stage, so I found myself foot-tapping on the sidelines or dancing only with girlfriends. Since I was head-over-heels in love with him I happily adapted to his wishes.

Just turned 17, I was unsure of myself in romance. Alvin was unlike anyone I knew in Nottingham, very mature and confident, especially onstage. He was completely focused on music, whether playing it or listening to other musicians. He turned 19 in December 1963, and it seemed to me that he already knew himself and what his path in life would be. An email exchange much later, tells another story. "From the day I met you, I was certain that you knew where you were going, you were very centered and focused," I wrote.

"I may have seemed that way but I was only guessing," he replied.

I had no picture of the future or that they might make a proper living with their band, no conception that being the girlfriend of a rock'n'roller was cool or even desirable. It was unchartered waters.

The Jaybirds played Chuck Berry, Bo Diddley, Jerry Lee Lewis, Little Richard, Ray Charles covers, all the music I loved. Alvin was already a dynamic rhythm/lead guitarist, extending his solos, and a confident singer, with effortless pitch and rock'n'roll phrasing.

In 1963 the general consensus was that rock'n'roll was a fad, something to enjoy while we were young. Even The Beatles thought their fame wouldn't last long. There is an early interview with them on You Tube in which they believe they'll last a couple of years. Ringo says he's hoping to one day open a ladies' hairdressers or even a string of them.

So how was it possible to think that The Jaybirds, who had already tried their luck twice in London had a future of more than a few years? Travelling around with these three guys was easy for me, a girl with three brothers, but I soon received an education in band dynamics. Alvin was the only one with a girlfriend and I was told that going to gigs outside Nottingham was not allowed, a band rule. One night in 1964, Alvin asked me along to a gig at The Regal, Ripley, which he said was a great venue. It seemed for once the others were making their own way there. I walked into the hall with Alvin and Leo came in from a side door. He took one look at me and said, "If she's here I'm not going on!" Leo sulked for a while and then relented and it was a great gig at a rockin' venue. He had over-reacted, something both he and Alvin were prone to do. Did I say they were both Sagittarius, an energetic fire sign, as were Little Richard, Jimi Hendrix, Jim Morrison, Frank Zappa, and quite a few other rock'n'roll front-line musicians?

Drummer Dave Quickmire was bothered by nothing and detached to a point of almost Zen mastery. Alvin would pick me up at The Newcastle, drive to Mansfield, pick up Leo and his bass. Then we would pick up Dave with his drum kit. "Evenin'," was all he would say as he climbed into the back seat, immersing himself in a book. At the venue, he would bring in his drums, set them up and sit and read. He would even read between numbers on stage, when Alvin and Leo were nattering. At the end of the evening, after dismantling and loading up his drums, he would sit and read while Alvin and Leo discussed the show and talked to friends and fans. Delivered home with his kit at the end of the night, he'd mutter "G'night", his second spoken word of the evening. I never saw Dave agitated. He was always self-contained, professional and an excellent drummer.

As Alvin was the driver he had the use of the van. It was our passion wagon and when Leo and Dave were dropped off we would indulge in well-hidden locations. We were both what they used to call "highly-sexed", but with the added tension of still living at home, and having the band around all evening, the release when we were alone was sweet indeed. I remember one rainy, muddy night, we parked in Billy Bacon's field in Basford and, as time passed, were oblivious to a sinking feeling. We were firmly stuck in the mud. Alvin went off and somehow came back with a guy in a vehicle, with a tow rope, who pulled us out of the mud with a wink and a smile.

My favourite Jaybird venues were the YMCA on Shakespeare Street and The Dancing Slipper on Central Avenue, in West Bridgeford where they played residencies. They played – The Rainbow Rooms, The Elizabethan Rooms – but the YMCA and the Dancing Slipper were the best Nottingham venues for rock'n'roll. Playing a venue regularly meant the band could build up an audience by word of mouth. Gradually these gigs became busier and busier and had an energy to which Alvin and Leo responded. The gap between audience and band was crossed through familiarity and this in turn increased the fun for everyone. Alvin performed with amazing confidence, every number tight and professional, with innovations going beyond the actual records they covered. Centre stage, he was happy and at home, looking out, engaging the audience, the pretty girls, a natural performer. He certainly looked the part of a young rocker.

The Jaybirds' repertoire was hot, rockin' music. A typical setlist included 'Twenty Flight Rock', 'Summertime Blues', 'Blue Suede Shoes', Larry Williams 'Slow Down', a personal jiving favourite, 'Peggy Sue', 'Money', loads of Chuck Berry, 'Roll Over Beethoven', 'Rock'n'Roll Music', 'Reelin' 'n' Rockin', 'Johnny B Goode' and 'Sweet Little Sixteen'. Later in the set they'd do a dynamic version of Ray Charles 'What'd I Say', which Alvin would take down low before bringing the song home with a pounding finish. Usually they ended with 'Ya Ya Twist' and they would be called back for encores. When he sang 'Little Queenie' – "There she is again standing over by the record machine, looking like a model on the cover of a magazine, she's too cute to be a minute over seventeen. Go go, go, Little Queenie!" – I knew he was singing this just for me.

I still love that song. It takes me right back to the time, just 17. Know what I mean?

chapter 12
The Jaybirds

Nottingham in 1964 with Alvin was extraordinary, full of music and adventure. The great thing about teenage love is you live in the present; too young to wonder how your childhood fucked you up, too young to carry baggage of previous relationships, too young to care about the future. Emerging from childhood, exhilarated by the freedom to take charge of your own life, it's a golden time.

If The Jaybirds were not playing, we often went to gigs, two of which stand out. There was Chuck Berry at the Odeon cinema, the man himself, performing his classics, duck-walking the stage which seemed odd rather than exciting. He didn't disappoint but somehow he looked a bit too old, not part of our generation. Support act was The Animals, fronted by Eric Burdon, with their soon-to-be-a-huge-hit 'House Of The Rising Sun', a memorable performance. The sparse, moody, intense arrangement was hypnotic and Eric's screaming vocals topped the night.

At The Dancing Slipper we saw Steam Packet, with Long John Baldry, Rod Stewart and Julie Driscoll, three singers up-front, and Brian Auger on Hammond organ. Their set opened with Rod alone at the front, mid-stage with a mic in hand, his back to the audience in super-tight satin pants, tall and skinny, his bouffant hair back-combed. We were totally confused. Was it a girl or a boy? It wasn't until he began to sing, turning to the audience and joined by even taller Long John Baldry and powerhouse Julie Driscoll, that we realised it was a boy. Julie amazed me that night, the first female, really exceptional, rock singer I had seen on stage. Their show was dynamic, loud, powerful, professional and impressive. At the end, Alvin and I went into the dressing room where he congratulated them and enjoyed a music-based conversation. Memorably, Rod was running around in only his underpants, laughing and having fun. It was a technicolor glimpse into another world, another energy, London vibes, very attractive.

Alvin loved going to the cinema on a night-off and had very broad tastes. We saw the Fellini films, *La Dolce Vita*, *8 1/2* and *Juliet Of The Spirits*. I loved these movies but really didn't have much idea of what they were about. Rather, like Rod in his underpants, they were a glimpse into another world, a world of beautiful people, glamour, mystery, craziness that existed a long way from Nottingham. How did Alvin know about these movies, so different from mainstream cinema? Maybe from his older sisters. Irma was an actress involved in the arts. Maybe Fellini movies were just shown in mainstream cinemas in 1964? He was always drawn towards the unusual in the visual arts, a world away from Constable's *Haywain*, and he definitely had a quirky sense of humour.

One memorable night we went to see Hitchcock's *The Birds*. Horror movies were big business, with Hammer horror films especially gory. You needed to be 16 to see these X-certificate films, so we all went as soon as we could pass for 16. The lure of the illicit, stuff forbidden to younger teenagers, X movies, smoking cigarettes, drinking alcohol.

The Birds was incredibly well promoted, with a remarkable trailer featuring Hitchcock talking about how we abuse birds and suggesting they would get their own back. Sitting in a room with stuffed birds, birds in cages, he sat down to eat a chicken, then decided not to. At the Odeon we sat in the centre of the balcony, front row, making it hard to leave. We settled down to watch in a hushed cinema and, as the plot unfolded, Tippi Hedren became a victim of various birds which we found more silly than scary. As big black birds settled on telegraph wires, we started to giggle, then laugh, then try to not laugh so as not to spoil it for everyone else. We lost control, buried our heads in our hands and into each other, thoroughly disgraceful, the horror lost for us.

At the other extreme, Alvin loved *Looney Tunes* cartoons that ran 24/7 in cartoon cinemas. Wile. E Coyote and the Road Runner was the favourite, and we spent hours laughing together over cartoons and comedy movies. We were still young kids having fun.

Nottingham friends Ruth and Jeff, who knew Alvin before I met him, remained friends with him throughout his life. Recently they sent me dozens of photos from these early Nottingham days, the four of us having fun. Alvin is mostly being mischievous, happy to pose with an empty champagne bottle as a drunk, despite not being a drinker. You can see that off stage he was relaxed, easy to be around, willing to join in with whatever was happening. I asked Ruth how she remembered young Alvin, his temperament. "He wasn't a show-off," she said. "He was very good-natured, lovely, fun, always lots of laughing, a big kid." That's my memory too.

Sam and Doris were lighthearted, good-natured and open-minded. I never saw either of them angry. Their home was an open house, Alvin and all his friends were always welcome. In true English style Doris would make cups of tea and sandwiches, plates of biscuits and cakes, for everyone who turned up. Sam might be pottering about in his shed in the garden, but he would come in to chat while we enjoyed Doris' delights. There was always music.

Most kids like to alone with their friends, without parents around. This was certainly the case with mine, but it wasn't with Sam and Doris. One or the other would strum a guitar along with Alvin, and sing. Sam's deep, bass voice was rich and warm. Or they might play records. Sam would play some of his vast collection from the deep south of America, blues players like Jimmy Reed, Big Bill Broonzy, Elmore James, Sonny Terry & Brownie McGee and even raw prison work songs. For me it was a revelation. This was not music played on the radio in the UK. I had never heard any blues. Alvin would put on the forties guitar players, Chet Atkins, Les Paul and Mary Ford, Django Rhinehart, Charlie Christian, that maybe Doris favoured. Theirs was a musical household unlike anything I had ever experienced. Families that connect through the arts are rare but not unattainable.

It was obvious to me they were a close, supportive family, enjoying a real family life, making music together and encouraging each other's talents. It was overwhelming for me. Our first Christmas together brought a visit with Alvin's sister Janice and her clarinet playing husband George. I remember a piano, clarinet, guitars and everyone standing around and singing. I liked to sing, but felt self-conscious and succeeded only in offering a smiling, clapping audience for everyone.

Sam and Doris supported Alvin and The Jaybirds in many ways. Doris was a great seamstress and made interesting clothes for Alvin, in particular a royal blue rayon velvet bomber jacket. It had knitted, fine rib collar, cuffs and lower hem band, and a zip front opening that was edged either side by embroidered Tyrolean braid. It was a favourite of his and there are many photos of him wearing it. In fact, he wore it so much it started to wear thin in places and I patched it to keep it going. Of course, Doris cut his hair. She was an excellent stylist. She would massage his back as he leant against a chair. I never knew the origins of his back problems, but they were certainly made worse by having a heavy guitar slung across his body. He enjoyed being massaged and I started to take on that role.

Sam was always available, day or night, to help out, especially with the van. When it broke down, which was a fairly regular occurrence, they would find a phone and wake Sam. Without complaint he'd head out to find them, fix whatever he could or tow them home. Once they got stuck in snow on Snake Pass, a perilous Peak District road, where the weather could turn nasty without warning. Sam left his cozy bed and set off to rescue them in the early hours, showing remarkable dedication to his son. Alvin was truly blessed to have been born to Sam and Doris Barnes, who supported his career in the way they did.

Sam had a great knack for problem solving. When Johnnie Clifton moved down to London he wanted to take his prize piano with him. JC's mother was a very religious woman and, since it was a Sunday, was dead set against the piano being moved. It had to come down the main staircase of their house. JC and Alvin, with no real planning, were on the stairs below supporting it against gravity. Mrs Clifton was on the top landing, pacing. "No good will would come of this," she repeated. "It shouldn't be done on the Lord's day." I stayed at the bottom, a silent observer. When the piano became wedged between the ceiling and the stairs, Mrs C's wailing increased several notches and Alvin and JC tried with no success to unstick it. Sam was called and, like Superman, leaped to the rescue. He looked at the problem for a while, suggested various maneuvers and low and behold all was quickly saved, the piano, the ceiling and Mrs Clifton's Sunday sanity.

Young Alvin and Loraine didn't fight or argue or fall out. We were great pals and life was an adventure, mostly generated by Alvin, which was fine by me. I had left school at 15 and, aside from my secret wish to go to Art College, had no ambitions. I was happy to have decisions about the future put on hold and just have fun, dance, enjoy the music and my gorgeous boyfriend.

In late 1963 Rudolf Gernreich, an Austrian born US fashion designer, invented the Monokini, a topless swimsuit. Rudi had been a dancer and wanted to liberate women from the corsets, suspender belts and stockings and ridiculous whirlpool bras of the fifties. His topless Monokini was a protest against repressive society, the baring of women's breasts a form of freedom. It was no secret that Alvin loved breasts. He was what was referred to at the time as "a tit man". In early 1964 we were out with Johnnie Clifton and his girlfriend Judy when we wound up at the house of a local guy JC knew named Mick, who sold clothes. The Monokini had stimulated other designers and there were now topless dresses and he'd bought some to sell to Nottingham shops.

It was suggested that Judy and I might want to take a look, so we went upstairs with Mick who left the room while we examined the goods. We both tried on a dress, which looked ridiculous, had a laugh and changed back into whatever we were wearing. There was a knock at the door and when I opened it Alvin stood there, his eyes dark, staring, his features fixed like granite. Not a word was said. With his right hand he landed a hard slap to my face, turned, walked away and quickly left the house.

The details of what happened next are lost in the mists of time. Distraught and confused, I discovered from JC that Mick had uttered a few ribald comments about us. Perhaps Alvin was worried I would walk downstairs to model this new fashion. Somehow, I got home. I got hold of him, we talked and explained and made up, but it only takes one incident. A line had been drawn and it was now clear to me that I should be careful about my reputation. My boyfriend had another side and I didn't want to call it out again. Women understand about defining moments in the dynamics of any relationship.

Alvin taught me to cook. My mum was always busy and organised so there was no helping her in the kitchen. I could do a fry up, eggs and bacon, and fried tomatoes, and prepare sandwiches, sharpen the carving knife on the back doorstep and shell peas. He taught me to makes omelettes, bonfire toffee and good pots of tea, like Doris made. He often chewed liquorice root and always smoked cigarettes as Sam had done, leaving them dangling between his lips when he played guitar. Eating out would be a curry, totally exotic to me. I would stick to an omelette and never ate a curry in all the time we were together.

At Toston Drive I watched fascinated as he changed all the strings on his big red GIbson. He stripped off the old strings, and showed me how to wind them into hoops and fasten off to keep in case spares were needed. He would spray polish the body, making it shine, the neck smooth and slick and ready for action. Then, beginning with the fat bass E, he'd take the pristine strings from their envelopes, attach them through the string retainer on the Bigsby vibrato unit, over the bridge and pick-ups and into the machine heads, pulled through before finishing the wind and trimming off the surplus string with wire cutters. The rest followed, all six strings ending on the high E. He worked with calm patience and dexterity.

Then followed tuning, pitching with a harmonica, individually stretching the high strings, retuning, playing quite hard, more retuning. The whole process took about an hour. He loved to play new strings, chords progressions, practice rhythms and runs, repeat passages, always lost in his personal music world. He would play guitar endlessly, but not sing along. He would learn new songs to cover and practice singing them at home, and sometimes he'd give me the lyrics so I could correct him or prompt when he forgot.

A self-confessed electronics nerd, he had two particular friends in Nottingham who were electronic boffins, Don Truscott and Johnnie Blatherwick. Don loved to build speakers and amplifiers and one day proudly told us he had split the garage roof while testing out some huge set-up on high volume, with the opening note of The Supremes 'Stop In The Name Of Love'. Johnnie would come and set up at Jaybirds shows and record the sets. If only we knew where those gems ended up. With a few friends we would go back to his house and play back the sets. "Blatherwick never had enough tea cups," recalled Ruth.

Blatherwick and Truscot were referred to by their surnames, like professors might have been, and Blatherwick stayed in contact with Alvin for many years after he left Nottingham. The phone would ring and Blatherwick would launch into a technical dialogue before he knew who had answered.

"Hey me ode! (Nottingham slang). You know that Ep 3Xz we were discussing, well I've found a 3Xw that does the job."

"Hi Johnnie," I would reply. "I'll get Alvin for you."

"Yes, mi duck, thanks."

Where are those Blatherwick tapes of The Jaybirds?

Leo Lyons, Manager, it said on The Jaybirds business cards along with his address and phone number. Leo was indeed the manager, taking bookings, dealing with fee negotiations, collecting the money, paying out to Alvin and Dave, later to Ric and Chick. Driving to and from Mansfield twice an evening to Nottingham gigs was effortless to Alvin, even on foggy nights. It seemed to me he had superhuman driving skills. He liked to jump red lights at road works that closed one lane.

At first, I was shocked when he did this, but then I realised he could see ahead and there were no CCTV cameras in 1964. On the road back from Mansfield, near to Redhill, there was a residential road up a hill that ran alongside the main road, with a pedestrian bridge across the A50 at the top. Up there in the dark, parked on the grass in front of a big detached house, we would navigate the gear stick and steering wheel for the evening's passion. Afterwards, back down the other side we'd rejoin the A50, gather speed down the hill and with the engine cut we'd coast to see how far the momentum would take us. A few nights we managed the two miles to the A6514, Valley Road.

There was no time limit, no need to get anywhere. We were kids playing, enjoying each other, in the moment, no responsibilities. Wonderful.

chapter 13
The Course of True Love

I was still working full time at the East Midlands Gas Board, filing work dockets in the accounts department. Some nights Alvin would pick me up from work to go to gigs. The Jaybirds van, parked outside waiting for me to leave, always gave me a smile and put a spring in my step at the end of a long boring day. In May 1964 I was fired, sacked for being persistently late in the mornings, my late evenings doubtless responsible.

I went straight into another full-time job, at Boots the Chemist, in a beautiful purpose-built shop on Pelham Street, on the road behind the council building. There was so much work available in those days that leaving one job and walking straight into another was easy. They put me on the surgical counter, where my hours behind the bar made the work second nature to me. I particularly enjoyed embarrassing dads who were sheepish about buying toilet trainer seats for their toddlers. I would display the whole range across the counter. It wasn't very kind of me.

Bizarrely, and this is true, during the time I worked there, Boots sold condoms for the first time. However, females were not allowed to sell them. If a man asked a female for a packet we would have to say, "Just a moment" and go and fetch the male on duty. This was considered less embarrassing for the females, but obviously it was not.

Boots was certainly more interesting than the Gas board, but fitting work in with my normal life was becoming more problematic. I had been smoking cigarettes since I was 13, roll-ups made with licorice papers and Old Holborn pipe tobacco, a habit I maybe picked up from Alvin. When we went for tea or lunch breaks and I rolled-up a fag, I got some odd looks from the other members of staff who asked what I was smoking. Eventually someone told me that women in prison smoked roll-ups.

None of this fazed me, being different felt ok and identifying with Nottingham social customs held no particular attraction. I wanted to be somewhere else, somewhere less brutal, less ordinary, more mysterious, more open and accepting, where no one knew me or asked about my life and my habits.

If not at work or with Alvin, music was still central to my life. I watched the brilliant Otis Redding live TV appearance on *Ready Steady Go!* and was on my feet transported, dancing around the living room into the place that was calling to me through the ethers. I played The Beatles' early albums over and over, singing harmonies along with the records, picking out chord sequences on the piano in the pub.

The Beatles released their second LP, *With The Beatles*, on the same day that John F Kennedy, the US president, was assassinated in Dallas. People have said, "You always remember where you were when you heard about it." For me it was precisely 17 days after I fell in love with Alvin and although I heard the news, I remember being more shocked when assassin Lee Harvey Oswald was shot dead outside the police station by Jack Ruby. That live murder on TV brought darkness and chaos to an America that had seemed Technicolor golden, the place of the future, the birthplace of rock'n'roll.

When Alvin played outside Nottingham, he would come to the house on his way back home. My parents were already upstairs, sound asleep in bed at the far end of the long upstairs corridor. Opening the back door when I heard the van, I would usher him into the downstairs lounge for an hour of passion before he went on his way. Over Easter 1964, he arrived quite late from a gig and it was almost daylight before he left and I went up to my bed for a sound sleep. In the morning I was woken by mum in a panic. There had been a robbery in the pub in the middle of the night. As there was no sign of a forced break-in the police thought it might be an inside job.

I was questioned. Naturally I kept mum about Alvin's visit, though they told me that they knew The Jaybirds' van was often outside the pub late at night. That was when I discovered that our lives were not private.
I denied he had been there that night so my parents wouldn't find out about our midnight trysts. I remember asking why they thought I would want to steal from my parents. It was a lot of cash, in a portable safe that was kept in a wardrobe right alongside my parents' double bed. The keys to the safe were on the huge key ring my dad always kept in his jacket pocket, which was hung over the wardrobe door. The thief had removed the safe from the wardrobe while they were asleep, and also taken the jacket before going down into the pub where they opened up the safe and took all the Easter takings,

£2,000. It was a long Bank Holiday, Good Friday, Saturday, and Sunday, with the banks closed. With inflation, £2,000 is worth over £30,000 today.

The police knew of a young local woman had recently eloped with her boyfriend and suggested that perhaps I was planning to do the same with Alvin. It was ludicrous. I knew perfectly well that neither of us were involved and we had no thoughts of eloping. I explained that Alvin was doing well with The Jaybirds and had a steady income, and so did I from my job, so there was no reason at all why we would have stolen the money.

Once the police had gone, I set off up Nuthall road to call Alvin and tell him what had happened, as obviously they'd interview him too. On the way, and now more awake, I realised that not telling them about Alvin's visit was unwise since the police on duty that night might well have seen the van outside. So, I decided to go into the local police station, and tell them he'd been to visit that night. They were understanding and took a further statement. What a strange Easter Monday. Later, Alvin and I went to Carrington Lido and spent the afternoon swimming, trying to relax in the midst of this surreal event.

In April 2012, sharing old memories with Alvin, he hadn't forgotten and sent me the following email: "Ay up me Duck (Nottingham greeting), Toston Towers, The Newcastle Arms, The Jaybirds Van. Remember that time The Newcastle Arms had that robbery and a copper came to my house and wanted to see my shoes to match it to the footprint they'd found. Knowing I was innocent I did my James Dean leery Rebel Without a Clue act and the copper thought I was definitely guilty and said so. I then phoned up the Chief Constable in my posh voice and complained that this policeman had accused me of the robbery. Poor guy had to come back the next day and apologise."

When I got back home late afternoon, my dad was raging. He started to push me about the room, shouting, furious that Alvin, who he mostly called "that lad", as in "has that lad been round again", had been a late-night visitor. I'm sure he knew that we were innocent of the robbery, it was just a father's reaction to the realisation that his little girl had her own life, and one he wasn't too happy about.

A few weeks later, my mother saw our window cleaner driving around in a brand-new car, and told the police. Nothing came of it, but he would have been the perfect fit for someone who'd had access to their bedroom and could have seen the portable safe in the open wardrobe. Also, his shoe print would have been on the small flat roof outside their bedroom, when he was cleaning the outside of those windows. Though there was no forced entry, it would have explained the shoe prints. It was easy enough for someone to hide in the pub or one of the upstairs rooms of the house, when the pub was open, and wait for everyone to go to bed.

It felt very strange that someone was maybe hiding and waiting for us to finish our secret passions. Nottingham was becoming extremely claustrophobic. It seemed to me that adventure and excitement would feature in our relationship.

Between my full-time work in the day and evenings out with Alvin, relationships with mum, dad and even my brother Stuart, were virtually non-existent. Unlike Sam and Doris, my parents had neither the time nor interest in meeting my friends. Graham was happily married to Valerie elsewhere in Nottingham, and Barry was living in London and working as a pilot with British Caledonian. After the RAF, he had worked as a steward for British Airways while training privately to be a pilot, his dream job. Barry had a few girlfriends but he fell for Yvonne, a stewardess with B Cal, and they were married in 1964.

Yvonne's family lived in Maidenhead where the wedding was held over a weekend. I was bridesmaid, along with Yvonne's sister, but I didn't want to join in the family celebration. The thought of being away from Alvin, even for a weekend, just made me miserable. He was my life at this point but he wasn't invited. Maybe mum thought that if she could prize me from his arms for a weekend, I would awaken from his spell.

When I was young, my brothers had been very important to me and I was not so estranged to refuse to be a bridesmaid but my attitude towards marriage was very cold. Knowing my mother had a lover had tainted the whole romantic ideal and I now saw it as a convention. The weekend was no fun for me. I was far too stubborn and confused, and probably put a bit of a damper on the event. I have vivid memories of the meal, the wedding breakfast, that started with a bowl of soup. After eating that I was already full up. I was unused to endless courses.

My lack of experience or interest in alcohol was another problem. I drank champagne for the first time, and my glass was topped up with wines and maybe even liqueurs. I was drunk, really drunk, so much so that in the car on the way back to the house to change I had to ask the driver to stop so I could throw up my lovely lunch by the side of the road. I was disgracing the family, and my mother constantly referred to it, even in the last years of her long life.

Back in the real world – my world – life with Alvin and the rock'n'roll Jaybirds was amazing. I wasn't planning our future, I was happy, secure and very much in love. We would babysit for Irma, Alvin's eldest sister, who had three small children and, sadly, had been widowed, losing her beloved husband Neil to cancer, just before I met Alvin.

Some evenings we would drive down the M1, 50 miles south, to the first services south of Nottingham, the famous Blue Boar at Watford. We'd have a coffee and a hamburger and enjoy the energy of the cars racing by on their way to London. One day we drove to the north of London, to Wembley and back, to collect some speakers that had been re-coned at Goodmans. We sat in a seemingly endless traffic jam on the North Circular road, but it was very exciting to think we were in London.

By now I knew that Nottingham was not where we were looking to spend our lives, but I was patient and happy to let life be what it was. I didn't want to change Alvin, he was quite acceptable just the way he was. So, it came as a bolt out of the blue when one wintery evening in early 1965, when we pulled up by my backdoor after a gig and all of our usual intimacy, he turned to me and said he didn't want to see me anymore. I couldn't believe what I was hearing. I was in deep shock, devastated. When I asked, he told me there wasn't anyone else. I would discover this was a lie, that he had met someone else, name of Heather.

The next few months were a nightmare from which I was unable to wake. I couldn't understand what had happened, what I had done wrong. In my mind, it had to be me who had got it wrong. But we had seemed so well suited, there was no friction, no arguing, we truly felt right together. My life stopped. All of our friends, Sam and Doris, my life didn't really exist without him. I felt alienated at home and at work, so I quit Boots and went back to working behind the bar at home. One night I went out to the cinema and Alvin walked in with his new girlfriend. He didn't see me but I knew I had to get out of Nottingham or I would go crazy.

The only place I knew a little was Bournemouth, the seaside town on the south coast where I had twice been on holiday, 200 miles from Nottingham and Alvin. On a Friday in May I went to the employment exchange where they set up an interview for me at a hotel seeking summer waitresses. On the Sunday I took a train through London to Bournemouth, where I was interviewed and accepted. I started work on the Monday. I shared a room in a house the hotel owned and all my meals were included. Ursula, the lovely Swiss housekeeper, introduced me to yogurt. I had left home to escape a broken heart. I would never return to live with my parents.

In a busy job, a new town, new people, gradually my life returned. Ironically, the most fun girlfriend I made, Suellen, had a musician boyfriend.

Roger Pope was the drummer in a band called The Soul Agents, along with Don Shinn, an excellent Hammond player, whom Keith Emerson cited as a huge influence, and Caleb Quaye, Ian Duck and Dave Glover. Roger and some of the band went on to a long and interesting career as Hookfoot, occasionally backing Elton John. An excellent soul band, they introduced me to amphetamines as an aid to all-night weekends dancing in the clubs where Wilson Pickett, Otis Redding, and Sam & Dave were nourishing my soul and healing my hurts.

This music had no nostalgic links with rock'n'roll to upset me and dancing was my first love, but still I couldn't understand how Alvin had been able to stop loving me. It wasn't that I was arrogant or vain. We had felt so right to be together, as if the future had a plan for us, and as if to confirm this here I was in Bournemouth again with close musical friends.

The summer in the busy hotel restaurant left little time for being miserable, and it was highly educational. The Hungarian breakfast chef, Joe, was a wild guy, long black curly hair, tattoos, broken teeth and gold earrings, his crisp, starched chef's whites a direct contrast to his exotic pirate look. When the large trays of fried eggs came up from the kitchen, he would scan them looking for any that had broken yolks. Then with one smooth move, sliding the spatula underneath the offending egg, he threw it backwards over his shoulder, where it hit the wall and slid down to the floor. One day he came up behind me and put his arms around me. Not only did I scream at the top of my lungs, I began to shake out of pure fear. That certainly scared him, which he deserved, having scared us waitresses for months with his grunts and growls. Payday in the hotel was always a Wednesday as Joe and the kitchen staff would go and get drunk and either be ill and absent or even more crazy for breakfast. The boss knew if they were paid on Fridays the weekend service would be compromised.

Being away from my parents, trying new and interesting things was just natural. Deirdre Beck advertised her model agency and I felt attractive enough to go and see what that was all about. Deirdre took me on her books, had me model and pay for a model portfolio with a local photographer, and showed me how to walk on a catwalk looking suitably serious and unattainable. It was easy and the other models were fun. We did shows in the Bournemouth pavilion and my photo was in the local paper a couple of times.

One evening a month Deirdre held a photographers' event at her studio. Under bright lights we would pose, in swimwear or nightwear, for a half dozen chaps with their Rollieflex and Rolliecord cameras, all very innocent by today's standards. Us models were not paid, it was part of our modelling course, though I'm sure Deirdre charged the men. A few times the photographers gave us prints, "glamour" shots I suppose.

One day three of us were sent out on a photo shoot to a rubberwear company. They were shooting for a mail order catalogue and we began by posing in wet suits which we squeezed into with lashings of talcum powder. After a while, thin latex nighties and baby doll pyjamas were brought into the changing rooms. We were all rather confused, but since they did cover us up with opaque layers, we went ahead and posed together, with our serious and unattainable expressions. We were so innocent and incredulous. "Why would anyone want to wear rubber pyjamas?"

The hotel closed when the season ended in September. I got a job as a filing clerk at a builder's merchants and, since the hotel's lodging house was empty, arranged with Ursula to have a room of my own. In November, for my birthday, I went up to Nottingham, my first visit back since I had escaped in May. I went to the town centre and into the Kardomah for a coffee, and there was Alvin, sitting alone over a cup of coffee.

He had changed physically. The slightly podgy teenage look with Elvis quiff hair had gone. His hair was very short, modish and his face more mature, slender, his high cheek bones a strong feature. Without hesitating I went over and sat with him, not knowing what to expect. He was definitely pleased to see me. We fell into a long conversation about what we had been doing over the summer. After a while I asked about Heather and he told me he'd had appendicitis, which became peritonitis, and spent a month in a convalescent home. The illness had caused his weight loss and dramatically changed his looks. While he was recovering, Heather complained. "Oh! When will you be well? I'm so bored!" This woke him up and ended the relationship. That appendicitis was a gift for sure.

In Bournemouth I had started modeling, in Nottingham Alvin had started taking photographs. He invited me out the next day to take some pictures. Warily, I agreed. He came to pick me up in a big black Austin Sheerline, a fifties gangster car with huge headlights. Apparently, the mudguards were held on with gaffer tape. The little Berkeley sports had been retired and the Sheerline, with its leather and walnut interior, had taken its place.

There was a side to Alvin that loved pranks, and he told me that, inspired by the car, he and Leo had "kidnapped" Dave Quickmire. First, they dropped Dave off, and then he drove the Sheerline around the block, screeching to a halt. Leo leapt out, grabbed Dave and bundled him into the back of the car, screeching away. As this was witnessed and reported to the police, he had another visit by them to explain his "crime". Obviously, Dave Quickmire was able to reassure them that he was the victim, and no harm was done, just a bit of fun.

On a sunny November day, we drove to Wollaton Park, not far from Alvin's home, a gorgeous backdrop for photos. We spent a few happy hours, me posing and Alvin shooting, both very focused and professional. The sun began to warm me and I felt relaxed. He suggested a pose looking over a small wrought iron gate at the top of some steps, and after taking the picture he walked slowly up the steps, kissed me gently and my heart melted. With that kiss we were back together. It felt completely right. He told me how much he had missed me, especially one night at The White Post cafe on the Ollerton Road. On the new juke box that also showed early videos, they played 'Go Now' by The Moody Blues. In the video was a blond girl walking away and it had made him feel sad that he had lost me.

Without realising it I had grown up that summer and felt more confident, with more sense of myself but I was not about to move back to Nottingham. Alvin was already planning to leave home again and try his luck in London with the band for a third time. I went back to Bournemouth. Maybe I wanted to test him, to be sure he was sincere. After the winter I went back to the hotel, this time for the season as a chambermaid, and I saved money from my small wage.

True to his word, he would telephone. We would talk on the pay phone in the hall of the house. He wrote letters and sent postcards, his visits, when he could get away, were wonderful. I had a room to myself and Ursula was cool enough to let us be together – against hotel rules. The first meal I ever cooked Alvin was here, steak and mushrooms and chips. Cooking it was a very intense operation and it was well received. And yes, it was also the first time we slept together all night. It was intoxicating, despite being a single bed.

After the summer season, I said goodbye to lovely, kind Ursula, packed my bags and in September 1966 I joined Alvin in London. I had saved £100 equivalent to £1,500 today, not a fortune but enough for a deposit on a tiny flat and a month's rent.

Now the fun really began.

chapter 14
Swinging London

In London Alvin was Alvin. Graham Barnes was no more, just a Nottingham memory. An early recollection of London in 1966 is being dropped off at Piccadilly Circus, facing the statue of Eros. The Jaybirds were off to audition at the BBC, hoping they might get radio work backing up singers, as they were still a covers band. I had just joined him from Bournemouth and had never been alone in central London before. Going down into the tube or trying to catch a bus back to where we were staying in Notting Hill was terrifying for me.

I decided to walk the three miles to our hotel, window shopping along the way. The crowds, the colours, the energy, the rush of people and traffic was on such an epic scale compared to Nottingham or Bournemouth. By the end of my first week, I had reasoned that the people coming up out of the tube looked no smarter than me. After traveling in and out with Alvin a few times, I took the plunge navigated it alone. We all smoked cigarettes and so did everyone else on the tube. No doubt it smelt disgusting, but as a smoker I never noticed.

The Madison was a musicians' hotel, quite a shock after the nice family hotel in Bournemouth. Some rooms had four or five beds and might be occupied by an entire band for months on end. Everyone smoked, and not just cigarettes. It was a social hang out for musicians, maybe the London version of the Chelsea Hotel in New York, but much smaller and very cramped. Obviously anywhere with a bed we could share made the environment fade into the background.

Leo was sharing a room with Alvin and moved out to a room of his own. Chick also stayed there somewhere, maybe in a multiple room, as he was the roadie. I knew about Chick only from a postcard sent to me from Blackpool, a long narrow card with a picture of Blackpool Tower on the back.

Dated Jan 1966, it was addressed to Miss L Burgon, at my Bournemouth address.

"Hello. Having a gas time today. Chick our pianist road manager & I have hired a Zephyr 6 and come to Blackpool for the day. We've just been up in an airplane, and it's all pretty great. Feel like a millionaire until I count my money. We've been doing a ton ten down the motorway with the radio blasting. Just having a look round the town then we're off back. I will write again soon and ring you at the weekend. All my Love, Graham XXXX "

As far as I know that was the first time Alvin ever flew in a plane, a joyride out over the sea and around the Blackpool Tower. "A ton ten", was 110 mph down the motorway.

Early in 1966, The Jaybirds had auditioned and been recruited as the band in a West End theatre production of *Saturday Night and Sunday Morning*, the play by Nottingham writer Alan Sillitoe, produced by Frank Dunlop. It was set in Nottingham, so for authenticity a Nottingham band seemed a good idea. Alvin rang me in Bournemouth with his West End theatre adventure stories. Memorably, one night Spike Milligan, who was appearing nearby in *Son Of Oblamov*, turned up on stage during his own interval. Ignoring the action, he laid down at the front of the stage, crossed his arms over his chest like a corpse and, having silenced the cast and the audience, declaimed loudly: "Henry the Eighth!" Amid confusion and laughter, he took a bow and left for his own show. Alvin had been to see *Son Of Oblamov* twice and loved Spike, no doubt recognising a prankster spirit similar to his own. *Saturday Night and Sunday Morning*'s run only lasted a few months.

The Jaybirds' drummer, the enigmatic Dave Quickmire, had opted not to spread his wings but to stay in Mansfield, recommending as his replacement Ric Lee, a drum student of his who had a similar, jazz-based rock style. During the West End theatre run, Ric met Ruthann, a professional theatre dancer. She seemed very confident, sophisticated and grown-up to me. I would discover that her father had left the family when she was young and her mother had passed away when Ruthann and her brother were teenagers. Growing up fast was unavoidable for her and, not unsurprisingly, she had a more serious view of life after the tragedies and financial hardship she'd suffered at a young age. Later in life we would become better friends than we ever were in the sixties and seventies.

Ric was living with Ruthann at her rented flat in Dulwich, where there was a room, for Alvin and me to move in and escape the madhouse Madison. We stayed there for a couple of weeks while looking for a place of our own and found a tiny flat on the fourth floor of an old Victorian house in Warwick Square in Victoria. The typical garden square was great on a fine day, somewhere to relax, maybe take photos. Our new home was within walking distance of the Tate, the magical art gallery by the Thames. The Salvador Dali paintings there introduced us to surrealism. Alvin would remain a fan of Dali, both his art and his outrageous persona, all his life.

The Warwick Square flat was really small, "compact" as an agent would say. It was fully furnished, which meant an old two-seat sofa and chair, a table with two dining chairs, and a cabinet cupboard that was a good size for storing LPs and a record player. Soon, living on the top of that, was a reel-to-reel tape recorder, a Simon, to turn the flat into Alvin's first home studio. A pair of decent speakers ensured that our neighbours could enjoy the music too. Our headphones enabled us to enjoy new stereo effects. Family's *Music From A Doll's House* was a favourite stereo album, with in-phase and out-of-phase vocals to add a 3D effect.

The bedroom was just big enough for a double divan bed, chest of drawers, a clothes rail, built-in corner cupboard with shelves and a full-length mirror on the door, which served to double the look of the space. There was no bedroom door, just an opening, so I put up a curtain. In the corner of the living room a door opened up to reveal a shower in a box. The "kitchen" was built into a space next to the shower, a small sink and, behind another door, a Baby Belling electric cooker. A freestanding fridge on the floor next to the shower held a bottle of milk and a tub of margarine. On the small landing we shared a toilet with two other flats. A single lady lived above us there. About once a month she would bring home a young man and enjoy a very noisy and, for us, entertaining hour of lovemaking.

Materially we had little in every way, but we had each other. I thought we had a perfect sex life but, one night, Alvin asked why I never had an orgasm. Well, I'd never even heard that women could have orgasms. It was news to me, raised in the age of innocence. Or was it simply ignorance? I had grown up without any sex instruction, only enthusiasm. When I first made love with my teacher boyfriend, one time it had felt like I was going to faint before I took control of myself. I guess that would have been my first orgasm but I didn't know what to expect and let it go. Now, in our very private flat, Alvin and I experimented with a variety of positions and stimulating situations and, at 20 years old, I had my first orgasm. My libido moved up several notches.

We had installed a big old black and white TV and covered the screen with a red spotlight gel, to make it a colour TV. One early evening, watching

Coronation Street, Alvin produced a hashish joint for me to share with him. At first, I thought it had no effect, but as the ludicrous Northern characters and plot became more and more absurdly comic I knew something had changed. I loved it. I had never enjoyed alcohol, but hashish, marijuana, grass, pot, whatever you want to call it, suited me perfectly. Sensual and creatively stimulating, it became my drug of choice. Whether listening to music, drawing, painting, taking photos, designing clothes for Alvin and me, cooking, playing house, making love, having fun, there was nothing that wasn't enhanced by a good smoke.

In our last telephone call in December of 2012, Alvin recalled how creative we had been in Warwick Square. I had brought my Singer electric sewing machine and made curtains from cheap Indian bedspreads, and clothes as I always had. Alvin's mum permed his hair, a tribute to Hendrix, recently arrived in London. We really were kids at play.

Money was scarce though I had managed to save the £100 working in Bournemouth. Even after paying the deposit and a month's rent, there was enough left over for me to live on for a little while. Alvin supported my ambition to become a fashion model but work was hard to come by, though I did do some modelling for photography students.

In reality, I was too short at 5'6" and much too curvy. Twiggy was the look of the day. I felt humiliated, treated like a piece of meat, and some photographers expected sexual favours, suggesting I would make a good glamour model. Glamour modeling was very tame in those days and didn't even involve topless work. There were some things that girlfriends didn't do, and I hated to be treated solely as a sex object.

Thinking skinnier might help, I was constantly on a diet, eating Limits biscuits for days on end and then bingeing, since my body was craving real food. As I was a well-proportioned size 12 (US size 10) someone suggested I try for work as a house model in a clothes company showroom. Laura Lee, the youth arm of the Eastex fashion company, had design studios and salesrooms in Kent House, just off of Oxford Circus in the heart of London's rag trade and close to Carnaby Street. This was a Monday to Friday, 9-5 job, mainly sitting around waiting to be called for fittings with the designers.

The best part was seeing the designer's workshop, expanding my knowledge of design and pattern making. Four times a year buyers would come for a couple of weeks and we would "show" the new range, putting on clothes they picked out to see the fit, the hang, and if it suited their business. It paid a reasonable wage and was secure and steady. I was used to working and supporting myself. It was important to me not to put financial pressure on Alvin. I knew his music required his full attention.

Alvin always made his half of the rent and bills from his music. For a while The Jaybirds backed an English pop vocal trio, The Ivy League. As a duo, Alvin and Leo played jazz classics for diners in clubs in the West End. Ric and Chick signed up to Man Power and I've no idea what kind of jobs they were sent out on. Alvin had to sell the air rifle he kept in the Jaybirds' van. Back in the Nottingham days he and Leo would use the van's headlights to stun, then shoot rabbits on their journey home. This was something he became uncomfortable about later.

Coming home one day, I found the flat sparkling clean and Alvin very pleased with his labours. It turned out he had taken some speed, and "got into cleaning". I was very appreciative. On our first Valentine's Day, 1967, he proudly came home with a big bunch of flowers for me. A naturally romantic man, he never forgot Valentine Day, birthdays or Christmas. We never bought expensive presents for each other even when money was plentiful, but his gifts were always special and thoughtful.

On New Year's Eve, 1966/67, our dear friends Johnnie Clifton and Judy turned up and insisted we experience the New Year celebrations in Trafalgar Square. It would be the only time we did and the memory stayed with Alvin. Squashed and squeezed as the crowds jostled, I squealed when I turned to find the hand on my backside was not Alvin's but a short Indian fella with a huge wide grin. Several times men leapt at me from the approaching crowd, and Alvin pushed them off. Having had a nice mellow smoke before we left home, this felt like hell on earth. Alcohol is definitely the proper drug for such events.

Before I met Alvin, he had already made two attempts to live and work from his music in London but failed and returned home. This time it was easier. He had a girlfriend to help support his mission, so two minds dreamed the same dreams. The new year, 1967, was a pivotal year for culture, politics, music and fashion. It was for us too.

chapter 15
Alvin Lee Emerges

In February 2017 I saw two museum shows, both celebrating the 50th anniversary of the 1967 Summer of Love, one at London's Victoria & Albert Museum entitled "You Say You Want A Revolution: Rebels And Records". Packed wall to ceiling over a dozen large rooms, the show featured posters, album sleeves butted together to run along the walls of all the rooms, fashions, festivals, news events and happenings, along with the music of late sixties London. In the central room was a wall-sized screen showing an edited version of the *Woodstock* movie. The 1969 Woodstock Festival had happened in New York State, but the 1970 documentary film featured so many English bands that it became a high point of this London show. There was Alvin, full screen. It was both bizarre and brilliant to discover those extraordinary times were now museum pieces.

Later that year, visiting family in San Francisco, I saw the De Young Museum's Summer of Love show which celebrated the events that had taken place there during 1967. Original poster art of the Love-Ins, the Be-Ins and Trips Festivals and Fillmore West concerts lined the walls, among them some from Ten Years After's amazing Fillmore gigs. The era's music played and sixties album sleeves were displayed, along with mannequins in glorious West Coast fashions, the tie-dyed, crocheted, beaded, embroidered, fringed leathers and personalized denims.

The argument that smoking dope makes people lazy and dumb was resoundingly squashed at both of these shows. Yet again I felt proud and truly blessed to have been a small part of this creative time, when the young openly celebrated life, inclusively, with joy, peace and love. We were part of an International tribe.

Years later I watched an interview with Carlos Santana. "Hippies were reincarnated Native Americans," he said. Certainly, the ecological values of the original Americans acted as early consciousness raising ideas for how to value the earth that was a home to us all. Hippies found a tribal connection and the early music festivals in the USA reflected that.

This was 6,000 miles from our little flat at Warwick Square in London but around the same time Alvin and I, 22 and 20 respectively, were playing house and getting high, smoking and listening to the same music: Bob Dylan's three pivotal albums *Bringing It All Back Home*, *Highway 61 Revisited* and *Blonde On Blonde*, *The Velvet Underground With Nico* and, of course, The Beatles' extraordinary development from *Rubber Soul* to *Revolver* and *Sgt Pepper's Lonely Heart Club Band*.

News from the West Coast of America offered a technicolor panorama that contrasted with the London's grey winter skies. The UK was swinging differently, revolving more around fashion, the mini skirt, dolly birds and Carnaby Street. Within the changing music scene, a growing underground blues scene was developing. Eric Clapton, once a Yardbird, joined John Mayall for the 1966 album *Bluesbreakers*, recorded at Decca's West Hampstead studios and produced by Mike Vernon. In mid-1966 Clapton left to be replaced by Peter Green.

In October 1966, Alvin and I went to the Marquee to see John Mayall's Bluesbreakers featuring Peter Green. Alvin was quiet, acutely focused on his playing. I remember him remarking that Peter was gradually turning up the volume of the guitar during the solos to increase the dynamics. The audience applauded the solos. The atmosphere in the Marquee was more like a jazz club, and he came away very impressed. The Jaybirds still had their financially safe gig backing The Ivy League, but it was leading nowhere. Peter Green no doubt triggered in Alvin memories of Sam's early blues records which he had played and loved but never seriously considered as the future of music once rock'n'roll had arrived.

What's Shakin, the June 1966, Elektra label compilation release, was a huge influence on Alvin. It featured five tracks by The Paul Butterfield Blues Band, tracks, including 'Spoonful' and 'Good Morning Little Schoolgirl', four by the Lovin' Spoonful, and three by an ad-hoc studio band assembled by producer Joe Boyd that included Eric Clapton and Jack Bruce, along with Manfred Mann singer Paul Jones and Steve Winwood from The Spencer Davis Group. Their tracks included 'I Want To Know', 'Crossroads' and Al Kooper's 'Can't Keep From Crying Sometimes'. These songs, along with the two by Butterfield, would form the basis of TYA's onstage set.

Most importantly, the electric, rock energy of those blues tracks showed how it was possible to take blues standards and revitalize them with shifting tempos and new arrangements.

This is what Ten Years After, as they would soon become, played in the rehearsal room. Not by imitating, copying or making cover versions, but by referencing Alvin's built-in personal blues library, courtesy of Sam Barnes, of riffs, licks and solos from the great blues masters. Everything he'd absorbed subconsciously through his childhood in his Nottingham home informed his guitar playing, the legacy of a white father who collected American black blues and prison work songs. What were the odds on this same music, the music on which he was raised, becoming the music of the day?

In the rehearsal room The Jaybirds did some soul searching and everything fell into place. They had never been interested in the tin-pan alley world of pop hits. Leo, a frequent visitor and appreciator of Sam's blues collection, fell right into it. The dynamic between him and Alvin now formed the core of the band. Bassists mostly stay on the backline and play with the drummer, forming a solid rhythmic foundation. Leo stayed up front, pounding the bass and pushing Alvin, who pushed Leo in return. On stage the strongest connection was between those two.

Chick Churchill, on keyboards, filled in with rhythms and riffs, the only member with formal education in music and, along with drummer Ric Lee, more than a passing interest in jazz. This added a further dimension, and it was shared with Alvin and Leo. It was jazz, not blues, that landed them their first gig at the Marquee. They were all very proficient musicians and, with the addition of Chick on keyboards, they were a tight unit who read one another well musically and could jam out energetically.

I remember Alvin coming back to Warwick Square from that rehearsal and clearly and calmly telling me that The Jaybirds were now going to play the music they loved and were unconcerned about whether it made money or not. It made sense to me. They had been drifting, unclear in their direction, focusing more on money to pay the bills, than their own music. Here was musical clarity. Alvin was happy. It was exciting to see a destination to the journey we were taking.

Meanwhile, Jimi Hendrix had arrived in London, and with the help of his manager Chas Chandler had put together The Experience and released the hit single 'Hey Joe'. His impact on all UK guitarists was immediate. Alvin was stimulated by his guitar playing and his rapid success was an affirmation that there was an audience for intense, guitar-based rock blues.

"Most guitarists... Jeff Beck, Jimmy Page and the like, I figured we all had the same influences, I knew where they were coming from," he told me. "But Jimi Hendrix was from outer space, he was a force on his own."

The Jaybirds became Jaybirds, then Jaybird, Blues Trip and even, for one Marquee appearance, Blues Yard. The name Ten Years After has its origins in a headline in *The Radio Times*, the BBC's programme listings magazine, that Leo came across: 'Suez: Ten Years After'. Alvin took to it straight away because it was abstract and, unlike Blues Yard, didn't put a limit on the type of music they would play. It was open-ended and you could not put 'The' in front of it.

Mr L Lyons, aka Leo, had doubled up as manager since the group's origins as The Jaybirds, taking care of business, organizing their gigs and auditions. A breakthrough came from an audition he arranged at the Marquee Club, in Soho's Wardour Street, through Jack Barrie who'd once promoted Jaybirds gigs in Norfolk. "It was the prestigious place to play," said Leo. The word was that John Gee, manager of the Marquee, was a keen jazz fan. So, on the day, they set up and choose to play Woody Herman's 'Woodchoppers Bal', a fast instrumental that showcased Alvin's guitar playing.

John Gee would write the sleeve notes on Ten Years After's eponymous debut LP: "I first met them one afternoon at the Marquee Club, in late spring of this year (1967). I was working away in my office when suddenly I heard the strains of Woody Hermann's 'Woodchoppers Ball'. Seized with curiosity, I entered the club and there on the stage were these four guys obviously having a wild (Woodchoppers?) ball. To this day I've never discovered how they came to be there, and I've never bothered to ask. I know that I was wildly excited with their playing and gave them a date to play the Marquee. Since then they have played several dates and had audiences on their feet screaming for 'encores'."

Their cunning plot worked exactly as planned.

At the end of 1966 The Jaybirds were smart young men in casual clothes with short hairstyles. I had experimented with Alvin's hair and, inspired by Vidal Sassoon's short Bob Cut, given him a cut with five points, one centre forehead, two over his ears and two more in the back. Our friend Judy Clifton, a model for Sassoon, had travelled with him around the country where he set up workshops for stylists to promote and demonstrate his cutting techniques.

Space-age minimalist fashion was associated with Andre Courrege whose mid-calf straight white boots, with rectangular cut-outs, were a huge success, endlessly copied on the high street. With his stark, geometric shaped mini-skirted dresses in black and white, Courrege was highly innovative and I had tried to style myself with this look, as some of Alvin's photos of me show. Mary Quant took Courrege fashion, naming short skirts "minis" after her favourite car. Good business sense.

Jimi Hendrix embraced the colourful clothes already seen on The Beatles, and Brian Jones of the Stones. I Was Lord Kitchener's Valet, on Portobello Road, introduced antique uniforms of the British Empire to London's groovy set. They opened two further branches in The Kings Road and Carnaby Street, where musicians had been style shopping since the earlier Mods look championed by The Who. A January 1967 photoshoot of the Stones taken in Hyde Park shows Brian Jones and Keith Richards in colourful velvet suits and Afghan fur, while the rest of the band still look more like bank clerks. Brian Jones seems to have been a fashion leader and a dandy. He and Anita Pallenberg spent hours dressing up for a night out, watched by Marianne Faithfull and recalled in her memoir *Faithfull*.

Not only was Jimi's music from outer space but so were his clothes, his hair, and his cool. Eric Clapton had a perm and so did Alvin after our five-pointed Bob Cut experiment. Our friend Ruth, a Nottingham hair stylist, reminded me: "Doris and I both did his perm, one on each side to get it done quicker." Much merriment was involved.

The "afro" proved to be a very easy hairdo for Alvin, especially when touring and performing. Go to sleep, wake up, run a big-toothed comb through it, good to go all day. Early in 1968, it was permed again, but as the perm grew out, I started to trim it into the long blond shag that suited him best. I was not trained to cut hair. It was a stoned and intuitive style, great fun to play with. There was a phase of him growing a short beard, in Scandinavia, which I loved, but he preferred to be clean shaven.

Alvin really disliked shopping for clothes, so it was way easier for me to find them for him or make them. I had been making my own clothes from the age of 10. Little girls have dolls they like to dress up and play with, and here I was with a full-grown glorious guy who was happy to let me experiment with his wardrobe. Alvin was my big doll to dress. We were so poor that one of his first pairs of trousers was made from my bag of sewing off-cuts, from four big patchwork pieces. With heavy curtain fringed bottoms, they show up on many magazine covers and photos from 1967.

In 2020, they came back to me through Toni Franklin, Alvin's Fan Club manager. It was emotional to handle them, to recognise the fabrics and to be reminded of the garments I had made and worn. Most of all they reminded me how much I wanted to make something fabulous for him while he was off gigging and I was home in Warwick Square; my secret, born from a desire to contribute creatively. He loved them when I fitted them for the first time, and he'd kept hold of them all the years, sending them to Toni for safekeeping back in the early nineties.

Once there was a little more money, and I was working near Oxford Street, I'd spend lunch hours in John Lewis' huge fabric department buying bright psychedelic prints for shirts with experimental necklines. Bright red needlecord pants were ok, but being cotton they shrank when washed and became shapeless. This led me to the curtain fabric department. I wanted a heavy fabric, as durable and practical as jean denim. That's how the "Woodstock" tapestry trousers came into being. That pair I made reversible, the seams bound with tape, but soon they were only worn one way. When they were washed and dried at the laundromat they also shrank and the solution was the heavy curtain fringe around the bottom, which actually added to their hipness. In a later interview, Alvin joked that Loraine, "the Wild One", had made his trousers from his mum's curtains.

I made two further pairs of tapestry trousers, one striped, the other a beautiful paisley design, turquoise motifs on a navy background. Neither were as popular with Alvin. What he wore was his choice. There was no such thing as normal day wear and different stage wear, whatever was put on in the morning was mostly worn all day, off stage and on. The trouser pattern I made was particular to Alvin and designed with extra fabric in the upper thigh and crotch area to allow for gymnastics on stage.

Carnaby Street, Portobello Road and Kensington Market all offered second-hand, antique clothes fashions, the florals, lace, silk velvets, lames, and battered old furs, old felt hats and amber and costume beads that became the hippie stock. Such sensual, luxurious pieces, from the twenties, thirties and forties were hoarded by upper-class English ladies who found them in storage boxes in their attics. Those thirties bias-cut rayon floral dresses were a particular love of mine. Rayon, one of the first man-made mass fabrics, had great hang for body, hip clinging designs that were cut wider into their lower skirts. They were great dancing dresses that moved with the body, accentuating sway and rhythms.

Alvin loved to be comfortable on stage and knitted jersey, from which all T-shirts are made, was a good choice. Later the purple Fillmore T-shirt, featuring Bill Graham giving it the finger, was a favourite. On one visit to Kensington Market, I came across some twenties glass-beaded flapper dresses. The fabric was a rayon knit and loose, like a T-shirt. I bought a couple, chopped off the bottoms, finished off the hems and one became the "Woodstock" top. On stage, in the dark, when the lights hit the beadwork the effect was electric, like fire flickering across his chest. They were magical tops for the big shows, a pure stoned brainwave.

On tour in Holland, Alvin had discovered clogs. He found them comfortable and practical and they became his only footwear for years, easy to slip on and off, great for travelling and for healthy feet.

Early publicity pictures shown Alvin in a mid-thigh fur waistcoat, with an orange paisley shirt beneath. It was actually a removable fur lining from a man's wool overcoat. Picked up at Kensington Market for me to wear, it worked for Alvin, so we shared. When I first gave up my day job in January 1968, I celebrated by resolving to dress in a way that showed the world I was a hippie. To start with, I dressed like a native American, with beads around my forehead and plaits at either side. Using a fringed orange patterned Asian Indian bedspread, I fashioned, trousers, a sleeveless top and a poncho. There are publicity photos of Alvin wearing the poncho and playing live in it.

My favourite memory of the bedspread outfit, complete with beads and plaits, was at the check-out in the local Pimlico supermarket. I was queuing up beside an elderly guy, who asked me: "Are you going to a fancy-dress party, love?"

"No, I always dress like this," I replied, a bit uncharitably. Oh, the arrogance of youth!

chapter 16
Ten Years After Foundations

As far as I'm aware there was no discussion with the rest of the band about image. Ruthann told me recently, however, that Chris Wright, who became their manager, had Ric wear a long black wig and a hat for one show, which was way too hot for a drummer, and there is indeed a publicity shot of him in a hat. Gradually their hair grew, Ric and Chick became more colourful in their clothes and Leo became a cowboy. Well it was all about personal self-expression and between his perm and hippie clothes, Alvin was taking the lead. They were all loosening up in their own way.

They had a musical direction and basic set, a suitable band name and an identity that evolved with the times, and out there somewhere was an audience who didn't yet know what musical good times awaited them. Ten Years After was ready for the road but they needed a team to support them. Chick had originally been hired as a roadie, but was now on keyboards. They needed a good roadie and, somehow, they found Roger "The Hat" Manifold. Once met never forgotten, Roger a larger than life Londoner could have played Fagin in Charles Dickins' *Oliver Twist* without a change of clothes.

It's safe to say that Alvin and TYA were fortunate to survive Roger's tenure as roadie. His knowledge of electricity was minimal. If an amp failed he would take out the mains lead and test for power by sticking a screwdriver into the plug he was holding, the other end still plugged into the mains. The UK has an A/C mains supply of 240 volts, more than twice the 110 volts of the USA, enough to electrocute someone. Roger's black hatted head would leap up behind the gear as his expletives turned the air purple.

A singer/guitarist has two items of electrical equipment and both need to be properly earthed so that the performer doesn't become the earth and get fried. It was Roger's job to make sure this didn't happen, but he didn't last long. He was lured away from Ten Years After by Mike Patto and can be heard on the Pink Floyd track 'Us And Them' on *Dark Side Of The Moon* album, talking colourfully about working with musicians, violence and death. It was Roger who introduced TYA to Andy Jaworski, who would work with them and Alvin for 22 years, a bedrock of all their work.

The old Jaybirds' Commer van was still stumbling along, but one day someone drove into the back of it and the doors would no longer close. Roger asked Andy, who had his own bodyshop, if he could fix it, which he did as best he could, though they couldn't afford to have the paintwork touched up. Roger collected the van and told Andy the boys were recording at Decca studios that night. Did he want to go? Andy went along and was fascinated with studio equipment and the recording processes.

Next time he saw him, Roger said he had a "bunch of wires that needed fixing, do you know anything about wires and things?" Andy said yes, and took them away, soldered and tidied them up. A few days later Roger came back and told Andy: "The boys are going on tour soon and they were wondering if you wanted to come along and help us out with wires and things." Andy was ready for an adventure. He'd never been out of England. He left his business, telling his partner Angelo he could have all of his tools as he was going to Denmark with a band.

This was a tremendous stroke of luck for Ten Years After, and especially for Alvin. Andy Jaworski officially joined TYA's crew in 1968 and worked alongside Roger Manifold until Patto stole him. Unofficially, he was at the many Marquee and other blues gigs round London during 1967, enjoying the band and helping out.

Andy was an incredible support to the band, to Alvin, to their management and to me. Intelligent, quick to learn, incredibly calm and even-tempered, a joy to be around. Over the years he developed more and more skills and became their tour manager. Andy got us up in the morning; "In the lobby in half an hour" his morning call. He organised our day, hotel check-outs, limos to the airport, boarding passes, limos on arrival, check-in at the next hotel, luggage and equipment on the plane and off. Gear taken to the venue and, with John Hembrow, set up, tested, checked so that when Alvin used the mike stand across the guitar neck he wouldn't electrocute himself. He mixed the band live for shows, looked after Alvin's equipment needs on tour, in the studio and at home, always there when called on.

After Roger left, Andy suggested John Hembrow as his replacement.

John began his TYA career as a fan of the band, turning up to regular gigs at The Manor House near to where he lived. He had a driving job and seemed ideal to replace Roger. Before the end of 1968 John had joined and, with Andy, formed the backbone and constant positive energy that touring bands need to function; all the US tours, reputed to be 28 or more, Europe, UK, Japan, nothing was ever too much trouble for Andy and John, the heart of Ten Years After. Their dedication and support were exceptional. They didn't just do the job – for the next six years and beyond, it became their lives. They kept the whirlwind from flying apart.

Andy retired from the rock'n'roll life in 1990, to live in the USA, near New Orleans, close to the family of his American wife Kim and their son Jason. John Hembrow stayed with Alvin in his later career, becoming more and more involved with him after Andy retired. John was with Alvin for 37 years, longer than anyone else connected with him. He now lives in London with his wife Penny.

But all this was the future. In 1967 The Marquee was TYA's springboard, a progressive underground venue with audience attuned to John Mayall, Eric Clapton, Peter Green, Jimi Hendrix, a Who's Who of rock. Alvin knew it was the perfect audience for the group. They listened, they applauded solos, and recognised talented artists in the same way that jazz audiences had done for years.

As a support band Ten Years After always set out to outplay the headliners. This was a standard approach in a very competitive world. Their earliest gigs at the Marquee included a regular support slot to legends like John Lee Hooker, whom Alvin felt uncomfortable trying to outplay. Alvin and Leo called it their "blow 'em off policy", a focused approach to gigs that quickly saw them move from support to headlining. Their reputation as a hard act to follow soon spread and bands refused to headline with Ten Years After as support.

By July 1967 they were a headlining band and by October had their Marquee residency, fortnightly on Friday blues nights. During the second half of the year they played at the Marquee 14 times in 26 weeks.

The role of the Marquee for Alvin and TYA during 1967 cannot be overestimated. Alvin and I would take a black taxi cab there, every second Friday evening. He was always quiet on the 20-minute journey, nervous in a way I had never seen him before. The anticipation and tension fed into his playing and over the next year his whole guitar style developed personally and creatively.

The Marquee audience was attentive, multiplying by word of mouth and through enthusiastic reviews in the pages of *Melody Maker* and *New Musical Express*.

The symbiotic, connected energy of everyone present led to some of the most innovative and experimental soloing of his career. Leo's intense, attacking style on bass pushed and drove Alvin. All of TYA grew and explored musically, and the songs of their basic set expanded dynamically to formalise TYA's identifiable sound. None of this was discussed or planned, it arose organically through live performance, Alvin and Leo especially.

I saw dozens of these Marquee gigs, looking on as their shows became captivating, immersive experiences, which seemed to move us all, band and audience, to a transformed level of what music has the potential to be. It was as if Alvin had been released from bondage, free to develop, to create, to fly, something compelling and increasingly exciting week after week.

Though the Marquee was the most respected small music venue in London, the stage was small, the ceiling low. The official capacity was only around 500, but in practice this was usually far exceeded. It was a heady atmosphere, like a live rehearsal space before an encouraging audience.

We all knew they needed a professional manager to replace Leo. Chris Wright, the son of a Lincolnshire farmer, had similar cultural roots to the band and found his way into the rock business through being social secretary at Manchester University. By virtue of the growing importance of UK universities as regular live music venues, it led to him "being one of the biggest music promoters in the country", as recalled in *One Way Or Another*, his autobiography. He was running a small local venue, the J & J Club in the Manchester suburb of Longsight, with Keith Bizeret, a fellow student and a Londoner with music business connections.

"The Jaybirds played the J & J Club for £15, our normal rate and went down brilliantly," writes Chris. "Keith Bizeret was impressed by their fantastic guitarist and vocalist Alvin Lee and suggested I try to manage them, but initially I was skeptical. Eventually, at Keith's insistence I took them out to dinner, got on well, and in a move that would change my life forever became The Jaybirds' manager."

Terry Ellis, who would soon become Chris's partner, had also been a social secretary, at Newcastle University. He too was working with agencies and music businessmen in London. Chris had begun to notice that he and Terry were undercutting one another to put on great bands, a source of frustration to them both.

In the summer of 1967 it became obvious to Chris that Ten Years After were attracting so much attention that it would be wise for him to move to London, to protect his interests.

He contacted Terry Ellis and they arranged to meet at The Marquee on one of Ten Years After's residency nights. Maybe they could work together in some way, rather than compete. Chris suggested they rent premises together in London. Though forming an agency was not his first thought, it soon became their obvious course.

A competitive but supportive relationship developed between Mr Ellis and Mr Wright, which was great for the bands. They formed the Ellis-Wright Agency. In the UK, they toured Ten Years After on the university circuit, where Terry and Chris had many connections. Terry would come to personally manage Jethro Tull, despite, according to his biography, Chris signing them initially. Terry and Jethro Tull worked well together. Chris was better suited to manage Ten Years After.

By the end of 1967 Ten years After were already forging a path with Chris, via The Marquee, Windsor Festival and first album release, that Terry was able to emulate with Jethro Tull in 1968. Everyone was setting down the roots for what would become the British blues boom in the USA.

chapter 17
First Festival, Album and USA Beckons

The 7th National Jazz & Blues Festival was held at Balloon Meadow, Windsor on August 11th-13th 1967, promoted by the Marquee and showcasing new bands from their Wardour Street venue. This was Ten Years After's first ever festival appearance, second from the bottom on Saturday 12th, list of 11 bands. They had 25 minute to put their "blow 'em off" technique to good use, receiving a standing ovation from an audience of 20,000 music lovers who were no doubt taken by surprise seeing Alvin play his intense guitar solos. The ovation was witnessed by Mike Vernon, which led to TYA's first record deal with Decca Records' niche label, Deram.

In their contract with Deram they could record albums without first having hit singles, a progressive attitude unusual at the time. Their eponymous debut was recorded at Decca's West Hampstead studios over five days during September 1967 in a four-track analogue studio. The first side featured new arrangements of tracks they had found on the *What's Shakin'* album, which they had developed at the Marquee and were far removed in tempo, feel and performance from the originals on the Elektra release. 'I Can't Keep From Crying Sometimes' and 'Spoonful' were both slower and more dramatic. This would become the hallmark of Alvin's performance, emotionally charged vocals and guitar solos that would shift from quiet, almost silent phases, then either build or punch into intense crescendos.

'I Can't Keep From Crying Sometimes' would develop over the next year at The Marquee into an epic virtuoso guitar solo lasting 20 minutes or more. It became my favourite Ten Years After live track for dancing, its dynamic contrasts moving me to blissful levels of self-expression.

I can't think of any other bands of this era who used dynamics in this way. It was something innate in Alvin who used dynamics to intensify the music and hold the audience attention. Add to this the availability of good hashish in 1967 London, both for Alvin and the audience, the music became a transcendental merger. Getting "out of your head" is the perfect description and allowed conscious control to move aside for instinctive exploration.

He was genuinely on an exploratory musical journey and loved to play for listening crowds, preferably crowds who had also enjoyed a little smoke, as he would have done. His competence on the guitar was at such a level that he didn't need to think and the less he did the more he flew. I'd glimpsed Alvin's dramatic use of dynamics back in The Jaybirds days on two songs by Ray Charles, 'I Gotta Woman' and 'What'd I Say', which Charles extended for the B-side of the single. Alvin would extend his guitar solos and take the vocals down very low and then crash back in for the climactic ending, much to the delight of his regular Nottingham audience.

Now, with Ten Years After, he would take that dynamic to an extreme and create extended solos that wove from the lowest to highest volumes. 'Help Me, Baby', which closes the album is slow, intensely moody and emotional. Starting deceptively quiet and instrumentally sparse, it always relaxed the audience, but the second verse is accented with a punch in the chest from the guitar, bass and drums. This brought gasps from the audience or involuntary jumps in their seats. Alvin loved making that type of impact and would tell me later that it was something he missed when he played more tastefully, after listening too much to critics.

Listening to this first album 50 years later, the songs that Alvin wrote himself astonish me. In several interviews conducted later, he says: "The first album was, in fact, basically our live set. We didn't have to think much or write anything and the album was recorded in two days." This is true of the second album, *Undead,* which was recorded live at Klooks Kleek on May 14, 1968, and their first stage set from start to finish, but not of the 1967 *Ten Years After* studio album.

It seems Alvin overlooked his first three self-penned blues tracks, 'Feel It For Me', 'Love Until I Die' and 'Don't Want you Woman', all on the second side. They're all catchy and competent songs based around classic blues riffs with lyrics about an emotion or a problem. As far as I know these are the first songs he ever wrote. They stand up well alongside the up-tempo opening track 'I Want To Know', written by Paul Jones under the pseudonym MacLeod.

Decca wanted hit singles, a conflict Alvin would face with all record companies. Leo, Ric and Chick had nothing against hit records, and would probably have been happy to see themselves in the charts. Alvin, however, believed that hit singles would have harmed TYA's standing as an "underground" band, especially in the UK. Record companies think in terms of moving units, making money as quickly as possible, before acts fell out of style and were dropped. Ten Years After miming to a single on the UK's *Top Of The Pops* chart show was a no-no for Alvin.

Mike Vernon, their producer at Decca, encouraged them to produce new material. Alvin co-wrote 'Losing The Dogs' with Gus Dudgeon, an engineer at Decca who would go on to work with Elton John and David Bowie. 'Adventures Of A Young Organ', an instrumental by Chick and Alvin, was a prophetic description of Chick's early life in the band. He preferred to stay well clear of band politics, preferring the company of pretty young ladies. Chick was the least complicated musician in Ten Years After.

John Peel, the UK's most influential underground DJ at this time, heard the band live at 3am during an all-nighter at Middle Earth, held at Camden's Roundhouse where he was deejaying. Initially he was a big supporter, inviting them to play live on his BBC radio shows, which were highly sought-after spots. Live versions of 'Love Until I Die', featuring an uncharacteristic harmonica solo from Alvin, and 'Don't Want You Woman' can both be found on the album, *Ten Years After, BBC Radio Sessions 1967*.

Live radio and TV appearances suited Alvin and TYA well. They would have felt and looked very uncomfortable miming along to backing tracks. This attitude split the thinking of the music media, with the musicians calling the tunes as well as playing them. This resulted in many legendary live performances on BBC2's *Old Grey Whistle Test*.

Ten Years After, released on October 27, was taken up and played in the USA on emerging FM stations, among them KMPX and KSAN in San Francisco, which was how Bill Graham first came to hear the group. The following February this most influential US promoter wrote to Chris Wright, as follows: "We are very interested in bringing Ten Years After to the Fillmore, for a Thursday, Friday, Saturday weekend. When you make your plans to bring the group to the States, we would appreciate price and availability for them. I might mention that we are now booking into May. We are also opening a Fillmore-type operation in New York City, that will be in full swing within a month. Please give us price and availability for that city too."

Odd to think that rock business was conducted by snail mail back in February 1968.

chapter 18
Warwick Square Creative Hub

By October 1967, we had been living in the tiny Warwick Square flat for one year but money was always tight. I was still working a five-day week as house model at Laura Lee frocks, travelling on the tube from Victoria to Oxford Circus and back in the rush-hour, buying sausages, the cheapest available, on the walk back home along Wilton Road and Warwick Way. Our typical evening meal was reconstituted Smash, dried mashed potato, and Surprise dried peas with the sausages, fried onions with Bisto gravy. We had Marvel dried milk powder in cups of tea and a few biscuits – Jaffa cakes were a favourite – for desert. Sometimes it was fish fingers, or omelettes, or beef mince, onions and tinned plum tomatoes to make spaghetti sauce. Ruth and Jeff, our Nottingham friends, came to visit, bringing a cooked chicken and vegetables, and I dare say Sam and Doris did similar. For the first few years, when we visited Nottingham I would load up a couple of boxes of tinned foods from my mum's well-stocked pantry. Early pictures of Alvin show a very skinny young guy. We had an emergency, catering-sized tin of Heinz Baked Beans that had been "liberated" from the hotel when I left. It was kept as a decoration on one of the three narrow bookshelves and travelled everywhere we would live to serve as a reminder of the tough early times.

So much was happening that being hungry or worrying about money was never really an issue. We weren't drinkers, which was one less expense. We did smoke. I rolled my own and Alvin's preferred mentholated cigarettes. He always found us a little hashish to aid our creative lives.

When I was out working Alvin was playing guitar, writing songs and sometimes drawing, making collages or cleaning the flat. There was always a drawing pad, pencils and paints in my life. I drew life portraits of Alvin sitting watching TV, and self-portraits. I painted a few pictures at Warwick Square that tell romantic tales and one night I had a psychedelic painting breakthrough, but I am running ahead of myself.

Alvin made soundscapes on his Simon reel-to-reel tape machine, experimenting with speeding up or slowing down the sounds. Late one evening, I had fallen asleep on the two-seat couch, he was making a tape of saucepan lids, spinning them on the table and slowing it down. Next thing I knew Alvin woke me with a grin, and played a tape of me snoring.

We often listened to current music, mostly through our good Lowther speakers on the floor, heads together on a pillow placed between the speakers for best stereo effects. Listening like this was a very serious and important part of our relaxation – Hendrix *Axis Bold As Love*, Traffic *Mr Fantasy*, Pink Floyd *Piper At The Gates of Dawn* and Beatles *Sgt Pepper*.

We still loved cinema but lack of funds made it a rare treat. There was a 24-hour cartoon cinema at Victoria station like the one in Nottingham. We'd walk up there for some *Looney Tunes* silliness, *Road Runner* featuring Wile E Coyote a favourite, and take home a carton of fresh milk from an automated machine in the station. There was a recording booth, which transcribed messages or tunes directly onto a black plastic record. I'm sure we made some silly stoned recordings, but I've no idea where they are. Train stations were a useful local amenity in those days. Twice we went to see Walt Disney's full-length classical music cartoon *Fantasia,* which was best enjoyed after a good smoke.

The *Fantasia* sequence of Leopold Stokowski conducting Bach's 'Toccata and Fugue in D minor' resonated with Alvin's love of repetition and dramatic use of volume. Thinking about this piece, I wonder how much it influenced the dynamics of 'I Can't Keep From Crying'? We bought a Bach album with this piece on and especially loved listening to it on stereo headphones. On the 2002 re-issued *Undead* album, an added experimental 'I Can't Keep From Crying' shows its development in the six months since the *Ten Years After* album release. Alvin's introduces it as "a cross between a Bach Fugue and something else".

We had an album of Beethoven Sonatas and No 23 in F Minor, *Appassionata,* another favourite that may have been the "something else". It certainly showcases the dynamics that Alvin introduced into his guitar solos. Beethoven was another Sagittarius who was able to express his dark as well as his light side through his music.

Another unique sound experience we discovered was on a world music album, *Kecak*, a monkey chant performed by maybe a hundred Balinese temple singers, "yatatatata tatata, yatatata tatata". Two groups of singers sat in a circle calling and answering, very fast, very hypnotic. One favourite for headphone listening was a Decca sound effects album – lawnmowers, car horns, a jet plane in stereo flying through your head. Turn over the first TYA single 'Portable People' and listen to 'The Sounds'. The most profound sound effect track did not make it to the record. It's an atom bomb exploding. Listening stoned, it was an intense experience.

Juan Serrano, a superb flamenco guitarist, caught Alvin's attention. His album *Ole La Mano*, released in 1962, was a virtuoso performance of fast, clean playing. On the cover image Serrano sits with his guitar and six hands, three on the neck and three strumming. We joked that he would need six hands to accomplish what he played. In 1969, strolling on a day off in San Francisco, we walked past a bar in whose window was a picture of a guitarist that caught our eye. It was Juan Serrano. The blurb said he paid an annual visit to this bar and played for a week, and that he was playing that very evening. We were amazed, and went in for a meal while we waited, almost in disbelief. He arrived on the small stage, on time, and a few dozen people watched him play an astonishing flamenco set. A magical encounter.

In Nottingham, Alvin had become interested in photography and made his own black and white prints. His darkroom equipment came to London with him and now he had a resident model, happy to pose and act as darkroom assistant. Drying negatives were suspended from cord strung across the corner shower cabinet, as were the wet prints. We had two large plastic trays on the table, one for developer and one for fixer. The main room light was made safe with a red footlight gel fastened around it. We discovered solarisation like Max Ernst and Lee Miller had originally done it in the thirties. Of course, we didn't know at first that it had already been discovered. When Alvin met John Fowlie, who became a great friend and the cover photographer/designer for four TYA albums, we learned all about solarisation from him.

Alvin quite often took photos of me in the flat to develop and print. I had black and red-haired curly wigs to alter my look, and I occasionally wore them in the evenings when we went out. Alvin took photos of whoever was about, Vince, Vivienne, using the kettle to distort images or putting Vince in my black wig. We were intrigued by the way it transformed him into a native American. It was all part of the playful way we lived.

This was our first year of living together, sharing the tiny space we called home. Surprisingly, we never got on each other's nerves or had rows.

Our personalities were complimentary. We were totally comfortable together. We were never at a loss for a project to work on or a conversation to engage in. Though the flat was tiny, we had very little stuff to fill it up, so there was room enough for all the various projects. Everything we needed was to hand, there was nowhere to go to look for materials to work with.

Warwick Square had a magical ability to accommodate the number of visitors we had. A picture from Alvin's birthday, December 1968, shows 10 smiling people and somehow it doesn't look overcrowded. Then again it helped that almost everyone was standing up with only Alvin seated. We made some good friends at the Marquee gigs, among them Vincent Tseng, a young Chinese student, with whom Alvin loved to discuss philosophical ideas. He was remarkably prescient, as early as 1967 discussing personal computers, the internet and world wide web. In stoned conversations we were futurists, space travellers, moon walkers, whole earth photographers. We had a sense that western culture was on the right path.

Vivienne Bidwell, an energetically creative blond hippie, was besotted with Jim Morrison of The Doors. A talented artist, she became involved with our creative activities. I had painted Warwick Square's walls in mauve and orange. Vivienne painted a mural, a highly stylised mermaid in a circular rainbow. It was still there when we left.

Simon Stable, a DJ who ran his own record shop on Portobello Road, wrote a column for the *International Times* and spent many hours getting high with us. When we first met him, probably at the Marquee, he told us his actual name was Count Simon de la Bedoyere, a French aristocrat. We couldn't decide if he was a Count, or if it was fanciful imaginings, though Alvin sometimes referred to him as "the Count". Status was unimportant. We made friends with those with whom we had something in common, which was enjoying a smoke, good music and being cool and relaxed. Simon ticked all those boxes.

We played all kinds of games, Pick-up Sticks and a card game called Contraband, where one player is the customs officer, and the others have to bluff and smuggle according to the cards in their hands. We doctored some cards to show various drugs and diamonds, which upped the stakes from watches and bottles of wine. In these early days Alvin loved to play these games, act silly and laugh a lot.

Our oldest friend from Nottingham, Johnnie Clifton, also living in London, was a regular fun visitor. Judy worked in the evenings at various up-market Kings Road restaurants, all called The Spot, Spot One, Spot Two. Very occasionally the four of us would dine out, a special favourite L'Artiste

Asoiffe, a fun and funky restaurant in Notting Hill. Later we took Columbia record boss Clive Davis there, an interesting evening. Johnnie launched a company producing high quality hand-made toupees, selling them personally through Elite barber shops. Mandeville of London would become his lifelong business, but there was always a rock'n'roll piano player waiting to come out to play.

There is a sound tape of an impromptu play that Alvin, Johnnie and I made one stoned night. Called *The Large Scorching Dragon!*, it's a Jack and the Beanstalk tale of magic beans. We heard that smoking banana skins got you high, so Alvin went to the local green grocer to buy bananas. He became self-conscious just buying bananas, so bought apples, oranges and then asked, "Oh, do you have any bananas?" We dried the skins out and smoked them in a pipe. They don't get you high. They will give you a headache!

Along with the Marquee residency, there were gigs all around England, in jazz clubs and colleges. After the first album was released there were music press interviews and the live recordings for BBC radio's John Peel. There wasn't too much pressure on Alvin yet. We didn't even have a telephone in the flat, so Andy Jaworski was tasked with driving round to keep us up to date. In those days of no mobile phones or internet, it's hard to imagine how we coordinated things. Life was simpler then.

Alvin wanted me to be with him more and as the band's gig load increased, it became more difficult for me to maintain my day-job. We made a deal that I would save up the £25 deposit to have a telephone installed, and when it was I could give up my full-time day job. I left Laura Lee frocks in February 1968 and for the next year worked through a model agency doing similar work but only during the six-week selling seasons. Luckily, I was a "stock" size UK 12/US 10, ideal for hanging clothes on. It also paid double what I had been earning working full-time.

Alvin's prankster side that in Nottingham involved "kidnapping" Dave Quickmire, emerged from time to time in London. Opposite the flat was a set of red public phone boxes. We wrote down the numbers of the phones, and on a few stoned evenings watched from our fourth-floor window as people walked towards them. Then we'd dial up one of the phone boxes. It was surprising how often people opened the box to answer the phone.

Then we'd make friendly conversations about what they were wearing, ask how they were, wish them well and say goodbye. We laughed to see them come out of the box and look around bemused. It was a bit like *Candid Camera*. One night a passer-by answered the phone as a cyclist pulled up at the red traffic lights. We asked our new telephone acquaintance to tell the cyclist, who was a friend, that there was a phone call for him. It was all good, clean, stoned, side-splitting, silly fun

Ten Years After fans were already starting to write in to the Ellis-Wright agency address on the album. This gave birth to Vicky Page, my alter-ego, and the Ten Years After Music Lovers Society. No one knew more about what the band, and especially Alvin, were doing, so I got to work writing about their progress and adventures. One evening alone, after a smoke, I doodled about with the name Ten Years After. Designing a red and white logo, with a 10 o'clock face, the top of the Y of Years slightly tilted so that it angled the same as the clock hands at 10 0'clock. This became the TYAMLS identity. Once I had that basic logo I worked with Vivienne Bidwell, who we renamed, Eowyn, to produce the society's magazine cover image.

The Lord Of The Rings, JR Tolkien's fantasy masterpiece had entered our lives. The Palantir is the stone in which events occurring in faraway places can be seen, and it seemed the ideal name for our magazine. I would nag the band and Alvin to write short articles or stories. Alvin produced the remarkable Green Gilbert, a common name for a hard and crusty piece of nose mucous. In one episode, Alvin's lighter-than-air super hero brings himself back down to earth by adding water to powdered potatoes, and thus becomes heavier. It was art inspired by the minutia of our humble diet. Then there was Leo's tale: *The Incredible Success Story Of Norman Link – Who Found Fame In A Different Way From Which He Sought It.* The magazine became my creative outlet for the next few years. Looking back at them, I'm not embarrassed.

In 2020 Gibson Guitars made a limited edition of Alvin's ES 335, as it looked at Woodstock in 1969, with four decals/stickers. He had started adding stickers to his guitar, and was among the first guitarists to do so. The first sticker he added was the TYAMLS logo, designed that stoned night back in 1967. At Woodstock, there were four decals, the TYAMLS logo, a peace sign, a mirrored marijuana leaf and a hippie with both hands raised in peace sign Vs.

The look of that red guitar summed up his interests and the era perfectly.

Young Audrey and Hector 1930s

Sam and Doris 1930s

Loraine's birthplace, Rose of England, Nottingham

Loraine's school photo,
Shirley Temple hair escaped,
looking cheeky, age 8 1955

Janice and baby Alvin 1945

Graham, Loraine and Barry. Shirley Temple hair 1948

Alvin with sand castles, about 6 years

Young Alvin with Sam at Butlins

Loraine, dad, singing Rudolf,
Coronation party 1953

Alvin's family
From bottom to top,
Irma, Janice, Doris,
Sam, George (centre
back) and two others

Burgon Family
From left to right, Graham,
Hector, Audrey, Barry,
Harold (in pushchair)
and Loraine 1952

Newcastle Arms, Loraine's home between the ages of 8 to 18

Coronation party at The Albany, with Loraine's dad (centre, back) 1953

Loraine, Brenda Lee
beehive, age 14 1961

Alvin Dean, Leo, Dave
Quickmire, Midland Beat 1963

Alvin and Loraine, second
night together at Locarno,
Nottingham 6 Nov 1963

Loraine, Sheringham 1964

Me, outside Toston Drive 1964

Burgon wedding, dad, mum, me, Barry, Yvonne, Valerie,
Harold and Graham 1964

The Jaybirds van, Sam on maintenance 1964

Alvin's Berkley Sheringham,
Norfolk holiday 1964

Alvin's James Bond, Toston Drive 1964

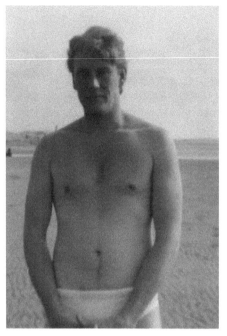

Alvin, Sheringham 1964

Alvin, outside Toston Drive 1964

Signature reads Graham, late 1965

Wollaton Park... and then he kissed me
November 1965

Me modelling for Alvin 1966

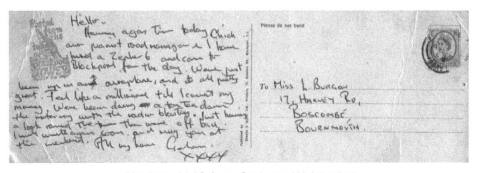

Blackpool P/C from Graham (Alvin) 1966

Alvin, first Christmas at Warwick Square 1966

Alvin's birthday with Vincent,
Warwick Square 1967

Alvin, Warwick Square
December birthday 1967

Warwick Square would grow with visitors. Harold's band - Life Without Mother -
Vivienne and Richard, Vincent and brother 1967

Alvin's collage, Warwick Square 1967

Alvin, with perm, and me,
Toston Drive garden 1967

Alvin and Sam (in my wig), Toston Drive 1967

Doris, Alvin and me,
Regent Street 1967

Warwick Square doorstep, Alvin, Harold,
Sam and Doris 1967

Alvin and me, the liberated hippie backstage London 1967

Ten Years After. From left to right, Leo, Ric, Alvin and Chick, by John Fowlie 1967

Alvin takes tea as the Don Martin character Captain Klutz, Warwick Square 1968

Alvin at home in Warwick Square with acoustic and red gel colour TV 1968

Me, the hat, at the BBC 1968

Alvin, Warwick Square 1968

Loraine's painting when Simon was tripping, Warwick Square 1968

Alvin and me,
we loved to talk,
Warwick Square
1968

Alvin contemplates the broken headstock on Big Red, his Gibson 335,
in the Marquee dressing room 1968

Bahamas P/C Alvin, my
nickname "Pod" 1969

JFK New York,
Alvin and me
December 1968

On the flight, my favourite so
un-rock 'n' roll, Pan Am 1968

Woodstock. Me, Alvin and
Dee Anthony, still image taken from
Pennebaker Woodstock Diaries 1969

chapter 19
Early Tours and Adventures

Scandinavia has always been the most liberal and progressive region of Europe. In February 1968, Finland, Sweden and Denmark welcomed Alvin and Ten Years After. Alvin met and became very close friends with English photographer John Fowlie, who lived in Copenhagen with his wife Eva. John was a hashish connoisseur and creative thinker, a stimulating and creative companion, and Alvin so loved his work that he insisted John become the cover photographer and artwork designer for most Ten Years After albums.

In 2018 I was pleased to see that two covers, *Cricklewood Green* and *Ssssh* made their way into the *1,000 Record Covers* book by Michael Ochs. Alvin would have been delighted, especially as they were placed next to two Steve Miller albums, *Sailor* and *Children of the Future,* Alvin's personal 1968 favourites, for their cover art as well as the music. Like poster art, album cover art in this era was highly experimental, the large 12" X 12" format of the vinyl LP an artist's dream canvas.

Alvin mostly enjoyed the early tours in Europe, though already there were signs of his struggles with the pressure of fame that came later. As a couple, we had become so close but the others in the band hadn't joined Alvin in his consciousness expanding activities. Separated from me on tour, he was not as happy as when he was at home. Yes, he could invite some lady into his hotel bed and for many young guys this would be one of the perks of being in a band on the road. Alvin had already enjoyed these perks since his mid-teens in Nottingham and Germany, and the novelty had long since begun to pale. Sure, it was a way to wind down physically after a show, when musicians are energized, wide awake, full of adrenaline and horny. With me, however, there was now a strong mental connection, which we both missed when we were apart. Unlike today, telephone calls were prohibitively expensive.

'I'm Going Home' was written for me in Scandinavia that 1968 spring. It wasn't a tender love song that most girlfriends might expect but a spontaneous celebration of his relief to be coming home, a great riotous, raw, raunchy, rock'n'roll outburst, a full-tilt guitar boogie of unrestrained energy and sexual expectation. I loved it, it was me, a sweet little rock'n'roller boogying with whatever energy was left in me at the end of a TYA show. 'I'm Going Home' would leave me dancing and sweating like Alvin. After Woodstock it became their anthem and we were told the go-to song played by US troops the night before returning home from Vietnam, full of the same energy of raw loving sexual anticipation.

"I'm going home to see my baby
My baby be good, going home to my baby, home to see my gal.
See my baby see my baby fine
See my woman treat me real kind
Gonna tell you about that good good love of mine.
I'm going home to see my baby."

When he was dropped off at Warwick Square and came back to me after a trip abroad, he always did the same thing. He held me, no words, just held me, really tight, for 5-10-15 minutes, as if this embrace was healing him, cleansing him, his heart relaxing from all the intensity of his time away. Stories, tales of times lived apart could wait, no words wanted, needed, just a deep loving re-connection, breathing out, together again.

One time after a long silent embrace, he quietly looked me in the eye. "Let's get married," he said. I wasn't expecting it. We were so happy together but the experience of my parent's marriage had left me thinking marriage was an old idea, a worn out expression of love, a gesture that stultified a relationship and gave it a whole load of unnecessary baggage.

"Not now," I replied "We are happy as we are."

Drummer Ric Lee and Ruthann were married that year. Ric wanted Ruthann on the road with him. Manager Chris Wright was upset about that. He thought it was bad for the band's image and female fan following. He didn't really understand the times, the band or their fans. He still thought like Brian Epstein who insisted Cynthia Lennon was hidden away.

I made Ruthann's pretty, pale pink, mini-skirted, silk wedding dress, with lace edging and lots of little covered buttons, a style that suited her and the times. Alvin and I didn't go to the wedding. I don't even think we were invited. The wedding dress was a commission, as were three further mini-dresses I made for her to wear on the second US tour.

During 1967, when I worked my nine-to-five modeling job at Laura Lee Frocks, it wasn't possible for me to go to UK gigs outside of London, except at the weekends. In truth Chris Wright did not want "old ladies" on the road, a common enough attitude in the music biz that was pretty well parodied in the 1984 spoof rockumentary *Spinal Tap*. There was a perception that "old ladies" would interfere in the finances and management of the group. Chris would discover that some artists, among them Alvin, were more stable with their partner for support. Many of the excesses of touring rock'n'roll bands in the sixties came about because their wives and partners were left at home.

When Alvin died in 2013 Chris was the first to email me. "When I first heard the terrible news, the first person I thought of was you," he wrote. "You always seemed to be perfect together, and I know how much you loved him, and probably continue to do so. I was most concerned that someone was in contact with you... I look forward to seeing you to reminisce about some wonderful old times."

In 2014, when Chris' autobiography *One Way Or Another* was published, we had lunch together in London, our first meeting in 40 years. Over a long lunch talking about the old days, Chris mentioned that in his long illustrious career the early days with Ten Years After were his most exciting and memorable of times.

He gave me a copy of his book and wrote a dedication in the front: "To Loraine, whose name I have consistently spelled wrong (Lorraine), and who is a much greater part of the story than even she knows!! She was a real rock to Alvin throughout, and without her the whole story could have been different. Loraine, you were great and also a real support to me. I hope you enjoy the read."

Though it contains some factual inaccuracies, Chris' book captures the excitement of Ten Years After's early days. There was a sense that new ground was constantly being broken. Chris was fearless in following up the leads that were presented, like Bill Graham's invitation to the Fillmore. There were plenty of times when the Ellis-Wright agency was up against the wall, juggling their cash flow, but like a western movie somehow the cavalry always turned up in time to save them to fight another day.

In February 1968, Deram released a single 'Portable People' backed with

'The Sounds'. Both written by Alvin, the A-side really was a lightweight song. I've often wondered if Alvin deliberately gave Deram something so unlike the band's music to encourage them not to release another single. 'The Sounds', his preferred A-side, stands the test of time, it combined the tracks from the Decca sound effects album, a staple of our stoned listening. He was determined never to play 'Portable People' on stage and 'The Sounds', with its background effects, was impossible to play anyway.

Chris flew the band to France to promote 'Portable People' on a French TV show, which can be found on YouTube. Alvin "performs" with a dark look and sneering attitude that the camera crew must have found very uncomfortable to film.

Alvin did not want to go. He was totally clear about that. I tried to offer logical reasons to just go and "get it out of the way". Andy turned up in the Transit van to collect him. I think Chris was also in the van. En route to the airport, they stopped at a traffic light and Alvin jumped from the van and ran off. They parked up and Andy gave chase. Alvin had run into a tube station. Andy spotted Alvin, and caught up with him on the platform. Somehow Andy persuaded him to go back to the van, sitting him in the middle so he couldn't escape.

Back at Warwick Square I knew nothing of this. Our new mustard yellow phone rang. The last voice I expected to hear was Alvin.

"Where are you?"

"In a phone box at Heathrow. I'm hiding!"

"What's happened?"

He told me the story of his "escape and recapture" in the train station and that he had now run away again and was hiding in the telephone box.

"The plane has been delayed. I called the airline and told them there was a bomb on board the plane!"

"You did what?"

"I don't want to go. They have just announced that there was a mechanical problem. No-one knows where I am or that I rang the airline."

Silence. Part of me thought it was hilarious and part of me was truly shocked. It never occurred to me or Alvin that he could have been traced and arrested. In 1968 airports were innocent, safe spaces with little surveillance. I was trying to find something to say, when he broke in.

"I just spotted Andy. Oh, I think he's seen me. I have to go, I love you!"

The line went dead. If only we'd had mobile phones.

Alvin's aversion to singles, particularly hit singles, was actually very wise. Ten Years After's progress was made in the underground music scene.

The pop TV shows, a holdover from earlier times, were at odds with the changes that were taking place in music and youth culture. This aspect of the music business was clinging on, but behind the times. Managers like Chris were winging it.

Alvin had a taste of fame on the Scandinavian tours. He was hoping to stay underground in the UK and lead a more low-key life at home. Touring the USA would confirm this as an excellent strategy for Alvin but this wasn't discussed with the band or his management. He would carry on ducking and diving around the questions of single releases for the next five years.

Meanwhile, there was business to be transacted. The five tracks that Alvin had written or co-written for the first album needed to be published. Chris did a deal with Getaway Songs Ltd. My memory is that there was an advance for Alvin of £1,000 that he did not get. It was used to buy the tickets for the first US tour in 1968, he did agree to this. Also, Alvin's songwriting on *Undead,* which included 'I'm Going Home', was signed to Getaway Songs. My understanding was that Getaway Songs did indeed get away with Alvin's royalties from the first two albums. It wasn't until 1971 that Alvin opened a royalty statement from a branch of EMI, who it seemed now owned the copyrights. Those were the first songwriting royalty payments he received from the first two albums and the *Woodstock* movie.

Chris Wright's book fails to mention any bad deals he ever made. Getaway Songs is not mentioned at all. The royalties used for flights for the first US tour are described as an advance for Ten Years After's band royalties. Chris admits that when he began managing TYA, he had no idea about music publishing, what it was or how it worked. Overall, he was an excellent choice and very successful as Ten Years After's manager. Alvin spoke affectionately of Chris towards the end of his life, even after he had uncovered deals that he believed might have benefitted Chris better than TYA. Those early years, when everyone was around the same age and lacked experience, created a unique bond. We were a group of people destined to meet and share this adventure.

chapter 20
Marquee London to Fillmore America

The music industry was splitting apart. Pop music was the old model, tied up tight by old, cigar-chomping music moguls. Chris Wright and Terry Ellis opted to call their company Chrysalis, a combination of their names, and they, along with Kit Lambert and Chris Stamp at Track, Chris Blackwell at Island, Richard Branson at Virgin and Tony Stratton Smith at Charisma, were young entrepreneurs, willing to take risks and explore the underground energy, wherever it would take them. One thing they had in common was a love of music and respect for the talented young musicians they represented.

There was no lack of work but the UK blues scene was mainly followed by young guys who took the music seriously. There were far fewer young women in the audiences for Ten Years After than there had been for The Jaybirds. The male fans were focused, intense, following all the solos, no girlfriends evidently, as there were at The Jaybirds rock'n'roll shows. Post gig confrontations with angry boyfriends hoping to paste Alvin for daring to be attractive had disappeared. Alvin was now approached with respect, for autographs and brief exchanges, all very relaxed.

When Deram released TYA's debut LP they issued a bizarre press release that harked back to the early days of Hollywood when actors were re-named, re-invented and re-packaged, however interesting their own back story might have been.

"Let us consider the facts," it read. "They actually met in a North Wales bus shelter, and this was the 'cue' they had all been waiting for!

"Alvin, tall moody and intense, brilliant guitarist and now the main musical 'thinker' of the band. Ex-pilot Leo the most highly-rated bassist in England, to whom the old American West is secondary only to music. And the terrible twins Ric and Chick, one well-loved and quiet and the other irrepressible and an incorrigible looner. Together their personalities fit as intricately and effectively as the firing mechanism of an H-bomb and potentially more powerful."

It was an insult to these young, hard-working, aspirational musicians, completely out of keeping with what was actually happening in the progressive music scene. That publicity release, and other publicity stunts, would turn up in the daily papers and even music press as facts. Gradually Alvin seemed to lose all interest in sticking to reality when he was interviewed and would often exaggerate. One such interview has to this day left me known to Alvin's fans as "the wild one, who made his trousers by cutting up his mother's curtains"!

It's lucky that 'Portable People' did not become a hit. It might have vanished into the mists of time had it not been for the arrival of YouTube. It's not a bad song, a sweet melody with cultural references to travel, when package holidays introduced British tourists to foreign countries they'd never visited before.

"One may have a bull or a pair of wooden clogs," sings Alvin. "They liked the Eiffel Tower, but they didn't like the bogs. They're the jet age gypsies with the supersonic sound, they're the portable people and they take themselves around."

On the B-side, 'Sounds' includes an early example of guitar shredding and is among the more innovative tracks that Alvin controlled. The cacophony reaches its climax when Alvin says "Stop", and the tape slurs to seven seconds of silence, followed by shredding guitar creeping back in from a fade to a reprise then to a fade-out. As a tribute to the dystopia of living in a modern megalopolis, it's probably even more relevant today.

TYA's first tour of Scandinavia, their first outside the UK, included shows in Finland, Sweden and Denmark. The lack of a common language and slow hand-clapping as a sign of appreciation was confusing and challenging. Scandinavians were ahead with music TV and they made their first TV appearances on Danish and Swedish TV, playing live instead of miming. Despite long and nerve-racking drives through snow laden landscapes, they enjoyed all the new experiences.

The workload of clubs and universities around London and the UK, along with time spent in the studio, interviews and BBC radio appearances left little time for analysis or self-reflection.

They were "taking off" but it was clear they would have to fight to retain control over their image as well as their music.

Initially the publicity people tried to involve and promote the whole band, but it soon became Alvin, the songwriter, singer and lead guitarist, who they were most interested in. Lead guitarists were the most exciting musicians of the era, Hendrix, Clapton, Page, Beck, Green, Townshend and Alvin Lee led the way in what was to become the defining live-gig experience. It led to thousands of young men taking up guitar or, failing that, air guitar, strutting and posing along to guitar solos in the privacy of their bedrooms, their hero's posters on the wall.

Bill Graham's Fillmore West letter was the catalyst for 1968. There was no hesitation from Chris Wright or Ten Years After. The only questions were logistical. How and when? The airfares had been secured. The issues of US visas, musician union rules, which had already been a part of their working in Europe, became more complex. There had to be an exchange of artists to and from the USA, one in, one out. As the early months of 1968 passed the first album needed to be replaced with new product to promote on a US tour.

A few studio tracks they'd recorded tried to capture the excitement and energy of their live performances. This became a big goal for TYA and Mike Vernon. On a Sunday in March 1968, an afternoon and evening session was booked into Decca's West Hampstead studios. The session was opened up to a couple of dozen friends and fans and alcohol was served in an attempt to create a live setting.

I was there and wrote about it in *The Palantir*: "Everyone had a great time, though few of those present seem to remember the last few hours after the bottles were emptied! I managed to hear back the tapes, the following weekend the results are terrific, especially a lot of the chat that went on in between numbers, which will probably be incorporated on the LP. Surprisingly to all involved, quite a few of the numbers will be usable, though some of the late tracks prove that alcohol clouds musical minds!"

Ric liked to drink, Chick also, Leo very little and Alvin was a doper, so looking back 50 years it is remarkable that this event ever took place at all. Alvin had no head for alcohol and would have found playing difficult after just one beer. As far as I know, nothing from that session was ever released. My enthusiasm – "The results are terrific" – is a mystery to me now but can probably be explained by my OTT zeal for the band.

Undead, the second album, was recorded live at Klooks Kleek at the Railway Hotel, West Hampstead, which, along with Bluesville 68 at the

Manor House in West Hampstead and the Fishmongers Arms in Wood Green, was a typically atmospheric music venue. Like the Marquee, it had a TYA audience. More importantly, it was adjacent to Decca's studios so after moving a mixing desk, cabling slung literally over rooftops and a plastic screen placed by Ric's drums, between Alvin's guitar stack and the vocal mic, all was ready. It was pretty basic compared to today's recording techniques and there was extra tension because they had only one evening, from 8.45 until 11pm, to record two sets, with a short break, from which the final album tracks would be chosen.

Rick Saunders wrote an enthusiastic review of the show in the July 1968 issue of *Beat Instrumental*, that included his half-time dressing room observation that he was "greeted by loud cheers from everyone, except Alvin (talking very seriously with a remarkably lovely girl in Indian gear)." That was me. He trusted me to give him good feedback on the sound and energy out front and I assured him it was sounding excellent. Alvin went out for the second half relaxed and able to forget any anxiety he might have had.

The *Undead* album includes as its final track the first recorded outing for the 5.24-minute version of 'I'm Going Home', which bounces along with early light and shade dynamics. There are already some rock'n'roll references in the solo and the intro. The riff, the energy of joyous release and tight ending are in place.

Everyone was knocked out with the recordings and Decca, who had initially intended to release *Undead* only in the USA, went with a UK release too. The solarised psychedelic cover was the first collaboration with John Fowlie (John Fowley, misspelt on the sleeve), who had connected with Alvin in Copenhagen earlier that year. When Alvin took me to meet John and his wife Eva in Copenhagen, we went to their apartment for dinner. After sitting down to eat, Henning, a close friend of theirs, appeared in a waiter's outfit, with white napkin over his arm, to serve the first course impeccably. I remember being slightly confused until everyone, including Alvin, burst into laughter.

The first American tour loomed and, though nothing was said, it was a given that this was a huge opportunity. The USA had been a mythical part of all our rock'n'roll lives growing up and for Bill Graham to have approached the band after hearing their first album on FM radio on the West Coast seemed extraordinary. As young adults all the alternative news coming from San Francisco was inviting. A consciousness revolution was taking place and soon they would be experiencing it in the flesh, in more ways than one.

The money for the band was very tight and there was no way that

Ruthann or I could join them. That was hard, had we been heiresses Chris would not have kept us in England. On the original leaving date in June we woke to be told that the US visas had not come through and it would be the following day when they were California bound. Alvin and I were tense with conflicting emotions. How would we not be? We went to the cinema to see *The Graduate*, appropriately American with its Simon & Garfunkel soundtrack.

Long distance phone-calls were prohibitively expensive, and we didn't even fully understand that California was in a different time zone, eight hours behind the UK. Chris Wright mentions he and Terry Ellis didn't communicate on that tour. "We couldn't afford to make phone calls, so we wrote letters, although I hardly received any of Terry's letters as I was always on the move."

Alvin sent postcards to me which, sadly, have been lost over the years. One was from the Sunset Marquis, in Los Angeles, a hotel card, with a picture of this huge very modern hotel suite, complete with kitchenette, on the front. I remember looking at this image and thinking how would he ever want to come back to our tiny home in Victoria.

I responded by sending him some photos of me taken by Vincent in the Warwick Square garden, posing in a pretty white Biba minidress. I posted these to Alvin along with shots taken of me inside the flat, posing in a wonderful handmade, psychedelic silk top and red jeans. All the photos are heavy on the model make-up and poses, as that was still a big part of my life.

This first US tour was a great success musically, though because it was organised so fast around Bill Graham's letter the date sheet was far from full. They picked up gigs as they went along thanks to their reputation as a live band. Arriving on the West Coast on June 13, a day later they headlined at the Cheetah Club in Venice, where a poster featured a serious Hendrix-haired Alvin and compared him with Hendrix, Clapton and Mike Bloomfield. "Catch a listen to Alvin Lee, who MANY consider to be the BEST BLUES GUITAR in ENGLAND TODAY!" The capitals are as per the original poster.

On June 24 they played the Whiskey a Go-Go in Hollywood before heading to San Francisco for shows at the Fillmore from June 28 to 30, with Canned Heat. This gig produced the first of their fabulous Fillmore posters, which continue to be the subject of books and exhibitions.

The Fillmores West and East created the perfect audience for TYA's music and Alvin's virtuosity. Like the Marquee in London the Fillmores elevated his sense of free-flowing experimentation. The US audience was totally involved from the first notes and called out and applauded in a way that the more introverted UK audiences never did. It was frustrating in the UK that audiences would sit, listen and applaud, albeit with quiet enthusiasm, and get up and dance only when the last number was announced. Then, having finally got to their feet, any number of encores were requested. In the US, audience were enthusiastic from the moment the bands were onstage. Their openness and energy made a huge impact on the UK bands who became popular there. It was obvious that the bands became more confident, extrovert and their music and performances progressed as a result.

Audiences were not only intense male blues fans, there were plenty of young women, with or without men, who came to get high and dance to the music. Left at home that summer, I wouldn't experience this until November 1968. I had no idea what audience they would find, and no doubt thought it would be mostly blues fanatics, guys, like it was in the UK and Scandinavia. It was perhaps fortunate I knew nothing about American groupies. Few bands had been out there and reported back on this aspect of touring.

In July the original Fillmore Auditorium closed and Bill Graham took over the Carousel Ballroom, which became Fillmore West. Between July 5 and 8, Ten Years After played on the opening night bill with the Paul Butterfield Blues Band. From Bill Graham: "The next night we opened at the Carousel, now renamed Fillmore West, with the Butterfield Blues Band and Ten Years After. Like Cream and Pink Floyd, Ten Years After was one of the English bands who exemplified something much different than what was going on in the American scene. I liked Ten Years After very much."

To have Bill Graham's seal of approval and to headline at both Fillmore West and newly opened Fillmore East in New York was a tremendous accolade on this their first US Tour. It guaranteed them headline bookings at venues across America.

They played ten nights, from July 12 to 21, at The Golden Bear, Huntington Beach, their first settled relaxation in 1968. From July 26 to 28, they were back at the Cheetah Club in LA. Then they flew to New York, to play at the Fillmore East on August 2 and 3, with Big Brother & The Holding Company headlining. This became a legendary gig for TYA and especially Alvin.

In 1968 there were very few women rock musicians and, with the possible exception of Grace Slick, none came close to the energy and performance levels of Janis Joplin, Big Brother's lead singer. Alvin and TYA stayed on to watch her extraordinary performance. Jamming after the gig was not typical but Janis was far from typical and after the audience had left she was back on stage with a few bottles of Southern Comfort and whoever would join in. It was a highlight of the tour that he talked about when he got back to Warwick Square. Not being a drinker, he didn't realise that Southern Comfort was liquor, with a high alcohol content. Watching Janis slug it back, he thought perhaps it was wine and did the same. There was some jamming and Alvin told me that Graham Bond got so drunk, he fell backwards off his piano stool and passed out. Alvin also passed out and woke in the middle of the night, curled up in a corner of the stage, not even sure where he was.

As for the speculation, did Alvin and Janis get together? He always told me he was terrified of her and I'm sure at that time it was true. Had she lived longer fate might have put them together somewhere for a wild night after he gained in worldliness. No doubt Janis fancied Alvin, grabbed his butt and called him "babycakes!" In her short and extraordinary life she enjoyed the favours of quite a few musicians.

Towards the end of their first US tour, on August 4 to 6, TYA played Steve Paul's Scene Club in New York. This was the first time Alvin met Jimi Hendrix, who borrowed a right-hand bass and jammed, left-handed. "He took the bass, turned it upside down and played an amazing solo. We just stopped and let him float off," Alvin said later.

Alvin respected Hendrix more than any of his fellow English guitarists because he could recognise their influences and backgrounds. Hendrix was a force of nature and Alvin was more than happy to acknowledge his gifts and talents. Confident of his own talents, Alvin never felt threatened by Jimi. It was clear to me when I heard them talking together that Jimi always spoke to Alvin as an equal.

Back in London I was often desperately lonely and found myself facing many personal dramas, both physical and mental. Ruthann reminded me that one of our stranger pastimes was to measure ourselves and share information about our hopefully shrinking bodies. Ruthann was still performing as a dancer in West End shows and on TV. I went to see her in the musical *Jorrocks* at The New Theatre in St. Martin's Lane and being impressed with how sophisticated and accomplished she was. I still felt like a stranger in a strange land. Nottingham was very provincial and without Alvin around my lack of London social skills made me very unsure of myself. An eating disorder was emerging as I continued to try for photographic modeling work, with some success, but I was often the target for unwanted sexual advances.

Photographer Roger Garwood was an exception. He and his soon-to-be wife Jenny Puddefoot became friends. Roger had his own studio and took some wonderful shots of me in clothes I'd designed and made.

Jenny had trained as an opera singer and had an astonishingly powerful voice, especially when singing unaccompanied in a small room. Eventually she would take over the Ten Years After Music Lovers Society and run it for Chrysalis.

I lost touch with her in the seventies and two decades later, looking at *Hello* magazine in a local supermarket, discovered she and Roger had divorced and Jenny had married Paolo Gucci. It was a marriage that was dramatically lived and ended quite tragically. I read her memoir *Gucci Wars: Jenny Gucci's Story*. What an adventure she had – a real life opera.

One day Jenny and Roger turned up and told me a photographer they knew, who had photographed Jean Shrimpton and been instrumental in her success, wanted to shoot pictures of me. We set off to somewhere in the countryside, met up with this middle-aged guy and went into a small wood. Roger and Jenny left us to work, and the next thing I remember was this man pushing me up against a tree and trying to molest me. Shocked and very cross, I made it clear that he was barking up the wrong tree. In the commotion Roger and Jenny reappeared to calm me to down, Roger suggesting it was all part and parcel of this guy's modus operandi and a great opportunity. I had so few friends that sulking or storming off in the middle of nowhere was not an option. I was, however, clear that I was not interested in a career that included being available sexually.

The chap shrugged and it was all quite lighthearted. He offered me a lift back to London, with Roger and Jenny following, and bought us all dinner at a fancy Italian restaurant. He hammered his car, an Aston Martin, through the narrow English country lanes. I glanced to see the speedometer at 140mph at one point. It was the fastest I have ever been in a car and if he was hoping it would impress me he was wrong. I was tense from head to toe. That was the end of any high fashion aspirations I might have had. I was out of my depth in this world and I knew it.

TYA's first US tour far exceeded the whole team's expectations. Everyone's confidence was high. Alvin was certain their music had an authentic US audience and felt a strong personal connection with the hippie's peace and love philosophy and their progressive, freedom-loving lifestyle. His only real surprise was their lack of knowledge about their musical roots.

"When I first came to America, I thought everybody would know Big Bill Broonzy and Lonnie Johnson," he told me. "I was very surprised that most Americans didn't have any idea who they were. I was taking American music, putting a little English energy into it, and bringing it back to America. It amazed me that so few Americans were aware of their musical heritage."

chapter 21
USA Tales, *Stonedhenge,* Flying London-NY- San Francisco

TYA left New York on August 7 so as to be home in time for the 8th National Jazz & Blues Festival at Kempton Park, Sunbury, three days later. This year they were fourth on the evening's bill, followed by Jeff Beck, The Nice and headliner Arthur Brown. Their musical progress was not lost on the crowd and they were in full "blow 'em off" mode, leaving a standing audience yelling for encores. We stayed on to watch The Jeff Back Group, with Rod Stewart on vocals, who had a hard time following them. Alvin was thoughtful, friendly to fans, answering questions about America.

The energy rose when The Crazy World of Arthur Brown took to the stage. Arthur wore white make-up and a flaming headdress. Seconds after he screamed, "I am the god of hellfire and I come to bring you, FFFIIIIRRREEE!" there was a dreadful crash as the corrugated roof of the rear stand gave way, collapsing onto the fans below. This brought everything to a halt, effectively ending the show as security and others rushed to the aid of those trapped. Ambulances took away the injured. Astonishingly, no one was seriously hurt.

It was fantastic to have Alvin home and to hear stories of San Francisco, Los Angeles, New York, Hendrix, Joplin and everything else. Despite my fears, he was relieved to be home and with someone he trusted, someone down-to-earth. Unfortunately, after a few days he told me that he'd brought home an unwanted gift, a dose of the clap. This hiccough seemed irrelevant and was easily dealt with. After all, I'd hardly expected him to stay physically faithful for 12 weeks. Chris Wright made us an appointment with a Harley Street STD specialist, whose one outstanding characteristic was a slack, loose handshake, which we all remarked on. A shot of penicillin in the rear and all was forgotten.

Alvin told me about the drunken after-show jam at the Fillmore with Janis Joplin and emailed me about it 2010: "It was Graham Bond (Hammond and sax player) of the Graham Bond Organization, who was the keyboard player in the Janis jam after the Fillmore East gig. He sat down at the piano, said 'Right boys, in the key of G', lifted his hands to play the first chord and fell over backwards unconscious onto the floor. His roadies just picked him up and carried him off, we didn't see him again that evening. Rock & Roll!"

He also told me about his fascinating experience at The Living Theatre, founded by Julian Beck and Judith Malina. *Paradise Now* was a cross between a play and pure performance art in which the fourth wall was dismantled completely. The performers came off the stage to confront the audience, with statements like "I am not allowed to smoke marijuana" while lighting up, or "I am not allowed to take my clothes off" while stripping off. Others were "I don't know how to stop the war" or "to be free is to be free of (fill in your own need)".

At one performance of the Living Theatre, they famously decided to take over the Fillmore. Bill Graham went onstage to tell them they could only take it over if they killed him first, which clearly out bluffed them. Like a few others, Alvin was perplexed by what the Living Theatre were all about but he was excited by events that stretched his thinking and imagination. Only an intelligent and open-minded man would have been able to open up and allow himself to travel beyond mainstream sonic boundaries.

Culturally, Alvin was most attracted to cinema and films that were obscure and surreal. Building on the Fellini movies, he took me to in Nottingham – subtitles were never a problem for him – we went to the Arts Lab in Drury Lane, lay on the basement soft-floor mattresses, getting high and watched the Jean-Luc Godard movies, *Week-end* (1967), with the long, traffic jam, car crash scene, and *Les Carabiniers* (1963) with the extended postcards scene. Godard famously said, "A story should have a beginning, a middle and an end, but not necessarily in that order." We also enjoyed Jean Cocteau's (1947) *La Belle et la Bete,* with the corridor of protruding arms each holding a candelabra.

The best gift he brought back was a bunch of fine US/UK albums from Tower Records in LA, where the group had been allowed by the record company representative to take whatever they fancied. It was one of the few social group outings and happened on all the tours but the bill – never discussed – was probably paid from their account.

No record stores in the UK boasted the size and scope of Tower on Sunset Boulevard. New releases were piled high at the end of each aisle, a musical wonderland. Their choices were left for their record company to box up and dispatch to the UK management office, and brought to our homes when they returned. Their arrival signaled a great day.

TYA's own live album *Undead* was released on August 10 in the USA and six days later in the UK. It reached 26 in the UK album charts and 115 in the *Billboard* charts. Though it missed the Top Twenty here and Top 100 in the US, it was pretty good going for a second album, especially as there was no hit single. In the US it was down to FM radio and the shows they'd just played.

Between an increasingly busy gigs schedule in the UK and Europe, TYA's days were filled with music paper interviews and BBC radio appearances. Since Alvin was the singer, guitarist, front man and, increasingly, the only songwriter, he was the favoured candidate for interviews. Chris tried to offer Leo, Ric and Chick for interviews, and they were all keen to do them but it was Alvin they wanted even though, paradoxically, he was the least keen. But Alvin was now the one steering their musical direction while the others were not that clued up about what Ten Years After were actually about.

This led to some rather opaque interviews. As much as they had all played together for some years, as The Jaybirds they had been a covers band, with no distinctive musical direction or philosophy. What was happening now was in Alvin's head and hands. He was following his instincts in the moment, not making plans. Despite being a dynamic extrovert on-stage, like many performers he was quiet off-stage, preferring to communicate through his music. He did not appear to have any personal need for extra attention or to explain himself.

On a lovely sunny Sunday afternoon towards the end of August, TYA played one in the series of free shows in London's Hyde Park. Playing early in the show because they had a gig in the evening, 135 miles away at the Winter Gardens in Malvern, Alvin was relaxed and confident, at home in the sunshine after all those weeks in California. It was wonderful to watch him play and observe how his stage presence had developed.

The Hyde Park concerts were a highlight of that summer in the UK. While Alvin was away in the USA, I had gone to see Pink Floyd play the first ever Hyde Park concert. They were perfect for the magical park which was full of the emerging London hippie crowd. As I was leaving I saw an elderly lady dancing in the sunshine, a huge smile on her face, in the midst of a circle of young hippies – a perfect image of the times and the sense of freedom that was spreading through the society.

At home we socialized with the same group of close friends, Vincent, Vivienne, Simon Stable and Johnnie and Judy. Visits from Sam and Doris, Ruth and Jeff and my young brother, now 18, using his first name Harold, and his own band Life Without Mother. Since I had left home, he had been making music, playing guitar and hoping that the music world might welcome him as it had Alvin. Our tiny home was a very secure nest for Alvin. It grounded him from all the extraordinary events to which he was exposed.

We still enjoyed lots of stoned creative silliness, and while Alvin had heard about psychedelics, especially in California, he still had not taken any. One evening Simon, aka "The Count", came calling and had some LSD with him, just one dose, that he would like to take with us for support and company. It was best to be in the company of people you could trust not to fuck around with your head when you were tripping.

Alvin had a few blues (amphetamines) and suggested that he and I would take one each to stay awake and keep Simon company. After a cup of tea to wash down the pills and some chat, I decided to paint, while Alvin began playing, writing and recording. What was that pill Simon took? After an hour, he was sound asleep on the sofa and remained so for the rest of the evening. Alvin and I were buzzing away. My painting began with a pencil squiggle across the page and turned into a psychedelic image, a loose abstract, unlike anything I'd ever done before. A few hours later Simon awoke. We were curious to know what his experience had been. He looked at my painting. "That is exactly what I was dreaming about!" he declared.

We were lucky at Warwick Square. The landlord was a great supporter of musicians but we were not the best neighbours and often played music into the small hours. Any complaints made to him about our noisy late hours fell on deaf ears. Particularly long suffering was the lady downstairs who used a broom or umbrella to bang on her ceiling. One evening, in her frustration, she came upstairs and banged on our door. Alvin answered. "Fuck off!" was all he said. I was surprised at his abruptness. We were outgrowing out first dear home, at least aurally.

Quite often in the small hours there was a persistent tap, tap tapping on the wall from the next building. I used to joke that it was the man next door boarding up his wife in the wall. Some months after we left the realisation dawned on us that he was probably also complaining about the music. Sorry mate.

In September they were back at Decca studios recording *Stonedhenge*, their third album. Alvin had written the key tracks, though Leo, Chick and Ric contributed short musical links. It was recorded over 12 days between gigging around the UK. With my day job now a memory, I was free to become ears in the studio and make cups of tea. They were great sessions with Mike Vernon confident to go along with Alvin's experimental ideas.

Visual artists use studios to experiment with ideas and techniques. They don't rehearse what they will draw or paint elsewhere and then go into the studio to make the finished artwork. However, the cost of hiring a sound recording studio was always high, so unless bands had more money than sense they would rehearse first so as to enter the studio already prepared, and record as quickly as possible.

The Beatles were lucky insofar as EMI, who owned Abbey Road Studios, allowed them unlimited studio time that wasn't charged to their account. This enabled them to experiment with techniques and ideas, opening up what recording could and would become. EMI's technicians, used to working structured hours, were not so keen on these young guys smoking dope, recording into the small hours, experimenting with ideas, instruments and the various acoustics in the studios at Abbey Road but The Beatles were so successful that EMI was happy to allow their experimentation.

I found a sensational photograph of Stonehenge in *Treasures Of Britain*, a book published by the Automobile Association. The mysterious stone circle, 5,000 years old, attracts millions of visitors to the UK, and the photograph was taken during the summer solstice with the sun rising at dawn through the main stones, and a circle of red light created by this phenomenon. The four huge stones were completely black in the night's shadow and behind them, on the horizon, the light of the dawn arises. It was a very strong graphic image that would stand out on a gatefold album in a record store or on a poster. Alvin loved it and thought *Stonedhenge* would make a great album title. However, they were told the cost of using the photograph was prohibitive and instead the record company used a painting of the image, a poor second best in my opinion. I remember my disappointment at the finished artwork. No one had told me the photo wasn't being used. Why should they?

Still, we did manage to add some eccentric musical credits: Count Simon (Stable) de la Bedoyere: bongos; Alvin Lee: guitar, vocals, Chinese fans, clog stomping; Leo Lyons: bass guitar, foot tapping, non-traceable cigarette tin clatter; and finally my own credit, as The Bird: Chinese finger fan holder. In reality, I held two fans while Alvin tapped out a rhythm on them.

There was also a list of miscellaneous personal incidents, titles and activities, among them: International Underground Consultant: Simon "very fine" Stable; Communications Link: Pete Drummond; Inscrutable Oriental Ear: Vincent Tseng; Transport Trigger: Leo Lyons; Silent Alarm Clocks and Ornithological Consultant: Chick Churchill; Locator of Wobbups: Ric Lee; and thunderstorm courtesy of God.

Good clean stoned fun was had at Warwick Square as Alvin and I dreamed up the album sleeve's non-too-serious credits, subtly acknowledging the friends who by now were an important part of Alvin's support team. We ended with: "The CDM is awarded to Andy Jaworski and John Hembrow, for services over and above the call of duty." I have no idea what CDM stood for. It's lost in the mists of time.

Ten Years After's second US tour opened on September 27 and 28 with two shows at the Fillmore East with Procol Harum and Country Joe & The Fish. Ruthann joined Ric for the two-months tour, and I was kept sane by the knowledge that I would join Alvin for two weeks at the end. Chris wasn't too happy that Ruthann was traveling with them, but Ric insisted.

No longer working full-time for Laura Lee, signing up with the model agency that found me seasonal modeling work for six-week stints paid twice the rate of the full-time work, and I had bought a great fitted pair of high-waisted men's pin striped trousers in navy wool with a fine line that fit fantastically. Later, the boss' secretary came into the models' room and said he wanted to see me in his office. Naively thinking he had noticed my well-cut trousers, I knocked and he called me into his office. He stood leaning against his desk and calmly unzipped his trousers before asking if I would like to go down on him. I stood there mortified. With Alvin away, I was at my most vulnerable and burst into floods of tears, explaining between sobs that I had a boyfriend and he had it all wrong. Apparently, tears are a turn-off. He fumbled about and angrily told me to go, which I was more than happy to do. Did I complete my six-week booking? I don't remember. I do remember feeling utterly wretched back at Warwick Square, lonely and bereft, but I never ever told Alvin.

This incident brought the curtain down on my modelling days. I now understood that as models, photographic, catwalk or in-house, you were considered sexually available. How disgusting the treatment of pretty women was back then.

The flight to America was unforgettable. I'd never flown anywhere before. I'd been to Heathrow airport to see Alvin off and caught the bus alone back to West London. My destination was San Francisco, via New York's John F Kennedy airport where I changed planes. About 15 minutes into the flight, a stewardess told me that a gentleman a few rows away wanted to buy me champagne. She pointed in the direction of a young chap with a smiling face. "No thank you," I told her. On all my subsequent flights this never happened again. The universe made a note. Despite his rock'n'roll dalliances, I had been faithful to Alvin from when we first met, even during our short break-up when I stayed in Bournemouth. It wasn't a principle, it was simply that I hadn't met anyone else who attracted me.

I had a window seat and experienced a visual effect called birefringence or double refracting, caused by the polarising effect of the windows, where you see rainbows on the sea all the way across the Atlantic. Why had no-one told me about this? It was wonderful, all that hashish smoking had fine-tuned my colour senses. We landed at JFK airport where I was to take an internal flight on TWA to San Francisco. Directed through some doors I waited for a shuttle bus to the TWA terminal, the most elegant futuristic building I had ever seen. It was the work of the Finnish architect Eero Saarinen, a smooth, white, abstract outline that suggested a bird taking flight.

Arriving in San Francisco, I wafted through passport control in a dream, my US Embassy visa already stamped into my passport. At customs the officer was astonished that I had brought only my little black modeling bag. I was wearing white clogs and didn't even have a spare pair of shoes. Exhausted from many hours traveling, I just followed exit signs and as I walked along an empty corridor noticed two guys coming towards me. The tall Californian with dark hair caught my eye. A few seconds later I recognised Alvin by his side, striding towards me grinning. How sweet it was. Without partings there are no reunions.

"One of these days boys, gonna see my baby, gonna see my baby coming down the road. She'll have my pardon, pardon in her apron, gonna see the governor, say release my man. She's coming down the road, boy, she's coming down the road. Red dress on, yeah! She's got her red dress on!"

After a car ride into San Francisco with Alvin's friend – I think his name was Richard – we dropped off my bag at the hotel, and then went to the house which Richard shared with a dozen other hippies. I felt like Alice falling down the rabbit hole. Nothing I had experienced in life so far came anywhere near this casual, laid-back, eclectic, friendly, colourful household.

A typical large wooden Victorian house, it had wonderful rooms with big windows that today would be called "desirable period features".

Sitting in this technicolor living room after two long haul flights to a time zone eight hours earlier than the one I had left 14 hours before was disorientating. Now I would enjoy marijuana, California style. I was used to rolling multi-skinned English style joints with heated hashish crumbled into a tobacco base. The American-style little one skin grass joints were deceptively sweet to inhale. I suffered a mild coughing attack, which no doubt helped the tetrahydrocannabinol (THC) to circulate faster into my blood and brain.

The pretty faces in the room smiled at me. Alvin glowed with a warmth that relaxed and welcomed me to his new world. A young woman came into the room smiling, someone asked her if she was ok. "I took some mescaline," she said. That was a real surprise to me. I hadn't come across any woman who was free enough to take a psychedelic on her own, without a partner. It caused a real shift in my thinking. As I was soon to discover, many young Californian women lived their own lives as independent individuals, free of the constraints imposed on them by a male-dominated society.

chapter 22
SF, Fillmore, Bill Graham, NY Christmas

In San Francisco a year after the Summer of Love, it seemed to me that I had discovered my true tribe. I felt at one with the sunshine, glorious colours, clothes, pretty people, loving smiles and hippie vibes. England seemed introverted, especially in cities where strangers don't tend to smile back at you when you smile at them. I'd been brought up in a social environment. I was outgoing, happy and curious, and found it difficult to contain my natural friendliness.

Finally, I had found a place where if I smiled people smiled back. It sounds so simple but it felt very profound. The women amazed me; so independent, confident, tanned, gorgeous but far more predatory than their English counterparts, and Alvin was their quarry. I had a rapid education in the US rock scene and the groupies who occupied it, so different from TYA's UK blues fans. Nevertheless, Alvin was oblivious to their advances, delighted to be with me after ten weeks on the road.

We crossed the Golden Gate Bridge to Sausalito, a wooden house-boats hippie community in San Francisco Bay. I saw beautiful custom-made soft leather clothes with beading and fringes, and the original Body Shop, with strawberry bath oils, hand-made soaps, massage oils and other sensual treats. Alvin was completely relaxed and happy, smiling and flashing peace signs to beautiful people. Back in the city, we went to Golden Gate Park, the tranquil Japanese garden, and everywhere we went we saw young hippies. It felt like paradise. We were high and full of wonder.

Between November 14 and 17, Ten Years After played Bill Graham's Fillmore West, the first shows I saw in the USA. It was a big open space, no static seating, with psychedelic light shows projected on the walls and ceiling.

The whole place pulsated with colours produced by overhead projectors, liquid dyes, oil on water, slide projections and 16mm films, all manipulated to subtle effects in time with the music, a totally immersive experience. As the bands played several nights and multiple shows, the lighting teams developed incredibly well timed effects to enhance the music's dynamics. They were as dedicated to their art as the musicians were to their music, as the audiences were to their own enjoyment and connection. It was thrilling and spellbinding, the perfect set-up, arranged to give everyone a memorable night.

Still photos from these Fillmore West gigs can't convey much beyond a glimpse of the reality. The San Francisco "Brotherhood of Light", formed in 1967, was a collective group of lighting and multimedia experts. Brian Epps, Ed Langdon, Marcus Maximist and Bob Pullum founded an organisation that still exists today, working in movies and touring with bands.

Bill Graham was extraordinary. Whenever a band would arrive at a Bill Graham venue, BIll would be there; relaxed, open, affable, hugs for the ladies, greetings and hand-shakes for the guys, enquiring how they were, how the tour was going. It was a fantastic strategy. No doubt one of his low-key security in blue jeans and a Fillmore T-shirt would have forewarned him that the band had arrived by walkie-talkie, so that Bill could pull off this magic synchronistic trick. For bands arriving after a few weeks at less welcoming and well-organised venues across the country, it was a total joy. They relaxed down a few more notches and totally focused on the music, knowing that Bill Graham and his team had their backs.

He invariably announced the band onto the stage. Bill can be heard online at Wolfgang's Vault, introducing "From England, Ten Years After". At the end of the show he was there with congratulations, ready to listen to any complaints. There were none. He ran the best gigs in the USA between 1967 and 1970 at his Fillmores in San Francisco and New York. Even the Fillmore West dressing room was unique. A large, open, dimly-lit room, around its walls was a raised platform area where groupies would sit alone on chairs and stake their pitch. It was more like a scene from a Fellini movie or the Reeperbahn in Hamburg than a dressing room. These ladies were very overdressed and exotic and, as far as I remember, not as friendly as most San Franciscan hippies. With names like The Black Widow, it was quite a scene, guaranteed to create a sexually charged energy to send the musicians out on stage.

When the band went on I sat on the floor with Richard and friends, smoking good weed openly and feeling the difference in the audience from the UK and how the band and Alvin reacted. It was so cool. If I had died and left the planet during one of those shows it would still have been totally cool.

As the music became more animated, the audience stood up and danced, arms held high and swaying like snakes, lithe bodies, hips moving to the beats; long hair on both girls and guys flying, with loose long skirts, dancing freeform, ballet moves and stretches, the light shows projected onto their bare skin, their faces, arms, shoulders, sometimes breasts, bare feet and legs. It was mesmerising, like little kids playing, having fun, quite unlike the sexily dressed posing found in an eighties disco. This was ecstatic dancing, the music, the weed, the lights all taking you higher, leaving all your cares behind in a spirit of transcendence.

In the US I learned how to let go, to dance to the music on a higher level than ever before. It was the highlight of every evening. As time and tours went on I would find a spot somewhere hidden in the stage wings where, hopefully, the audience wouldn't see me. Then I could clearly watch Alvin singing and playing guitar and dance, transported in a trance, often sweating as hard as he did. 'I Can't Keep From Crying' was wonderful to dance to. I felt all the notes and the rhythmical changes and dynamics through all my body. How lucky I was to be in these places and times with such an extraordinary partner.

I know not everyone dances and later, especially post-Ten Years After, Alvin had a huge following of guitar players, mainly males.
Their involvement with his guitar playing was probably quite personal, imagining themselves as great rock players. Alvin would come to be called a rock star, a superstar, a rock god, but November 1968 he was spreading his wings, carried along with the times. As I wrote about the Marquee, getting high and feeling the freedom to experiment with no expectations from the audience was a buzz for him. The Fillmores took his playing to a new level. On rare occasions he might even play a number twice, or get lost in a solo, or forget for a moment which number they were playing. He figured his equally high audience probably didn't even notice.

As an art form, rock or jazz music is very forgiving. Alvin's philosophy was that if you play a bum note, do so again so it seems intentional. A live show is the ultimate experience of being in the present, each note giving way to the next. If you go "wrong" don't stop, keep going, bluff, find your way back with confidence. The chances are no one will notice and you will keep the audience with you.

People find their own way to get high, some run or jog, go to the gym, play sports or enjoy sex, all of which release endorphins and give them a high. Music and dance are still mine, Alvin's virtuoso guitar playing my focus. The connection it brought to him with his audience was an energy loop. When it works, the audience connects with the musician. Everyone gets high.

Walking around the streets of SF in 1968 was wonderful, the greeting a smile and flash of a two-fingered peace sign. We were never happier in any city. In thrift stores we bought two funky hats, fur over felt trilbies, a couple of fringed leather jackets. Headshops were filled with psychedelic posters, buddha statues, incense holders in all shapes and styles, pipes and bongs, which we couldn't take back home. I wore patchouli oil for years, especially when traveling through airports after having finished off a joint on the way there. Its smell overpowered the residual smell of weed in formal environments. A huge store called Pier One near Fisherman's Wharf was a cornucopia of ethnic fabrics and wonders from around the world. In a San Francisco house we visited, a big street billboard of the sky and clouds was used as wallpaper to cover a couple of walls. A sun-shaped circular mirror reflected the yellows and oranges from the facing wall. It was fantastic use of space.

The Beatles double white album was released around this time and we were invited to the home of John Wasserman, an underground DJ, to hear it. Leo joined Alvin and me at John's spacious city home on one of San Francisco's characteristic sloping roads. His large basement was devoted to music, with a great HiFi system and wall-to-ceiling shelves filled with record albums. There was no furniture, only bean bags, the popular alternative to sofas in SF, truly a listening room in which to chill out. Drinking hot tea and smoking great marijuana, we settled down and listened for the first time. Conversation was unnecessary, only a glance at the all-white album sleeve. John placed the needle onto the pristine black vinyl surface. All four sides, one followed the other as the tracks and arrangements drew us further into a transfixed state. My memory says that we played it through twice. It sounded that good.

Los Angeles was the next stop. Alvin and I stayed at the Hollywood Hills house of Lennie and Sandy Poncher, the West coast music agent and his wife. It appeared quite opulent with chandeliers and a grand piano in the lounge, but it was somehow not that big a surprise to discover the piano was out-of-tune and the outdoor lounging chairs collapsed when we sat in them. It was very different to the funky realness of San Francisco. America,

I realised, is not one country but many local and state cultures. Hollywood revolves around the movies. We settled into our room and I changed and walked downstairs to be greeted by Lennie, who looked me up and down. "You look great, but those shoes have to go," he said, smiling. White wooden clogs were just not Hollywood.

The band few off to some gig out of town and while they were away, I was left in the hands of Sandy Poncher, which wasn't really great for her, I'm sure. What do you do with a kid from London lacking in sophistication? "Let's go shopping. I'll take you to Country Casuals," she said.

We went to this big store, full of clothes that were not my style but were Sandy's. She spotted a silk scarf she liked in a few different colours, picked up one of each and handed them to the assistant on the big wooden accessories desk. The assistant rang them up on the till and Sandy gave her a credit card, the first I'd ever seen. I really didn't know what it was. After a few minutes the assistant said, "I'm sorry madam, your card has been declined," which also meant nothing to me. Sandy was not pleased. We left the scarves, left the store and drove back home while she told me how embarrassed she felt.

Back at the house she spent the next few hours ringing around to her friends telling them. "I was with my guest from London, can you imagine how embarrassed I felt?" Nothing in my previous life had prepared me for this drama. I was speechless, somewhat bemused by the whole event. It was like being in a foreign language movie.

On this, my first two-week US trip, I ate everything I was offered after having starved myself and lived on Limits diet biscuits in the UK. This meant eggs, bacon and sausages for breakfast, with pancakes and maple syrup, huge hamburgers with melted cheese, fries and large super-thick ice cream milk shakes, and sundaes like knickerbocker glory. It was a dairy, fat and sugar rich diet, which resulted in me gaining half a stone and breaking out in spots. Not long after this I cut down on eating meat, only chicken and a little lamb in the UK and no meat at all in America. I did enjoy the fish dishes in the USA, especially clam chowder and, in Boston, a succulent white fish called scrod.

In the USA I discovered honey as a healthy option to sugar, to add to tea. Alvin loved honey in his tea and I still use it to this day. In California I started to become interested in diet, how to cook food to maximise the nutrients and what constituted a healthy diet, and how animals were cared for and the hormone treatments that were already being given to cattle to stimulate the muscle growth. Naturally these hormones also found their way into the people that ate them and explained for me the bigger butts and thighs I saw on many Americans.

When Ten Years After returned to Los Angeles they played The Shrine Hall on November 29 and 30, supporting The Moody Blues and The Jeff Beck Band. I have vivid memories of watching The Beck Band from a balcony with Alvin. On vocals was Rod Stewart, whom I had last seen with Alvin at the Dancing Slipper in Nottingham in 1964 with The Steampacket. We were amused and mystified when Beck stood directly in front of Rod as he sang, as if to hide Rod, who had quite a height advantage, from the audience. Ronnie Wood was on bass guitar and within a few months I would meet Krissie, Ronnie's extraordinary English girlfriend. Ronnie, Alvin, Krissie and I would become close friends in 1969 but that was all to come. It was the first time hearing the Mellotron, used by The Moody Blues, which could emulate strings and sounded very lush on 'Nights In White Satin'.

That was the last gig of the tour. I had flown in via New York and so had Alvin, Chris Wright, Chick and Andy Jaworski, and we wound up back there. It was here I met Dee Anthony, who had become TYA's American manager when Chris Wright realised he needed someone who knew the US music business. Dee was a larger than life New Yorker. Alvin and I had much stoned fun with him and, in a way, he represented for Alvin something of the relationship that Elvis had with Col. Tom Parker. He grew close to Dee in a way he never did with Chris. It's all about personalities and fantasies. I think Dee helped Alvin to feel safe in America in a way that Chris never could.

Dee took us to Fifth Avenue, where spectacular Christmas decorations bedecked the stores and many jolly Santa Clauses lined the streets ringing bells to entice us inside. We visited Bloomingdales, the nearest department store in New York to Harrods, and Alvin was delighted in FAO Schwartz, the huge toy store. He bought Rock 'em Sock 'em Robots, a Marx toy with two plastic robots, the blue bomber and the red rocker, with boxing gloves in a boxing ring. Joysticks operated the arms, the aim to land a punch to the opponent's spring-loaded head. Hit right the head pops up to be re-loaded and repeated, most knock-outs is the winner. Johnnie Clifton and Alvin staged a memorable contest at Warwick Square on Alvin's 24th birthday. Christmas in New York was a buzz. Fifth Avenue wasn't filled with hippies but there was plenty of love in the air.

In New York Alvin and I stayed at the house of Sandy Bennett, the wife of Tony Bennett, for whom Dee had worked as tour manager. It was a beautiful home and Sandy was a lovely, generous, hospitable lady. We had a charming bedroom where we slept on our first waterbed. Heated water in December was a sensual delight. Along with some good weed, the enjoyment of Sandy's waterbed goes some way to explaining why Alvin and I look so relaxed and connected in photographs taken at JFK airport and on board the Boeing 707 TWA flight back to London.

Waiting for the flight home at JFK, we were a great Christmas melee, Chris, Chick, Andy J, Alvin and I, Dee with his teenage daughter Michelle, who would become a highly successful music business lawyer and also Executive Vice-President of Universal Music Group. There was Al Rosenstein, Dee's lawyer, Val, Dee's English wife and Sandy Bennett, dressed in a stunning black leather mini skirt, silk blouse, a funky, maybe Mongolian, lamb fur coat and matching hat, like a WWII pilot's helmet. She totally stole the fashion show.

Al Rosenstein turned and smiled at me and asked if I wanted him to take a photo of Alvin and I. He had seen me busily snapping away. I handed over my camera, he took one and handed it back and then a few minutes later took the camera from my hands and had us stand for another. We had swopped sides, and grinned even wider, both in funky SF thrift store hats. I would end up wearing Alvin's hat for the next year.

In April 2009 I sent these pictures to Alvin, along with some Warwick Square photos. He had not seen them in 40 years. He emailed back.

"Thanx for the pics. Warwick Square that place was so tiny. The tape recorder was a Simon, I'd forgotten all about that machine, I still have some dodgy demos I recorded on it. It's funny, I thought that when I looked at pics from all that time ago, we would look all young and innocent, not imagining what lay ahead, but in fact we both look pretty worldly and confident. By NY we were obviously up to speed with fur hats, bright eyes and ready to rock. LotsaLove. B.Goode. Alvin"

These pictures are my personal favourites of us together. Not too many were ever taken of us, so thank you Al Rosenstein. You spotted the magic of that day. On the flight home I took a photo of Alvin returning to his seat next to me. It remains another favourite image of him for me. He was so young, so open-faced, so relaxed and so completely un-rock'n'roll.

chapter 23
Move to Belgravia, Last Intense Marquee Gig

Back in the UK, we knew we had outgrown Warwick Square, our precious little first home, the creative incubator for the adventure that was Alvin Lee and Ten Years After. Johnnie Clifton introduced us to Perry Press who had just launched his estate agency, Pereds, in London. Perry set out to find us a flat on what was still a limited rental budget, £12.50 a week. According to Chris Wright, the 1968 second US TYA tour took $32,000 gross (maybe the equivalent of $400,000 in 2018) but left the band with a $5,000 debt. Chrysalis was very overdrawn. Terry Ellis went to LA at New Year and persuaded Mo Austin to sign Jethro Tull to Warner Bros in North America for an advance of $40,000. That cleared Chrysalis' debts. The company's cash flow problems were at an end.

Before the 1967 Ellis-Wright agency became Chrysalis (Chris/Ellis) in 1968, Chris came to Warwick Square and took Alvin and me out for dinner at a nearby Italian restaurant. He was very charming and explained to Alvin that he and Terry wanted to expand their management and bookings operations. Their idea was to have a record label and a songwriters' music publishing company all under the banner and logo of Chrysalis. It was obvious that Chris needed Alvin on board with this, as Ten Years After was the most successful of their bands. Their performances, record releases and Alvin's songwriting formed the foundation of their business during that exceptional first year.

It was clear to me that this expansion would create a conflict of interests. How would Chris Wright, as their manager, guarantee that a deal with Chrysalis for records or songwriting was the best available? After all, the job of a manager is to get the best deal for their artist. I raised the question but Alvin, although a bit surprised, was persuaded by Chris's comforting reassurances. He offered Alvin 0.5% of the new Chrysalis company, but nothing was offered to the rest of the band which didn't sit well with Alvin. It was Alvin whose agreement Chris needed. As his manager, he had 20% of Alvin who thought that an offer of 0.5% was an insult. He turned the offer down. In truth, we had no idea about business, no lawyer to turn to and were completely out of our depth.

Chrysalis did become management, booking agents, record company and publishers and that 0.5% would in time have been worth many millions. Much is written about artists and bands being ripped off by their managers but the reality is more elusive. The pressure of touring, writing and recording is as much as most musicians can handle. Managers took advantage of this simply because they discovered they could get away with it.

Alvin would always sign contracts with Chris and they formed a publishing company, Chrys-a-lee, for his songs. I stayed away from the business side as much as possible, preferring to focus on Alvin who I knew was already struggling with success. A few years later I went with Alvin to Chrysalis when he signed a new contract. We had discussed showing the contract to a lawyer first. In the office, with just us three there, I asked Chris if we could have a copy of the contract so an independent lawyer could check it over before Alvin signed. It was the only time I tried. Chris smiled, looked at me and said: "I'm not asking you to sign anything." Turning back to Alvin, he asked: "Is there a problem Alvin? Don't you trust me?" Alvin signed the new contract and that was that, the end of our attempts to get impartial legal advice.

As I said before, Chris was the right man to manage Alvin and Ten Years After. His courage in the first year, blindly leaping into unknown territories, was extraordinary. I don't know if all the deals were good deals and there's no point in speculating. Alvin always trusted Chris and the good relationship between them lasted until the end of his life. Ironically, as you will see, a pot of gold was waiting for Alvin that had nothing to do with music.

In December 1968, there was a quick visit home for Christmas. We had lunch at Alvin's with Sam and Doris then I went back to the pub, to my parents, for a second lunch. I remember lying down in the late afternoon, when all that food felt like it was pressing on my heart and might kill me.

For all the years we were together, whenever we were in Nottingham we always slept apart at our parents' homes. We both still had rooms with single beds. My parents would not have let us sleep together as we were unmarried.

On Boxing Day we were back in London for a celebration gig at the Marquee, billed as their Christmas Party. Was this the Marquee gig when in his excitement Alvin got carried away, threw his guitar around and split off the headstock below the machine heads? I took a photo of Vincent's hand holding the severed top, the guitar leaning against the graffiti on the dressing room wall. It has its first two stickers the TYAMLS fan club sticker I designed, its first sticker, attached under the strings, and the peace sign on the top body horn the second.

Alvin's Gibson ES 335 was his working guitar and not yet the iconic instrument of Woodstock it became. He referred to it as Big Red but he treated it as a tool for the job, not some precious artefact. In the damaged headstock photo it has the original dot inlaid neck, which was not harmed and so not replaced. However, it would have gone back to Gibson for repair and this may be the reason his red Fender Stratocaster turns up on images and videos from 1969.

In the New Year of 1969, Alvin and I left our home of two years at 80, Warwick Square. In our last telephone call in late December 2012, Alvin recalled how incredibly creative we were there. We were always engaged in some creative pursuit, or expansive conversations, whether alone together or with our friends.

Moving from the fourth floor down four flights of stairs was very intense. Roadies John and Andy and Alvin and I formed a chain. I had packed up our few earthly goods and we passed boxes down to where John, at the bottom, loaded up the Ford Transit.

Our next home didn't last long, only about two months, but it was so quirky it deserves an honourable mention. It was a rented flat just off Belgrave Square, 32 Grosvenor Crescent Mews, a cottage that would once have been a coach house at the back of a larger property. This first home that Perry Press found for us had a first floor rented flat at the back of the property. There was a large lounge, kitchen, bathroom and a bedroom, which had a smaller locked room inside that contained someone else's property. Between the lounge and the bedroom was a hallway with large whitewashed windows, and when these were opened you looked directly at horses in their stables. Lilo Blum's Riding School occupied the whole ground floor of the property. From here the riders would cross Knightsbridge to Hyde Park, for hacking, trotting and cantering around Rotten Row.

Having horses stabled below you was quite an experience. In the night, particularly in bed, we could hear them moving and making lovely horse sounds, blowing and whinnying through their noses. If you opened the large hall windows the smell of horses in their stables would drift up. When we'd had a smoke with our evening visitors we would open the hall windows and surprise them with our beautiful four-legged companions. There were no other windows in this flat, just skylights. During the short time we lived there it once snowed quite heavily. When the skylights were covered all daylight disappeared. We lived in a darkened flat for some days waiting for the snow to melt.

In 2018 I looked up Lilo Blum on Google and discovered she was still very much alive and 91 years of age. Her 90th birthday was held at The Dorchester Hotel, near to her Park Lane apartment that overlooks Hyde Park, and 100 people attended. She is a legend in riding circles.

One evening Alvin climbed through the lounge skylight and walked around the rooftops. Remember as a teenager, he'd got into trouble at school walking around the outside of the building on first floor windows. I knew nothing about that in 1969. I never tried to stop his adventuring spirit and watched as he disappeared through the skylight. He was gone for some time maybe a half hour but I don't remember being worried. When he returned he said he'd managed to get onto the roof of St George's hospital on the corner, and had an amazing view across Hyde Park Corner and into Buckingham Palace gardens.

Belgrave Square was a very upper class, up-market part of London and we discovered it was very uptight. After moving in and emptying out our cardboard boxes we put them outside to wait for the rubbish collection, we were contacted and told to take them back inside until the correct day to put them out. We noticed that when we went out of the front door and walked down the mews, net curtains at the windows would twitch. Our hair and dress were far from typical of the upper classes who called Knightsbridge their home.

I think it was a flat that today you would call shabby chic. In reality it was very low on furniture. There was a double bed and a wardrobe in the bedroom but all I remember in the lounge was a large dark oak dining table. We fitted a cord carpet in the lounge and placed on top of this a patterned rug, which would move with us. Living on the floor had appealed to me since our visit to John Wasserman's listening basement in San Francisco. From somewhere I acquired a saw and sawed off the lower legs of the dark oak dining table, so we could sit around it on cushions at floor level.

I wasn't sure the owners would appreciate this new table height. I wrote numbers 1, 2, 3 4 on the pieces I had sawn off and their corresponding leg stumps.

There was insufficient time for Grosvenor Crescent Mews to become a creative hub like Warwick Square. On the lounge wall was a large blackboard and Alvin and I and most visitors would add something with coloured chalks. Photos of the blackboard images show small lines high up, made by Alvin, Vince, Johnnie all trying to add the highest mark. We tried our best to enjoy ourselves in our new spacious living room. Pictures of Chris Wright enjoying a smoke and playing a clarinet under a peace poster, show we were always ready for fun.

One memorable evening when Chris Wright was present, a friend arrived with his girlfriend and they decided to play the board game Risk, which involves aggressive tactics to control the world. His girl declared herself a pacifist, declined to make hostile moves but despite this she won the game. It was an interesting experience for the alpha males.

Stonedhenge was released in early February. Decca's four-track recording studio was very limited, which was frustrating for the band at a time when recording was becoming freer and more experimental. The album's first side showed TYA's jazzy influences, while 'Going To Try' and 'No Title' are wonderfully loose and playful. All four wrote short link tracks to separate those written by Alvin, and this added to their share of songwriting income.

'Hear Me Calling', with a great descending riff, was released as a TYA single and even played live. It was picked up by Slade whose version appeared on their big selling *Slade Alive* LP in 1972. Snatches from the illustrious Sound Effects album are dotted throughout, with surprising touches. The friends who appeared under aliases in the credits all came to some sessions and added good vibes or bongos. Blessed as The Bird, I held Chinese finger fans that Alvin played on 'Skoobly-Oobly-Doobob'. He always welcomed friends who turned up. He was no fan of closed studios and enjoyed making work fun.

It was from Grosvenor Crescent Mews that we set off for Ten Years After's last gig at the Marquee, on February 25. The club was now too small to cope with the number of fans that TYA attracted. Despite it being mid-winter, the temperature inside was at boiling point and sweaty from the reportedly 1,200 who crammed in. Alvin was nicely stoned from a smoke and transported with the energy of his home fans.

During one ecstatic long solo, probably in 'I Can't Keep From Crying', more than halfway through the show, I watched from the wings as he slowly became entangled in the mic stand and his guitar lead. Turning to free himself, a few moments later he fell to the stage and passed out, mid-solo. John Hembrow went onstage and took off his guitar. Alvin began to come around but didn't move. I went to him, sat down on the stage between him and the audience, held him and asked if he was ok. He said he couldn't get up with everyone there. He was obviously embarrassed. He said he felt awful. There were no curtains on the low Marquee stage and it soon became clear this was the end of the show. The audience was asked to leave. We were told that 14 people had fainted in the crowd that night.

Once the audience had all left, Alvin slowly recovered enough to be taken back to Grosvenor Crescent Mews. He was very upset, mortified that he had let down the audience and felt completely responsible and not at all well. Chris Wright was with us and we decided to take him to St George's Hospital, the accident and emergency department. A doctor examined him and we were told that oxygen starvation had caused him and 14 audience members to faint. Thankfully, he only needed plenty of hot sweet drinks and a good night's sleep to recover completely.

When Alvin was onstage for a show and the set had started, he was committed to giving the audience the very best he could. Part way through a show his guitar might slip out-of-tune, especially during a particularly intense solo. He would power through, working with what he had and adapting his playing to accommodate the situation, re-tuning as he played or between numbers. If he broke a string during a solo he would tear it off and carry on. When Big Red had the Bigsby tremolo unit, he could change a string on stage between numbers very quickly while chatting to the audience, tune up and carry on.

He had just one guitar on stage, no back-up, plugged straight into his amp and speakers, with no effect pedals at all. He thought effect pedals made guitarists all sound the same. The range of sounds he developed were nuances of his distinctive techniques. He used a big triangular pic, which he would hold between his teeth when using his right-hand percussively or finger picking. Tortoiseshell, with his name printed on, it would be thrown into the audience at the end of the evening. If he used blues harmonica on a number and he could blow well, it would serve as a bottle neck as would the microphone stand or a wooden drum stick, left ready by Ric on the front of his kit.

His simple and uncomplicated workmanlike stage set-up rarely got in the way, broke down or caused him any confusion or irritation. His quest was for Big Red to become an extension of himself and liberate his technique, to offer maximum freedom to soar into space unhindered and uninterrupted. John and Andy would set everything up perfectly for him to be confident with his amps and speakers when he walked on stage and plugged in his guitar, an impeccable team.

chapter 24
Scandinavia, Another London Move, Krissie Wood

In early February I travelled with Alvin and TYA to Sweden and Denmark. It was only a week and three gigs but I really enjoyed my first outing to countries where I didn't speak or understand the language. In Scandinavia, and later in Germany, I was always taken for a local. In restaurants, all the band and Ruthann would be given English menus and I would be given one in the local language.

Scandinavian audiences were male heavy, similar to British audiences, more blues fans. One of the things I loved about Scandinavian and European tours was not understanding very much of what was said. It was so relaxing. Those snippets of conversation that in the UK or USA would attract your attention and involve you emotionally in some way, just wafted past my ears as an aural landscape of sounds unknown or maybe part recognised. As the touring became more intense it became very therapeutic. With my little understanding of them, Scandinavian languages became rhythms, tones, energies and somehow very musical. I always wanted to know the basics such as, hello, goodbye, yes please and no thank you, to be friendly and polite.

It was in Copenhagen 1969, that I met John Fowlie and Eva and was pranked, by their friend Henning dressed as a waiter. We went out to a smart restaurant in central Copenhagen where John produced a ready rolled joint that we smoked there after our meal. Apart from being excellent hashish, it was tremendous to feel that free. We wouldn't have found a quality restaurant in London where that was possible.

I think it was on this tour that we went to a Swedish live sex club. Ruthann and me, with Alvin, Leo, Ric, Chick and Andy Jaworski stood right at the back of the seated Stockholm club, facing the stage. Ruthann had been on stage in London musicals, and was curious to experience this novelty. I was just plain curious.

It was clean and well-lit with comfy surroundings and plenty of red and gold in the curtains and trimmings. On the stage a man and a woman energetically performed a variety of athletic sexual positions. The man appeared to have a huge penis that amazed the band. When they finished he left the stage and walked close to where we were standing, we noted he wasn't very tall which might have created an optical illusion. For the next act two young ladies took the stage. Softer lighting and music made their intimacies seem less of an act and I remember feeling voyeuristic watching their performance.

The star of the evening was a strapping young lady barely dressed in something erotic. She went around the audience straddling men and touching them up, whilst carrying on a hearty and, it seemed, hilarious Swedish dialogue. We had no real idea what she was saying but no doubt it related to their endowments. There was plenty of laughter and ribald, encouraging comments shouted back. I was struck by how healthy and harmless it all seemed and how different from London's seedy, sexy Soho strip clubs. As the young lady made her lascivious way towards us our men got cold feet and sidled towards the end of the row, slinking off into the bar. Their bravado had failed them. Ruthann and I stayed put and enjoyed the spirit of her show. We might even have been the only women in the audience. I talked with Alvin afterwards about how it had seemed so much healthier than in England where prurient attitudes were the norm.

Back from Scandinavia we became aware of a new imperative to deal with in London. We heard that the curtain twitching neighbours of Belgravia thought we looked like the sort of people who might be taking drugs. It was definitely time to move home.

Just three days after Alvin's Marquee collapse – sadly their last ever Marquee gig in these early years – Ten Years After started their third US tour but I was not going with them. I would be flat hunting. Ruthann was now a permanent fixture on tour. Since I had been to the US the previous November and seen the groupies and confident young California girls, it was tough going to Heathrow and waving Alvin goodbye for several months.

Andy Jaworski was on all the US tours but John Hembrow was not yet permanently with them. Chris Wright went on the early US tours and took on some of the driving and support, according to his biography. He was also learning the music business ropes in the USA, connecting with important contacts and keeping an eye on his hottest property.

Perry was tasked with finding another home for us in London. We seemed to connect and got along well together. Perhaps he felt sorry for me and came to realise that I still didn't have many friends in London. He introduced me to another musician's girlfriend, correctly intuiting that we would get along well. Christine Alice Marcella Findlay was the girlfriend of Ronnie Wood, whom I had briefly met at The Shrine Hall in LA the previous November, playing bass guitar with The Jeff Beck Band.

Krissie Findlay, who married Ronnie and would later become better known as Krissie Wood, was living with Woody in a lovely cottage in the English countryside near Henley-on-Thames. Perry drove me down to The Old Forge, Fawley Green, partly on the M4 motorway and then through twisting, turning little country lanes. This was in March when spring was starting to break through the landscapes and I was charmed by the beauty of nature that day. Like Alvin, I was an urban person. I'd never lived in the countryside. I'd spent very little time in it and actually felt very little connection to it.

I had made a chocolate brownie hash cake for us to share, and Krissie would often reminisce about first seeing me walk down her front garden path holding this small cake in my hands. She opened the old, dark-oak front door to reveal a classic English cottage of uneven oak beams and leaded-light windows, a wood fire alight in the inglenook fireplace. The Old Forge was a cornucopia of intriguing and beautiful objects and colours, surrounded by its own small, pretty lawned garden with roses literally growing around the door. It was the dream cottage of so many fairy stories and urban escape fantasies.

Krissie was extraordinary, beautiful and gentle with her own unique style of dressing and homemaking. She would have been wearing something feminine with white lace or colourful embroidery, perhaps velvet, maybe teamed with faded denim dungarees. Her eclectic style would be right at home in *Vogue* magazine today and I sometimes wonder how much of her own intuitive fashion style found its way into the designs of the sixties and later.

Whilst I was already experimenting with US thrift store clothes and my funky trilby-style fur hat, which I'm sure I was wearing that day, Kris certainly influenced and expanded my fashion horizons. I was probably dressed in the long brown, khaki embroidered dress that can be seen in a series of photos taken at Grosvenor Crescent Mews.

Luscious velvet cushions, curtains, vintage fabrics, rugs and patchwork quilts, pictures of Beatrice Potters's animal drawings and some of Woody's early drawings hung on the walls. In the kitchen were pots and pans, brass wear, an ever-present big enamel teapot and a patchwork of assorted old pottery mugs, cups and saucers, plates, bowls and dishes of all shapes and sizes.

Asleep on a kitchen chair was Beano, a beautiful grey cat with white markings who was always laid-back even by cat standards. He reminded me of the cats we had as children, who trusted me so much that I could dress them, tuck them in my doll's pram and take them for a walk. Beano would lie on Kris's lap and accept any attention she gave him, tickles, strokes, playing with his paws.

On a sideboard in the kitchen's mix was a large bird-cage and perfectly still on the perch was Sadie, a turquoise and yellow Macaw. I knew she was a parrot though I'm not sure that I had seen one before and certainly never been in the same small room with such a large parrot. White and black feathers surrounded her penetrating eyes, and her large curved beak was capable of cracking open a Brazil nut.

Kris's mum Pat told me that when she had visited she had assumed at first glance that Sadie was stuffed. She realised how wrong she was when, with her back to the cage, Sadie had let out an ear-splitting shriek. Those shrieks were extraordinarily loud and occasionally went on for some time. Woody painted Sadie life-sized a few times and on one painting added real feathers that she had shed. It was stunning.

We drank cups of tea, ate chocolate hash cake and talked about our lives. Kris and I were both the third child and the only daughters of our respective families. We talked about our men. Kris had been with Woody since she was 16, as I had with Alvin. She loved Woody in a sweet, trusting, childlike way and talked of how they slept together curled up side by side, like spoons. There was an instant connection between us. I was relieved to find a friend who had as deep a love and commitment to her boyfriend as I had to mine. It became a burden when most women I met had eyes for Alvin. Now I had a friend who did not.

When Kris came and visited me in London we went off to Portobello Road, very close to where Johnnie and Judy lived with their black and white cats Fleur, Felix and Molly on Ladbrooke Grove. Kris was a delight to be with and my friends were charmed by her. We all went out to Portobello and shopped for nothing in particular, enjoying the antiques and knick-knacks, the beautiful, the odd, the weird and the wonderful, expensive and cheap, with no regard for their status, only their attraction.

As a friend, Kris was a perfect distraction who helped me to enjoy life. She was much more familiar with London than me, having spent her teens around West London, the clubs and music venues. Open-hearted and generous, she loved to cook to feed people. Whatever she did was filled with grace and beauty. That was the essence of Christine Alice Marcella Findlay. In truth she was guileless, a rare quality, and she would speak spontaneously, sometimes uttering things that might seem silly, but not to me.

Not long after we first met, we were in a taxi together in the West End.

"How old are you?" Kris asked me.

Age wasn't something we'd discussed until now.

"I'm 22," I replied

"Oh! That's great," said Kris immediately. "That means I will still look good when I'm 22."

Slightly puzzled, I asked, "How old are you?"

"Twenty," she replied.

There was such an unguarded honesty in this exchange. It has stayed with me always. Kris was a beautiful young woman, but she was deeply insecure about her looks for most of her life.

Perry found a new home for Alvin and me, a two-bedroomed mews cottage with an integral ground floor garage, a very sought-after amenity in central London. The cottage, at 26 Gloucester Place Mews, was owned by a Scottish Laird, the Chief of the Farquason clan. His wife, Frances, who I met there for approval as a tenant, had been a *Vogue* editor. I liked her mews cottage and she seemed happy enough with me. Our next door neighbours were a couple of American guys who turned out to be draft dodgers protesting against the Vietnam war. As a pacifist, they had my complete sympathy. With the curtain twitchers of Belgravia behind us, their presence reassured me that here was a home where we could comfortably relax, get high and play music.

The living room corners had been rounded, which made it feel like the inside of a castle turret. It had red fitted carpets and white painted walls, a red sofa and armchair, and a real open fireplace which was bliss in the winter, the first real fire either of us had experienced. The ceiling was high and a staircase along the far wall led up to two bedrooms and a bathroom finished in sugar pink, Frances Farquason's favourite colour. It had a feel of faded luxury and seemed very spacious after our two years in tiny Warwick Square.

On one lounge wall was a large mirror that doubled the size of the room.

By a weird coincidence my new friend Krissie, being a Findlay, was a member of the Farquason clan, which meant that Captain Alwyne, Frances' husband, was her clan chief. We didn't know this at the time of course.

The rent on new home was £25 per week, twice what it was for the Belgravia flat. Despite a record contact, three albums released, tours of the UK and Scandinavia, and three tours of the USA, it still felt beyond what we could afford. Well so what. We had thought that about Warwick Square when we moved into there. I took a load of photos and sent them to Alvin, who wrote back enthusiastically and said how much he was missing me. He was about six weeks into a 12-week tour.

Fortunately, this was a furnished rental as we still had very little of our own. A long low set of shelves below the large lounge mirror were perfect for our growing vinyl record collection. When Alvin returned to his new home our HiFi was upgraded to a state-of-the-art space age looking turntable, a gorgeous and perfectly functioning piece of engineering: the J A Michell Transcriptor Hydraulic Reference Turntable, which Stanley Kubrick would use to express the modern age in *A Clockwork Orange*. A Quad amp and our Lowther speakers completed an extraordinary HiFi system. Acoustically, it was a brilliant listening room, with garage space one side to insulate us from the neighbours and, with the American hippies to the other, no one banged on ceilings, walls or doors to complain. Bliss.

The Simon tape recorder would be replaced by Alvin's first Revox tape machine. Increasingly there began to be more money than we needed to survive and this was mostly spent on tools like the Revox, a Uher portable tape machine, a Bolex Super-8 movie camera and the Rolliecord 35mm camera was replaced with a Nikon F. This camera traveled everywhere with Alvin in his brown leather school satchel, along with song-writing notebooks, cigarettes, lighter, harmonicas and his deep-red Swiss army knife. This had tools that helped with guitar restringing, tightening up loose screws, small scissors to trim nails, a small toothpick and a tiny pair of tweezers that neatly held the very end of a one-skin marijuana joint so as to get the last puff without burning fingers. The Swiss army knife was his essential piece of kit, though I rarely saw the blades used.

Before Alvin's return from the third US tour, Perry introduced me to his friend Kim Gardner, a bass player who lived only a few streets away with Roy Dyke. Kim had also been in a band with Woody a few years before and knew Krissie. After hanging out together a few times I sensed a physical attracted to Kim. He was smart and funny as many English musicians were. It was the first time since 1963 that I had felt an attraction to another man. I was 22 years old and full of hormones with no outlet. Alvin was across the other side of the Atlantic, no doubt enjoying female company.

Pure sexual attraction is extremely difficult to ignore or control, and it became obvious this was a two-way attraction. One evening Kim called around to see if I was in, cups of tea and a nice mellow smoke did nothing to squelch the attraction, quite the reverse. We wound up in bed together. It was very exciting to just fuck someone with no real thought or emotion involved. Pure lust is intoxicating and carnally satisfying but I was relieved when Kim left for his own place.

I knew that would not be the end of it and remember us being at Kris's in the country for an evening, though I have no recall how we got there. We stayed overnight on the living room couch. I do recall that after getting high in the early evening I had felt claustrophobic and suggested a walk, in the dark through the little village graveyard nearby. Kris stayed at home. The next day Woody arrived back at the cottage from his Jeff Beck tour and being there with Kim suddenly seemed wrong. It was the first time I had really met Woody and this was not the circumstances I would have chosen. Yes, this was the sixties but loose sexuality by women, by musician's old ladies, still didn't feel ok.

Kim and Woody were old friends. They laughed and joked and caught up and I hid away in the kitchen with Kris feeling awkward and trying not to let it show. Later, back in London at Kim and Roy Dyke's flat with Perry, I took Kim aside and told him that our little fling was at an end. I was confused to see him look quite crestfallen and realised that casual, lusty sex is not necessarily casual at all.

It was some weeks before Ten Years After's tour ended and when Alvin returned I was unprepared for the level of guilt and remorse I felt. In my anguish, I thought it might ruin my relationship with Alvin. The level of my self-punishment was extraordinary, something I had never experienced before. I made up my mind to say nothing at all to Alvin and try to not let it change anything. I was sure that Kris, Perry and Woody would say nothing to Alvin. That at least I felt certain about.

My draft dodging neighbours were sweet and funny and helped to make the time pass. They also gave me a couple of pills, which they said were psychedelics. When Alvin came home he loved the new house, held me close and was, as ever, really relieved to leave his rock'n'roll life behind. I was still struggling internally with what I felt was my disloyalty to him. He briefly met the new neighbours and was interested in the psychedelics they had

154

given me. "Let's take them," was his immediate response.

Hoping it might help me overcome the strangely distracting guilt of my fling with Kim and bring us closer, I was game. We took them and after a while, when they started to come on, it slowly dawned on me that there was no way to hide what had happened. I felt completely transparent. Lying was impossible and stupid, a state of mind I always experienced with psychedelics. We were laying on the bed kissing and cuddling but I was so distracted I starting to feel scared and physically sick.

"Let's go downstairs a minute. I need to talk to you," I said.

Looking bemused, Alvin followed me down and as we sat side by side on the sofa and I told him about Kim and my fling. He was very calm, perhaps the drug helped him be open-minded. I only remember him shrugging and saying, "Oh well, I have probably had about a dozen women on this tour. Forget about it. I love you, that's all that matters."

He was right. My fear evaporated. My anxiety left. A dozen women? I shrugged too, massively relieved to have brought everything out into the open.

What drug had we taken, I've no idea. Later we knelt on the carpeted floor trying to paint a picture together. The carpet pile seemed several inches deep, so it was certainly hallucinogenic. The drawing/painting was quite odd, surreal, but it was fun and we laughed and later we made love and we were back as close as ever. The amazing result of all this was that I was never ever left at home again.

From now on, I was on the rock'n'roll bus full-time.

chapter 25
Guitarists Galore and Jimi Hendrix

With a mews cottage and garage in central London, the next essential was a car. Alvin bought a soft-top vintage Triumph TR3 in maroon, a fairly cheap car at that time. Heading out west to visit Krissie and Ronnie Wood on the newly constructed Westway – before it was officially opened – was so tempting. Ronnie was back from tour and Krissie and I wanted to get together and introduce the boys. It would have been in May 1969 and I was excited for Alvin to experience the English countryside and magical Forge Cottage. We all got along well and, best of all, Kris only had eyes for Woody and I only had eyes for Alvin. We could all relax and get high, laugh, play and have fun. Woody, quick-witted like most sixties British musicians, was the first of the London musician's gang to accept Alvin as a bloke rather than a musical threat.

On May 6, TYA headlined the Royal Albert Hall to a packed house and a riotous reception. In the UK there was no question that Alvin Lee and Ten Years After had arrived. This date was part of a short UK tour, a Chrysalis promotion with Jethro Tull and Clouds. In effect TYA, the biggest draw, were being used by Chrysalis to provide an audience for Tull and Clouds, a common strategy of Chrysalis in the UK. Was it best for Ten Years After? Were we seeing the conflict of interests we had discussed before Chrysalis formed? It was certainly a music business decision rather than a strictly artistic or musical one.

On June 24, TYA played the end-of-year student ball at Queens College, Oxford, along with The Pretty Things and Pink Floyd. The Pretty Things had released their exceptional album *SF Sorrow*, an early concept rock-opera, in late 1968. Alvin and I watched them. They were an impressive, exciting, tight group of musicians, physically the antithesis of their name, which may be why they were destined to be so underrated. Fame and fortune in the sixties wasn't only about talent and musicianship. Looks and luck also played a big part. *SF Sorrow* was released in the same few weeks as The Beatles' *White Album* and The Rolling Stones *Beggars Banquet*, bad timing.

In Oxford, Ten Years After played late evening, a perfect time slot for them, when the audience was loose enough to boogie but not too loose to fall over. Performance timing was important and later in the year this would prove especially true. In Oxford they went down a storm with the celebrating students, typical of their gigs night after night. They were on a roll and Alvin, their dynamic frontman, was tightly focused. They had given up trying to fit into any existing musical molds and, instead, made a collective decision to play the music they wanted, whether or not it put food on the table.

This decision liberated their playing and resulted in a natural commitment to stretch themselves, to push their musical boundaries. To hell with musical fashion or formula or the interests of the music biz, the moment and the muse were the only criteria. Ironically, this integrity produced a rapid increase and connection with their audience as well as a management contract and record deal. Alvin's drive was further fueled by the competition from his guitar contemporaries, Peter Green, Eric Clapton, Jeff Beck and Jimmy Page, who were all Londoners. Alvin had arrived from Nottingham "out of town", 120 miles north of London, and there was no welcome mat at the end of the M1.

Decades later I had an enlightening conversation with Ray Majors, a fine guitarist who was on the London scene in the sixties and played with Mott The Hoople and The Yardbirds, among others. Ray told me that Alvin caused a big upset within the guitar-playing clique in the capital when he arrived on the London scene in 1967. They were surprised and very impressed by Alvin's talents but were they welcoming?

Egos and testosterone probably didn't allow for that. These guys had played in the same bands. Eric Clapton and Peter Green played with John Mayall's Bluesbreakers, Clapton, Jeff Beck and Jimmy Page all played in The Yardbirds. They knew each other and socialized together. They had the scene to themselves and, like many tight communities, didn't welcome newcomers who might take a slice of the action.

Is this the popular image of the late sixties, hippies, flower power, peace & love, musicians getting high together and jamming the night away? Obviously not, but this was the English music scene and it was different from the blossoming rock scene in the USA.

These legendary bands – The Yardbirds, John Mayall's Bluesbreakers, Peter Green's Fleetwood Mac, The Nice, Graham Bond Organisation, Savoy Brown, Family and Ten Years After – set out each evening to "blow the other band off". The opening bands played to win the crowd and make it difficult for the next band to play. Being a "hard act to follow" was a great compliment.

In 1967 and 1968 London's blues bands were at the cutting edge of the second British invasion of the US and about to take this black American music back to its roots, albeit modified by British drive, competition and enthusiasm. Fate dealt a surprise card with the unexpected arrival of Jimi Hendrix who blew the tight clique of guitarists wide open. Hendrix had a similar grounding in the US to many of the UK's guitarists, playing as a backing musician and on recording sessions for successful frontmen, including Little Richard.

Chas Chandler, formerly bassist with The Animals, believed that transplanting Hendrix to London would give him the audience he sought. Chandler was well aware of the guitar rivalry taking place at UK venues like the Marquee Club, Klooks Kleek, Eel Pie Island, the Fishmongers Arms and the Manor House. Jimi had been in New York, a musician without a band, getting high and jamming in the clubs in the way that jazz musicians had done for decades. In bringing that energy to London, he put the cat amongst the pigeons, a sudden presence in London's after-hours music hangouts like The Bag O'Nails and The Speakeasy where he approached bands to sit in and jam with them.

One night when TYA were gigging at The Speakeasy he asked Leo if he could use his bass to play with Alvin. Leo turned him down. Unlike the USA, it wasn't the norm for musicians to jam spontaneously. It was a slow loosening process helped by their experiences on tour in New York and the West Coast. When Hendrix arrived in London in 1967, however, Eric Clapton and Alvin suddenly had curly hair. For Alvin it was easy. Doris, his mum was a hairdresser. I never knew who did Clapton's perm. It was a hairdressing homage to Hendrix.

At The Speakeasy I was standing with Alvin when Jimi came over to talk. They had a quiet conversation which was certainly based in mutual respect. It was obvious that Jimi saw Alvin as his peer. We had loved his first album *Are You Experienced*, and Alvin, who was not over impressed by his English contemporaries, was truly excited by Hendrix's playing. I was struck by Jimi's gentlemanly courtesy. He seemed confident and comfortable with himself, neither shy nor pushy, just really at ease in his skin, which made him very alluring.

I don't ever remember being attracted to any other musicians when I was out with Alvin. I simply didn't notice anyone else. Jimi was a rare exception. He caught my eye that night, but apart from a polite smile and hello, his interest was fixed on Alvin. Years later I read that Jimi loved blonds but, ironically, I had worn a jet-black wig that night. It was hard to decide whether he was Jimi or Hendrix. Onstage he was definitely Hendrix but off stage in a quiet conversation he was Jimi. There was a complete contrast between the two.

In the late sixties and early seventies Alvin was in the top five guitarists on the blues-based rock scene. There was Hendrix, Clapton, Lee, Beck and Page. A portrait in *Rock Dreams,* illustrated by Guy Peellaert, with text by Nik Cohn, showed five English guitarists dressed as gangsters, with violin-shaped guitar cases; Beck, Lee, Clapton, Page and Pete Townshend, muscling in on a sleazy New York city scene. Alvin was the only one not from London or the Home Counties.

Hendrix and Clapton were considered the two top guys but Jimi was certainly in a class of his own. "Hendrix had come from outer space," Alvin said. I knew that Hendrix was outstandingly original but, naturally, I thought Alvin was the best of the rest.

Alvin became known for his dexterity and speed which some saw as flashiness. He even gained the nickname Captain Speedfingers, as if he was aiming solely to play as fast as he possibly could. That was not the case. His speed wasn't done for effect, nor was it a product of taking speed or cocaine, as has been suggested. Alvin's drug of choice was a good smoke, hashish or marijuana, which should have slowed him down if anything. During the ten years while I was with him, 1963-1973, he was never a drinker or a user of hard drugs. He just loved a good joint. It relaxed him and gave him great focus, almost a Zen approach to his guitar work.

His guitar playing was very jazz influenced. Jazz informed the technical art of his playing, blues the phrasing, sustain and feedback and rock'n'roll the drive and energy. These three aspects were his grounding, learning by ear, listening, copying, practicing, adapting and innovating, using all of that experience to create his own musical signature. Today's young guitarists listen to these early rock guitarists to learn their styles, riffs and solos, or they may work from guitar tablature, a system that identifies instrument fingering and allows a player to master guitar parts without needing to learn to read sheet music.

Alvin played from a transcendent place inside himself. On stage during a solo he would allow his fingers to work with as little conscious interference as he could achieve, moving into expanded, altered states of consciousness. That's what being high from a good smoke is all about, being "out of your head", out of your normal control, while keeping enough control so that the structure doesn't fall apart. In Alvin's case, Leo's bass guitar, Ric's drums and Chick's Hammond organ maintained the structure with solid rhythms and forms, which underpinned his extemporisation and allowed him to fly.

In the space between the backline of the band and the front row of the audience, Alvin worked like a lightning rod, channeling riffs and arpeggios as if he was possessed by an invisible force field. We were all spellbound. Some solos developed from loose experimental forms into structured pieces with light and shade, like revered classical music compositions. Alvin was at his most free and creative during these years with Ten Years After. The muse held him by the hand. His talents, the changing culture and receptive stoned audiences, the musical competitiveness and availability of good venues all came together, in the right time, at the right place.

All of TYA had their roots in jazz and all listened to and learned from players of the forties and fifties. Alvin learnt from Charlie Christian, Barney Kessel, Wes Montgomery, Joe Pass, Charlie Byrd, Tal Farlow, Les Paul, Django Reinhart and George Benson in his early incarnation as guitarist with Jack McDuff. He also studied great country pickers like Chet Atkins and sonic visionaries like Les Paul, and multi-talented rock'n'roll guitarists Scotty Moore and James Burton. I thought it astonishing that these guys hadn't been to music college or learned to read music but had developed their talents by ear and practice, practice, practice.

Alvin had perfect pitch when he sang. He never had to struggle to hit notes or hold a tune. His vocal range was wide, his phrasing and ability to move from trembling whispered blues, through melodic jazz to full-tilt yelling rock'n'roll, while maintaining the rhythm and structure on his guitar, was a feat managed by few others. Most bands of the day had separate singers and guitarists on the front line. Whatever field of music Alvin would have gone into, he would have become a virtuoso, given his natural musicality and obsessive tenacity.

Guitarists at the highest levels put in thousands of hours of practice and develop their skills over many years, first by listening to other earlier players and working out how they had played something and then practicing to a level where they can define their own styles.

This was what the rowdy students heard that night in 1969 at Queens College. Alvin was a young guitar maestro. There was no question about his ability to consistently deliver a superb set with Ten Years After, one that enthralled and engaged an audience and left them stomping and yelling for more.

Later, as I walked with Alvin through the multi-spired, ancient buildings of historical Oxford back to our transport home, the ethereal electronic strains of Pink Floyd's music floating on the warm night air made a perfect soundtrack to this magical summer's evening. The calm beauty of the night and the happiness I was experiencing was enhanced by knowing that in 10 days I would be in America with Alvin and Ten Years After as they embarked on their fourth tour of the USA. The end of their second tour in November 1968 had introduced me to the US scene so I was excited by the prospect of leaving the UK for 12 summer weeks of rock'n'roll.

Little did we know just what an historic and extraordinary tour this would turn out to be.

chapter 26
Rockin' in the USA

By the start of the summer 1969 tour of the USA, Ten Years After had enough of a buzz about them on FM radio to ensure a following wherever they played. They had spent around seven months out of the previous twelve gigging, being interviewed and travelling around America, and now, eight years after Alvin and Leo first met, they had found a receptive audience that fed energy back to them in a way that was quite different to the English and Scandinavians. It stretched them to give more, work harder, play even better.

In the UK they drew an audience that was mainly young guys, some of whom were blues purists who would quiz Alvin in arcane detail. "You know in 'Spoonful' where you hold the sustained note in the solo, you hold it for 20 seconds and Eric (Clapton) holds it for 17 seconds. Why is that?" Alvin always remembered this question and often re-visited it, in a suitable nerdy voice, in moments of stress.

America was different. The audiences were more mixed, young guys and young girls loosening up, a whole generation getting high and shunning the culture of their parents. They loved these English bands, not only for their musical ability but also for their looks, their long hair, their colourful clothes, particularly their tight jeans and velvet trousers. Their English girlfriends visited London's antique stalls in Kensington Market and Portobello Road, bringing home beautiful finds and encouraging their guys to experiment with vintage fabrics and styles. I found and made wonderful clothes for Alvin which he was adventurous enough to wear.

I had taken to wearing a big funky fur hat that we had found in a San Francisco thrift store the previous year. In fact, we found two hats, and can be seen wearing them in two photos of us from December 1968, at JFK airport in New York. They were taken when we waited to leave after two weeks, at the end of their second three-month US tour, my first trip abroad.

The fur hat I wound up with had been the one that Alvin wore. He discarded it but I preferred the way it looked with my new multicoloured wardrobe. Having quit work and the need to dress conventionally, I was using wild fabrics to make into exotic clothes. It was a visual statement about the sense of freedom I had after leaving behind the straight 9-5 world. As time went on my clothes became more and more adventurous. Alvin loved it and would encourage me to go further. Like little kids we were playing dressing-up and the world was our playroom.

In the USA I was surprised by the saggy-assed jeans and shapeless, washed out t-shirts worn by young US males. There was talk about English musician's tight pants and even speculation that they might be gay, this fuelled by a language misunderstanding. In the UK the slang term for cigarettes was fags which was US slang for gays, so a rock musician's innocent request "Have you got any fags?" brought strange looks from fans. Still, their behaviour left no confusion. Rock groupies were happy to report their preferences for chicks.

Despite the feminized look, rock was a softly macho world. The men loved and needed women for support but not as competition. Very few bands featured women players and there were only a handful with women singers, among them Janis Joplin and Grace Slick, competing with the men at this time.

On July 13, TYA played the Singer Bowl at Flushing Meadow in New York with The Jeff Beck Band. Whilst Ten Years After were onstage Led Zeppelin, who were in town, turned up backstage. They stood below the side of the raised festival stage, attempting to pelt the band with unopened juice cartoons and the like. I was standing there and saw everything that happened, the whole drunken episode. They were all very drunk and their aim was crap so no harm done. Nothing like that had ever happened before. It was bizarre. John Bonham and their tour manager Richard Cole seemed to be the ringleaders. In the dressing room afterwards Chick, our organist, who had been hanging out with Zeppelin, whispered to me that Jimmy Page was intending to grab my hat and piss in it. Yes, my funky, fur hat from San Francisco.

There was a strange, tense vibe with much sniggering and sly looks. I had been backstage in the UK with these guys before with no such dumb behaviour or edginess. It became apparent that when abroad, these Englishmen felt they could behave like naughty schoolboys. My perceptive friend, photographer Dick Polak, would later coin the phrase "terminal adolescence" to describe the antics of musicians on the road, encouraged and supported by management and record companies. Being out of control of your life gives someone else the chance to be in control of it for their own ends.

In 1975 I met Jimmy Page at his west London home, the Tower House in Holland Park, when my girlfriend Krissie Wood was living with him. Kris told me that Jimmy was embarrassed about threatening to piss in my hat. I was surprised he'd remembered, though of course I had. He was very gentle and took the opportunity to apologize to me for the incident. We operate on many levels and carry guilt like an unhealed wound.

Back in 1969, later that night the Edwin Hawkins Singers soulful choir came on stage to perform 'Oh Happy Day'. I had never heard a live gospel choir. The extraordinary fusion of so many rich black voices was intoxicating, joyfully infectious. A gospel arrangement of an 18th Century hymn, this was the first such track to cross over and become an International hit reaching number four in the US charts and two in the UK. Their huge vocal sound and positive energy transformed all of the earlier nonsense. The evening ended with an onstage jam with Jeff Beck and Jimmy Page, Robert Plant and Rod Stewart, Ric Lee, our drummer, and Glenn Cornick from Jethro Tull, performing 'Jailhouse Rock'.

Alvin made a connection with Robert Plant, Led Zeppelin's lead singer, that night in New York. He was obviously embarrassed by the negative vibes and we three went back to Robert's hotel room where he and Alvin talked about music and America. Robert was stunning and, like Alvin, dynamic and extrovert on stage, with his Leo goods looks and lion's mane of golden curls pacing the stage with intent and command.

Here, away from the spotlight, he revealed himself as a thoughtful and intelligent man. He confessed he envied me and Alvin being able to travel together on the road. He spoke tenderly about his lady back home in England and how he wished he could bring her on the road with Zeppelin. What I saw of the Led Zeppelin "pack" that evening made me understand why Robert left her at home.

Richard Cole writes about the Singer Bowl incident in his Led Zeppelin book *Stairway To Heaven*, beginning by remarking that Jimmy Page watched Alvin playing. "He's just great," Jimmy is quoted as saying. He goes on to write that John Bonham, who'd been drinking all afternoon, was restless to leave and became irritated, hurling an open juice cartoon which drenched Alvin and his guitar. This, says Cole, resulted in Alvin's playing being wrecked. "He struggled through the group's remaining songs."

Well, I need to set the record straight on this one. A few small cartoons were thrown, but none were open and none hit him. Alvin and his guitar were unscathed. I don't think he even noticed and if you look for the reviews of the show online you'll see that it was a triumph for the band with no mention of the OJ incident. More to the point, Alvin had grown up in Nottingham, a city where young men had no choice but to fight well. If Bonham had drenched Alvin and his guitar that night I'm pretty sure Alvin would have jumped off the stage and landed a few punches on the drunken Bonham.

Whenever I was asked "What's your name?" in the US, the next question would be "What are you?" Well, the first I could answer but the second took me awhile to figure out.

"What am I?" I asked whoever was enquiring.

"Yea, what are you, what sign are you?" I soon learned that my astrological sign was an important a part of my identity, second only to my name.

"Oh! I'm a Scorpio," I would say, at first quite innocently, no edge, until I realized this had a powerful effect on people, especially guys.

Their reply, "Wow! You're a Scorpio, far out man!" was accompanied with a look that suggested I had acquired a new status. As my two Scorpio grandmas had been seen by mum as a big negative, this was very liberating. I would soon get used to being called "man", a convention yet to reach the UK.

Alvin was Sagittarius. In the sixties rock era, a number of the frontmen and women were fire signs, which seems too much of a coincidence to me. Alongside Alvin, Jim Morrison, Jimi Hendrix, Keith Richards, Frank Zappa and Tina Turner were or are all Sagittarians. Eric Clapton is an Aries and Robert Plant and Mick Jagger are both Leos. Fire sign characteristics, as you might imagine, include dynamic high energy, creativity, focused directness, leadership and well-developed egos. Fire signs are also fun and want to give people a good time. Just like fire they want to warm us up, get us partying, a perfect fit for rock'n'roll. Ten Years After had two Sagittarians up-front, Alvin and Leo, doubling the fire energy.

Being November born hadn't been a big deal until I got to the USA in 1969. According to astrology, I was intense, powerful, very sexy and dangerous... which was far out, man! Not that I felt powerful or even slightly dangerous; intense, yes, sexy, I could relate to. I was happily very sensual and life on the road suited my senses. Most days we would travel to a new city, a new hotel, a new venue, meet new people, with a loud rock'n'roll show to dance and sweat to at the end of the night. My senses were being stimulated all day every day, and snuggling up with Alvin in fresh crisp sheets every night was bliss. I love hotels. You never knew what you'd find and as the band became more successful the hotels became more luxurious.

Most US hotel double rooms had two queen-sized beds, a large TV and super-efficient bathrooms. American plumbing was a revelation, after the UK where plumbing was Victorian/Edwardian, very old and tired, with showers that dribbled and toilets that needed several hefty tugs to flush. In American bathrooms the showers were dynamic, invigorating affairs that not only wash you well but stimulate and tone your body, setting you up for the day.

Anonymous hotel rooms were perfect for after show winding down, with a few new friends, a good smoke and some excellent music. We had a small travel kit to customize the hotel rooms. I always packed a couple of fringed, embroidered shawls which were draped over the big, plain lampshades to soften the light and radiate a sexy coziness in these clean, bright boxes. Alvin had a travelling record deck like a small suitcase, with the two stereo speakers in the lid. It was excellent sound quality and as long as we had other band members or road crew in adjacent hotel rooms we wouldn't disturb less rock'n'rollin' guests.

On both the East and West Coasts company representatives from London Records, their first US company, would turn up at the hotel and offer the band whatever they needed. In Los Angeles, as before, this meant a trip to Tower Records where they were given the run of the store, offered any albums they wanted. It was an Aladdin's cave for musicians and no bill at the check-out.

Steve Miller Band's *Sailor*, Quicksilver Messenger Service's *Happy Trails*, Procol Harum's *A Salty Dog*, Dylan's *Nashville Skyline* and eponymous albums from Blood, Sweat & Tears, Crosby Stills & Nash and Blind Faith were snapped up by us. I vividly remember the topless pre-pubescent girl holding the super-sleek silver airplane on the Blind Faith cover piled high in Tower Records. The image seemed inappropriate. It was hard to know why exactly, but it was also very beautiful.

More obscure, and often played, was *Presenting Lothar and The Hand People*, a favourite album Alvin picked out at Tower by instinct. The final eight-minute track, 'Space Hymn', is excellent for stoned listeners winding down late at night. If humour was required, many happy hours were spent in the company of The Firesign Theatre's albums *Waiting For The Electrician or Someone Like Him*, and *How Can You Be In Two Places At Once When You're Not Anywhere At All*. The clues are in the titles.

Winding down after a gig, full of the adrenaline and excitement from

performance, would take Alvin several hours. Smoking good weed, listening to music and having a laugh with visitors helped. When everyone had left, we would be very relaxed. I would massage his back and his legs to relax him and help with the discomfort caused by his
heavy electric guitar, worn across one shoulder and swung around during the show.

I had no training but another excellent effect of a good smoke was to slow you down and tune you into whatever your hands touch. A soothing massage of loving gentleness worked deeply into the muscles would shift the knots and tensions of the day. Tenderness lead to sensuality. Massage is wonderful foreplay. These days sex therapists teach it. Back then the gods of marijuana were my instructors, Panama Red, Acapulco Gold, Thai sticks or good old homegrown.

Alvin was quite a masseur himself and from time to time I would bury myself face down in a soft bed and have his magic hands work with gentle soothing pressure over my body. How sweet it is. Will I tell you what you now want to know? Was my young rock'n'roller a good lover? Listen to him playing the solo on 'I Can't Keep From Crying Sometimes'. The inventiveness, teasing the notes, exploring the structures, sustaining the intensity and the climactic crescendos… musicians reveal themselves through their music.

Sound asleep in the morning; I was by the hotel phone, Andy Jaworski, TYA's wonderful, efficient, ever cheerful and patient tour manager on the other end. "In the lobby in half-an-hour."

Regardless of how much or little sleep we'd had, the show was on the road. Time to blast the shower, dress, pack the bags and portable record player. Then the phone would ring again. "Bell boys coming for the bags."

Once the bags were taken we would go down to the lobby, where a few really determined fans might have gathered, though TYA invariably booked into the hotel under pseudonyms. In Alvin's case, he reverted to Graham Barnes but the smarter fan might have known that. American fans were like excited puppies, eager to talk and ask questions but often, when the chance arose, they would be tongue-tied and manage only, "Wow! Alvin, man, great gig."

By the late sixties rock bands no longer attracted the hordes of screaming young girls that had made touring for The Beatles more like a game of cat and mouse. Up to a point, it seemed that if you were cool around people they would be cool around you, hang around, get records autographed, take a few photos, maybe lay a couple of discrete little one-skin joints on you.

I had a perfect stash place for these gifts in my funky fur hat.

Once, caught in the rain, the hat became very wet. I put it on a hot radiator, which split the skins on the top. As they'd been sewn onto a man's felt trilby hat, there was now a gap on the top into which I could pop a few little joints and feel secure they wouldn't be found. Only the band and their immediate travelling crew knew what I kept under my hat.

From the hotel lobby we went straight out to waiting black limousines. Traveling in limos might seem costly but, in reality, it's not much more expensive to ferry a group of people to an airport in limos than it is in taxi cabs. Usually, Alvin and me, Leo and Andy J, would be in one and Ric and his wife Ruthann and Chick in the other. Often, we would have management with us, English manager Chris Wright and his American wife Chelle whom he met in March that year. Chelle enjoyed a smoke and we became great touring buddies.

A partition in limos separates passengers from the driver, so I could delve into the funky fur hat and enjoy a little smoke on the way to the airport. Alvin, Andy J and I were the "heads" in this traveling circus. Chick and Leo would smoke occasionally but Ric never smoked dope, preferring his pints of beer. Chick also enjoyed a drink. Ruthann claimed she was totally straight, though we noticed how she would get giggly from the smoke in the limo if she and Ric rode with us. We called it a free contact high.

I remember Ruthann getting wound up by the vagaries of late flights, less than ideal hotel rooms and lack of available food after a late arrival in a hotel. It seemed like misplaced energy to the stoned me. I saw my job as being a patient and amenable travelling companion to Alvin, supporting his days to get him in the perfect state of mind to deliver a fine performance night after night.

Limos took us to the airport where porters took away our bags. We'd follow Andy J, wait to be given boarding passes and told, like children, what time to be at what gate. Alvin and I liked to go off and explore gift shops which were surprisingly parochial. In Texas we learnt about "The barbed wire that fenced the West" and admired hand-tooled cowboy boots, belts, even saddles and bridles. We liked to try on cowboy hats.

In Arizona we found Mexican artifacts, colourful pottery and embroidered clothes and rows of large, lethal-looking desert scorpions set in clear plastic paperweights. All over the South-West could be found crafts and artifacts of Native American tribes, the turquoise jewellery and soft doeskin, beaded and fringed clothes which had such a strong resonance for hippies. In Las Vegas you could continue gambling on one-armed bandits all the way to the departure gate. At the airport in Anchorage a stuffed polar bear in a case transfixed me with his glass-eyed gaze. I marveled at the size of this ferocious yet so attractive creature. Some airports had early game machines and one I loved, despite my pacifist nature, was called Night Bomber, a link to my childhood and two brothers who were mad about planes.

On a 12-week tour we would find ourselves in a half dozen different airports some weeks, a hell of a way to experience a culture and a country the size of the USA. Our 90-day tickets allowed us multiple stopovers within the US borders. It was reckoned that no UK band toured the US more than Ten Years After: 28 tours in seven years, with each one lasting around 12 weeks. They wouldn't have coped so well without Ruthann and me. We helped to stabilize and to an extent normalize the bizarre life on the road.

Luckily, we all loved flying. In my case it was a throwback to my airplane-mad brothers. On the earlier tours, however, especially on the East coast, some of the travelling was done by road. We loved the immense, endless landscape of a country that was a technicolor fantasy to us in the UK. In fifties England, American culture, even prior to rock'n'roll, was an optimistic, aspirational dream and so attractive. It was epitomized by big, gas-guzzling, chrome and high-gloss classic winged cars, which some English rock stars bought and imported back to drive in the tiny country lanes back home. Harley Davidson bikes, those classic cars and American trucks, huge rigs so well cared for by their drivers, were testament that we had crossed 3,000 miles of the Atlantic.

At fuel stations, we watched in amazement as truckers filled a water bucket and conscientiously washed down the outsides of the cabs. In the UK lorries were often dirty, diesel fuming heaps with graffitied witticisms scrawled into the dirt, my favourite, "also available in white". Service in diners, motels and shops was friendly, helpful, communication easy and informal. Even for a band of exotic-looking, long-haired English freaks, locals were generally more curious than hostile, especially when they heard us talk. "Are you guys from England? What's it like?" or "You're from England, groovy!" depending on the size of the town. *Easy Rider* was released in July 1969 but I can say, hand on my heart, the hostility that greeted Peter Fonda and Dennis Hopper never came our way. I never met anything but goodwill and warm welcomes in this foreign land, though the guns were a mind-fuck for us English.

We were so young, on this summer 1969 tour. I was 22 and Alvin 24, two kids really, but since we'd both left school at 15 years old and had been out in the world for seven or more years, we didn't feel as young as we were.

We had a confidence that carried us through the many new situations we encountered. As time went on and TYA became more famous and earned more from touring, the motels became five-star hotels and the internal flights in America became first-class, but I am skipping ahead. In the summer of 1969 it was still early days and touring was a full-on travelling experience designed to get the band's music to as wide an audience as possible. Each day's drive or flight would take us to a new city, a new hotel, a new venue and, better yet, a new crowd.

Arriving at our next destination, more limos waited at the airport. We would wait around while our luggage was collected, then driven to the hotels, checked-in, our room keys given to us and a bellboy allotted. We'd identify our luggage and give him the room number and make our way to the room. Everything was organized for us with no requirement to do anything other than relax and be happy, a perpetual rock'n'roll roller-coaster ride.

With the arrival of our luggage, the sound system was up and music was playing, shawls draped on lampshades and, if last night had lacked sleep or we were feeling frisky or both, there was a do-not-disturb sign to hang on the door and fresh sheets in which to snuggle. As a couple, travelling was truly fun, but for the single guys, Leo and Chick, I guess the afternoons were a bit dull. Later at the gigs, they could find willing companions for a night of fun and games.

It's easy to see why bands found hotel wrecking and general mayhem-making a way to pass the time and expend pent-up energy. Many managers disapproved of having "old ladies" on the road. It was felt they interfered with business or might deter female fans. In reality, like women in most work areas, they added stability and ameliorated male behaviour. Still, there would be a whole lot less romantic mythology and lurid tales about the rock'n'roll lifestyle without the excesses and the groupies.

Alvin never wore a suit or shirt and tie which some five-star hotels demanded for their restaurants. We ate early evening, mostly in the coffee shops, or used room service. In the more tourist friendly cities like New York, San Francisco, Boston, Los Angeles and New Orleans days off were scheduled. Alvin preferred as few days off as possible. He was on tour to play music not visit the sights. Everything was organized so that when the band walk out on stage, into the spotlight, every evening, they were in the perfect mood and environment to play. At least that was the plan.

chapter 27
Woodstock

By the summer of 1969 Ten Years After had played three US tours, June-August 1968, October-December 1968 and March-May 1969, and on their fourth they arrived in the US to play the Newport Jazz Festival on Rhode Island on July 4, Independence Day.

This was the first and last time that Newport would include rock bands on the bill. TYA had covered Woody Herman's classic 'Woodchopper's Ball' on their 1967 live album *Undead* and perhaps that had brought them to the attention of George Wein, the Newport promoter. However, Jeff Beck, Jethro Tull, Blood Sweat & Tears and Led Zeppelin were also on the bill that year. TYA managed three or four extended soloing numbers but some guy who was concerned that the fences might be not strong enough interrupted their show. Rock offered too much excitement for Newport.

While we were in New York there was talk of a festival being put together for late August in upstate New York and a buzz was developing about it. US manager Dee Anthony was very enthusiastic, telling us that the young festival producers had a simple plan. They had found a place in the countryside to hold their festival and had booked all the major British rock acts that were touring the US that summer, assuming they would ensure a big crowd. Naively they had no idea what they'd set in motion. They expected an audience of around 30,000.

From New York we headed out to the West Coast for more gigs and festivals in Seattle and San Diego. The band was in fantastic form that summer, rockin' audiences at venues both indoors or outdoors. In San Francisco at the Fillmore West, TYA headlined over the Ike & Tina Turner Review. Tina and her Ikettes gave a fantastic, high energy performance. When Ike held aloft their current album and did a promo on stage, the hippie audience was bemused. They weren't used to direct selling in the old showbiz manner.

This was the second time I had enjoyed Alvin at Fillmore West. The two Fillmore auditoriums, West and East, both run by the legendary promoter Bill Graham, would become my favourite venues. I loved the crowd of young hippies, the air pungent with aromatic marijuana joints shared along the rows and the incredible, psychedelic light shows. It all made a perfect setting to relax and enjoy Alvin's inventive explorations on Big Red.

On Sunday, July 20, we had flown into San Francisco after two great nights at The Grande Ballroom in Detroit. Along with many millions around the world, we watched Neil Armstrong take his "giant leap for mankind" on TV. Monday was a day off before the three nights at the Fillmore. Walking around with Alvin, enjoying the mellow street vibes, my eyes caught the white-on-red headline in capitals, "MEN ON MOON" on the front of the *San Francisco Chronicle*.

After dropping 10 cents into the vending machine I had a piece of this historic event which I somehow felt part of in this land of the free. America, the land of possibilities, had the sense of community I had been looking for since I'd run away from Nottingham, where I felt like an alien. Here, 6,000 miles from my own country, I had found my tribe and finally felt completely at home.

Hippie friends who lived in Haight Asbury in those years say the reality was more complex. Youngsters had come from all over America looking for their tribe. Naturally there might be troubled souls among them and this created darker problems for the welcoming community. As visitors, rock'n'roll world tourists, we were quite oblivious to those issues. Later spiritual seekers have told me about going to ashrams in India, looking for peace and finding fellow seekers were troubled souls there too. How else would it be? Looking for peace suggests a need or a lack of it.

On Saturday, August 16, the night before Woodstock, Ten Years After were performing at Kiel Auditorium in St Louis, as part of the Newport Jazz Festival. It was an unusual gig in a theater with an all-black audience. On the bill before them was Nina Simone, who was magnificent, very intense, focused, and we watched spellbound as this feisty musician played out her heart to an audience of her brothers and sisters. She ended her set with her classic anthem 'Young, Gifted And Black'. It seemed like she was throwing down the gauntlet at the feet of the white rock band due to follow her. The audience loved her and gave her a noisy standing ovation, well deserved.

Alvin was really impressed by Ms. Simone. He was quiet and focused when the band took the stage. Having been performing since his early teens, he had developed a great ability to read an audience and give them what would work for them. I'm sure this wasn't done consciously but by instinct and experience. That night, along with the jazzy 'Woochopper's Ball', which demonstrated his speed and skill, he emphasised the blues numbers in TYA's repertoire, focusing on building his slower, bluesy guitar solos.

This was the blackest audience that I ever saw them play to. I don't remember white faces in the rows of seats. At first, they were quite detached but Alvin's skillful playing seduced them. During one number an old guy got up from the audience front row and strolled to the stage. He put out his hand and felt the fringes on the bottom of Alvin's trousers. Looking up, he smiled at Alvin who returned his smile. Happy with what he found he went back to his seat. Alvin carried on playing through the whole encounter. The applause confirmed that they were impressed with these four white English boys' interpretation of their music, and appreciated Alvin's guitar and vocal work.

Early in 2009, Alvin emailed me and asked if we could talk about Woodstock to help jog his memory. It was the festival's 40th anniversary that year and he had interviews lined up. I reminded him of the old black guy from St Louis. "I can still see his face looking up at me," wrote Alvin. "I've tried to draw him a few times." It was a strong connection.

On the Friday and Saturday we'd caught glimpses of dramatic news items about Woodstock on the TV in our hotel rooms: that it was the largest audience in history, that the freeways had been closed, that it was a national disaster. We couldn't wait to get there and see for ourselves. Half a million hippies all gathered to get high and boogie in a field! We were hyped up about going there. How could we not be? We rose at 5am to catch a flight from St. Louis to New York where limos waited to drive us to Woodstock.

The freeways were blocked so we were driven to the festival base, a Holiday Inn five miles from the festival site. Outside, on the "Welcome to the Holiday Inn" sign, usually reserved for "Bill and Sue's 50th Anniversary" or "Welcome Michigan Ford Dealers Convention", it just said "TRANQUILITY BASE", a nod to the men on the moon. Bands touring the USA get used to staying in Holiday Inns, opening the door to find bland, though clean, lobbies, with bland, though clean, staff politely welcoming their motley crew. The scene in "Tranquility Base" might have been on the moon; no bland, clean, straight people in sight. It was crowded wall-to-wall with hippies, mind-blowing. It seemed we had taken over a small part of the universe. I thought it was fantastic.

An organising hippie greeted Alvin and the band. "Hi guys, you will be going out to the site in a helicopter, performing and flying straight back out.

Just the band, no old ladies. You'll only be gone about two hours."

The "old ladies" were me and Ruthann. Thanks to the mighty rainstorm that was brewing, this two-hour round trip would turn out to be famous last words. Alvin and I went off for a huddle. We had been watching this event on the news for two days. Staying at a Holiday Inn some distance away was the last thing I wanted. My tribe was gathered out there in those fields. I had to join them.

Alvin was fantastic. He got it, no problem. "Man, my old lady comes, or I don't go on," he told him.

"Listen man, Joe Cocker's old lady is up the road in a diner waiting for Joe."

"Well that's fine for her but not for me," I said.

Calmly but directly, Alvin repeated his threat not perform.

"Okay, she will get to come but not with you," he said. "You have to go now but there isn't room in your helicopter. I promise I will get her on one."

Phew! A hug and a kiss and off go Alvin and the band.

I'm still in the hippie Holiday Inn, distractedly chatting with Ruthann. Ten minutes pass. I never take my eyes off of the guy who passes us from time to time. Each time he passes, we remind him of his promise and after a half hour of this, he says, "Okay, let's go." He'd evidently realized we were not going to join Joe Cocker's old lady at the diner.

We are taken to a field where a large twin-blade Chinook sat on the ground, filling up with doctors and nurses. We joined them. As we boarded, it occurred to me that I hadn't actually asked Ruthann if she wanted to go or to stay at the Holiday Inn. She was very straight, no drugs, didn't smoke or even drink, so maybe she wasn't as keen as I was to fly to a huge muddy field full of hippies. I do know today she's very glad she went.

Having never been in a helicopter before, the noise of the rotor blades and the lift from the vertical take-off was a sudden rush. Strapped in with the big side-door open, we came over a hilltop and banked as we passed over this huge field of multicolored people, the rainbow tribe horizon to horizon, a sight as awesome as it was overwhelming. A disaster area?

You must be kidding, this looked like heaven to me. We landed and walked to the backstage area. The crowded hillside reached away in the distance. I will always be grateful to Alvin for supporting me, for making sure I flew those last few miles to that extraordinary scene. What a fine friend.

Once backstage with Alvin, it was obvious their managers were hard at work securing the best spot for their bands. Even though this was now a free festival – the fences were pulled down and an ear-to-ear stoned grin was the main accessory – the businessmen were still doing what they love best, hustling. In the early nineties, R A Pennebaker, legendary rock documentary maker, re-visited the *Woodstock* movie footage to produce the excellent *Woodstock Diaries*, which included a number of bands left out of the original movie. More delightfully, for me personally, he added a brief backstage shot of Alvin, Dee Anthony and myself walking down a set of steps. Alvin and I look stunning, bedecked in colourful silks, tapestries, beads and fringes.

Though it would massively perpetuate and enhance the festival's legend, the *Woodstock* movie was way into the future and being filmed was not the main consideration for the bands. The focus of their performing was this huge crowd. There was no thought on their part that they would wind up in a film of such huge importance. The filming was unobtrusive and did not interfere with the music making. There was no stopping to re-film numbers, re-position cameras, no sound or light checks. It was shot in true documentary style, recording the events as they took place.

In the added Pennebaker footage, Alvin and Dee are in intense discussion. Dee was giving an update on TYA's performance slot, and also hustling on behalf of Joe Cocker. Then the dark clouds rose over the hill. The storm had arrived and everything changed. Without the storm, Alvin and TYA would have performed in daylight on the Sunday afternoon. Daylight is never the best setting for high-octane electric blues rock. The high-key contrast of black night and intense spotlights enhances the drama. An audience immersed in darkness is more liberated as they lose the sense of being seen.

The storm took over the day, not simply a rainstorm but a huge primeval force unleashing itself. Relentless, rolling black clouds, torrents of cold rain and high winds made the technicians anxious for the onstage equipment. On either side of the stage were scaffolding towers supporting not just a vast array of PA speakers, but intrepid climbers after a better view of the performers. They looked fragile in the onslaught.

The tarpaulins that had shielded the stage during smaller, earlier showers were totally inadequate and soon came adrift, flapping about like untethered sails on a yacht. The stage area resembled a galleon in a storm at sea. In the *Woodstock* movie, announcer Chip Monck's voice is cool and calm for most of the time but in the face of the storm he become louder, more strident. "Please move away from the towers. Please move away from the towers. Hold onto your neighbor, man. Sit down and wrap yourself up. We're gonna have to ride it out."

The audience, all half a million of them, had enjoyed two days of great music and authentic community spirit. They were flying high, and weren't about to be brought down by this fearsome, climatic event. Country Joe braved the deluge and encouraged them to concentrate en-masse to stop the rain. He led a chant: "No rain, no rain, no rain, no rain!" until he had to quit because the torrent threatened to electrocute him while he held the microphone. Mass singing broke out. 'Let The Sunshine In' from the musical *Hair* was ambitiously optimistic.

There was no backstage in the sense of dressing rooms or hospitality areas or administration that you might expect at a festival, only empty rigging trucks that served as waterproof shelters. The bands waiting to perform, and by now there was quite a backlog, found shelter where they could, mostly in the trucks. Those that were tokers got steadily more stoned from the freely available marijuana. Leo joined us in the back of a U-Haul with a dozen people. We offered him a passing joint which he momentarily declined, then happily relaxed and joined in. It was the only way to stay mellow in an electric storm.

Alvin and I were also both cigarette smokers and as the hours passed the supply we thought we would need for the quick journey in and out of Woodstock ran out. At one point, Alvin was so desperate for nicotine he was offering $20 for one cigarette but there were none to be had. By the time he went on stage he'd forgotten how many joints had substituted for cigarettes.

Nevertheless, everyone remained pretty chilled backstage. How could we not? We could hear that huge audience singing, chanting, with no shelter whatsoever. It was an awesome inspiration. Rumours spread backstage that the straights, the CIA, or some such, had "seeded" the clouds. We weren't sure if this was possible or even what "seeding" the clouds might mean, but the idea that the straight world might feel so threatened by this peaceful gathering that they would engage in expensive sabotage was strangely empowering to us.

Earlier, while Ruthann and I were waiting at the Holiday Inn for our ride with the medics, Alvin had walked out alone into the audience and around the lake. It gave him a buzz to witness the energy of this massive crowd and he would bring this same buzz to his performance. Ten Years After had played at festivals in Europe and the UK, among them the National Jazz & Blues Festivals, but these were tiny compared to Woodstock.

It was remarkable that despite the blocked roads, Andy Jaworski and TYA's intrepid road crew had made it through with the guitars, amps and drums. Andy had to leave the blocked highway and resort to miles of trails that went through woods and eventually past the lake where hundreds of naked kids were swimming, bathing and having fun. That was when they knew they were getting close. When he asked someone the way, he was told: "I don't know, man, follow the music."

TYA were scheduled to perform, in the afternoon, before the storm and they had made all the usual preparations. Alvin and Leo got together to tune guitar and bass. This was in the days before electronic tuners and Alvin would tune his Gibson guitar unplugged, using a harmonica for pitch. Unable to tune his bass unplugged, Leo would stand by Alvin who with the head of the bass against his ear, to better hear the note, would tune it. Having tuned up, they were ready to take to the stage, waiting with their guitars on, when the deluge arrived. The stage was quickly flooded, making electric guitars, amps and microphones potentially lethal. We went for cover and the guitars were tucked back in their cases.

I don't know how many hours had passed before the storm ended, maybe four or five. Darkness had fallen when Ten Years After finally took to the stage at 8.30pm. Nature's intervention, and some clever footwork by Dee, had moved their time slot from daylight to darkness. The gods had anointed them. Every night, before he went on stage, Alvin held and kissed me. Tonight was no exception. I could feel the excitement and tension in his body as he set-off with a stoned smile and twinkling eyes. I followed him onto the stage, looking as always for a hidden spot to dance and sweat to the music, my daily release, my personal work-out, my transport to boogie bliss. Here at this huge gathering, I expected a tremendous full-on rock show.

There was a bank of PA speakers on the very front right-hand side of the stage, and that was where I headed. I was in line with Alvin but hidden from the vast audience that stretched away, way, way into the distance, as far as the eye could see, to the horizon of the hills. Fires had been lit to warm and dry-out wet bodies and clothes. Billowing smoke and flickering gold and orange glows silhouetted tens of thousands of people, primed and ready to celebrate in this perfect setting. It was like a painting by Hieronymus Bosch, a medieval throng gathered to dance and rejoice with the gods of rock'n'roll.

As a result of the storm, band's time slots were shorter than usual. Alvin had chosen five numbers: 'Spoonful', 'Good Morning Little Schoolgirl', 'I Can't Keep From Crying Sometimes', 'Help Me' and 'I'm Going Home', mostly numbers that could be improvised and extended. Ric's drum solo 'Hobbit' was added and would provide a very useful break.

Alvin approached the microphone and in a short, friendly greeting complimented the crowd for coping with the storm. They opened with

'Spoonful', the classic blues New Yorkers already knew and loved.

This got the audience's attention, its classic seven-note riff already familiar. With blistering speed in the solos, it was a useful warm-up exercise for Alvin after hours of standing around in the cold and damp.

The audience was also warmed up. Alvin and Leo next launched into the opening bars of 'Good Morning Little Schoolgirl', an intense riffing blues by Sonny Boy Williamson they had made their own. The instrumental opening, a repeated tight four-bar riff with the guitar and bass played in harmony, revealed they were badly out-of-tune. In the damp air, the tuning of both guitar and bass had slipped. They should have checked before going on but many hours of good weed had put a small dent in Alvin's professionalism.

They were far too out-of-tune to continue and had no choice but to stop the number. Alvin apologised briefly to the crowd who seemed quite happy, stoned, easy. Many were New Yorkers, who had already seen Alvin perform at the half dozen Fillmore East gigs over the previous two years. He and Leo went back to their amps either side of the drum riser. Alvin re-tuned his guitar but Leo found himself in front of 500,000 people, out-of-tune and unable to do anything about it. Alvin moved back center stage and again they let rip into 'Schoolgirl', still out-of-tune with each another.

My God, what level of adrenaline was now surging through them. Unbelievably they had no choice but to stop again and slip behind the Marshall stacks while Alvin tuned Leo's bass out of sight of a half-million stoned people. I remember it all so well because by this point my head was spinning. A problem like this had never happened before.

Alvin came back to the microphone, made an announcement that ended with him exclaiming "I wish I was dead!" and the two stoned, adrenalised guitarists tore back into 'Good Morning Little Schoolgirl'. Alvin belted out his lyric that got the song banned by some radio stations in the US: "I wanna ball you, I wanna ball you all night long." This slipped past the censors in the UK easily because balling is an all-American pastime.

The bizarre false starts added another layer of tension and as a result the music seemed even sweeter. During 'Schoolgirl' Alvin and Leo played head-to-head in the solo, making it more like a musical sparring match than a duet. The pent-up energy of the day and all the waiting around finding its release at a locomotive pace. Leo, an extremely physical bass player, thrashed his right hand and gyrated from the top of his head through to his feet, as if assaulting his instrument would deliver more power to his playing.

Alvin spun lick upon lick of superspeed webs of sound, he and his guitar somehow merged. The guitar became an extension of his body through which his consciousness was wailin' and rockin' effortlessly, directly communing with his muse. As they were both right-handed players they were able to work face-to-face like this without collision, each pushing the other's performance, sometimes barely inches between their heads. Working hard, they began to sweat and in the chilling damp night air, steam rose from them like two horses galloping towards the finish line. It was spellbinding, and if the wet crowd needed something to get up and boogie to, then Alvin, Leo, Ric and Chick gave them a musical rocket up their butts. Towards the end of 'Schoolgirl' Alvin broke a guitar string but on this stage at this time there was no chance of changing it out front, so Ric's energetic drum solo 'Hobbit' was added earlier than usual to give Alvin a chance to nip behind the amps and replace the string.

'I Can't Keep From Crying Sometimes', the soulful blues written and first recorded in 1928 by Blind Willie Johnson, came to Alvin's attention on the Elektra compilation *What's Shakin'*, the only track from Al Kooper's Blues Project. In Ten Years After's 20-minute version, Alvin's extended guitar solo had become one of his most creatively structured showcases.

It opens with light, jazz chord progressions, moving shapes up and down the guitar neck, interjected with repetitive chord picking. Alvin's vocals are soft, soulful and sweet, with heavier, angrier accents for lyrical emphasis, the words minimal, repetitive. The verses give way to inventive jazzy guitar solos. Particularly powerful was the de-tuning and re-tuning of the low E string, as the high crescendo solo ends and the vocals return to complete their epic interpretation.

I had seen TYA play 'I Can't Keep From Crying Sometimes' many hundreds of times, watching as it developed from a five-minute basic version into this superb 20-minute classic. For me it was always exhilarating, totally engaging and transporting, physically and emotionally, holding me in the present where nothing else existed at all. The best recorded version I have come across is the full version live at the Isle of Wight Festival of August 1970. I have never heard a more perfectly constructed guitar solo. It is a pinnacle of its genre, true rock genius. If Beethoven – another Sagittarius – had been an electric guitarist, he might have come up with this before Alvin.

'Help Me', by Willie Dixon and legendary Chess producer Ralph Bass, was well-known as a blues classic from Sonny Boy Williamson's rendition. I love this song. For me, it presented Alvin at his hottest, sexy best, tall, well built, a gorgeous handsome classic face, framed by long full blonde hair the looks of a Viking god. Early audiences were mainly men and maybe some girlfriends, and while the men would get off on his guitar virtuosity, his hypnotic power, the women were attracted to his sheer physical beauty.

Alvin was now center stage, playing a long wailing guitar solo, a stream of consciousness vibe, building all the while into more repetitive, furiously fast guitar figures dancing over the steady, sultry riff of the organ, bass and drums. His guitar, the big, red curvy Gibson was like a woman in the throes of orgasm, seduced, willing, crying and moaning. Alvin would grab a drumstick or the microphone stand to improvise a bottleneck, and slide up and down the neck of his guitar, the notes merging into a shredding, soaring crescendo.

At its climax Alvin was back at the microphone shouting the verse, insisting on his raunchy demands. "I don't feel so sleepy, just feel like lying myself down." Then the volume drops right down again, with low slow insistence, menacing seduction. "If you don't help me baby, I gotta go out on the street and find someone else to love." Back up to high volume and the frantic desperate guitar, bass, organ, drums thundering below the repeatedly screamed, "Help me... baby.... help me!"

In this number Alvin and Ten Years After delivered themselves to the crowd with compelling contrasts of light and dark, high and low volume. I loved it. Every night, 'Help Me' was my personal turn-on, my transport to ecstasy. Alvin may have been performing for 500,000 people, but this didn't water it down. I would be in his arms again that night, no need to go out on the street and find someone else.

"I'm going home... by helicopter," was Alvin's final introduction, announcing the encore that would become immortalized in Michael Wadleigh's 1970 *Woodstock* movie, but that was all to come. For me, 'I'm Going Home' is the greatest, raunchiest love song ever written. Alvin wrote it on tour in Scandinavia while I was pining for him in our tiny love-nest in London. It's a rock'n'roll love song, a full-tilt celebration of sensual expectation. Leo was told by soldiers he met in US airports returning from Vietnam that it was the song they played when they knew they were coming home to their wives and girlfriends.

Here at Woodstock it became Ten Year After's great boogie climax. The intro features Alvin alone on guitar, a tight, six bars of runs and shapes, a high-key up-beat celebratory opening. Then the band and the vocals come in, "I'm going home to see my baby," the repeated refrain, the thrust of the lyric, the heart of the song. This is pure rock'n'roll, with a solid driving up-tempo rhythm designed for swaying, sweating, stomping and clapping. Alvin's rock'n'roll roots get an airing, an aural montage of luminaries like Tommy Tucker, Duane Eddy, Bo Diddley, Chuck Berry, Elvis Presley, Jerry

Lee Lewis. 'Dimples', 'Blue Suede Shoes', 'Mean Women Blues', 'Whole Lotta Shakin''. 'Boom, Boom, Boom Boom'. This was Alvin returning to his teens in Nottingham, when The Jaybirds were a covers band with a great repertoire that got everyone up and dancing.

To me this was the rock equivalent of action painting, plucking riffs, lyrics, adding and mixing, creating a new masterpiece every night, like Jackson Pollock dripping and splattering colours. Eventually he takes down the volume to tease, holding everyone in the grip of his lightning fingers. Leo slapping the bass, Ric's minimal straight drum tempo, Chick cheerleading, hand-clapping to bring the audience into the song, all support Alvin's moans, screams, and sultry vocals. "I'm going hooooooome, baby, hoooome, child, home, home, home." Finally, and straight to the point, "Look out baby, I'm comin' to get you, one more time" and the whole band crash back in at full-tilt volume. Alvin was now the total rock'n'roller, riffing and hollering his heart out with Ric, Leo and Chick driving the song along, giving every last drop of energy and adrenaline they have left. Noisy, exuberant, relentless, a great rock'n'roll finish, which always left the crowd hollering for more.

Tonight at Max Yasgur's farm, from out of the dark, smoldering landscape, hundreds of thousands roared, clapped, screamed, yelled, and whistled their approval and gratitude. Alvin Lee and Ten Years After had played a stunning set and they loved it. Half a million were transformed from muddy misery and joined together to celebrate themselves, a triumph, an enchanted generation whose legacy was no war memorial but a peace memorial, a beacon of hope.

From my hidden dance spot where I had been stompin' and shakin' my money maker, I was soaked with sweat and high as a kite. Alvin looked across at me as he did during 'I'm Going Home', with his stoned, twinkling eyes and broad grin, as happy as I had ever seen him. It was a perfect, magic night. As they finished someone rolled a large green watermelon onto the stage. Alvin lifted it up, first to his crotch, in a gesture which surely indicated his satisfaction at a great performance, then onto his shoulder, a gift from the audience to the band. Though someone was paranoid enough to suggest it might have been injected with LSD, we were very happy to eat it.

Were we going home by helicopter? No, of course not. We were stranded for hours in the psychedelic fields before cars took us back to New York. The coming down from the show was sweet and relaxed. I wandered with Alvin around the edges of the vast crowd in a delicious stoned high. We joined small groups of friendly freaks gathered round improvised bonfires.

We found great warmth, friendliness and hospitality, a little food here, a mellow toke there, smiles, gentle conversation, cool congratulations. Simple sweet bliss of community and belonging, peace and love, easy vibes.

No cigarettes though, even though we offered $50.00 a time. What a bummer nicotine addiction is!

chapter 28
Riding with Dee and LSD

Dee Anthony was at Woodstock but Chris Wright was not, one of his greatest regrets. I have been told that Dee, of newly formed Bandana Productions, was a member of the Mafia, as was Frank Barcelona, head of Premier Talent, which became the biggest rock booking agency in America. Whatever the truth, Alvin connected with Dee on a human level.
He was a larger than life New Yorker, and he gave Alvin confidence and the encouragement to be fully himself on stage. Wisely, he liked to get high with us and that validated him to Alvin. He trusted Dee, leaving him to handle business so he was free to focus on the music.

On East Coast gigs around New York, Dee would drive just Alvin and me in his Cadillac, all three of us on the front bench seat, me in the middle, Dee driving. My overwhelming memory is of stoned, silly storytelling and an incredible amount of laughter. Being with Dee was like stepping into a movie. The rest of the band would travel in a station wagon with Andy Jaworski, and I'm told they weren't pleased that Alvin was singled out. Was it a deliberate ploy on Dee's part? Probably – but a gap was already opening up. Rock guitarists were the revered musicians of the era. Alvin was also the singer and the main songwriter. Realistically, they couldn't expect equal billing or equal attention and this created discontent.

Three moments with Dee stand out for Alvin and me. The first was on the road somewhere in the east. We had checked into a small motel on the edge of a town where the evening gig was to be but had no weed. "No problem," said Dee who took off with no further explanation. I unpacked enough for the show and settled down to relax on the bed, watching TV with Alvin. There was a knock on the door and Dee came in with a broadsheet newspaper, loosely held together, which he plonked down onto the table. To our delight and laughter, it fell open to reveal a large pile of marijuana plant tops, dried of course, small branches, leaves, seeds heads, not how weed would usually arrive. Smiling, Dee said: "A job for you Loraine!" By now, I was pretty good at cleaning grass of seeds and twigs to make a smooth one skin joint but this was probably the largest pile of weed I had ever tackled. How and where Dee had located this in the back of beyond was a mystery he wouldn't divulge.

The second fond memory is of Alvin and me relaxing in our room early evening at Loew's Midtown in New York when the phone rang. It was Dee. "You guys need to come over here, quick, you won't believe this shit!" A taxi ride through Central Park to Dee's office found him sitting behind his desk, alone, holding on to its edge with a wild look in his eye and several joints in front of him. "Smoke this," was all he managed to say. It was like a scene from Alice in Wonderland. I smiled at Alvin, raised my eyebrows, shrugged my shoulders and lit up.

The first hit told me it was something chemical. I smiled wider and passed it to Alvin. He inhaled and grinned too. We three sat and grinned at each other. The lights twinkled brighter, the room breathed and the office became a spaceship in which we all traveled through the universe for several hours. Conversations became philosophical, mystical, surreal, hilarious and spasmodic. The connection between us that night was absolute and needed no discussion. Travelling back through Central Park, we especially enjoyed the red, amber and green traffic lights as they dripped colours like abstract paintings onto the rainy walkways and roads.

The third event occurred when we were traveling back from an East Coast gig with Dee in his Cadillac, which was fast approaching two years old. "Built in obsolescence," he said. "I'm trading it in next week." I'd never heard of the concept before. We were in high spirits after a good show and Dee was on a mission to get home to his lovely English wife Val. They were trying to start a family without much success and Dee needed to get home to hit a window when Val would be particularly fertile. I'd never heard of that concept before either. As we approached New York Dee's dialogue about his looming task and the need to perform on time got funnier and more absurd.

Then the Cadillac's indicators stopped working and when it began to rain the windscreen wipers gave up the ghost. The Cadillac felt as if it was haunted. None of us could stop laughing, we were hysterical. Visually impaired, we crept up Eighth Avenue. Dee ploughed on, the clock ticking. Then there was a very loud metallic clunk. The muffler had dropped off the bottom. "Built in obsolescence," we chorused as Dee pulled up at our hotel to drop us off. We waved to him as he went off, his car sounding like a motor boat, for his appointment with his fertile wife. I'm happy to report that the first of their three children was conceived that night and the newest model Cadillac bought later that week.

The biggest schism in Ten Years After was about drugs. Alvin fully embraced the hippie ethos of the times, as I did. It wasn't anything we discussed. We just loved it, it resonated. Getting stoned together was fun. It kept us relaxed, happy and mellow, especially with the increased pressures of touring. Very soon we would start experimenting more with psychedelics which we would also enjoy together. Leo and Chick, who had never been serious stoners, weren't interested. Ric stuck to his beer.

Alvin was opening up and expanding his thinking while Ric, and Chick especially, were settling into a comfy slippers style of touring. The schism was projected by the band as divisions engineered by management, whom they thought wanted to move Alvin towards a solo career. In reality, this was the farthest thing from Alvin's mind. He loved the audience the band was attracting and, overall, he trusted the band, his road crew, the management and all the other aspects of support that went into him being free and comfortable on stage. The years 1968-1972 were some of the best for him musically and personally. I was with him on the road as well as at home, and this brought stability to his life. In short, he was enjoying his music and his life.

Just after Woodstock, TYA played the Pasadena Rose Palace in California for two nights. We spent a few days in LA and took our first LSD trip on a night off. It was quite mild and Barry Hill, the USA roadie, and Andy J were with us, in time-honoured tradition staying straight and not fucking with our heads.

This first trip was mostly spent in and around Barry's house and yard, checking out the wonders of nature, the grass and plant life which, due to the hot climate, was way more vibrant and intense than in England. The grass on bare feet felt almost like plastic and we spent some time pottering and pondering this fact. The evening culminated in a drive, with Barry and Andy, up into the hills above LA. The city was laid out like a carpet of sparkling jewels below us, with stars in the night sky circling above our heads. We had good guides for an awesome first encounter with transcendent reality.

We flew back up to San Francisco, by now my favourite city, for three more nights at Bill Graham's Fillmore West, our favourite venue. During this tour we were being filmed, as was Terry Reid, a support at Fillmore West. The film that had been sold to Alvin and TYA was to be called *Rock 70*, about English rock bands on tour in the USA. Joe Cocker was also filmed for the movie. Looking at the TYA schedule and the pressure of touring in the summer of 1969, I wonder about the film crew and their intentions? I don't think that Alvin or anyone in the band took it seriously or really believed a worthwhile movie would result. They were so low key, interviews here and there with the band members, live recordings. How naive we all were.

The movie they constructed wound up being called *Groupies*. The production team were obviously much smarter and more devious than we had credited. There is an interview with Alvin lying back on our bed in the hotel room with me next to him, my facial expression betraying my thoughts. They were asking him about groupies, the impression given that we knew what was going on. In fact, this was only a few minutes in an interview that lasted at least half hour and the only moment when groupies were mentioned. When they'd finished with Alvin, or he'd had enough and left, they asked me questions, filming for a further 15 minutes.

Again, these were innocuous questions about touring, none of which they actually wanted or used. *Used* is appropriate. We were all used. Though *Groupies* has only ever been a cult film, it certainly doesn't present Alvin or TYA in a good light. The film makers had a hidden agenda. We were beginning to realise that just because people had long hair and hippie clothes didn't meant their philosophy wasn't centred around old "breadhead" value systems. From then on Alvin became much warier of people's motives, which led to fewer interviews and a creeping disillusionment with the media.

After San Francisco, we headed south to the Texas International Pop Festival, which it's estimated attracted 120,000 to 150,000. TYA played on a pleasant sunny afternoon and we were delighted to find so many young freaks and heads in Texas. Backstage each band had a caravan dressing room and I recall a very pretty young lady, completely naked, visiting caravan after caravan. Quiet, stoned and smiling, she spent a while with us enjoying a smoke, her nudity somehow calming and very natural.

The warm dry weather, sunshine and smaller crowd, made this a chilled-out gathering. Despite there being as many great rock bands as Woodstock, this was a size that worked for the music. Without the intervention of stormy weather, however, it didn't become an historic human event. We heard on the music grapevine that Woodstock had so freaked out the government that festivals would now have limits put on crowd sizes. Woodstock had been and would remain the biggest ever festival crowd, the victim of its own success. Huge gatherings of peace- loving young people were threatening the American dream.

Sssh, TYA's fourth album was released in August. Recorded at London's Morgan Studios between gigs during June, it was their first to be made outside of Decca studios and their first using an eight-track desk. As a result, *Sssh* is loose and experimental with an energy free from the music business system. The mixing has some nice overlaps and gives the album a sort of structural whole. 'If You Should Love Me', a love song by Alvin, expresses how close and happy we were in 1969. "I love the way you walk and the way you talk to me," he sings. Of the eight tracks, seven were written by Alvin, all except 'Good Morning Little Schoolgirl', which had now become a strong stage number. Alvin was always trying to write songs that would become good live numbers; 'I Woke Up This Morning' was one that worked well.

The mixing, by Alvin and Andy Johns, had to be fast. Alvin wasn't interested in making it tight, or cleaning up all oddities on his vocal tracks. Laughter and comments can be heard, alongside loose shouting and stretched vocal gymnastics. It is a stoned album, aimed at an audience listening on headphones and being surprised by little hidden touches. There is a great YouTube video of 'Bad Scene' live on a US TV show. *Sssh* went to 20 in the *Billboard* top 100 and four in the UK album charts, their highest positions to date. Alvin's writing, musicianship and ideas were in harmony with the times of which he was a part.

John Fowlie's album design showed a solarised, doubled up photographic image of Alvin's face on the front, a perfect stoned image, published in the compilation *1,000 Record Covers* by Michael Ochs. The gatefold version has a similar processed, enlarged pair of Alvin's eyes when opened out, a nod to Kubrick's *2001* with this inside photo. The back cover, a straight photo of the whole band, is overlaid with Alvin's notes about recording, about how he tried to capture the much fuller experience of TYA's live sound.

Recently I've read articles where Ric, in particular, says that the cover, which featured only Alvin's face, generated an angry response from the band. Again, this sums up how in touch with their audience Alvin was and how out of touch some of TYA were. It's ridiculous. The image is distorted, far from self-promotion on Alvin's part. I remember finding it more disturbing than attractive but it was strong and timely. Fame had arrived, money was being earned, success could be enjoyed but some egos were feeling hard done by. This is the nonsense that happens in bands, it destroys what they have worked so hard to achieve.

The end of this extraordinary tour found us back in New York, via Chicago's Kinetic Playground where we played with Bo Diddley as support. I remember watching Bo Diddley with Alvin and discussing how strange it was that TYA were headlining over him. Bo Diddley's inimitable songs and rhythmic flow were a feature of Alvin's Jaybird years in Nottingham.

We were in New York for two more nights at the Fillmore East, four more exciting shows. New York had really embraced Alvin and, in the theatre setting, the Joshua Lights worked hard to give the shows a tremendous backdrop. For one show I sat out front, to the side on a balcony, relaxing and immersing myself in the energy of the crowd. That night is imprinted onto my memory, an unbelievably fine evening. They were also the last shows of this historic tour. We were exhausted and looking forward to going back to London, to the mews cottage that we had hardly lived in.

There were a couple of days off in New York and Alvin decided this was a good opportunity for us to take more LSD. It would be the most epic, transformative and memorable of all the trips we took together. Much of the day was spent out and about, first on the subway, then in the Bronx Zoo followed by the Botanical Gardens. We returned to our hotel, Loew's Midtown, by cab and when we stepped from it Joe Cocker was walking out of Loew's surrounded and followed by the *Groupies* film crew.

Alvin stopped and asked Joe how he was doing. Eyebrows raised, looking up to heaven, Joe smiled. "Just fine man. Crazy stuff, as you see."

chapter 29
Cricklewood Green, London Life with Dear Friends

Back home in England it became harder for Alvin and me to relate the psychedelic experiences, the rock'n'roll life and the increasing fame to our friends and families, but we were blissfully inseparable. It had been a sunny summer in the UK and we'd only been home for a day when Andy Jaworski knocked on our front door. He burst into Gloucester Place Mews in great excitement.

It turned out that before the 12-week US tour he'd sprinkled some "grass" seeds in amongst the rows of tomato plants his parents were growing in their back-garden vegetable patch, in Cricklewood. The seeds had enjoyed the compost, the daily watering and the sunshine and were now a fine row of marijuana plants that towered over the vegetables below. Neither his mum nor dad had any idea what their 20-year-old son's horticultural experiment was and, luckily, neither did their neighbours.

"Wow, man!" What else was there to say about such a bounty? Andy took a polaroid photo of his crop in the vegetable patch, then cut it down and hung it upside down, best he could, to dry out in his dad's garden shed, explaining to his parents that it was a type of herb he had grown.
That polaroid can be found on the front cover of *Cricklewood Green,* TYA's fourth studio album. It's pinned to the wall above John Fowlie's mantlepiece, to the right of the "gold coke bottle with tits" photo that looks burnt on the right side, and above the photo of John's grey cat whose meows opened side one of the album. The Cricklewood Green crop was hidden in plain sight since the album's release.

About 11am most mornings there was a knock at the door which I would open to a grinning Andy. "Good morning, you need to try this." He would deposit a bag of his latest blend in my hand and come in for a cuppa tea and some feedback. He was "curing" his plants in various substances. I think brandy was one! We had no idea after a few days what the difference was or if there was a difference. Cricklewood Green was a mellow smoke whichever way it was dried or cured and obviously a bounty from the gods during a period of frantic rock'n'roll life.

In the autumn of 1969, Ten Years After somehow fitted in recording time between a UK tour and a European and Scandinavian Tour. *Cricklewood Green* was recorded at the most renowned recording studio of the day, Olympic Studios in Barnes, where The Rolling Stones, Led Zeppelin and Traffic had all recorded. Olympic was totally noncorporate, Cricklewood Green could be smoked openly in the studio and the control room. Andy Johns, the engineer, was a lovely young man with immense talent to support but not intrude on the recording process. Alvin was determined to keep writing and keep improving his music despite the increasing pressures on him.

Recording *Cricklewood Green* was a great experience for Alvin. Finally, the band were able to work at the most sought-after studios in London. Being able to smoke certainly shifted the energy in the control room, though how the rest of TYA felt about this is anybody's guess. Having worked hard for many years, their songwriting guitarist/singer was high and feeling free from constraints. He really had earned it.

The album is loose, full of invention, sound links and hidden treats, stereo effects and a fair splash of psychedelic lyrics and instrumentation, reversed and panned sounds. Friends arrived to contribute. 'Love Like A Man' was the single that escaped and Alvin insisted its B-side was the long album version at 33rpm, with the three-minute single edit as the A-side at 45rpm. Later Leo recalled hearing the B-side played in a bar on a juke box at 45rpm, the Mickey Mouse version.

The lounge at Gloucester Place Mews was a great music space and I supported Alvin's daily life as chief cook and bottle washer, so he was free to write with no interruptions. Sometimes I would go out with Kris on a funky clothes search to Portobello Road or Kensington Market, spending only pennies to buy wonderful fabrics and clothes from bygone days.
We must have looked spectacular, two pretty young blondes, iconic "chicks" of the day, tripping around the clothes stalls trying on this or that, checking ourselves in the mirrors, admiring each other, laughing, having fun.

We were unaware we might have caused ripples in the fabric of 1969 London consciousness. We were just kids having fun.

I made clothes for many people, including a pair of tapestry pants, like Alvin's, for Doug D'arcy who was new to Chrysalis, lived around the corner and dropped in from time to time. Recently I saw Doug reminiscing online about those days, his trousers and Alvin, whom he described as "avuncular". I had to look it up. "Avuncular: kind and friendly towards a younger or less experienced person." Kind and friendly was a very good description of Alvin at the Mews. It was how we hoped our home would be for visitors.

We had all kinds. I remember Keith Emerson and his wife Elinor coming to visit. Elinor, who was Scandinavian, kept slapping me heartily on the back, declaring, "We are so lucky to have these great rock'n'roll musicians in our lives!" That had never crossed my mind but I didn't say so. I knew we had nothing in common. Rolling a joint to pass around and making tea for everyone who turned up was my go-to modus operandi.

Sometimes it was just plain useful for dealing with music business nonsense. One day we had a visit at Gloucester Place from Bill Harry, the new Chrysalis publicist, who had been sent to try to find something interesting about Alvin that would get him into the daily papers. This filled Alvin with horror. He was very happy that he could go anywhere unrecognised. He wanted to hold on to his anonymity, though he couldn't really tell that to the band or his management. Becoming famous, recognisable in the USA, Europe or Scandinavia, was ok but he needed to come home and live a low-key life, to relax, regenerate and enjoy himself.

Two invented stories that did make the press, and both may have been Bill's doing. One was about how the band played naked at a free concert in Chicago, which is hilarious and so highly improbable but it's still out there. Written by Richard Green, a journalist on *NME*, it quoted Alvin fresh back from a US tour in 1968. "Nudity is really very popular out there. It's a minor revolution against society. When you first get over the hang-up of playing without clothes, it's quite fun." As I've noted earlier, there was a prankster in Alvin and from early on he had a general disrespect for the press and publicity stunts.

One Bill Harry plant that did make the papers involved Ruthann and Ric's Alsatian dog Nicky, who was set up with a mike, to "sing" blues, to "howl" to the music. "She is in the studio right now laying down some tracks, this would make Nicky the first canine blues singer in recording history." The band are all posed in the pictures with serious faces. Alvin is permed and wears an Indian bedspread cape of mine and tapestry pants, kneeling next to Nicky and appearing to play Big Red. Leo has his bass, he, Chick and Ric all have downcast eyes.

At the Mews, Bill Harry explained with some patience that if Alvin had something going for him like Leo the bassist had, with his cowboy clothes and his horses, it would be easy. Leo could have ridden his horse down Oxford Street and made the front pages of the tabloids. Hunting around for inspiration, Bill suggested that as Alvin liked to wear wooden Dutch clogs, perhaps he could buy a dozen pairs and be photographed with them. We were kind. I made tea, rolled a joint and offered it to Bill, who said, "Ok, but I usually fall asleep if I smoke dope." We smoked, drank tea, smiled and Bill, true to his word, nodded-out on the sofa for several hours. Alvin and I got on with our day. Eventually our sleeping publicist awoke, looked at his watch with surprise, made his excuses and left. There were no pictures of Alvin's clogs though there was a spread in a tabloid about me in a miniskirt and maxi length sheepskin coat.

The long Welsh sheepskin coat was part of a venture into sheepskin clothing that came about through Johnnie Clifton. JC was a huge fan of North Wales where he and Judy spent much time. Alvin and I went with them, all four of us crammed into their classic split-screen Morris Minor. We had a memorable holiday on a farm down a long track with five-bar gates that Judy jumped out to open. The farmer and his wife were super proud of their new Formica fifties kitchen cabinet, though to buy it they had sold a fabulous antique wooden Welsh dresser.

It was an experience far away from rock'n'roll, in the Welsh mountains around the Dovey valley in the shade of Cader Idris, a frozen giant of a mountain, a welcomed holiday. Johnnie had come across a source for cheap Welsh sheepskins and the standing joke was that all around us were his agents in the field, the sheep. On our last muddy day, Johnnie drove off into the hills, exploring a narrow road, mile after mile of winding track with no way of turning around. Eventually we arrived at a farm, where a lovely chap leant on an open gate with a quizzical expression as we passed him and drove the car into mud, grinding to a halt at the end of the farm road.

Alvin, Judy and me got out to push. We girls unwittingly positioned ourselves either side of Alvin, in line with the wheels. He always had luck on his side. When we pushed the wheels spun and splattered us both in mud from head to foot. The car lurched off and we were able to turn it around, only to see our gate-leaning friend looking just as nonplussed as he had when we passed him. What splendid entertainment we had offered him in his remote home, a tale he would no doubt regale the locals with in the pub that night. We drove past, looked and smiled at him. His face remained intact, his stoic expression unchanged.

Our friend Simon Stable would walk down the mews in his oversized white sheepskin coat, his briefcase clutched at his side, his long black hair and small head topping it off. In 1970, Simon would marry the lovely Judy Dyble, first singer with Fairport Convention. Alvin was to be his best man but we arrived too late after battling with Kensington traffic and getting lost several times. They were married for 20 years until Simon's passing, far too young, in 1990. Sadly, Judy left us in July 2020 after suffering various health problems.

Alvin and Simon had a deep connection through music. At 297 Portobello Road, Simon ran a brilliant record shop, Simon's Stable, next door to Forbidden Fruit, an eclectic clothes shop with a peacock painting covering the main window. His record stock included all the underground groups and he wrote a regular column for *International Times*, and articles for *Music Now* and *NME*. He did one of the best interviews with Alvin, published in May 1972 in *NME*.

When Simon came to visit us at Gloucester Place Mews, he would often bring with him interesting or unusual Portobello area hippies. A great aspect of these few, pure hippie years was the belief that if a friend arrived, whoever came with them was completely accepted and welcomed with a cuppa and a smoke. We were unfazed by the people we met. There was Honk, a gentle giant of a man who played bass guitar, and Spider, whose name came from his ability to climb down walls from upper floor windows should the police arrive. Simon had his first LSD "experience" with us at Warwick Square. We had taken amphetamines to keep him company and he had fallen asleep. Many decades later Alvin told me that the Orange Sunshine we took with Simon in London had been smuggled, unwittingly, by Dee Anthony. Alvin had hidden it in his travelling record player and asked Dee to carry the machine through customs.

We invited Simon to come around during the day and trip with us. After two trips we no longer felt the need for someone straight with us so all three of us took a tab. We smoked some Cricklewood and as the Sunshine came on Simon said several times: "Mmmmm. Dear me this is very strong indeed!" We realised that his first experience, which he had slept through, had most likely not been LSD.

We had listened to Van Morrison's *Astral Weeks*, much acclaimed by critics, without really getting it. That day we put it on the space-age record deck, turned up the Quad amp, and the Lowther Speakers gave us a HiFi experience unlike anything we'd known before. Van's vocal delivery, his poetic lyrics drew pictures, whilst Richard Davis' incredible melodic bass lines wrapped around us, the violins spun gently up to the ceiling and dripped their way down the living room walls. Even the obscured image of Van's face in the foliage of the album sleeve became transformed into a spiritual icon. Did we play it twice or three times? I forget. There seemed no point in playing anything else as the hours meandered.

Over the years *Astral Weeks* has become one of several albums I cherish but play very rarely. My instinct says that if I ration them, they won't lose their time machine magic. Music is such a nebulous, ethereal yet transformative medium.

At some point at Gloucester Place Mews, Krissie and Ronnie Wood moved in. They were between homes when the lease on Forge Cottage ran out. Their next home was a flat in the same building on Sloane Street where Perry Press had his estate agents. Jeff Beck had broken up his band the week before Woodstock, where they had been scheduled to play, leaving Woody out of a job.

At Gloucester Place they put their possessions somewhere in storage, though naturally they brought Sadie, the big turquoise Macaw. Her cage sat on a table in the window. Every morning, she would politely say "Hello" in parrot fashion when I went to put the kettle on. A large parrot with a piercing eye and a brutal beak is both wondrous and unnerving. Stoned, I would study her and talk to her, even venturing to stroke her neck, through the cage bars. She appeared to love this and would almost purr, making contented sounds. Part of me was uncomfortable at her being caged. A bird should be free to fly, I thought.

Woody painted a wonderful life-sized portrait of Sadie, and attached some feathers she had shed. Woody and Kris eventually gave Sadie to Chessington Zoo; where for all I know she might still be alive.

The four of us took an Orange Sunshine trip at the mews, starting early one evening, and when we were riding high the doorbell rang. Kris, Woody and Alvin froze and I went to the door. It was drummer Micky Waller, who Woody had been playing with in the Beck Band. Jeff breaking up the band was a drama for everyone and talking to Micky was the last thing Woody wanted to do at that moment. A quick plan was hatched. I let Micky in and the other three said, "Hi man, see you later, we're just off to bed." The three of them crept up the open stairs that led out of the lounge, waving to Micky as they went.

I sat with Micky for a little while, listening as he poured out his heart to me. It was all about women and how dreadful they had been to him. In my high state, I recognised that his negative energy about women would almost certainly attract more of the same, though it would have been unkind for me to say so. Another part of me was waiting for the moment when I could politely send him on his way and resume my tripping with the others.

After a while I was able to tell him that I also needed to go to sleep. He was so wrapped up in his own misery that he didn't seem to have noticed that we were in fact all wide awake and buzzing. I saw him off through the front door and returned to find Woody, Kris and Alvin laughing their way back down the stairs.

While Woody was with us, his career was in high drama, as he and Rod Stewart were joining up with Ronnie Lane, Ian McLagan and Kenney Jones from The Small Faces. They would become The Faces. In Alvin's opinion this was the best and most creative period of Woody's career, both for his art and for his music. Chris Wright almost took on The Faces but was put off by the contractual and legal circumstances that needed to be dealt with. Billy Gaff was willing to take on that challenge and would successfully manage their time together as a band.

Alvin's home life and his close friends were an anchor that helped balance out life on the road, with the increasing pressure of writing songs, recording and being available to give interviews. Sam and Doris continued to visit at Gloucester Place Mews, just as they had at Warwick Square. Doris really enjoyed having a smoke with us and though Sam gave it a go, he decided it wasn't for him. Ruth and Jeff came with them for one visit. My parents visited briefly but were only offered cups of tea. In the small kitchen the cement floor had broken up in one section, leaving the linoleum worn through. It was the only really shabby thing in an otherwise very desirable property by London standards. After they got home, mum rang. "Your father is horrified," she said. "You bring them up so well and then they come to this!" No surprises there then.

An old friend from Nottingham, Andy Collinson, turned up while on his honeymoon, though I don't think his new wife was with him. I was in the midst of cleaning out the seeds on a whole pile of Cricklewood Green. After a cup of tea, he left and returned half an hour later with a Bible he had bought for us. It turned out he had become a born-again Christian and was horrified about us smoking marijuana. He thought there was a in danger of the devil making off with us. He didn't stay for long and he was really tense, annoyed that we wouldn't take him seriously.

Vincent Tseng visited from Manchester where he was now at University. We smoked and watched Laurel & Hardy movies, finally watching one in reverse. A house and a car, wrecked in a retaliatory tit-for-tat episode, remade and reformed themselves, a fine surrealist movie show. When Vincent left we walked backwards up the stairs shouting "Night good, night good."
He reminded me of that in 2018.

Johnnie Clifton arrived early one evening. Kris and I were in Alvin and Woody were not. We girls were rolling and enjoying a hashish joint. I made Johnnie a cup of tea and he shared the joint, before leaving for his next port of call. About two hours later we were still smoking and talking when there was a knock on the door. I opened it to find Johnnie ashen-faced. "What was in that joint?"

"Good hashish," I replied.

He told us he had set off down the road in his car but the parking meters on either side of the road had begun to sway. So he pulled up, parked and sat in his car for two hours, holding on to the steering wheel, trying to regain control of himself. "I had the car window open and heard a plane fly over and somehow I followed the sound of the plane all the way to Heathrow airport (10 miles away). I heard the engines reverse for landing, and even the wheels on the tarmac of the runway, as it landed."

Wow! Kris and I listened in amazement at his surreal account, all brought about by the same smoke we had. For years Johnnie was certain we had given him something far more psychedelic than hashish. Giving anyone anything other than what we said we were offering was not something we would have done, completely against everything I believed in. I was very idealistic.

One afternoon when only Alvin and I were in, a knock at the door revealed the whole of the soon-to-be Black Sabbath, circa 1969. Chrysalis had suggested that they all go around to Alvin's to ask him about touring in the USA. The lounge filled up with these nice guys from the Midlands, not far from our Nottingham roots. I have a clear memory of carefully moving between them, mostly sitting on the floor, with a tray of mugs of tea and plates of biscuits. I rolled some joints and listened to Alvin's advice on rockin' in the USA, as Ozzy, Geezer and gang gazed up at him with rapt attention. Later the conversation shifted to choosing a band name and Alvin told them he thought the proposed Black Sabbath would be a very bad idea in America.

chapter 30
Touring UK and Europe

Alvin and I had fully embraced the peace and love culture of San Francisco. It truly was like another planet. Yes, we had hippie friends in London, though the underground scene was much more introverted and limited to a few areas, clubs, record shops, art scenes, cinemas, like The Electric on Portobello road, and one on Baker Street that showed movies at midnight. I remember we saw a movie there called *The Trip* starring Peter Fonda and Denis Hopper. There were some great music and arts clubs, among them UFO on Tottenham Court Road. Most London hippies stayed indoors with their friends getting high, listening to good sounds. A great HiFi, a rack of albums and some psychedelic posters along with Indian fabrics, velvets cushions, and burning incense transported us from grey Britain to sunny California.

London was "Swinging", with mini cars, mini-skirted dolly birds and style hungry guys who bought their clothes on Kings Road in Chelsea, Biba's on Kensington High Street and any of a dozen shops on Carnaby Street. Chris Wright had a flat on Kings Road, where his Californian girlfriend Chelle crossed the Atlantic to join him in August 1969. She found his modern flat furnished in a minimalist style, that is no furniture. Alvin and I went with Chelle and Chris to a furniture store on Tottenham Court Road where we convinced Chris that a fabulous purple sofa was the way to go. Chelle, transported to London from Sacramento, would visit Alvin and me and hang out, getting high and telling us stories about the hippie life she had left back home.

I connected with Chelle and we remain good friends to this day. It was great to have her on tour with Chris. She was easy going and loved to get high, and this naturally brought Alvin and Chris together. Chris was quite reserved, businesslike, most of the time, but with Chelle he loosened up, enjoyed a smoke and had a good laugh. She was the first girlfriend from the TYA team with whom I could really hang out. All the other wives and eventual girlfriends were straight – no problem with that but no fun for me.

Now that Ten Years After had outgrown The Marquee and similar clubs, the Albert Hall beckoned. One of my early visits there was in February 1969, to see the Jimi Hendrix Experience, now considered an iconic rock gig. Alvin was away on the US tour and by now I was quite a connoisseur of sound quality and performance, the essential connection between the audience and the performers.

Support band Soft Machine, whose music I didn't know, mystified me. They seemed like good musicians who were determined not to play anything together, but when Hendrix came on stage the audience and energy suddenly became far more electric. He looked fabulous, a visitor from another much-more-cool and languid galaxy. Hendrix's charisma held your attention, extraordinary, in command, focused, brilliant, intoxicating. At times he was distracted by his equipment, his amp in particular. This would quieten the audience, so the show never seemed to really gel or maintain a level to take everyone into a higher connection.

When Alvin played his immersion was intense and it was rare for him to disconnect but with Hendrix that night, I just wanted him to become happy with his sounds and performance, so I could relax. I remember talking to Alvin about Hendrix playing with his teeth and behind his head. It was showmanship, said Alvin. "He doesn't really pluck the strings with his teeth, his right hand on the neck is making the notes ring." Nonetheless it was memorable to see Hendrix.

Overall the sound quality at the Albert Hall was not good. It is a large open space, completely circular, an acoustic nightmare, especially for loud rock music, though Alvin would do his best to overcome these handicaps. The Woodstock summer had boosted their confidence and all the UK shows were sold out. 'I'm Going Home' was a great closer and soon fans were yelling for it from the moment the band walked out on stage, all the more so after the *Woodstock* movie was released in early 1970. When TYA returned to the stage after 'I'm Going Home', the encores would all be Chuck Berry classics from The Jaybird days. Alvin would be flying high, reconnecting with his teenage exuberance. I would be dancing, yelling and clapping along, using up the last vestiges of energy I had left. I loved getting back to the dressing room with him, both high, both sweaty, another great night.

Sssh, was released in August 1969, reached number four in the British charts and 20 in the US *Billboard* chart. Outside of London some of their best gigs had been in universities with the students, the circuits that launched the careers of both Chris Wright and Terry Ellis. Now they had outgrown universities, Chrysalis put together their own short package tours in concert venues around the UK, often in bland local authority buildings.

Their December 1969 tour saw them headlining at Newcastle City Hall, Birmingham Town Hall, the Southampton Guildhall, the Albert Hall in Nottingham, Bristol's Colston Hall, Edinburgh's Usher Hall, the Free Trade Hall in Manchester and the Royal Albert in London – no chilled-out security, psychedelic light shows, funky dressing rooms or colourful groupies in sight. Luckily, the audiences made it all worthwhile. After the Marquee era there are no UK gigs that really stand out. They were all good, all well organised, no riots, the music was great, everyone went home happy.

On December 12, when TYA returned to Nottingham and the Albert Hall it was a great triumph. It was not as memorable as when they had played the Nottingham Palais in 1968, a Mecca dance hall. It was jammed to the rafters. Family and friends arrived: Ruth and Jeff, Sam and Doris, and my mum and dad and sister-in-law Val. It was a very cold night and dad, having got mum away from the pub for the evening, headed to a nearby pub and insisted they drink whisky macs – Scotch and ginger wine – to keep them warm. Afterwards, when we met them downstairs in the Palais, mum was very drunk. Someone turned on the revolving dance floor, with mum lying on it like a Pharaoh, going around and around much to everyone's amusement.

In Europe there were more incidents, more unpredictability, more highs and lows. Here there was still an element of the wild west, the new frontier. Scandinavia had taken to Ten Years After very early and their venues, security and audiences were focused on everyone having a great time and getting high with the music. It seemed that Scandinavia was the hippest part of Europe. Amsterdam has had cannabis cafes since 1972. I have always considered the Dutch to be the most advanced westerners, the least hysterical and most sane.

There were no rock'n'roll shows in Spain or Portugal, Spain because Franco was still the dictator-in-charge and Portugal because it was too out of the way. Alvin and I were both huge Salvador Dali fans and going to Spain might have included Barcelona and a trip to Cadaques to sit by the sea, drink coffee and maybe even glimpse our hero.

Germany was and remains a huge rock'n'roll country. At the end of a show "Zu-ga-be" was the loud, repeated collective chant, its literal translation "extra" so it was the equivalent of "More, More, More" in the UK and USA and the slow intense hand-claps of Scandinavia. We mostly traveled around Germany in a bus, enjoying the long, straight, fast autobahns and landscape, the huge, dense forests of pine trees and mountains, and the occasional Gothic castle.

Germany was great, well-organised, efficient, exciting. The German promoter, Fritz Rau, would tell us about his decadent life in the thirties. He had been a boyfriend of Marlene Dietrich, Germany's most famous movie star and singer. Like Dee Anthony and Bill Graham, Fritz Rau was a huge personality with a passion for rock'n'roll and jazz. He felt music was a force for good that could unite the world, his dream to take bands to perform behind the Iron Curtain in communist countries. His company Lipmann + Rau would continue to promote in Europe throughout the seventies and eighties and he was Alvin's only choice in Europe. He understood that though we didn't share a common verbal language, what we had in common was a musical sensibility.

In contrast to Fritz Rau, Italian promoters were a posse. It took at least four or five of them to put a gig and a band together. In the morning, when the TYA crew were keen to get to the gig and set up for the evening show, they would have to wait around. The promoters would all need to go to the hairdressers, for shaves and trims and general tarting up. Then nothing could happen until after "manjiare", eating lunch which concluded with drinking strong expressos.

"Manjiare, manjiare," they would shout, fingers to their mouths and sad, hangdog expressions. Finally, Andy, John and the crew would be taken to the venue where they were now under time pressure to set up and be ready for the show.

Francesco Zanavio, the "leader" of the posse, liked to pose and lounge around the band in the hotel with a sidekick or two. Was there anything the band needed? On the day of our arrival at the Rome hotel we sat around in the lobby for a while, getting to know them. Ruthann and I were ignored and far from happy when the conversation turned to the band's extra-curricular requirements.

"Do you need anything, any women?" they were asked.

It was like we were in a movie, an Italian cliché. A tour of Italy was proposed. We would stay on a yacht, sailing around the Mediterranean coast from gig to gig. Payment was to be a Ferrari each.

The Italian audience was 95% male, like the good old early UK blues audiences, but for a different reason. Italian society was still very strictly Catholic. The only girls likely to attend rock shows would be disreputable, not nice Catholic girls. It seemed so odd after other countries where the audiences were mixed. The shows were just as hot and rockin' as everywhere else and by now the basic set would be augmented by tracks from the current album. Alvin would still get high and fly his fingers to new places on the neck but given the number of shows and numbness of travel, the drive and excitement was diminished. This level of touring was relentless, and so new that managers had yet to work out how to pace the workload to satisfy everyone's needs.

We had a day off in Rome. Chelle, Chris, Chick, his new girlfriend Suzanne, Alvin and I had a limousine to take us around the sights. Chick and Suzanne met at the 1970 Isle of Wight Festival, where some of TYA stayed overnight at her large family house. Alvin took some fine photos in Rome. We were all blown away by the Coliseum. Knowing something of its history the crowds and the spectacle, there was a resonance with rock'n'roll. At the magnificent Trevi Fountain some Italian lothario made a pass at Suzanne when Chick wasn't looking. It was nothing much, just another cliché. Suzanne opted to tell Chick, embellishing it a little.

Back in the limo Alvin, who was sat in the front with the driver, spotted the hapless lothario in the crowd and pointed him out to Chick. Lowering the window, Chick reverted to his Nottingham youth, gathered a mouthful of mucous and launched a "gob" – a spit – from the window. Despite there being a crowd, his aim was immaculate. We watched transfixed as it performed a perfect arc and landed squarely on the Italian's face.

From there things went rapidly downhill. The guy launched himself at the car, unwisely putting his head and torso through Alvin's open window looking for the culprit. Realising he was outnumbered, he started to withdraw but Alvin, now also in Nottingham youth mode, grabbed him by his clothes. How he got his Dutch wood-clogged foot out of the footwell and kicked the guy several times before pushing him away is a complete mystery but remains a memorable image for me. He was certainly flexible. The driver, doubtless in a state of shock, put up the electric window. Alvin got his camera and took photos of the guy's face pushed up against it.

Alas, our getaway was hampered by a traffic jam, which no one had noticed. The Italian leapt on to the car bonnet and attacked the windscreen, which started to move. The energy in the car was fit to explode. Chris was very freaked out and Chelle was trying to pacify him and Chick. I felt numb, detached like an observer, not part of the action. Growing up in Nottingham I'd witnessed many episodes of mindless violence and learnt to stay calm.

Just as it seemed the windscreen would give way, the traffic in front moved off and our driver accelerated, causing the Italian to lose his balance and be thrown off of the bonnet. Looking back as we drove away, we saw a commotion in the crowd, as you might imagine. The Italian was on his feet, shaking his fists but not daft enough to give chase. Alvin's attack on the guy was not really justified. It was clearly an overreaction, probably based on touring frustration bottled up and needing an outlet. Thinking about it now, perhaps our lothario put two and two together when he saw Suzanne in the back of the car.

Back at the hotel Chris reported our drama to Francesco and gang, who took it all very seriously. They were worried the guy might have Mafia links and offered to stay with Chris that evening with a gun or to give Chris a gun. Of course, this only served to make Chris more anxious, positively paranoid in fact. They thought his reactions a bit over the top. The hotel offered a shoe shining service and Chris put his shoes outside his room that night. In the morning they had disappeared. I don't know who or how or where, though I'm pretty sure it wasn't Alvin. It turned out to be the only pair of shoes he had with him. Cool-headed Chelle, with Chris in his sock feet, had no choice but to take a taxi to the elegant Via Veneto to get him a new pair. I'm sure it stopped him worrying about the Mafia.

In Rome we went to a brilliant restaurant, in huge, arched, brick wine cellars. Francesco was at his preening best, the food was amazing and he took charge of what we ate, as in "When I eat spaghetti, everyone eats spaghetti." The restaurant was on two floors, with entertainers on each one, a group of guitar playing Romans on ours, and a lady who sang opera aria requests on the other. When they switched, we gained the opera singer, but as none of us knew any arias we were happy with whatever she sang. The wine flowed, the food was excellent.

Sitting with Alvin on one side and Francesco on the other, my tolerance of his antics was getting low. After deserts, coffees were ordered and Irish coffee was on offer. I suggested to Francesco that it was my favourite and that he would really love it. I knew that he was unaware it was alcoholic. I sipped mine and Francesco, finding it delicious, drank his down like an expresso and ordered another. Gradually they took effect and completely disoriented him. Returning from the loo, I passed him on the stairs looking very much the worse for wear, quietly gripping the handrail.

Italy was certainly memorable.

Chapter 31
Woodstock Movie and Robin Hood Barn

The pace of life, this total day-to-day involvement with music and the world of Ten Years After, was a world now expanding like the ripples of a pebble dropped into the still surface of an endless lake. We were all taken over by it, a different reality than the world of hopes and dreams we had all inhabited for years. I remember once reading a quote by the British actor, Michael Caine, to the effect that when people discover they can make a percentage from your talents, you will never be out of work again. How true.

We weren't oblivious to what was happening in the bigger world, nor did we think that everything was wonderful out there. In London we lived next to two young American draft dodgers who, like many young men, had decided they didn't want to go to Vietnam. We didn't think they were failing America, they were seen by my peace seeking sixties generation as sane human beings. We admired the drive and energy, the demonstrations and marches against that war which eventually helped bring it to a faster conclusion. It also led to more discussion about subsequent wars that the West would embark on, hopefully helping to bring an end to war.

The assassinations of President John F Kennedy, his brother Robert and Martin Luther King, had marked the sixties with violence that was shocking to us English people. While we were in New York before Woodstock, we heard about the brutal murder of Sharon Tate and her associates in Los Angeles. In December 1969 the world learnt of the hippie cult weirdness of Charles Manson but it had already become apparent to us that growing your hair long, smoking marijuana and tripping with psychedelics didn't necessarily produce a peaceful, loving individual.

However, Manson and his cult of lost young girls was inconceivable to us. His dark, intense stare on the news, his personal hypnotic power, did seem to reach out from the TV set into the room. It was easy to understand that by using sex and drugs he dominated and distorted those lost young girls' minds.

It was very chilling, as was the fiasco at the Rolling Stones' Altamont gig in December. Fortunately, the *Woodstock* movie did much to counteract the idea that the hippie project was over. On a US tour a few months after the festival we were taken to a Warner Brothers editing suite to watch Ten Years After's proposed movie segment. Director Mike Wadleigh loved the high energy of 'I'm Going Home' and the camera loved Alvin's face.

We were told that Warners had offered their state-of-the-art editing facilities in return for a deal over the ownership and distribution of the finished documentary. So, the hippiest film crew ever assembled played with technology and discovered the potential of split screen in a 70mm wide screen movie. They had three days of live music and documentary footage of the crowd and local residents. Split screen would allow them to use far more of that footage and produce a truly involving, unique rock festival film.

Ten Years After were very fortunate to make it through to the final three-hour movie. Other performers, who were more famous than them at the time, ended up being cut, while the management of Janis Joplin, Jefferson Airplane, Grateful Dead and Canned Heat declined permission for them to appear. *The Woodstock Diary 1969*, the remake by D A Pennebaker in 1994, used original footage that includes some of the performances originally omitted.

In early 1970 we went to the New York premier of the 70mm *Woodstock* movie. There was Alvin on the giant screen, his beautiful face so photogenic, his pyrotechnic guitar playing as mesmerizing as his soulful voice. "I'm going home, to see my baby," he screams – the song he wrote in Scandinavia when I was left at home in London. In the USA while on tour, in airports, we came across American servicemen returning home, happy to tell us it was played around the US camps the night before.

In 2018, I met Henry Gross, a member of Sha Na Na, who was the youngest performer at Woodstock. He was so pleased. "The blond from *Woodstock*," he said. "I sat next to you at the New York premier in 1970. Me, then you, then Alvin, I often wondered what happened to you. You guys were like twins, you had an extraordinary energy together, as if you were from another planet." That was how it felt to me at the time. It was lovely to hear after five decades that was how we also seemed to others. We had grown so close during our psychedelic excursions and touring together.

On the night of the premier we were astonished by what we saw. Our experience of the Sunday was many hours sheltering from torrential rain. The storm sequence was epic. The crowd became an energised tribe, beating on tin cans and hurtling themselves through the mud like little kids, their spirits undaunted. The whole movie reflected the energy and beauty of Woodstock. The local people, initially anxious about the influx of so many thousands of young hippies who looked so alien to them, were overwhelmingly delighted to realise what a fine generation they were.

Max Yasgur, the farmer on whose land it was held, made a speech to the crowd that was so touching. "I'm a farmer," he said. "I don't know how to speak to twenty people, let alone a crowd like this." The audience cheered. "The most important thing that you've proven to the world is that half a million young people can get together and have three days of fun and music and have nothing but fun and music, and God bless you for it."

Pete Townshend acknowledged that the *Woodstock* film elevated The Who to their place in American rock aristocracy. "It wasn't just The Who, everyone who performed at Woodstock enjoyed mythic status, once the film was released," he wrote in his autobiography *Who I Am*.

Alvin had little idea what the effect of being in this movie would have on him, his career or Ten Years After. It was overwhelming, thrilling and beyond their wildest fantasies. Their appearance in *Woodstock* would sky-rocket them to a totally new level of fame, increasing their nightly audience from 3-5,000 people in Fillmore style venues to 20-40,000 people in football stadiums and arenas where netball and ice hockey are played.

Woodstock's general release was on March 26, 1970, seven months after the festival, during which time nothing much changed for us. The movie's budget was $600,000 and at the box office it took $50 million. It was shown at the Cannes film festival in the south of France and at the Academy Awards it won the Oscar for Best Documentary Feature.   Michael Wadleigh has revisited the *Woodstock* footage for both a 25th Anniversary and a 40th Anniversary Director's cut, adding 40 minutes and a number of performances, Janis Joplin, Grace Slick and the Jefferson Airplane among them. In 1996, the *Woodstock* movie was inducted into the Library of Congress National Film Registry. Thus, it was embraced by the US establishment as an important cultural artifact.

The sixties defined my life and my beliefs, and Alvin's too. On his last album *Still On The Road to Freedom*, the track 'Back In 69' laments his feelings about the loss of those values. My renewed email exchanges with him in the last years of his life were often about this. I tried to bring him some good news, some green shoots from the seeds planted in those days. His widow Evi graciously told me how grateful she was that I had brought those "hippie ideas" back into his life.

In 1970 my mother and sister-in-law Valerie saw *Woodstock* at a cinema in Nottingham. They both thoroughly enjoyed the film, and made positive remarks to me about the young hippies. They were impressed to see how young Graham Barnes had transformed into Alvin Lee, a widescreen rock god. It must have seemed as alien to them as it would had he turned into an astronaut walking on the moon. Sam and Doris were always unreservedly delighted with Alvin's increasing success. They had already been to many Ten Years After gigs and loved the music he was now writing and performing.

In London, Alvin and I smoked something good, maybe some Cricklewood Green, took a taxi and headed down to the Odeon in Leicester Square. We bought our tickets, and got up close to the 70mm widescreen, as we had for Kubrick's *2001,* and enjoyed the whole film again. No one recognised Alvin. We were able to experience the responses of curious young London hippies as they applauded the bands and laughed at their stoned American counterparts. The cinema audience gave a standing ovation at the end, a very rare event in the UK. It wasn't that long ago that visits to a cinema ended in a rendition of the National Anthem. We had to stand still for 'God Save The Queen'.

Though fans often recognised Alvin after gigs and increasingly wanted his autograph and to offer their thanks for a show, we were pleased that in London he could go out and about to cinemas, camera and music shops, occasional restaurants and even The Speakeasy, the cool basement club favoured by musicians. I remember us going to Mr Freedom, a trendy boutique on the Kings Road in Chelsea, where he encouraged me to buy my first hot pants. They were tan velvet with a dungaree-style bib, adorned with an appliquéd satin abstract landscape, great for travelling in though I'm not sure I would have dared buy them if he had not been there.

Gloucester Place Mews, where we got high and listened to great music, became a great creative hub, just as Warwick Square had been. We were so available there. Increasingly the front door bell would ring and a stream of friends, family, musicians and Chrysalis staff arrived. We had no idea how to satisfy our need for a personal life. We talked about it, about how it had become party central. Eventually it dawned on us that we now had enough money to buy a fairly comfortable house in the countryside with easy access to London, probably in the same area where Kris and Woody had been living when we first met them, somewhere in the Thames Valley about 40 miles to the west of London. This was a job for Perry Press, regular visitor and smoking chum.

On a sunny day in May 1970 we set off with Perry to look at three properties. The first was a small farmhouse with some land, owned by the widow of the pilot who died in the famous 1958 Munich air disaster in which eight Manchester United footballers died. The farmhouse was a nice home but it lacked the magic of The Old Forge.

The second house Perry showed us was called Robin Hood Barn, the coincidence for two Nottingham people almost cartoonish, located a couple of miles outside the small Berkshire town of Wokingham in an area called Merryhill Green. Dating from the thirties, it was a half-timbered barn that had been dismantled and re-built a short distance away from a group of farmhouses. It had 4.5 acres of land, probably 2.5 acres around the house cultivated into a beautiful mature garden, vegetable area, garages and a circular drive entrance. Another two acres were a wild U shaped, hedged field that enclosed and gave privacy to the garden.

We were entranced when the front door opened and a lovely elderly lady invited us in and asked us to call her Granny. She showed us through the entrance lobby and opened an inner door which revealed a two-storied minstrel's gallery, double height to the ceiling, and an oak beamed Inglenook fireplace with a wood burning stove. Through small, leaded windows and glass doors we could see a magnificent lawn and garden laid out with mature trees and tasteful flower beds. A wide staircase led up to the minstrel's gallery, along which ran a bench and more leaded windows. Three bedrooms, two with bathrooms, led off the gallery and a further small staircase led up to three attic rooms with sloping ceilings and dormer windows looking down onto the garden.

Back on the ground floor there were two good sized rooms, a lounge with double aspect windows, an open fireplace and across the galleried hall a dining room. The kitchen had an oil-fired Aga cooker, perfect for country kitchens. Granny opened the French doors and we walked out into the garden. She made tea with homemade cakes and scones, which we ate, sat by the trees enjoying the sunshine, the birdsong and squirrels, the peace and the fine clean air. She told us how she and her husband moved into the house when it was newly built and how they planted out the garden with small trees that were now mature. She had two sons who were married and had moved away, but now she needed to move to a village near to one of her sons in Newdigate because the house was too big for her.

As we left, she showed us the grooves on the front door beams where her sons had come home from school and propped up their bikes. We had found our next home, and the price – £24,500 – was just affordable. Perry had one more house viewing booked on the other side of Wokingham, Lock's Barn, and we said we might as well take a look. It struck us straight away that it would be a perfect home for Chris and Chelle, so we phoned them when we got back. They viewed it with Perry and agreed. They would live one side of Wokingham and we would live the other, which helped keep Alvin and Chris connect during the next few years.

We bought The Barn, as it came to be known, and moved in during August 1970. That summer, between hectic touring and recording, we would head off there on Sundays, taking Chris and Chelle, or Kris and Woody or Johnnie and Judy, always with Perry Press. Arriving completely unannounced, Granny would beam at us all and bring us tea and homemade cakes. It is no surprise the house had such a warm, welcoming energy. Everyone agreed it was a magical place.

My challenge over the next few months was to learn to drive. Alvin loved to drive when we were in Nottingham and living in London there was no need for me to learn. Now however, living in the country with the nearest shops four miles away in Wokingham, I would need to drive. I took lessons at the British School of Motoring on Baker Street and passed my driving test the second time.

We were out in the Triumph TR3A when Alvin stopped, swopped seats and I drove it for the first time. It was much more fun than the BSM car. The first week we were living at Robin Hood Barn was the first time I drove on my own. I set off in the TR3A and it jumped down the road like a kangaroo. No one had mentioned the manual choke needed to warm it up from cold. About a mile from the house I was ready to give up, go home or have a nervous breakdown. I drove into the car park of a pub, leaving the car running while I sat shaking.

Gathering myself together, I gave it another go. The engine now warm, purring smoothly. I completed my first solo adventure. Back at The Barn, Alvin thought it was hilarious and taught me how to use the choke when starting a car from cold. I loved driving that little two-seater sports car on the country lanes and took to driving down new roads wherever I found them. Alvin bought a Jaguar, a Series 1 XJ6, the state-of-the-art Jaguar brought out in 1968 to replace their classic 1960s models. It was about a year old, metallic brown with cream leather upholstery and walnut dashboard. He drove it fast and well and it took us to gigs all over England. I was given the Triumph TR3A. What a great first car.

One night, after a gig in Manchester, we set off to drive 200 miles back home in the XJ6 quite late, well after midnight. There was virtually no traffic and the route back took us down three motorways, M6, M5 and M4, so Alvin decided to see how fast we could get back. I wish I had noted our speed, at least 120-140 mph. It was a dream drive down the empty roads, a fine clear starry night, perfect road conditions, listening to music and looking forward to home. We had covered about 150 miles when up ahead a police car with lights and siren pulled onto the road. We slowed but he stayed just ahead of us and indicted for us to pull into the hard shoulder.

The car doors opened and two policemen sauntered over to the driver's window. "Good evening, sir, would you mind waiting here a moment. Some friends will be along soon?"

Five minutes passed and behind us the flashing lights of another police car grew nearer and parked up. Two more policemen joined the first two. "We've been following you down the M5," said one. "Would you mind waiting here a moment?"

After five or ten minutes a third police car arrived, lights flashing and parked up. These two police were not so relaxed, must have been a hairy drive.

No one had asked Alvin to "step out of the car". They must have realised from the first whiff of his breath that he hadn't drunk any alcohol though the smell of cigarettes and patchouli oil was pretty strong. This was probably a car that all six would like to have owned themselves. There was plenty of respect shown but the conversation was pure Monty Python. The occupants of the third police car took over the dialogue.

"We have been following you since the M6 sir. You were doing well over 100 miles an hour."

No point in denying this.

"Yes, officer," said Alvin calmly. "I wanted to get home.

The roads were empty."

"Do you realise that fox hunts come across this road?" asked one of the lawmen. This was too silly by far.

"At three o'clock in the morning?" replied Alvin incredulously.

There was a sudden sense that we had entered an alternative reality. It took all seriousness out of the situation. There was a certain amount of embarrassed spluttering. The policemen from the first two cars wished us good night and left while Alvin gave his details to the humbled copper who had raced at top speed for over 150 miles on a starry night to give out a speeding ticket.

chapter 32
Bliss At The Barn, Not In The World

During 1970 it became obvious that Alvin could become a huge superstar. Nothing was standing in his way except himself and his own musical wishes. On March 8, 2013 just after Alvin died, Chris Wright emailed me: "Looking back, he was a huge star at the time," he wrote. "It was only his decision to take a step back that diminished his profile to the extent that it did."

Woodstock, released in March 1970, gave TYA massive global exposure. Alvin's performance and photogenic good looks had turned him into an Elvis for his generation. Up to now, the increasing fame had a trajectory that was steady and just about manageable, even logical. Yes, there was increased pressure but the space left for creativity, song writing and even some relaxation was ok. Alvin was 25, fit, healthy, solvent, happy, even contented at times. The future was not something we ever talked about. It was great to be so focused in the now, to be living each day as it arrived.

In August 1970 we arrived at Robin Hood Barn with our portable sound system, a few albums and camped out in the lounge. We didn't know how to turn on the Aga in the kitchen, or the central heating. There were logs and we lit a fire in the lounge grate which we used to boil water in a kettle for tea. We went out to get fish and chips for supper and a few provisions for breakfast. Somehow (perhaps from Granny) we had a mattress and we spent the weekend in simple bliss, living, loving and listening to mellow music. I remember cooking bacon and eggs in a frying pan on the open fire. We had been left some curtains which opened to reveal the garden wrapped around us. It was glorious.

Having always rented furnished places in London the little we packed would arrive with John Hembrow the following week. On Monday we drove off to Reading to turn this empty house into a home. We needed pretty much everything. We were really playing house and it was fabulous fun. Four large, abstract red, long-pile Scandinavian rugs were bought and stitched together, along with two layers of underlay to make a floor level listening room in the lounge. It was obviously an unusual request for the carpet shop who luckily had an expert carpet layer. They were happy to accommodate our odd ideas. The sound system was installed with low shelves for the growing vinyl record collection. I made red velvet curtains, with wide fringes for the double aspect windows. From somewhere we bought big red flags, Russian and Chinese, and a delivery of polystyrene balls arrived on a windy day. Deposited outside in an old grain store, one bag burst and gave us plastic snow down the drive on an autumn day. I sewed up the flags and filled them. Our listening room, inspired by John Wasserman's SF listening room, was complete.

Having enjoyed the water-bed at Sandy Bennett's, we had a wooden platform built in the bedroom with a big rectangular container on top. A bright pink carpet was fitted around it and over the platform and the water bed liner and mattress were installed, with a foam pad on top. The bed was made up with Peter Max linens in psychedelic designs, brought back from America. I made purple satin unlined curtains, which filled the room with purple pink light when the sun shone through in the morning. My sense of freedom from convention turned much of this lovely oak-beamed barn house into San Francisco circa 1967.

Somewhere we saw advertised a secondhand billiard table, which with oak panels fitted over the baize was transformed into a dining table. Alvin bought a pinball machine, which also lived in the dining-cum-games room. I painted the kitchen bright orange, and all the pipework in rainbow shades. With a small oak table and a pretty oak dresser, along with the Aga and butler's sink, the kitchen became quite *Wind In The Willows*. We brought a tall white fridge freezer and Perry gave me a collection of food pictures he'd cut out from magazines. I made my first collage, covering the white of the fridge with mouthwatering images of food.

With money still tight, we found the cheapest and, as it happened, the most colourful psychedelic striped carpeting for the three attic rooms. The middle one became Alvin's first real home studio. Most of the songs for *A Space In Time* and *Rock'n'Roll Music For The World* were written there.

Whilst he spent his evenings in the attic studio I was in my first actual sewing room below. It had been two rooms and when Sam came to visit he and I set about demolishing the lathe and plaster dividing wall. I loved working with Sam. He had all the building knowledge and skills while I was his labourer.

With a sofa-bed and its own bathroom, this was also a spare room, where Sam and Doris stayed on their many visits. It wasn't until the nineties that Doris told me they were kept awake the first hour by the washing machine in the scullery underneath that I turned on at bedtime. They never complained. In the first attic room Doris painted murals of Egyptian gods and hieroglyphs, her great passion. She had started to use oils and produced excellent paintings of Robin Hood Barn and the garden.

It was the garden that brought us the most joy and wildlife surprises. The roof space above the attic was populated by bats which circled as a flock at dusk, catching insects. We spent many early evenings watching them against the darkening sky. We learned that a small stone thrown up would imitate an insect and bring them swooping down nearer to us. In June, their breeding season, we discovered small baby bats clinging desperately to the leaded windows of the bedroom. I would open up and rescue the helpless little newborns and take them back up and pop them through the attic hatch, hoping they might survive.

One dark evening after supper and a good smoke, I had an impulse to go out into the back garden while Alvin was engrossed in TV. Some distance from any ambient lights, we had a really dark sky and the stars and constellations were clearly twinkling against velvety depths. A movement from the tall trees at the end of the long lawn and a large light-faced barn owl, its wings outstretched, swooped slowly down towards me. It flew closely over my head, and I turned to watch it complete its arc up over the outlined roof of the Barn and disappear. It had been a silent encounter, no flapping of wings, no calling out, just superb control of body and environment. My heart was lifted. Part of my being merged with the bird in flight as I stood in my garden.

Writing and recording sometimes until early sunrise, Alvin was astonished by the volume and variety of birdcalls when the dawn chorus started up. Early one morning, he fetched me from my sewing room where I was immersed in some project. We sat in the open dormer window listening to the divine cacophony, watching the stars' last twinkles as the sun came up. Getting high on the road and in the city had been fun but out here, enveloped by nature, was a whole other level of high. Were we ever happier?

No, we never were. It was our best home, the most freedom, so easy, creative, a Goldilocks house. It was just right.

Winter was a countryside surprise. One sunny winter morning we woke to find the lawns, all of the bare branches of the plants, shrubs and trees coated and outlined by hoarfrost, sparkling and twinkling in the sunshine. That was a magical sight you will rarely see in a city, but another arrived soon enough. Waking one morning we looked out to find a dozen cows, munching the grass and flowers. They looked surprisingly big in a garden. We called our part-time gardener, Jack Millard, and he called the farmer who came and nonchalantly walked them down the drive and into the lane.

Jack had been looking after the garden with Granny for many decades, so we kept him on for his two days a week. He was a lovely, gentle man, and when we were home I'd take him out cups of tea and talk with him about garden issues. Gentle as he was, he was a countryman and not very happy that city people like us didn't want him shooting the ever-growing population of rabbits, especially those that munched on the young chrysanthemums he had grown. "Jack, there are so many pretty flowers in the garden already," I said. He looked at me as if I was speaking Chinese.

When we came home in the dark and swung the car into the drive rabbits would be hopping, jumping and running from all sides. We had molehills on the lawn and Jack said he had to draw the line at moles. Next day Alvin and I had a smoke and went out to the offending mounds, standing one on each side. We talked to the moles and told them, quite seriously, that if they carried on burrowing under the lawns theirs would be a story with a sad ending. However, if they turned around and headed for the field just beyond the lawn, they could dig there to their heart's content. Yes, it was a 50/50 chance but they did turn around and head for the field. Jack had told us the way to kill moles was to open up a molehill and put broken glass in it. "They run along sniffing the earth, cut their noses and bleed to death," he said.

It was a culture clash but it never got out of hand. One day Jack looked downcast. He'd trodden on a wasp's nest and they'd flown up his trousers and stung him. "I had to jump behind the raspberry canes (for modesty) and take off my clothes to get rid of them," he said. From time to time Mrs Millard would bake Alvin butter shortbreads, which Jack would bring down in a cake tin. I'd return it to him at the end of the afternoon. "See you next week Jack," I said.

"Yes, you will, unless I fall down a wormhole," he'd reply in his soft Berkshire accent.

One afternoon, Alvin and I were relaxing in the garden and grey squirrels

– "tree rats" Jack called them – were playfully running and scooting their way across the lawn up into the trees. Unlike city squirrels, these were wary and wild then one came close, about 40 feet away from us. Alvin took some hazelnuts, and threw a couple at the squirrel who ate them with delight. He spent the next 20 minutes inching slowly across the lawn, getting closer and closer, throwing hazelnuts. Eventually the squirrel ate from his hand.

We christened this lovely, plump grey squirrel Cyril and he would come over to us whenever we were outside. If I sat on the lawn he would jump into my skirt lap. I would throw him off and he would jump back for more. When I stood up he would run up one leg, across my shoulders, and down the other side. Sitting on my hand to eat an apple, I was captivated by his dark, almond shaped eyes and the dexterousness of his little hands. These simple interactions were as far away from the city and the world of rock'n'roll as you could get, an antidote to the stress of touring. Alvin was relaxed, calm and peaceful, and his songwriting benefitted. He had asked Chris for six months off. In the event he had three months and their 1971 album, *A Space in Time* grew out of our idyllic life. It was certified as a platinum selling album in the USA.

We were listening to Erik Satie's *Gymnopedie*, Cat Stevens' *Tea For The Tillerman*, Donovan's *Gift From A Flower To A Garden*, Pink Floyd's *Meddle*, George Harrison's *All Things Must Pass* and Paul McCartney's *Ram*. They provided the random musical background to our home-edited "on-the-road" movies. We were both filming on tour, Super 8mm and 16mm. We had a projector and editing kits and would project movies into the listening room where a roll-down movie screen was hidden behind a beam. Sam double glazed an opening he cut between the listening room and the projection/editing room.

One sunny morning I sat outside, alone, drinking tea when a large peacock butterfly landed on a big flower on my gold flowered pants. There it sat motionless on my thigh, folded up its wings and swayed slightly in the breeze. Maybe it was there 5-10 minutes, I sat still and gave it my full attention until, having rested, it fluttered away. Pure magic, I was deeply happy and at peace.

Insects are more plentiful and bigger in the countryside. A large hairy spider in a small white sink was dispatched with hot water from the tap. One day, in the kitchen, an electrician was sizing up work we needed doing when I spotted another huge 2" hairy fella. "I'll run the hot tap onto it," I said.

The electrician looked at me with disdain, took a spider's leg gently between his fingers, opened the nearest window and popped it out. "You don't want to be killing spiders, they're good luck," he admonished. We felt duly ashamed of our city ways.

A few days later, up in the attic showing off our new lovely home to visitors, another big hairy spider sat staring at us from the wall. Armed with newly acquired spider knowledge, Alvin stepped forward and gently caught its leg, which fell off, as the 7-legged beast ran up his arm. Spider dancing and squeals ensued. Mature oak beams are a haven for spiders. I discovered that a washed-out honey jar and a postcard was the easiest and most efficient method of removal. There was one on every mantlepiece.

Badminton was our favourite garden activity. Shuttlecocks don't roll away like tennis balls. We rarely put up a net or made it competitive, except with Chris and Chelle at Lock's Barn where they also had a set. Alvin bought an archery set and a target which he used a few times, but it wasn't really his thing. I took photos of him posing, bow drawn like Robin Hood. Among the other photos I took of Alvin there is one of him fitting an extra pick-up to the Sunburst Gibson 335 he used at the Isle of Wight, and one of him sat on the small motorbike he bought for zooming around the country lanes.

Visitors were all dear friends and family. At Robin Hood Barn we no longer had random people – Chrysalis staff or friends of friends – dropping around at all hours. It wasn't that we didn't like people, it was more that we needed a counter balance to life on the road. Sundays when we were home, there was always a classic roast dinner to enjoy. I had mastered the art of slow cooking a leg of lamb overnight in the Aga's slow oven, whilst roasting potatoes in the hot one. Lamb or a chicken was our Sunday lunch, as it had been when I was little. Never fans of beef or pork, we didn't eat much meat. Vegetables were a staple in pasta sauces or for pizza toppings, with great English cheeses adding proteins. Overnight visitors would be given a full cooked English breakfast with sausages, bacon and eggs.

When the photographer John Fowlie stayed with his wife Eva, they brought their friend Henning and his lady. In the morning all of the milk had gone, as had all the eggs. "Henning only eats eggs and drinks milk," I was told. In those days, on Sundays there were no shops open. We survived.

Johnnie and Judy, Ruth and Jeff, Simon Stable and his wife Judy Dyble, Kris and Woody sometimes with Lucy, Perry who especially appreciated a Sunday roast, my brother Harold and his girlfriend Barbara. I remember we were playing topless badminton when Harold popped into the garden with a cheery "Hello". Sam and Doris visited regularly and once my parents Hector and Audrey came to visit. There are photos of us all posing in the garden with a yellow fairground painted horse I'd bought at the Furniture Cave, a treasure trove of the practical and the unusual on Kings Road in Chelsea. Sam and Doris look relaxed, my parents don't. Alvin and I look somewhat tense. It was a collision of worlds. My mother loved the house, but was still not sure about Alvin. After all, he now had way more power over me than she had ever managed.

Alvin was very happy at Robin Hood Barn. He became very prolific in his attic studio. We stayed up half the night working on our creative projects and slept until late morning. Every few hours I would make a cup of tea and take it up to his studio, and he would play me something he was working on. Then a while later Alvin would make us tea and come to see my project. Our creative household flowed easily.

Early evening after supper we might watch TV for an hour, especially *Star Trek*, which Alvin found completely absorbing. Captain Kirk was his role model, Spock's logical thinking was a big influence and Scotty coping with the unexpected mechanical engineering challenges also resonated. Meanwhile, back on earth, US President Richard Nixon had declared a war on drugs. To us it seemed ridiculous. People were far more relaxed, peaceful and loving as a result of marijuana. The gulf between the old, mostly male, white politicians dictating to the young rainbow tribe epitomised by the *Woodstock* movie was illogical and destructive. The old, deep grooves of war were best served by people consuming large amounts of consciousness numbing alcohol. Drunks are more often aggressive, and not self-reflective.

Nixon was the first politician who made my hackles rise, his face, his voice. He, Spiro Agnew and Henry Kissinger was a trio that embodied all the fearful, self-interested, repressive, narrow thinking that we hoped to transform. I would watch him on the news and try to engage Alvin in the politics of the day. Perhaps he was wise to realise that getting wound up by the news didn't help.

I felt he wrote 'I'd Love To Change The World' as a response to my attempts to engage him more with the politics of the day. The lyrics confused people. They're a paradox, with opening verses that rant a smorgasbord of media headlines, the so-called issues of the day. "Everywhere are freaks and hairies, dykes and fairies, tell me where is sanity?" The chorus seemed to echo how so many of us felt. "I'd love to change the world, but I don't know what to do, so I'll leave it up to you." It was a task that felt overwhelming.

George Harrison's 1971 Concert For Bangladesh awakened the world to both human suffering and our potential to organise outside of government. It enabled musicians to get together to generate large amounts of money and goodwill, to show that people joining together have the power to do good and raise consciousness about appalling issues. Cynicism and non-action, leaving the world to the politicians, is a dangerous abdication of our actual power to make a better world for future generations.

John Lennon was on the right lines when he said: "The establishment will irritate you - pull your beard, flick your face - to make you fight. Because once they've got you violent, they know how to handle you. The only thing they don't know how to handle is non-violence and humour."

chapter 33
Memorable Tour Stories, Rock Deaths

It was reassuring for us to know that when we locked up Robin Hood Barn and headed for the airport, Jack would keep an eye on things when he was working in the garden. Making sure it was left shipshape was my job and I have a vivid memory of Alvin sitting in the big black Daimler limo waiting for me to finish putting out the rubbish. One time when we got to Heathrow Chris Wright confessed to me that he'd spotted our two long blond-haired heads on his journey to the airport, and thought we were both "chicks". It was only when he had his driver pass us for a closer look that he realised it was Alvin and me.

There were so many tours, cities and venues that it's difficult to recall individual concerts unless an incident occurred that lodged into my memory. I didn't keep a diary, living as we were in the day, in the fullness of each moment. Being so totally present is a blissful feature of young lives.

Before the *Woodstock* premier in March, and our later move to Robin Hood Barn in August, the 1970 spring tour of the USA, which started in mid February, was the last pre *Woodstock* tour. The first half dozen gigs were in East Coast universities, and then the Fillmore East and Boston Tea Party, each for three nights, two shows a night. Heading west after two nights in Detroit at The Eastown Theatre, we flew to Vancouver, where a day off invited a ski trip into the mountains. Alvin and I did not ski and somewhere there is video footage of the rest of the band entertaining themselves on the snow slopes, which we both shot on our cameras.

From there it was San Francisco and four nights at the Fillmore West, which always felt like home. These shows were with Buddy Rich on the bill. Bill Graham disliked drum solos by rock drummers and booked Rich to show the SF hippies what a drum solo really was. It was unfortunate for Ric that he put TYA on the bill that night. Graham acknowledged that Ric wasn't the worst example, and I remember watching Buddy Rich and really enjoying his virtuosity and his show.

Ric's drum solos served another purpose for Alvin, Leo and Chick, giving them time for a mid-set cigarette. Personally, I enjoyed watching Ric's solos. The ability to do something different rhythmically, with all four limbs, seemed an extraordinary feat of athletic co-ordination. When I'd had a good smoke, it was compelling from the side of the stage.

From San Francisco we went to San Diego, where a day off brought about a psychedelic adventure, this time with mescaline, a rare and beautiful drug; hard to find and often lost amongst the more easily available LSD. Mescaline is a compound version of the peyote cactus, the substance used by native Americans in their spiritual ceremonies.

It was my personal favourite. I found it the most loving of the psychedelics and the least unpredictable. Mostly a colour enhancer, it produced less intense visual hallucinations, and if someone you found difficult arrived, you would feel love for them. It was also highly energising and on that day in San Diego we spent what seemed like hours trampolining across the two beds in the hotel room, bouncing from bed to bed.

We were staying on a very high floor, above the sightline of planes coming into land at the airport, with a multi-lane freeway below us. There was a balcony where we stood for some hours watching the sun go down. The sunset overwhelmed us and the dark night sky enveloped us. The flashing lights from the planes and the light streams from the freeway were a delight. Listening over and over to Procol Harum's *A Salty Dog*, we looked out over San Diego port, home to the US Navy. For the record, at no point were we tempted in any way to jump off of the balcony.

The rest of the band were indifferent to these treats and if they were unhappy that Alvin was indulging no one mentioned it. Maybe they didn't know. At his core Alvin was a professional musician. Our tripping took place on days off, never on a day when there was a gig.

Via two auditoriums, in LA and Seattle, we headed east for a gig at Ludlow Garage, Cincinnati, memorable for its large communal dressing room. The support that night was a new band called Alice Cooper. Although we were used to seeing musicians in all manner of exotic clothes, these guys had taken it to the next level with heavily sequined frocks and heavily applied make-up. The guitarist had a kind of cape sleeve that he was checking out in the dressing room mirror, slowly raising and lowering his left arm to watch the impact below the guitar neck.

Ten Years After were quite subdued watching this carnival and seemed almost conservative in comparison. As the seamstress with the band I was fascinated. Little did we realise we were watching the future of one strand of rock'n'roll emerging from its pupae into fully fledged butterflies. Alice was a good opening act which warmed up the bemused audience, but their theatrics in no way diminished the effect of Alvin's guitar wizardry on the Ludlow Garage crowd. The effects of *Woodstock*, whose premiere we would see in New York at the end of this tour, were yet to impact the shows.

Our psychedelic adventures had brought us closer. He still loved to have a smoke, get on stage, close his eyes and travel musically to the edges of his consciousness. Big Red, the cherry Gibson 335, was so comfortable, like an extension of his body, and his mastery of it so complete that he could bypass the limits of his own critical thinking.

Decades later in a 1988 *Guitar Speak*, online interview he said: "I like the freedom to feel your own way, don't play exact guitar, never read music. I play from the hip, like a gunslinger. I'm a jammer, often play something good, and never play it again, I don't remember what it was. I play by instinct and from adrenaline.

"Sometimes I think I'm firing a machine gun, when I'm playing guitar. I think in more dramatic visuals like that. I don't really think about the guitar at all, it's just there, direct from the brain to the amplifier.

"I sometimes get a little out of control, it's like you get your car on a tight corner, not too sure if you're gonna come out of it. Just go for it, that's the excitement to me, the excitement of playing, go for it."

Smoking helped Alvin to focus and be calmer on stage. The top-quality American grass was abundant. Perhaps it levelled out his adrenaline. The gigs needed to be well organised on every level, so Alvin would be relaxed. Only then could he surrender to the moment and produce unexpected magic. If the band have an act, a show that night after night is a slick repetition of their hit records, that is very different. Not better, not worse, just different. I've heard people say, "They sounded just like their records," as praise. Well these sixties bands were aiming for something more typical of the jazz era, improvisation, surprise that created a connection between themselves and the audience.

Cricklewood Green, their fifth album, was released in April to great reviews and amusement over the title. It went to 14 in the *Billboard* 100 chart and four in the UK where it stayed for 27 weeks. It was the pressure from Deram that resulted in two versions of 'Love Like A Man' released as a single, the A side a three-minute pop edit at 45rpm with the B side the seven-and-a-half-minute album track that played at 33rpm. Alvin was fighting to have their extended tracks, solos and all, put out, both to challenge the whole notion of the three-minute single and to limit mimed pop TV appearances. Integrity and authenticity really did matter to him. He knew his audience and had no interest in becoming a pop phenomenon. He was 25 years old, not 15 and still fantasising about being Elvis.

This was probably frustrating for Leo, Ric and Chick, the other members of TYA, though I'm sure they knew by now that Alvin had a better instinct for the direction of the band. His ear for the music and culture of the day, and his songwriting, were garnering more praise with each album. Now none of the others produced any material of their own. Alvin didn't have time to help them become songwriters. There was little enough time for his own writing.

A sell-out tour of England and Scotland, again in institutional civic settings of town and city halls, at best designed for classical music, kicked off at London's Lyceum, by far the most atmospheric and funky venue of the tour. In *New Musical Express*, Richard Green wrote: "Alvin still dominates the stage and his wizardry with the guitar becomes more interesting with every appearance. He is unquestionably one of the fastest guitarists around but this does not mean, as is the case with many others, that skill is sacrificed for speed. His closeness with the other members of the group, has if anything become even tighter than before."

After a vivid description of the highlights of the show and the audience's enthusiasm, he concluded: "A deserved triumph for Ten Years After who have come a step nearer to 'the world's most exciting group' tag."

We undertook the Scottish part of the tour by bus, stayed in hotels and stopped one rainy day on the shores of Loch Lomond where we skimmed flat stones that bounced on the surface through the raindrops. In the UK, hashish was far more easily available than marijuana but I think Alvin had come to prefer marijuana for playing on stage. Luckily, we still had a good quantity of Cricklewood Green. How lovely to travel your homeland promoting an album obscurely named after the weed you were smoking.

After closing the tour at Edinburgh's Usher Hall on May 26, we headed back to London for a couple of weeks of Alvin being interviewed about *Cricklewood Green* and *Woodstock*, battling to avoid *Top Of The Pops* but accepting BBC radio sessions. At least on John Peel shows they could play live and transmit some of the stage magic through the radio.

On June 12 we set off back to New York for the next long tour of rock'n'roll land. This was a pivotal summer tour we crossed the Atlantic in a huge new 747, a jumbo jets, more like a small cinema with rows and rows of seats, three either side and four across the middle, seating up to 400+ passengers. For internal flights in the USA we now travelled first class, but the transatlantic flights were seldom very full. On night flights back to the UK, we could even find seats on which to stretch out, lie down and sleep.

My most embarrassing memory of my entire time travelling with TYA occurred just before a full transatlantic flight when we were separated in the aisle seats of different rows. Waiting for take-off I leafed through the inflight magazine and came across an article about Alvin and TYA. Being naturally gregarious, I chatted with the friendly, middle-aged American lady sat next to me.

"Are you a student?" she asked.

"No," I replied.

"Why are you going to America?"

It seemed harmless to tell her that my boyfriend was in a rock band and we were headed for the USA to tour for three months. She didn't seem especially interested. Then the devil got hold of me.

"There is an article about them," I said, opening the inflight magazine.

She looked at the article, looked at Alvin and Leo across the aisle, un-buckled her seat belt (we were still on the ground) and jumped to her feet. "Hey!" she shouted. A few hundred heads turned around. "We have a pop music group on the plane and they have an article in the magazine." She was certainly excited by this point "Here they are!" She pointed to Alvin and Leo. "Perhaps they will give us some autographs."

It turned out that she was in charge of a group of several hundred American tourists heading back home to the US of A after a trip to London. Ahead of us was seven hours in the company of middle-aged lovelies who dutifully filed down the aisle with their inflight magazines, had little chats with Ric, Chick, Leo and Alvin, and collected their autographs along the way.

Even now, about 50 years later, I still cringe, and suffer physical discomfort recalling this little tale of misjudgment. Alvin looked at me in disbelief from across the aisle, raised his eyebrows and, with a sanguine shrug, accepted his fate. Leo was well pissed off. Ric and Chick put on a good act of being delighted to talk to all these folk and explain the ins and outs of touring America. I don't remember what was said to me directly when we disembarked. My mind is kind and memory selective. It was the longest, most uncomfortable seven-hour flight of my life. It seemed endless. I stayed very quiet, hoping to become invisible.

Starting on the East Coast, the second gig was at Crosley Field, Cincinnati, Summer Pop Festival, a glorious hot sunny day. TYA played early, at 12.40pm. We had flown to the local airport in a small plane, disembarked on the tarmac and walked to the airport building. All around us were huge swept-up piles of large insects, periodical cicadas, of the Great Eastern Brood, who emerge every 17 years. The sight was horrifying, yet none of the locals seemed disturbed.

As the band tuned up and got ready to go on, Ruthann and I walked around Crosley Field among the early crowd. I noticed there were still dozens of cicadas in the sky around us, and I found it difficult to be around these bugs. Ruthann shrugged, seemingly unaffected by them. Close to us, maybe 20 feet in the air above us, one hovered and seemed to be looking at me. I knew it would swoop. As it did I moved the unaware Ruthann between myself and the flying attacker. It landed on her right shoulder and I nearly passed out as she casually brushed it off.

We headed for the stage, stood to the side behind them. A cicada landed on Alvin's back on his shirt and stayed there for most of the set, occasionally creeping around. It was the only time I was really pleased to leave a show.

Back to Boston for Don Law's Tea Party and Bill Graham's Fillmore East. This may have been the Fillmore East visit when Ruthann and I became snake handlers. A hippie guy turned up back stage with a small sack, out of which he retrieved two three to four-foot long snakes, a reticulated python and a boa, both nonvenomous constrictors and too small to be dangerous. He offered them to us. Ruthann and I wore them draped around our necks on the side of the stage. They extended their heads and gently swayed to Ten Years After's rock'n'roll.

After the show in Boston we went to a party in an apartment, which was unusual. The place was pretty full, especially the bedroom, where a crowd had gathered. In the top of the wardrobe was some kind of a small wild cat that kept hissing at the crowd of onlookers. It didn't seem very cool to be keeping this wild creature as entertainment.

Woodstock had already impacted on the crowds and there were shouts for 'I'm Going Home' as soon as the band set foot on stage. The Aragon Ballroom in Chicago on this tour was memorable as BB King was one of the support acts. It seemed extraordinary that in a couple of years TYA were headlining above such blues luminaries. Alvin and I watched some of BB King's set. He was a focused and full-on performer.

It was a gift to watch him.

The next morning, we took a flight to Toronto for the Transcontinental Pop Festival. On the ride to the airport we finished off all the grass we had. Mostly we were high when we went through customs. We knew we were never ever carrying anything because we'd smoked it. It was fun to meet authority with a happy smile. Lining up with our suitcases we were about four people back from Chick in one of the lines. I know Alvin wasn't watching Chick or he would have spotted the customs man ask him to hand over his wallet. I watched in disbelief as the customs man casually opened Chick's wallet and pulled out a small one skin joint. It wasn't hidden. It was sitting in the money compartment but he went for it as if he knew it was there all along.

To this day I wonder how this customs officer knew to ask Chick for his wallet. It was bizarre. Chick was not a regular dope smoker. It turned out that at a party the previous night in Chicago someone had offered Chick a one skin grass joint. Rather than light it up, he had taken out his wallet and put it in there. Because he was not a smoker he had forgotten all about it until the customs man asked him for his wallet.

The moment I saw the guy take the joint out of Chick's wallet, I turned to Alvin. "Let's try another line," I said calmly. "This one is very slow." Alvin didn't resist. We left the line and joined one further to the right. We quickly got through and casually walked past Chick, who was watching the guy go through his luggage. When we were out of the customs hall, I asked Alvin if he'd seen what was happening with Chick.

"No, what was happening?"

"He just got busted," I replied. His expression was more disbelief than shock.

Fortunately for TYA, the gig was the next day, which was time enough for Chris Wright to bail Chick out. It was some time before the whole episode was resolved. The priority was to make sure that Chick wound up without a conviction that would have limited his eligibility for a visa to work in the USA. It was a horrible irony that Chick, who was not a regular smoker, was the only member of TYA to get busted. He'd also been busted on their first US tour for jaywalking in Los Angeles. All he did was cross a road in the middle of a block, as we do in the UK, but he got a ticket.

The Trans Continental Pop Festival involved a train crossing Canada, with bands on board, stopping to play gigs in big venues along the way. The list of performers was staggering, among them The Band, Janis Joplin, Traffic, Grateful Dead, Delaney & Bonnie, Buddy Guy, Mountain. It visited

Montreal, Toronto, Winnipeg and Calgary. In Toronto on June 27 and 28 it stopped off at the Canadian National Expo Grandstand but TYA only played on the evening of the 28th.

In the afternoon Alvin and I watched Delaney & Bonnie, soon to go on tour Leon Russell and Joe Cocker, billed as Mad Dogs & Englishmen. It was a huge success for Joe on the back of his *Woodstock* performance. He had told us how much he disliked having his band as backing vocalists. The Mad Dogs Tour was a gift to him with great back-up singers.

Alvin and TYA played a great set. The Canadian audience enjoyed themselves and were attentive, without the frenetic energy now manifesting in the big US festivals. Later Alvin and I stood on the back of the stage and watched Traffic. We had enjoyed their music since *Mr Fantasy* and in Toronto they were only a three-piece, with Chris Wood on flute and saxophone, Jim Capaldi's tight drums, and Steve Winwood who was spellbinding in the darkness, playing Hammond organ lead parts, rhythm and the bass lines on the pedals, whilst singing the lead vocals. His focus and calm virtuosity were extraordinary.

Closing the show that night was Janis Joplin. I had never met her and was unaware that she had previously come on to Alvin. I remember the two of us standing talking on the back of the stage behind some form of backdrop that hid us from the audience out front. The roadies were getting the stage ready for her when, suddenly, there she was in all her glorious colours, velvets and sequins. She spotted Alvin and came bounding over, standing squarely in front of him. She smiled, laughed her raspy laugh and made small talk about touring and music for five minutes. Electric sparks flew from her.

Alvin had her total attention. She glanced but never spoke to me, until she said "bye" to us both, laughed and left. For five minutes she paced in front of us like a prize fighter, stomping, yelling and singing out, warming up her voice and her body. Then she was gone out front into the audience's embrace. We watched through the side opening for a few numbers, then Andy came to fetch us to go back to the hotel. I'd witnessed a true legend for an unforgettable 10 minutes.

Janis was so vibrantly alive that night, so joyful. How was it possible that less than four months later, October 4, she would die from a heroin overdose? Hers was the second in a sad toll of deaths that affected us deeply. Jimi Hendrix died on September 18 and the following summer Jim Morrison died in Paris, on the second anniversary of Brian Jones' death, supposedly by drowning on July 3, 1969. Brian, Jimi, Janis and Jim were all 27 years of age.

On December 19, 1971, Alvin would enter his 27th year and I was determined he stay away from heavy drugs. Luckily, he disliked alcohol or pharmaceuticals of any kind. He still preferred to smoke marijuana or hashish and sometimes take a psychedelic, none of which are toxic. I understood that you cannot endlessly travel and tour, standing in the spotlight, giving your best, night after night, without some form of after-show relaxation to allow you to sleep and be ready for the next show.

Bill Graham was asked by the writer John Glatt if success had spoiled rock music.

"No," he replied. "It's the inability to cope with success that's spoiled rock, it was the inability to cope with success that killed Janis Joplin and killed Jimi Hendrix, it wasn't the drugs. If you spoke with them you would see they just didn't know how to handle the adulation that was heaped on them by the music they created. Neither you nor I would ever know what it's like to walk on a stage and have a half a million people tell you that you are a queen, that you are a goddess and everything you do is just fine."

chapter 34
Woodstock Effect, USA, Isle of Wight

Throughout the summer of 1970 promoters all around the USA were putting on festivals, encouraged no doubt by Woodstock to believe that either the counterculture or their bank balances would grow. Some were opportunists and some had experience. Alvin and TYA turned up, went on stage, delivered the best music they had in them that night to increasingly demanding audiences. It was becoming apparent that people wanted their own magical Woodstock through those who had played there. TYA now carried that magic in their DNA.

Woodstock would remain the pinnacle of festivals because the states and towns of America had seen what took place there and local laws were being passed to limit the chances of it ever happening again. The hippies were now viewed as a political threat to straight America, not merely colourful entertainment on the TV news.

Some festivals had problems with fans not wanting to pay because they felt music should be free. I guess that also came from *Woodstock*, where making it a free festival was depicted as a gloriously altruistic moment. Realistically, however, musicians couldn't tour the USA for three months at a time with the multitude of costs involved yet play everywhere for free. It was all very well joining the anti-war and ecology movements, but we had to be practical.

On July 17, TYA headlined The Spectrum in Philadelphia, a vast open circular arena with the stage to one side, in front of 18,000 fans, one of their biggest audiences. When Alvin walked to the front of the stage, screams from women could clearly be heard above the general applause that always greeted the band. I saw a look of disbelief on Alvin's face as he scanned the audience. Never before had women screamed and he seemed to freeze at the sound. The show was great, the women calmed down and got into the music but this level of hysteria was far from relaxing.

On July 19, in the Baltimore Civic Centre, the excitement was too much for a big black security official. Alvin and the audience were having a great time together. He was flying, in the middle of a guitar solo in about the third number, when the official marched onstage towards Alvin's microphone and told the crowd to sit down. Alvin looked up, stopped playing, unplugged his guitar and strode off stage, followed by the rest of TYA.

I was standing on the side of the stage with Chelle as this big guy, whose arm was in a plaster cast, paced slowly past us, circling the now silent, empty stage. The crowd of 13,000 was not silent. Instead of calming down, they seemed intent on starting a riot. As he walked past us again, I shouted at him. It wasn't a compliment. He stopped, looked calmly at me, raised his arm and yelled, "I broke this arm on one women, and I'd be happy to break the other one on you."

Considerably out of my depth, and grateful to have Chelle by my side, I said nothing as he returned to his pacing. Out of his sight, I slipped backstage and headed to the dressing room. Alvin was scowling but very pleased to see me with a first-hand report. I told him about the security guard and suggested that the only way to stop a riot was to have him removed from the building and resume the concert. I didn't mention his threat to floor me. It was unlikely to have helped get Alvin back on stage, which was what we all wanted. He understood my advice and Chris Wright was sent to negotiate the trouble maker's removal from the building.

Maybe 10-15 minutes passed in the silent dressing room. There was nothing to say. Chris reappeared with assurances that the guy had been removed, not only from the stage but also from the building. Once he left the stage the audience had calmed down and it was all clear to go back on. We all headed back to the stage, and the show continued to its usual fine rock'n'roll conclusion. The following year at the same venue, I spotted the same security guy who, being very tall and black, stood out clearly near the front of the crowd. Before they went on stage he was removed. We couldn't take the chance that he was any smarter at dealing with rock'n'roll energy.

On July 21, they played one of the most beautiful venues, the Red Rocks amphitheater built into a mountainside near Denver, Colorado, at 6,400 feet above sea level. It is a stunning venue, possibly the most beautiful in the world. Unfortunately for TYA there was a very strong wind and their

Marshall stacks crept across the stage and had to be anchored down with ropes. It didn't stop Alvin from having a great show. He was testing the idea that if you have a smoke at a higher altitude, you will get even higher. It was hard work for Andy and John and the road crew. The audience of 10,000 was receptive and never knew about the onstage problem.

We stayed in Denver, the Mile High city. Dee Anthony was with us and he threw an after-show gathering in the penthouse suite in the hotel where we were staying. I guess Dee was also getting over-excited about the band's success. Alvin and I stayed in the suite and enjoyed the privacy of the balcony in the sunshine the next morning. Mile high living indeed.

On July 22 we were at the Los Angeles Forum, another 17,500-seat arena, but it was not a cool gig. A semi-contained riot was instigated by the security, as it invariably was. In front of the rectangular stage, set up in the centre at one side, was a line of security cops with nightsticks standing side by side. Many appeared to be wearing earplugs; one had put a bullet in each ear. Their aim was to keep the fans away from the band.

Ruthann and I had a good view of all that was happening from the left side, at ground level. On either side of the stage was an almost continual trail of cops carrying out fans whose only crime was to stand up and dance. Directly in front of Alvin, on the front row, maybe 15-20 feet from the stage a young female fan was being clubbed by several cops for not staying seated. She too was carried out. It was discovered she was having an epileptic fit.

This particular gig was a huge turning point for Alvin. He was at the front of the stage and could see everything that was taking place. Somehow, he got through the show, knowing that stopping would surely cause a riot. Afterwards we talked about what had happened. He felt personally responsible that his music and performance was the cause of people being hurt. It wasn't something he had ever pictured and he was very upset and overwhelmed by the gig that night. This was a far cry from the intimacy and crowd connections he had so enjoyed at The Marquee and the Fillmores.

Alvin spoke about the LA Forum gig to Gavin Petrie, the editor of *Disc & Music Echo*: "Los Angeles I didn't like. There's a civil war between young people and the police there. The police are so heavy handed. They don't believe in putting up with anything. I don't know why they have a line of policemen at the front of concerts. If the police freak out and start clubbing people, that's when the trouble starts."

If scenes like this had been repeated every night, I think Alvin would have quit much earlier than he did. The next four nights were in Texas, in the Convention Centres and Coliseums of Fort Worth, Dallas, Houston and San Antonio. I don't recall any major incidents. Following this, three nights at Bill Graham's blessed Fillmore West restored a balance and a better connection with the crowd and the music.

On August 7, we were at The Goose Lake Festival in Jackson, Michigan. There is footage online of Ten Years After's encore of 'Sweet Little Sixteen', preceded by Alvin's typical scream, which he did while breathing in rather than out. He'd practiced and perfected this technique at home.

It was a very hot night and all the band were wet through with sweat. Part way through the encore's first verse, Alvin looks across to Leo as if to say, come on man let's go, and casts a similar glance back to Ric. You can tell they are lagging. Anger is driving Alvin throughout the song and the solo, and at the end he drops his guitar, Big Red, onto the stage, then gives it a hefty clog-footed kick before heading to the back of the stage. Ever the professional, he turns back to the audience, throws his guitar pic into the crowd and takes a bow before turning to leave. The road crew rescue the forlorn guitar which is squealing with feedback.

Was this the night when he walked into the dressing room and, in one swift movement, cleared all the drinks and titbits from the tables at the side of the dressing room? It was a night when his bottled-up anger had found its outlet. Alvin was not an angry or violent man. If he had been a drinker rather than a stoner, maybe it would have been another story. I was never ever frightened of his occasional outbursts. Instinctively I would stay quiet and just be there for him. It was understandable that he would flip out from time to time. This man I loved so much needed a calm companion, a safe space. That was my job.

Alvin would never rant and rave. He might say something to one of the band if he felt there'd been a weak performance and might even have shouted in exasperation, but when it was done he'd let it go. He was just as hard on himself, able to admit his own onstage failings. This probably impacted him more and he found that harder to just let go. Early on I remember discussing with him that live music by its very nature was ephemeral. Wrong notes disappeared as soon as they were played, and were followed by the right ones that wiped out their memory in the audience. It didn't stop him from always striving for better and cleaner playing, though never just faster.

Two nights at the Capital Theatre, Portchester in New York, ended this tour on August 11. Then it was back home to the UK after breaking new American territories, as the record companies would say. I likened it to the wild west energy, where a few amateur promoters and inexperienced security men forced the band into tight corners. The record companies and the "can do" attitude led to high and low experiences for the band and their support team. We were still a tight group, the only partners travelling with the band were Ruthann and myself. Chick and Leo were still alone, but that was about to change.

Back in the UK, on Saturday August 29, we set of for the Isle of Wight, just off of the south coast. We flew out in a four-seater plane with Chick and the pilot, taking off from an actual field in the south of England. Part way out the pilot let Chick fly the plane by watching the instruments for a short while. After landing in another field, we transferred to a bubble helicopter to fly over the immense crowd at East Afton Farm, Freshwater.

What an amazing sight to fly over. The official estimate is 600,000-700,000. Alvin and I had flown into Woodstock separately in big, twin-bladed US army Chinooks with no windows, just an open side door through which we saw the crowd over the hillside. A year later we were together, with Chick, in this little bubble chopper, seeing another huge crowd laid out in front and below us. We all marvelled at the sight, the excitement in the bubble was palpable. Fate was waiting for Chick on the island that night. We had no idea.

It was a five-day event held one year after Woodstock, which the promoters hoped to rival and eclipse, a ridiculous idea since sixties culture was not about competition. However, money was now being made, serious money, and that was distorting everything. The line-up was spectacular, and included The Who, The Doors and Jimi Hendrix, who would die 18 days later. Joni Mitchell performed 'Woodstock', the song she had written in a New York hotel while that festival was in progress. Her management had stopped her from going due to commitments in NY the next day, though no doubt she watched it on the TV news where it was the top feature for the whole weekend.

My memory and impression of the IOW was of a great gig for Ten Years After, who appeared as sunset turned to night, a perfect time. Where Woodstock had been a large outdoor stage, with wet bare wood ravaged by the storm for their set, this stage was relatively small and well organised, as good as it gets for a festival. After two weeks with no gigs, the band was fresh, connected and ready to deliver a strong, tight set. Alvin was relaxed and radiant. 'I Can't Keep From Crying Sometimes', their 20-minute epic, was superb. Alvin always said he would have preferred this song to have been in the *Woodstock* movie as it was a better representation of the band at that time. Sadly, it hadn't been filmed at Woodstock.

However, 'Crying' did appear on a 1971 Columbia triple album release titled *The First Great Rock Festivals of the Seventies: Isle of Wight /Atlanta Pop Festival*. The Isle of Wight tracks, including the whole unedited live version of 'Crying' is in my opinion the best recorded version that I have heard from the plethora of renderings available. This is Alvin and TYA at their pinnacle.

Edited footage of the 1970 Isle of Wight Festival can be seen in *Message to Love* directed by Murray Lerner, which includes five minutes of 'Crying', with Alvin in the spotlight, clear, focused and professional as ever. There are shots of roadie John Hembrow tucked between the backline and the drums, at one point seen nodding his head to the music. John told me recently that 'Crying' was his favourite Ten Years after track. "It was why I joined the band," he said.

We didn't linger after Ten Years After's set. We were keen to get back to Robin Hood Barn, our new home. Chick, Ric and Ruthann, Leo, Chris Wright and Chelle stayed on at a small country house that had been provided for them. The owner, Mrs Fieyve-Gould, had two unmarried daughters and one, Suzanne, would become Chick's wife. Alvin and I missed his departure from rock'n'roll bachelorhood, but one further adventure was in store for us that night.

We flew back with Andy in the four-seater in the dark towards the field we had left from earlier that day. Just ahead of us a similar plane landed, its vision impaired by the summer fog from the hot day. We saw it overshoot the field and wind up in a hedge. Luckily, no-one was hurt. We were already in the descent approach but our pilot decided not to risk the landing and pulled back up into the night sky. He re-arranged our flight path, cleared us to land on the main runway at Gatwick airport. We touched down like a small insect among the jumbo jets, grateful not to have ended up in a hedge.

Five days later we flew to Berlin along the special air corridor allotted to this divided city, changing altitude to conform with regulations. In Berlin we stayed at the Kempinski Hotel, once a famous haunt of the SS officers and their ladies, not necessarily their wives. Crossing the lobby in the afternoon on our way to the gig, I was fascinated by the many glamourous older ladies in their powder and paint, sat taking tea. I wondered what their stories were.

The gig in Berlin was at the Deutschlandhalle, an arena so vast that half of it had been curtained off for the stage to be set up. Jimi Hendrix headlined, following Alvin and TYA. We watched some of his show. He seemed lost without The Experience, unsure of his musical direction, stranded between his past and a future with the Band of Gypsies. Less than two weeks later he would leave us. Alvin was never in any doubt that Jimi Hendrix was the master guitarist of the hippie era.

Alvin and Chris jamming!
Grosvenor Crescent Mews 1969

Me and Krissie,
Sloane Street 1969

Alvin and me test
the self-timer at
Woody and Krissie's
Lower Sloane Street
flat, with painting of
Sadie The Parrot

Me and Krissie sit on the chopped off table, Grosvenor Crescent Mews 1969

The blackboard drawings, Grosvenor Crescent Mews 1969

Robin Hood Barn, rear

Me and Woody, Sloane Street 1969

Alvin relaxing, Grosvenor
Crescent Mews 1969

Chelle, Albert Hall 1970

Robin Hood Barn,
Chelle, Chris, Alvin,
me, Mrs Earl and
Granny Earl 1970

© Hopper archive

Me, Albert Hall 1970

Shawls and our travelling record deck, Boston hotel 1970

Me and Alvin in the lobby at Loew's Midtown in New York, tripping 1970

Alvin and Chris Wright and, below,
Johnnie and Judy Clifton, at the
L'Artiste Assoiffe restaurant in
London's Notting Hill 1970

Alvin with the key to the front door at
Robin Hood Barn September 1970

Garden at Robin Hood Barn, mum, dad, Doris,
Alvin and me 1971

Inspired by his surroundings, Alvin shoots his bow and arrow at
Robin Hood Barn 1971

From left to right, Leo, Alvin, me, Ruthann, Ric, Jack Cunningham,
John Hembrow, Andy Jaworski, Chick, Chris Wright, Chelle,
Elvis at Las Vegas 1971

Andy Jaworski and me on the road
at the airport 1971

Mylon and Summer,
Atlanta GA 1971

Me as wardrobe mistress at
another hotel on the road 1971

At the Coliseum, Rome, Francesco, Chelle, Suzanne, Chick and me 1971

Me, Chick and Suzanne USA 1971

Me with Leo and Chick 1971

Cyril the squirrel at
Robin Hood Barn 1971

Me in Rome posing 1971

Alvin's 'Space In Time' studio at Robin Hood Barn 1972

Alvin tries out his new fish-eye lens at Robin Hood Barn after our return from Japan the night before. Me checking the mail watched by Perry Press who will show them Hook End the following day May 9, 1972

Outside St Martin-in-the-Fields church in Trafalgar Square before Chris and Chelle's wedding. Johnnie and Judy Clifton, Andy Jaworski and Dorothy, me and Alvin
March 15, 1972

Judy Dyble, me, Simon Stable,
Lucy Daniels and Krissie at
Robin Hood Barn 1972

Woody, me and Krissie,
Hook End pool, winter 1972

Me on the balcony of a Bourbon Street hotel in New Orleans 1972

Me, Sally, Ruthann, backstage somewhere USA 1972

Me in the company of groupies in an American dressing room 1972

Me and Alvin, Jamaica 1972

Alvin's studio at the Glass House on our Jamaican holiday 1972

Alvin's art shot of himself and me at a New York chandelier store 1972

From left to right Sally, me,
Chelle, Ric, Ruthann, Andy and
Supertramp Europe 1972

Me and the polar bear Anchorage,
AL. en route from Japan 1972

Me and Mylon, Jamaica 1972

Joe, Hook End 1973

Mylon with big spliff, Jamaica 1972

Loopy, Hook End 1973

Me and Saracen, Marlow 1973

Me and Jim, Wookey Hole 1973

Jim at Wells
Cathedral
1973

Jim and me, Rainbow Rooms 1973

Me at Hook End window 1973

Lee Popa (record producer) took the photo and sent it to me.
He was at Hook End the day Alvin died and was the last producer to close
down the studio there that day. It has not re-opened since.

In Spain, last photo of me with Alvin and Evi 2006

chapter 35
The Garden, NY, Fame Beckons, Elvis In Vegas

The next US tour, in November, kicked off in New York at Madison Square Garden. At JFK we were met on the tarmac by limos and a police motorcade that took us straight into the city without passport control and immigration. We stayed at The Pierre Hotel on Central Park. A motorcade to Loew's Midtown on Eighth Avenue would have been very over the top. Alvin would never use a restaurant where they insisted on him wearing a tie, preferring a more relaxed coffee shop to eat. There was no coffee shop in The Pierre, so we ordered room service, which arrived with several staff, on a trolley that became a table, with a linen tablecloth and silver service. I had fresh salmon, still a favourite of mine. Alvin had a fillet steak. It was probably the best meal in all the hotels and cities where we stayed.

All of this high living, the motorcade, the hotel and our now first-class internal flights, had been organised by New York publicist Connie De Nave whom Dee Anthony had taken on for Ten Years After. They wanted to capitalise on the success of *Woodstock*. I believe Alvin was even offered film parts and to appear in an advert for toothpaste. A photo session was arranged for Alvin with a young Richard Avedon. After taking some classic portraits of Alvin, Avedon called me over and took a wonderful double portrait of us, with me in "The Hat". We were sent a copy but sadly it has vanished.

Connie De Nave held a dinner for Alvin and me, maybe at her home. There was half a dozen of us around the table, including Dee and his wife

Val. The conversation turned to a proposal to market Alvin and me with an article in *Cosmopolitan*, using the photos by Richard Avedon, as a glamorous rock'n'roll couple. The photos were gorgeous, but this was a crossroads. It had nothing to do with Alvin's music. We discussed it at the table, in front of everyone, and both of us felt it was not the right direction for either of our lives. Connie was obviously disappointed. I suspect she thought that I was meddling, holding Alvin back from great celebrity opportunities. I knew him far better than any of these people and that what they were asking was far outside his comfort zone, let alone mine.

Near the end of his life, in an email about this book, Alvin wrote that he was concerned for his privacy, that I might let people know too much about where he was living and his private life, and that fans might try to find him. "I nearly became famous once," he wrote. "I don't want that to happen again."

When we stayed in New York the room phone would ring early. I would answer it as I always did. It would be Connie. "Hi, it's Connie, is my baby there," she'd say, or, maybe, "Is my sweetheart there?"

Alvin's eyes would roll but he knew she couldn't be avoided. She would tell him about interviews she'd lined up. One day she took me to one side and said, "Wherever Alvin is, your grey eyes are always watching him?"

I was surprised that she would say that, or that it would be a problem. "I love Alvin that's why I'm here," I told her. "Of course, I watch him, everyone else watches him too."

Connie operated on a New York level that was far beyond my relatively innocent perception of the world. It made me very uncomfortable.

Madison Square Garden has a capacity of 20,000 and Ten Years After sold it out. Although it was a vast stadium, the acoustics were good and it was a tremendous gig for them. Many fans there had been to their Fillmore East shows over the previous two years and this was the nearest to a home crowd in a stadium they ever played. I was out front, half way back, dancing among the standing crowd on the sprung floor that night. When they got to the encores, TYA quite literally rocked The Garden. The floor moved up and down as fans jumped in unison. When I stood still I moved up and down with the bounce of the floor. I had just had my 24th birthday and Alvin's 26th was a few weeks away. Only seven years had passed since we first met on a winter's night, on the steps of Nottingham's Rainbow Rooms.

Unknown to us Clive Davis, head of Columbia Records, was on a talent raid at The Garden that night. He had heard that TYA were unhappy at London Records, and wrote about Alvin and TYA in his autobiography

Clive – Inside the Record Business.

"Alvin Lee, lead guitarist, had become a major star overnight following his appearance at Woodstock (and in the subsequent documentary film). As a performer he had the ability to excite an audience quite apart from the quality of his music. I personally liked his musicianship, though the critics gave him mixed reviews; even so it didn't matter. He had a stage presence that suggested raw sexual energy, and he could whip an audience almost into a frenzy."

"Ten Years After had a very successful show that night. It was clear they had a star's aura about them onstage and Alvin, in particular, brought the crowd to its feet several times."

I think Clive must had slipped out before the bouncing floor encores, but he had seen enough to be convinced to offer a million dollars to sign the band. Though that figure was one I never heard until I read it in his book, four decades later. He went on to write:

"Ironically for all the artists mentioned in this chapter, there were only a few 'million dollar' deals made. Ten Years After, Neil Diamond and Pink Floyd. These three deals will stand the test of time."

The first album Columbia released, *A Space In Time*, became a certified platinum record and stayed in the charts for six months. We went to Clive Davis' office in the Black Rock, the skyscraper that housed Columbia Records, to sign the contract. We went up in the lift and into a large reception room, where Clive shook hands and greeted everyone. He introduced us to all the other Columbia executives in the room and later took us on a tour of their offices. I was impressed by his party-trick ability to remember all our names, as well as the names of the staff in these vast offices.

TYA gigs now took on a life of their own, with actual riots caused mostly by overenthusiastic security or fans. In vain attempts to get them to sit down, those at the back of the vast arenas pelted fans at the front who stood up. Alvin and Ten Years After never encouraged people to stand up, it was their music that got people out of their seats. Alvin was never an entertainer who encouraged fans to dance or sing-a-long. He kept his focus on his music.

After *Woodstock,* it seemed many who went to see TYA for the first time hoped they might experience an astonishing cultural event, a sort of secondhand Woodstock transcendence. As soon as they appeared on stage, cheers would be littered with shouts for 'I'm Going Home', and this would continue during breaks between numbers. Alvin still saved 'I'm Going Home' for the end, not to tease the audience but because it was a rip roaring rock'n'roll rebel yell, always the ideal closer.

The encores still returned to Chuck Berry, 'Sweet Little Sixteen', perfect with its American place names, often where they were playing that night. It always took Alvin back to his teen years in Nottingham and me back to mine with my rock'n'roll sweetheart. A persistent crowd would get the band back for 'Roll Over Beethoven' and 'Johnny B Goode', a medley of classic Chuck. Alvin knew them all and brought them back to life. Chuck Berry aside, no one rocked them like Alvin and Ten Years After.

Most fans were cool after the show ended. Some would wait to talk and some were in awe of Alvin and reluctant to make a fool of themselves. Alvin had sussed out that bands were more likely to create a hassle if the limos came to the stage door and the band raced into them, than if they were relaxed and stayed to talk and sign autographs for a while. At least that worked for their level of fame; if you were a multi-million selling pop star, good luck.

There is no way to quantify the effect of KMPX, KSAN and similar FM Freeform radio on the success of the sixties progressive musicians and the music scene that developed. These stations were one of the pure joys of travelling around the USA on rock tours, in stereo equipped limos, late in the evening after a gig. Still energized from the shows, needing to wind down, smoking some nice mellow weed, listening to the latest album releases, with no news and few station identifications. It felt like a new era of elevated human consciousness had arrived. The freaks were running the show

My favourite fan experiences occurred when travelling back from stadium gigs, down dark freeways, in two limos. Fans, also driving back to town, would spot the two darkened cars and drive alongside, winding down their windows and yelling across. "Yeah Alvin! Woo hoo! Woo hoo! Alvin!" We'd wind down the electric windows and wave and shout back, "Yeah Man!" with FM station belting out rock in the background. This would go on for some miles and occasionally get hairy as concrete bridge supports came into view. "Watch out man, be cool!" We'd wind up the window, so they'd focus on driving. It was great to have this after show exchange of exhilaration.

One afternoon on the west coast, there was a knock at the hotel room door. I opened it and found a pleasant looking young couple. They asked if Alvin was there. "Just a minute," I said, shutting the door. I asked Alvin if he wanted company. "They look cool," I said. He smiled and shrugged in the affirmative. I went back and let them in.

After hellos and handshakes, they sat down. Then the guy said, "You wrote a song, 'I'd Love To Change The World', but I don't know what to do?" Alvin smiled at him. "Well I can tell you what to do man," he went on.

It turned out he was a member of a religious cult and had come to recruit Alvin so he'd become a member too. He knew all the answers to life and exactly how the world could be changed. Obviously, Alvin was sufficiently famous to make it all possible. We smiled a lot. I rolled smokes and offered them a toke or two. After maybe 20 minutes we told them, thank you but they needed to leave as Alvin had to get ready for the gig. They understood and left without any fuss. There were no arguments about beliefs or anything else.

As the band became more famous and more money came in, we stayed in more expensive hotels. After the Pierre in New York, there was the Georges IV in Paris and the Kempinski in Berlin. It was interesting to see how the 1%, as we call them today, live. In Hawaii we stayed at the Kahala Hilton, a modern five-star hotel built on stilts over a dolphin pool. It had a white sand beach, a large swimming pool and a golf course. Walking around was like being in an Elvis movie.

We were told that Spiro Agnew, Nixon's vice-president, had stayed there the week before. In our room there was a fresh pineapple on a tray. Its top came off to reveal perfect cubes of sun-ripened pineapple and small forks. It was incredibly sweet, ripe and delicious, a revelation for this Englishwoman.

When TYA played the Convention Center in Las Vegas in August 1971, we stayed at Caesar's Palace and went to see Elvis at the Hilton International. Dee Anthony had seen him the year before and was so blown away he insisted we go too.

All of the band went, along with Chris and Chelle. We sat around a table and had an official photo taken, as you do. This was a big deal for Alvin and me, as we had both been Elvis fans for ages. The 1969 comeback special showed he could still rock, despite his army years and dreadful, cheesy movies. Now, here was Elvis in Las Vegas, with an orchestra, in jumpsuits, doing the karate moves.

When he sang 'Teddy Bear', a man shadowed him with a basket of little teddies that he handed out to adoring female fans crowding around the stage. During another song he handed out white scarfs that his shadow repeatedly hung around Elvis's sweating neck. The fans screamed. They loved the show. Here was the King of Rock'n'Roll up close and personal. Alvin and I were very quiet, stunned, stoned on good weed. It was a tragedy to watch, a commercial crucifixion. When Alvin and I later learned about how manager Col. Tom Parker's gambling addiction made Elvis his cash cow, it wasn't a surprise. We saw it all in the darkness that night.

Las Vegas was the most bizarre city in the USA. When we stepped out of cars the heat was dry and overwhelming, like stepping into an immense oven. When we flew in, we walked through the airport corridors with rows of one-armed bandits. A team of pink suited, pink haired ladies manned the Hertz car rental desk. Astonishing.

When we pulled up at the hotel and walked through the main door I thought we'd made a mistake, as it seemed we'd entered a gambling casino. After the gig, back at the hotel, we were drawn back down. We watched the roulette, the blackjack, the old timers at the rows of slot machines with buckets of quarters to feed them. We played a few fruit machines and the biggest one-armed bandit with a huge arm that ate big dollar chips. Clunk, clunk, clunk, three cherries lined up. It spat out more dollar chips, which we put back into the machine until there was only one left. I still have it.

As ever, Alvin never wore a jacket and tie, which was insisted on in five-star hotel restaurants, so we would eat in the coffee shops. He wanted to be relaxed, incognito, comfortable, me too. Having been brought up by a mother who loved to dress up, I wasn't interested in any of that either. I liked wearing hot pants, platform shoes, no bra, no make-up, long blond hair flying looking drop dead gorgeous with my stunning long-haired old man. I liked flying first class within the USA, the compartment full of boring, expensively suited businessmen who would look disapprovingly at the band and then at me with drooling envy. It was a subtle first-class act of rebelling. I was helping to broaden their minds.

Gradually in the US, I dressed more and more outrageously and Alvin definitely got a kick out of it. We were a team. At gigs, when the band were onstage, fans would often come up and ask if I was Alvin's girlfriend. When I said yes, they would ask silly questions and always say, "Oh, you are so lucky to be with Alvin." It became quite irritating. They had no idea of me or my life, or just how lucky I actually was. Eventually I took to saying I was a groupie and had only met him the night before. That never led any further. Then I could do what I really loved, dance my ass off and enjoy the wonder of Alvin's music as I always had.

In New Orleans we saw Dr. John at The Warehouse. He was funky, focused and full of voodoo trinkets and costumes, both disturbing and exhilarating. Their summer evening gig at The Warehouse was extremely hot and when Alvin came off stage he was soaked to the skin. When I went to embrace him, the sequins on his beautiful black antique shirt had melted and came off on my hands. The shirt was ditched, replaced by a red Warehouse, US football-style shirt similar to the purple Bill Graham's Fillmore one. These became favourite stage wear and were easily laundered by the hotel service.

We took a ride around the old French quarter of New Orleans in Allen Toussaint's Cadillac. He pulled over and shouted up to the balcony of a beautiful old house. Two sexy ladies appeared, laughing and shouting back to him. Suddenly we were in another movie scene, with loud funky music on the car radio as its soundtrack.

Many attractive young ladies were in hot pursuit of Alvin. These weren't the groupies he'd met on earlier tours when I was left at home in London. They were often very beautiful, and had spent months waiting for Alvin from the *Woodstock* movie, the silver screen hero, to come to town. They'd spent a day bathing and tarting themselves up with Alvin's conquest in mind. It was a challenge for me, living out of a suitcase, travelling every day, to look good, but I was never jealous. I was certain he wouldn't go off for the night with anyone. However, Alvin was very hot-blooded, easily flattered, turned on and distracted by some long-legged, long-haired, bra-less beauty coming on to him. Which brings me to a memorable event in New Orleans.

After the Warehouse gig we stayed at a lovely hotel on Bourbon Street with classic wrought iron balconies. The hotel had a disco bar downstairs and, unusually, Alvin suggested we go down for a drink. When we got there, we noticed a young women and her boyfriend, who had been at the gig. She was stunning, with a curvaceous body and revealing top. We all sat together. The music was too loud for conversation. She got up and walked towards the bathroom. Shortly afterwards Alvin, too, went to the bathroom. Maybe five minutes went by. No one returned. The boyfriend looked sheepish. I got up to leave. He jumped ahead of me and blocked the doorway. I asked him where his girlfriend had gone and he smiled. I slapped his face and pushed past him.

I was cross and out of control. I went to the front desk and asked for the key to our room. The receptionist looked flustered and declined to give it to me. Now I saw red. Marching to the lift, with vague shouts behind me, I was quickly in and up to our floor. I ran to our room and pounded on the door, yelling to be let in. After a few minutes the door opened a crack. It was Alvin, also looking sheepish. I pushed past him. No sign off the girlfriend.

"Where is she?" I was calm but obviously looked menacing.

"In the bathroom," he said calmly. "I don't want you to hurt her."

Before I could reply there was a knock on the door. Alvin opened it. The boyfriend. "She hit me," he said, looking at me.

Alvin was astonished. "She hit you! She hit you!" he repeated, shaking his head in disbelief.

The bathroom door opened and the girlfriend came cautiously out. When she got near me I grabbed her half-exposed breast. It felt strangely soft, not at all pleasant. "Is this what you came for?" I said.

In truth, the anger had left me. The whole charade was fast becoming a farce. Alvin was still reeling with shock at the idea that I would hit this sweet looking hippie man. I sat down and rolled a joint, lit it and passed it to Alvin. We all sat and smoked the joint and soon enough they went home to their own lives and we carried on our rock'n'roll way. He'd been taking topless photos of her. I enjoyed the eroticism.

The next day Alvin took a half dozen photos on me on the balcony. In some I look magnificent.

chapter 36
Riots and Craziness, Even at The Barn

Late in 1970 Mylon LeFevre and his band Holy Smoke played half a dozen gigs with Ten Years After. Mylon cut quite a figure in his black leather jumpsuit with white top stitching, emblazoned with white crucifixes. It wasn't often we would catch the support bands, which was a shame as some were excellent and would go on to fame and fortune. We caught some of Holy Smoke's last numbers and were intrigued by Mylon's act which had more to do with English musicians like Joe Cocker than the more laidback US performers.

Mylon was as up front off-stage as he was on stage. With his long black curls, black moustache, long Elvis side burns and dark eyes, he reminded me of portraits of the King Charles II, who was known as The Merry Monarch. On one early gig with Mylon's Holy Smoke Alvin was particularly physical with his guitar, as he had been since be back in the Marquee days. Mylon was watching as Alvin threw it around and bounced it on the stage, and when he came off-stage Mylon didn't mince his words. "Hey man! What are doing throwing your guitar about like that? That ain't respectful!" Alvin had done it for so long that no one had ever questioned it, but after that he rarely did it again, only when very stressed.

When we were close to Mylon's Georgia home we went to visit and met his gentle wife Ann and daughter Summer. Ann was a stunning Southern lady whom I liked very much. She taught me how to make an intensely sweet desert called cherry cobbler. Mylon had plenty of boys' toys including a Harley Davidson, which Alvin took for a ride with me on the back.

When we pulled up back at the house, he was feeling confident and accidentally did a wheelie. I clung on somehow.

Above the couch in the living room, where Summer was bouncing as little girls do, hung a holster with a hand gun in it. We looked at each other in surprise, but I don't remember Alvin being as forthcoming as Mylon was with him and asking about it. We had entered a foreign land and were too polite to ask the locals about their habits.

It was plain to see that Alvin and Mylon got along well. He hadn't many close men friends so I was pleased that this might help him to get more enjoyment out of gigs they both played. Ann and young Summer left a great impression on me and given me a very different take on Mylon to the uninhibited rocker on stage.

From 1970 there were disturbances at TYA gigs, just as there were at gigs all over America following the Kent State shootings that inspired Neil Young to write 'Ohio'. One occurred at the Chicago Coliseum in November. "A guy got up and started yelling at Alvin," a fan called Eddie Lee told me. "He was shouting 'It's all your fault' at him. Alvin stepped back to the mike, said 'Shhiiittt!' and walked off the stage. The crowd at the front had seen this exchange and was naturally pissed off at the guy, who was led away. I was right in front of the stage and people had wanted his blood. A few minutes later the band came back on and it was Alvin that tore the place down."

Another incident was at Kiel Auditorium, St Louis, on August 28, 1971. Security guards were shining their torches on the crowd up front and Alvin admonished them. "Stop waving your torches about," he shouted.

A fan, Kevin Basil Carmody, was standing in the stage wings near where I was and had a better view of what happened next. "As they were pushing forwards there was danger of a crush," he told me, "and a table that was there was put up on the stage to one side by some people in the crowd. The security guards got the table and threw it back into the crowd and that was how the riot really started. Shortly after the table arrived on stage, all hell broke loose. Alvin walked off followed by the band. He shook my extended hand thus giving me the pick he'd been using and headed straight to you. My girlfriend and I headed out the stage door to the street."

The closest we ever came to dying on a tour happened in November that year. The gig was at Boston Gardens, promoted by Don Law, a well-known promoter who put on gigs at the Tea Party there. The show was stopped several times due to fans rushing the stage, and a riot was on the cards. We wanted to get away as quickly as we could and the limos were ready and waiting for us. Chris and Chelle were with us, probably Leo too. The only way out was through the huge car park. We were in a queue waiting when we were spotted by fans leaving for their cars. We were trapped. Fans pushed their faces up against the windows, and when some climbed on the roof it began to buckle under their weight. Our only option was to put our feet up against the roof of the limo and pray. The driver hooted, wound down his windows and ordered the fans off of the roof. Luckily, they understood and the jammed cars in front made way for us to escape.

There were other dangerous nights, the worst from my point of view at the Cow Palace, in Oakland, which holds 14,000. It was across the bay from San Francisco, where Alvin felt safe to get high, and we had enjoyed some good weed before he went on. It was stadium seating, which means the fans sat on the floor, a few thousand of them stretching back. As they played, those at the front stood up and those at the back threw stuff to get them to sit back down.

Alvin, eyes closed was playing a fine solo, flying into his own transcendent universe, when an empty bottle smashed onto the neck of the guitar. It exploded right next to his left hand. He stopped and the band stopped and the audience stopped. He unplugged and left the stage in a daze. I followed him back to the dressing room.

He was in a state of shock, as in a trauma. The bottle had missed the fingers of his left hand by inches. He sat, head down, rubbing his thumb over his fingers, not speaking for quite a while. Calmly, I massaged his back, shoulders, neck, and head saying very little. Gradually he began to relax and come back down to earth. He didn't want to go back out, but he knew that 14,000 people wouldn't leave unless he did. We could hear them cheering and shouting for the band to come back out.

He was off stage for maybe a half hour. All the band were quiet and sympathetic. The stage was swept and the guitar cleaned up. He sat and retuned it, which helped him to re-connect. He walked slowly back out onto the stage to a welcoming and chastened audience and finished the show.

In interviews around this time Alvin spoke often about the problems of touring, and not the pleasures. Musical integrity was a phrase he used, he felt the band was becoming a travelling jukebox. Tours and record sales were producing ever-increasing sums of money, which finally brought financial security. It was ironic that Woodstock, the festival, had been a blast, but *Woodstock*, the film, had increased their fame to a level that was more inhibiting than liberating. Music writers praised them and spoke of *Woodstock* bringing TYA overnight success when in reality they were enjoying a good, thriving musical career pre-*Woodstock*. Alvin tried to explain this over and over in interviews, all the while trying over and over to understand it himself.

Decades later, after hearing of Kurt Cobain's suicide, I realised that what he and Alvin had needed to hear was that the "crazy fame" does not last. The stratospheric lift off, being discovered, having hits, over-exposure and intense fan worship will not last. It will not be there for the rest of your life. Relax, take control of the money machine, pace it to suit your musical yearnings, don't be manipulated by the percentage takers or you will burn out, flip out or run for the hills. This hot and heavy burst of fame is temporary, a crazy energy that will not destroy you unless you let it. Most of all, it will not stay with you. Alvin would later tell me, "I understand how Kurt Cobain felt and what happened to him."

Whenever we were back home at Robin Hood Barn, there was calm and a balance that was what made touring possible. The Barn was a universe away from the crazy unpredictability of life on the road. It wasn't too big or too small, nor too tucked away out in the countryside, it felt relaxed and comfortable. Alvin had the privacy to be creative and in my sewing room below him I could hear him playing and singing whilst I played with fabrics. We were lucky to be able to be alone together, to enjoy a rare connection.

There was absolutely no input from Alvin about how the house was decorated, furnished or organised. He was 100% happy with my taste and choices. There were no domestic discussions of any kind. Bills and paperwork were my domain. We had separate bank accounts and my household allowance was left to me to manage. When we toured I would spend very little so there was a nest egg when we got home.

My tastes were very simple, even frugal, but I never saw it that way. I just didn't desire stuff. Making my own clothes from the age of ten had been my pleasure and it remained so. My one luxury was shoes and boots, which I couldn't make myself and this was the era of platform soles. The Chelsea Cobbler in upmarket London and Andy's, the famous custom bootmaker to the rock stars, in Shepherd's Bush, were favourites. My favourite shoe shop was Goody Two Shoes in New York, and while Alvin was doing interviews in NY I would head off to get great shoes. Chelle had a hat shop she loved to visit in NY and we had some trips together, shoes for me and hats for Chelle.

My other love in New York were the two big modern art galleries, the Guggenheim and MOMA. In London Alvin and I had visited the Tate, and been knocked out by the Salvador Dali collection. That was the start of a lifelong love of Dali and Surrealism for both of us, and acquisitions of art books and posters.

As a gift Alvin bought me an easel, some canvases and a set of oil paints, but with no instructions I didn't know how to work with the linseed oil and turpentine to thin the paint. One day Alvin set up the easel, projected a slide he had taken of an autumn tree onto a canvas, and painted through the projection, a great first oil painting. I was really annoyed and told him it was cheating. I was projecting my own discontent onto his creative inventiveness.

We were both still smokers, nicotine as well as hashish and marijuana though for a few years we tried to quit. It was especially hard in the UK as joints are rolled with tobacco and hashish, at least marijuana could be rolled pure in a little one skin joint. I'd visited a health store on Baker Street, looking for an herbal alternative. I think it was the first health store in the UK. We tried a number of types and settled on Barmora, a dark, strong herbal mixture in a honey base. We got some funny looks when we rolled it up without hashish and lit it on planes when the no smoking sign went out. Alvin never did quit smoking for long and I was 40 before I finally quit it for good.

The last psychedelic experience Alvin had when I was with him was at Robin Hood Barn in the summer of 1971. Andy came to visit, bringing some mescaline with him, and I made the decision to not take any but to be there for them. Andy and Alvin took a tab each. I made tea and rolled quite a strong joint of hashish and after a while they went off into the garden. Such a lovely day, I sat outside and could hear them climbing in the trees, which were not very high. Later Alvin came to me and said, "I don't think that mescaline is any good."

Somewhat surprised, I said, "That hash was very strong. I don't think you'd have gone out and climbed trees, if the mescaline was no good!"

He saw the logic and we both laughed. Later on I found them both relaxing in the garden room, with the back door open and Cyril the squirrel having fun climbing around the wooden railings of the minstrel gallery.

Recently I talked to Andy about this trip they shared. Later he and Alvin were up in his home studio. "Alvin was playing chords on guitar and I started to sing along, and make up words. I'd never done anything like that before." I thought that was extraordinary. They had been friends for years and mescaline had opened them up and allowed them to connect on a whole other level.

Heavier and deadlier drugs were around the music world, though not with us as TYA was never into drugs. I came across some young women who loved to take Mandrax, a heavy sleeping pill, and then fight the effects by going out dancing. That was never my scene, just as alcohol never had been. We heard about cocaine but my instinct was it was not for Alvin or me.

The Barn was somewhere away from rock 'n roll and we hadn't wanted it to change, but you cannot control your fate. It seemed harmless enough to let Mylon come to visit and stay a few days with his friend Steve Saunders, another southern musician. Mylon and Steve both came from families of Christian preachers. The LeFevres had their own successful TV shows, though Mylon was not a part of their work. Steve had been a child preacher. His parents had schooled him to preach and make money for them. His was a miserable story, in his mid-teens his parents had fleeced him of all the money he had earned.

Neither Alvin nor I had any religious background from our parents and knew little about what Mylon and Steve told us. We figured they were both pleased to no longer be part of their family's businesses. They stayed the night and the next day were going up to London for some meetings. We were to be away for a few nights at some UK gigs. We gave them keys to the house when they left for London and said it would be ok for them to come back the day we were getting home.

When we got back in the early evening, Mylon was sitting in the main room but there was no sign of Steve, who Mylon said was tired and had gone up to bed early. Steve was sleeping on the sofa bed in my sewing room which had an en-suite bathroom. We had something to eat, tea and smoked some joints. We were tired from travelling and about 11pm we all went off to bed. Five minutes later, Mylon was knocking hard on our bedroom door. He'd been to check on Steve and found him unresponsive. We went across the landing and, sure enough, he was unconscious in his underpants on the sofa bed. I had no first aid training and neither did the boys. I got them to get him upright and try to walk him. We took him into the bathroom and splashed cold water on his face. There was absolutely no change. Luckily, he was breathing. They put him back on the bed. I remember clearly that Alvin and Mylon, both nicely stoned, slouched on the floor, their backs against the wall.

It was only then that Mylon told us that while they had been in London, Steve had become upset after falling out with a girlfriend there. They had returned earlier in the day and he'd gone up to bed. Mylon hadn't checked on him for some hours before we got back. We had no way of knowing how long he'd been unconscious. Mylon said he'd probably taken a load of his heavy-duty sleeping pills. Much as I was annoyed with Mylon for his carelessness, I was much more concerned for Steve. I told them I was going to call an ambulance. Mylon protested. He was worried about the police coming around. Alvin said nothing. I'm sure he trusted whatever I would decide.

I was very angry that this was happening in our home. I looked at Mylon and told him, "Your friend is unconscious. He has probably taken an overdose. If we don't get him to a hospital and he dies here, how will we explain that to the police?" I wasn't interested in his answer. I left the room, went downstairs, called 999 and explained the situation to them. Unlike today, there were no mobile phones, no internet, and no connections except the land line. We were hidden away down a country lane and I wanted Alvin and Mylon to go out there to guide them to the house.

Before they went out, there was one more thing. "Where is your stash of pills," I asked Mylon. I was direct and not to be argued with. "I will flush it all away while you go to the hospital and deal with this. If the police come, they are not to find anything here."

He went to his room and came back with a washbag containing several pill bottles. He and Alvin went out the front door, down the lane and after about 10 minutes re-appeared with two ambulancemen. It's unlikely these guys had seen a home furnished as flamboyantly as Robin Hood Barn. Dangling down from the top bannisters was a pair of plastic legs in fishnet tights.

Once in the bedroom they checked Steve for signs of life, then strapped him, into an upright hospital trolley chair. With only a blanket over him, his head flopping, he looked so vulnerable. They took him downstairs into the ambulance and set off with Alvin and Mylon with him in the back. I closed the front door, got Mylon's washbag and took it to the loo. I emptied out the pills and flushed them away.

Our little stash of weed was hidden in a jam jar in the garden. It seemed to me that once they arrived at the hospital and saw how bad Steve was, they might very well inform the police. Alvin and Mylon came back in a taxi in the early hours. They told me that the ambulance driver had lost control at high speed, and had spun it in the road. For a few crazy seconds Alvin wondered if they were all to die

The hospital was quick to act. Steve's stomach was pumped, emptying it of anything that remained, which would help them identify the drugs he had taken. I imagine Mylon was able to tell them what strong US sleeping pills he was travelling with. Once they had taken Steve off to intensive care and his name and details had been given by Mylon, there was little they could do, so they had come back.

There was no point staying up all night. We all turned in and the next day went back to the hospital to find out how he was. Steve was kind of conscious when we arrived. He was high, like he was drunk, as he would remain for several days. On the second day they told us he had got out of bed in the night, found an elderly lady on an adjacent ward and got in bed with her. He was on the mend.

While we waited, Alvin and Mylon made music together and it was arranged that we would go to Roger Daltrey's house in Sussex the following week to record in his small studio. Roger and Heather, his tall, red headed, buzzy New York wife, lived in the village of Hurst, quite near to us, and Perry Press had taken us to meet them. Their home was a classic little country cottage, and Roger proudly showed us all the building work he had done on it. There were low overhead beams where Heather had to duck to avoid bumping her head as she walked through the kitchen and sitting room. Not long afterwards they sold up and moved to a large old Tudor house on the Kent/ Sussex border, with acres of land and lakes where Roger set up a trout farm. Alvin and I visited one day with Perry, and Roger took us out for a drive in one of his collection of antique cars.

After a few days, Alvin and Mylon were getting stir crazy. They came into Wokingham and wandered about while I was food shopping. We all went our separate ways and when we met back at the car Mylon was very animated. "Man, I just met Jesus on the High Street," he told us, laughing. "Least he said he was, but maybe I shouldn't believe someone whose face is covered in glue!"

Steve recovered and returned from the hospital. The police never visited and, this being Britain, there was no invoice from the hospital. Steve had three days bed and board and suitable treatment courtesy of the National Health Service. I remember being relieved that he didn't have to find money, which he would not have had. He was very repentant and full of apologies and wrote a song to that effect, which he would record for us.

At the weekend I went into Wokingham again food shopping, and when I got back to the Barn, Mylon was downstairs looking worried. He told me that Alvin had found Cyril the squirrel badly injured in the garden and he was upstairs and very upset. I went up to our bedroom and found him in tears and quite inconsolable. Perhaps Steve's overdose and the need to keep it all together had really been too much for him. Finding Cyril was the final straw. Alvin was a man who was able to cry, no surprise with such relaxed, loving parents.

Cyril was in an outbuilding, the half-timbered grain store, in a box with a towel around him. He had lost blood and the wound looked like he might have been attacked by a cat. I found the number for a vet and we took him to be seen. The vet wanted reassurance that this was a tame squirrel and believed us when he saw how plump Cyril was. He gave him some injections but warned us that he probably would not survive, as "wild creatures are easily traumatised". He also told us that squirrels only live a couple of years and he was quite old. Cyril did die that night and the next morning I put him in a shoe box, surrounded him with roses and we buried him in the garden. We talked about Cyril four decades later. If you've ever read *The Little Prince* by Antoine de Saint-Exupéry, you will understand why.

The next day we drove off to Roger Daltrey's with Mylon and Steve in the back of the car. Finally, relieved of all my responsibilities, I wept for Cyril for most of the drive. I felt guilty for allowing him to become so tame that his awareness of the dangers in his environment had been compromised. The guys were all very quiet. We played music as the English countryside slid past us. At some point Mylon said to me, "Man, it's a drag you flushed all my stash."

I was not impressed and told him so. I was unable to understand how he could be so ungrateful when a potential tragedy had turned out ok.

chapter 37
Cap Ferrat, Jamaica, Patto

Roger Daltrey had converted a barn on his property into the studio with living accommodation. We spent a few hot summer days there and I relaxed by the lakes. The music making was very healing. When Mylon and Steve left for America and we returned to The Barn we were grateful for the peace and quiet. They had brought us quite a rock'n'roll whirlwind.

When we bought The Barn we were told there could be changes in the roads around us. A road ran through the field next door, but it was a small country lane with little traffic. Now we heard this quiet lane was to become a slip road to join the M4 motorway a few miles away. Estate agent Perry, our friend and regular visitor, gave us updates about the road. We were very private in the back garden and a bigger road meant we would be more exposed, especially in the winter with fewer leaves on the trees.

A two-acre strip of the field next to our garden and the road belonged to a local doctor, and we thought that if we could buy it we could plant a high hedge along by the new road to protect our garden. Robin Hood Barn was our home. We really loved it and we had no desire to leave. While Ten Years After were beginning to earn better money, we didn't have much to spare and were stretched with our £15,000 mortgage. The universe had us in its sights however, another totally unexpected surprise, a game changer, was in store. We had no idea what would happen before the year was out.

In February of 1972, we spent 10 days in a villa at Cap Ferrat in the South of France. All of Ten Years After brought their old ladies, the only time we all lived together, and we were self-catering. TYA had hired the Rolling Stones' mobile recording studio and Chris Kimsey, their regular producer, also stayed at the villa. They experimented with the various rooms for drum, instrument and vocal sounds but never seemed to settle into as comfortable a recording mode as they had at Olympic Studios in Barnes.

The kitchen was huge and basic but somehow Ruthann, Suzanne, Sally (Leo's new lady) and I managed to cook friction-free meals together. We visited the local supermarket, filling up three trolleys with fresh foods, bread, wines and beers. One afternoon the four of us drove along the main road that runs to the Italian border, then up, up and up a winding mountain road that cut through the mountains. When we were quite high up, we stopped to eat and drink with the Mediterranean twinkling below us.

Just two tracks 'Convention Prevention' and 'You Can't Win Them All' appeared on the 1972 album *Rock & Roll Music To The World*. In 2018 the tapes were rediscovered and a tenth disc added to the TYA collectors boxed set included Alvin's 'Holy Shit'. Chris Kimsey was surprised by the quality of the music from all those years ago but at the time they weren't too impressed with the experiment and were happy to return to Olympic later in the year.

The French trip wasn't a holiday for the band. Did we take holidays? We once stayed in a farm in North Wales with Johnnie and Judy who were regular and welcome visitors to the Barn. Johnnie always gave solid, emotional support to Alvin, a true friend, and sometimes we'd go up to London and visit them with their household of lovely black and white cats, Fleur, Percy and Molly. When Clive Davis came to London, after TYA had signed to Columbia, we met up with him, Chris and Chelle Wright at the funky L'Artiste Asoiffe restaurant in Notting Hill. Clive swept in and declared loudly, "Geez, this place is so quaint." Apparently when they got out of their limousine outside, a passing local openly declared them "capitalist pigs!"

Alvin pleaded for time off after US tours and we spent time in Jamaica, visiting Chelle's friend, Tina, an artist, and her husband Aaron, an architect. It was about 11 pm when we arrived at their house. Under a clear sky, lit by a full moon, we stood out in their garden by the ocean enjoying a local smoke. The moon was casting our clear shadows as if it was daylight, and in a huge bordering bush hundreds of fireflies were dancing. Their lights flickered spasmodically as they flew, endless changing light patterns. The grass was lush, as was the vegetation, and the sound of crickets mixed with frogs croaking, calling and responding in a continual chorus.

Nights in the English countryside are silent except for the occasional hoot of an owl. Here the night was alive, electric, as if the volume was cranked up to the maximum. Above the Northern horizon, where Cuba lay, there was a lightning storm which lit up the banks of clouds. Running along the line of the horizon were groups of clouds at differing depths lit with lightning against the dark sky. We were too far away to hear the thunder, but the cosmic Caribbean light show was epic.

My arms were bare. The night was hot but a gently breeze ran over my skin. The air was heavily scented with tropical bloom perfume. All of my senses were alive, it was a blissful environment. "This is paradise," I said to Alvin. "If there was a garden of Eden, this is how it was." Alvin smiled as we marvelled at the wonders around us. It was the start of a romance with Jamaica for both of us for many years to come, our first experience of a tropical paradise.

The next day we went into Ocho Rios and arranged to rent a house, with a swimming pool, near the beach in Mammee Bay. The rental included a lady who cooked for us and took care of the house. Later Mylon and Ann flew out to join us, renting a car at the airport and driving for two hours along the superb North Coast.

When they arrived, Mylon was fidgety. We asked him about the drive. "Man, it was pretty, but I was thirsty," he said. "I wanted to stop for a beer, only there were all of these New York niggers hanging around outside the bars." Perception really is based on our own experiences and not actual reality.

After a few days Mylon was chilled out with the locals and enjoyed the good Jamaican weed. Some beach musicians came by with a drum box and guitar, Mylon got into their playing and realised this was not New York. I noticed that after about three days of Jamaican sun and smokes, I felt a deeper level of relaxation that ever before.

Jamaicans are warm hearted, relaxed, fun loving and friendly. In the cities of Montego Bay and the capital Kingston, there was more crime and social problems but Ocho Rios was small, a tourist centre, with great markets for fresh fish, chickens, vegetables and tropical fruits, all huge, luscious and abundant. I learned that if I asked the price for an avocado it would cost much more than if I asked for pear, as they were locally known. The market women called out to me, "Hey, sexy girl, come here, see what I have." They looked Alvin up and down and asked me if I had any children. When I said no, they tutted and clucked, sucking their teeth, laughing and shook their heads.

The people were poor but no one went hungry as there was food growing everywhere. Jamaicans are fit, strong, handsome people and the women are up front in every way, liberated, running the island long before women's liberation was invented. Children in their smart khaki shorts and shirts might walk several miles to school and back which made them strong and healthy. Most days it rained at 6 pm, a warm downpour that stops after a half hour, leaving everything dripping and fresh. I stood under the corner of the roof guttering enjoying a natural shower.

On our next visit to Jamaica Andy Jaworski and his girlfriend Dorothy came along. We rented the same small house, arriving there in the dark, but the following morning we were woken by shouts and banging. A new house was being built next door – not so relaxing after a US tour. The agent apologised and for a little extra up-graded us to a large modern house further down the bay. The Glass House was surrounded by stunning plants. The amazing insect life included dragonflies in turquoise, red and yellow and some had black bodies and transparent wings with a black stripe. They seemed to float as they dipped and bobbed above the swimming pool.

One day on a path I found a huge moth, jet black velvet with a raised tail that reminded me of the shape of a Vulcan bomber. Another time Alvin and I watched for five minutes as a spider climbed down onto the surface tension of the swimming pool, walked the length of the pool and climbed out the other end. One evening we sat at sunset on the end of the boat dock and watched as, 20 feet away, an octopus climbed out of the sea, slowly slithered across the dock and slid back into the glistening water.

Angular black frigate birds flew over the ocean, pulled in their wings to form aerodynamic darts and dove into the water to reemerge with a fish in their beaks. John Crows, a type of vulture, circled languidly overhead with outstretched wings with fluttering tips, scouting for road kill and carrion. Freestyle garbage collectors. Huge spider webs adorned overhead electric cables. Bejeweled hummingbirds darted and hovered around the luscious open blooms of the Angel's Trumpet, Frangipani, Hibiscus, Heliconia, Bird of Paradise and Lignum Virae (Tree of Life), the Jamaican National flower.

One time, arriving at Montego Bay airport, we walked across to the car hire and met Paul and Linda McCartney who had also just arrived. Though we had never met before, we smiled at each other as kindred spirits, and muttered a greeting. We all knew why we had chosen to relax on this island.

The second day at the Glass House Alvin returned from the beach and said he'd been talking and smoking with one of the builders from the previous house. It seemed the man had fallen off of the roof, only a one-storey building, and the foreman had sent him for a walk along the beach to recover. In Jamaica we heard those common phrases, 'No Problem', 'Everyting Irie' (alright) and 'Soon Come', a very loose indication of when something might happen. The music on the beaches, in the bars, was still calypso, 'Island In The Sun' and 'The Banana Boat Song'.

Alvin was happy to swim, eat, smoke and relax. One day he and Andy hired sea scooters to zoom around Mammee Bay. Our bedroom was a large suite with sofas around a coffee table where Alvin placed his tape recorder and notebooks. Alvin always had a guitar close to hand, played for pleasure, and it was bliss for me to sunbathe on the adjoining balcony listening to him play. After half a year of touring that involved crazy intensity on every level, it was a delight to see him unwind, relax, have fun.

In early 1972 Ten Years After toured the UK, playing a dozen universities over three weeks, as they had in the past. It was much more relaxed and lower key than they had experienced in the last few years and very welcome for that. Mostly we could drive to the gigs and drive home afterwards. Chris and Chrysalis were going along with Alvin's need to make touring more mentally manageable.

In late February, for three gigs in Scandinavia, we traveled on a bus with Patto, the support band. Alvin had suggested them to Chris for the tour. Alvin had known Mike Patto back in the days of The Jaybirds when they slogged up and down the M1 motorway and met up with bands in the Blue Boar services. Back then Patto's band were called The Bo Street Runners. Now, as Patto, the four-piece included Ollie Halsall, an extraordinary talented guitarist and pianist who was deeply unpredictable. Mike Patto was also very much larger than life and the two of them were quite a duo on and off stage. Their drummer, John Halsey, was also a tremendous live wire and a wit, only their bass player Clive Griffiths was low key. Life off-stage was one long laugh, exchanging banter and stories and piss taking.

Patto were stoners and Alvin and I were delighted to travel with them at the back of the bus, smoking and laughing. The rest of the band and their ladies stayed at the front by their own choice. At one city Ollie Halsall spotted a baby grand piano in a hotel lobby, sat down and played, classics, jazz and rock'n'roll, uninhibited solo pieces, for a good half hour. We sat and watched. No one from the hotel interfered. If you can play so astonishingly everyone applauds.

After a break, the short Scandinavian tour was followed by shows in Germany and we were looking forward to spending more time with them but when we climbed onto the bus there was no sign of Patto. Alvin asked where they were. Ruthann told him that Patto were no longer travelling on the same bus. Apparently, the instigator was someone from the band. We were told his name. He had complained to Chris. What was our crime?

Being too noisy? Having too much fun? Simply enjoying ourselves? The outcome was that Patto travelled and stayed separately from TYA.

Alvin, overcome with emotion, started to weep. He could have been angry but he was in a state of shock and disbelief. It was more than he could bear. Leo, Ric and Chick certainly wanted to keep the band going, to carry on touring and they all knew that Alvin was backing off from the fame he felt was claustrophobic. It was an unbelievably mean and dumb thing to do to him. The band was a democracy, it was three to one in favour. In my view this was a big nail in the coffin for their future together.

I didn't tell Alvin how I felt, not at the time anyway. In my mind TYA was never a competition, never an us and them situation. They had all worked hard to bring the group to this position of success. Allowing it to fall apart made no sense. Keeping Ten Year After together was the rational thing to do, so there would have been no point in me stirring things up. Calming the waters, keeping the energies harmonious, was part of my nature from a young age.

There was the bigger picture, too, that involved Andy and John and the road crew, special people who were brilliant and devoted to their jobs. Recently I learnt from John Hembrow that when there were months and years between TYA tours Alvin kept them on and paid their wages, even when they were touring with him as Alvin Lee & Co. Alvin was a decent person who thought about the lives of others. He fully understood the economics of the music business and his role in their lives.

chapter 38
USA, Japan, UK, The Future Beckons

Early 1972 was busy with touring. Eight days after returning from Europe we were off to the USA for three weeks, covering the whole country and winding up in Stockton, California, at the 28,000-seater sports arena of the University of the Pacific on April 29. The gig was promoted by Bill Graham who in 1971 had closed both Fillmores, West and East, but In San Francisco had opened the 5,400 capacity Winterland. Ten Years After were filling stadiums and arenas all around the USA.

It was a beautiful sunny day and the gig was excellent. I shot a movie of the band, the crowd and backstage which has made its way onto YouTube. What didn't make its way was Bill Graham spotting me filming and gesturing me to stop. No one argues with Bill. There was also footage of someone being put into an ambulance on a stretcher backstage. I was told that he had been shot by someone he knew. Again, someone asked me to stop filming.

On May 4, TYA played The Budokan in Tokyo. We flew to Japan across 6,000 miles of endless Pacific Ocean, crossing the International Date Line and losing a day. It was their first Japanese trip and we were told they were only the third rock band to tour Japan. Chris and Chelle were with us and the support band was another Chrysalis act, Procol Harum, who were heavy drinkers. Their set was piped into TYA's dressing room. One night they played the same number twice. They also went walkabout at airports and had to be rounded up for flights, usually from bar stools. By comparison TYA were really a dull, sober and professional band, so we didn't socialise, though Ric and Chick probably did. There was no marijuana to be found in Japan, so Alvin and I had a week off which wasn't a problem as it's not physically addictive.

In Tokyo we stayed at The Hilton, in a Japanese suite. Once inside the door we took off our shoes to cross the threshold onto the tatami matting, made from rice straw. Living at floor level, in the day we sat on cushions around low tables and in the evening two mattresses were laid side by side, with pillows and a wonderful large duvet. The bathroom had a deep rectangular wooden bathtub. All of the suite's walls were shoji opaque screens. The decor was minimal and soothing, room service offered a massage service, we asked for two. The masseurs arrived together and we lay a few feet apart on our mattresses for joint massage therapy. I decided Japan was the most civilised country on earth. Massage was a normal, everyday part of life.

The next day I went down to the lower floor of the Hilton to the bath house. Alvin was not so keen on the idea. Again, it was private and civilized. I was taken to a wet room where there was a western bath, steam cabinet and massage bed. Sitting naked on a small wooden stool, the smiling young masseuse soaped me with a large natural sponge. Handing it to me, she pointed down to indicate that I wash myself in my private areas. She rinsed me off by throwing buckets of warm water over me. Somehow it all took me back to my infant self. It was charming.

I was put into the steam cabinet, then scrubbed down with salt on a soft brush and finally plunged into the bath of clean warm water. After being dried with soft white towels, I was in heaven lying on the massage bed for a full body massage. She spoke a little English and taught me a few Japanese words, those I always tried to learn in any country; hello – kon'nichiwa, goodbye – sayonara, please – onegaishimasu, and thank you – arrigato.

We were taken on a trip to a large open air 1972 fashion expo, where stalls sold mainly denim mini-skirts to young Japanese ladies. For some time, I'd loved the graceful old Japanese culture of kimonos and fans, and I thought mini-skirts were unattractive. Most of these girls didn't have long, lean, swinging London legs and were quite flat chested, so kimonos suited them perfectly. It was the only country we visited where Alvin was not especially attracted to the women.

In a huge department store Ruthann and I made for the antique kimono section and were dressed there by assistants who showed us how to put on a kimono and obi belt correctly. Alvin and Ric were suitably impressed and amused as we sashayed in a very elegant way. We both bought some kimonos, Ruthann an exquisite wedding kimono with stunning embroidery.

Adjacent to the Hilton, just through a large, beautifully carved wooden archway was the Hie Shinto temple. The colours, incense, bells and shinto hangings were in stunning contrast to the highrise Hilton and the rock'n'roll Budokan. The centre of Tokyo was a very busy modern megalopolis where people wore western dress. Only here and there were remains of old Japan. Some older men, women and monks still wore kimonos and greeted one another by exchanging low bows.

This was early days for the Budokan as a music venue and the 10,000-capacity crowd had little idea how to behave at a rock show. The floor was unseated and about 60 fans kept backing up together and rushing the stage. On either side of the stage were security police in smart full uniforms, groups of three or four poised together in crouching, martial arts poses. Whenever one of the stage-rushing fans made it onto the stage, they would all pounce on the hapless fan and drag them away. This went on continuously.

There was a balcony from which fans jumped onto the stage. One nearly landed on Ric's drum kit. The stage jumper was pounced on and dispatched. Security stopped the concert three or four times. Alvin and the band traipsed off into the dressing room and waited while order was restored, then traipsed back out and carried on. It was the most disrupted gig I ever saw them play, but it ended with everyone happy. They had enjoyed themselves and nobody died.

The next morning at the hotel, there was a group of gentle fans who had brought small gifts for everyone. They were very humble and apologised for the behavior of the stage-rushing fans, who they said were glue-sniffers. They were grateful to have photos taken with Alvin and the band and not pushy in any way. Coming as we had from a US tour, the contrast was huge. US fans were casual and pushy, but of course we were used to that and comfortable with it. Left for us at the hotel reception were a half dozen letters from fans, again apologising for the crazy glue sniffers who had disrupted everything and tried to spoil it for everyone. They were poetically written and full of charm.

I wrote about the Tokyo concert in the TYA fan club magazine which I was still putting together, though I had handed over the running of the club to a friend, Jenny Puddefoot. "Fans wrote saying it was a pity this had happened as it was obviously very unnerving for TYA, and the concert was shorter because of it, as the officials felt a full-scale riot might emerge."

From Tokyo we travelled to Osaka, from where we took an hour coach ride to Kyoto to visit the famous Golden Pavilion, a Zen Buddhist temple on a lake, surrounded by gardens, the Japanese equivalent to visiting a stately home in the UK. It was a tourist excursion, the only such outing I ever took with Ten Years After, and we walked around the lake which was tranquil. On the first US tour they had gone to the top of the Empire State Building in New York, the Grand Canyon in Arizona, the Muir Woods in San Francisco, and the Redwood Forest over the Golden Gate Bridge. When I joined Alvin on later tours, these sightseeing events were a rarity. Nevertheless, every time we were in San Francisco, late after a gig Andy would drive Alvin and me down Lombard Street, the famous winding hill, as fast as he could.

In Osaka, a much more industrial city, TYA played two nights at the Koseinenkin Hall, to 3,500 people. This was where we heard Procol Harum play the same number twice. It was all theatre seating and there were no glue sniffers. One night when we got back to the small modern hotel room, we lay on the bed and watched TV without understanding the dialogue. We were surprised when a landscape scene was accompanied by the sound of people grunting and groaning.
We turned down the sound and realised we were hearing lovemaking from the next room, easily heard through the thin walls. I can report that the sounds of passion are both universal and international. It reminded me of the noisy, rampant neighbour above us at Warwick Square, six years earlier and 12,000 miles away.

The second night, with nothing to smoke to unwind Alvin post show, I looked at the hotel room folder and discovered that despite the late hour we could ring down for a masseuse. A rather elderly lady arrived and indicated to Alvin to strip off and lie on the bed. Rather than watch her technique, I took a long hot relaxing bath and emerged to find Alvin sleeping like a baby.

Some of the same fans who had been in Tokyo had travelled to Osaka and were there in the morning with more smiles and gifts, taking more pictures. They gave us great feedback about the gigs in Osaka. From their perspective TYA had been very successful on this first tour of Japan. For Alvin and the band, it was very different to all the earlier tours, full of charm and grace. They looked forward to returning one day.

There was a break before returning to Olympic to record *Rock & Roll Music To The World,* their seventh studio album. Some of the band, and Chris and Chelle, went to Bali. We talked about it but nothing in the world was as appealing as spending the summer months at Robin Hood Barn. We had hardly been there this year.

We flew back to London over the North Pole, where we stopped at Anchorage to change flights. Alvin took a wonderful photo of me looking at a huge stuffed polar bear in a large glass case. Decades later we both agreed it was a favourite image. I'm wearing a Biba jacket that was reddish toffee colour with big cream spots. I loved that jacket. It travelled all around the world, and in a 2009 email Alvin sent me photos of it in various tour locations, winding up on the bed at Robin Hood Barn. "The Red Coat diaries," he wrote. "The Italian Job.... benissimo!!"

Back in the UK, Perry Press called with news about the two acres next door that we were trying to buy to protect our privacy. Could he come down? Jet-lagged as we were, this was news we wanted to hear. Alvin had bought a new toy at the airport, a fish-eye lens for his Nikon. Photos of Robin Hood Barn taken that day with the fish-eye lens include me going through the pile of mail the postman had delivered. Perry has black curly hair and is dressed in black, head to toe as he always did, decades ahead of fashion.

We were appalled to discover that the doctor who owned the field was asking £90,000, ridiculous. It was only two years ago, in May of 1970, that we had bought The Barn with its 4.5 acres for £24,500. This was an unimaginable increase. Perry told us that 100 acres of land, which included our magical Robin Hood Barn, had been earmarked for development for housing and industry. This was why the land values had increased so dramatically.

We were shocked. This was a disaster. We loved this house and our life in it. We couldn't envision living here surrounded by houses and industry. It was too much to take in. We had started our journey from Japan in good spirits, looking forward to coming home, but we went to bed confused and exhausted. Perry asked if it was ok for him to stay the night as he had a property to look at nearby in the morning. Of course, it was ok. He had stayed many times.

In the morning we tried to get our heads round these developments, with little success. Perry asked if we wanted to go with him to see the property he was inspecting. It seemed like a good distraction. We drove over in the Jaguar XJ6 that had been sitting in the garage for most of the year. Driving always relaxed and focused Alvin. We drove through Henley-on-Thames where Perry pointed out the gates to Friar Park, George and Pattie Harrison's home which he had found for them.

He told us about finding this run-down Victorian Gothic 100-room mansion and 60 acres in early 1970. Catholic nuns, who lacked the funds to maintain it, had owned it. To save on electricity, they had a small, plastic light fitting hanging from the central chandelier in the main galleried room. Carved wooden panelling had been taken from walls to build confessionals in the dining room. The stories went on and on. It had been left to run down; apparently it had a low price for such an extraordinary property. Some years later I read it was £140,000.

After Pattie and George had bought it, Pattie had overseen the restoration work, no small task. Perry told us her attention to fine detail, quality and taste was superb. Money was no object for a Beatle.

We carried on out of Henley into the countryside for 10 more miles through Peppard and Sonning Commons, driving on ever smaller country lanes. It was a lovely May morning, the early summer foliage was breaking out and the blossoming fruit trees were in full bloom. English countryside is picturesque, especially at that time of year, when the new greens are emerging. I asked Perry if he had anyone in mind for the house we were going to look at. He said he did, but he didn't say who.

Down a narrow single-track road, overhung with trees we came to an open pair of large wrought iron gates which Perry said to drive through. We drove round the circular gravel drive and pulled up outside the front door. The impressive house was on top of a small hill, with gardens and countryside falling away. Large bushes of brilliant rhododendrons were in bloom and there were tall mature trees of many varieties. The stunning garden was well maintained. Perry rang the doorbell and the large oak front door opened. We were greeted by the owners, Geoffrey Marks and his wife. Perry introduced us all. The Marks were typical English country folk, friendly and proper, as was their home.

We were given a tour of the house, through oak panelled reception rooms, up the galleried main staircase to all the bedrooms and the attic rooms, and the self-contained staff flat; down the back stairs through a corridor with two old unused kitchens, past the rather small modern kitchen and out into a large stable yard, with a beautiful old timbered barn; past the outdoor swimming pool, through changing rooms, with a sauna and into an indoor tennis court, once a dairy that had tiled walls. What a place this was. It was stunning.

Outside there was an archway through to five large greenhouses, all filled with fruits and vegetables grown for the house. A large orchard led to a small bungalow, where we were introduced to the couple who lived there. He worked in the garden and she worked in the house. There were woods and across the lane a large field, in all 50 acres. The Marks were planning to keep a small plot of this field, far from the house, to build a smaller house for themselves. There was more outside, a weighbridge, large hay barn and bull pens in some disrepair. The Marks walked us back across lawns to the car and we all shook hands and said goodbye.

They walked back into the house. We drove around the circular drive and stopped out of sight of the house, outside the entrance. Perry produced a joint. We smoked and talked about what we had just seen. What an amazing place. It was very similar to The Barn, red brick and half-timbered.
The half-timbered empty barn had caught Alvin's eye. "That barn would make an amazing studio," he mused. "How much are they asking for it?"

"£250,000," Perry replied.

Alvin was quiet. "If the two-acre field next door to Robin Hood Barn is worth £90,000, and we have 4.5 acres of land, that's £225,000," he said.
"It would be amazing, if we could sell The Barn and buy this property."
In our hippie philosophical way, we concluded that if it was meant to be. It would be lovely synchronicity. We should go for it as we always had.
We drove back through the countryside to The Barn. Perry left for London to explore all the possibilities.

chapter 39
The Barn Door Shuts, Hook End Awaits

We went to sleep that night pretty confused but agreed to go with whatever fate had in store for us. We had moved into Warwick Square, Grosvenor Crescent, Gloucester Place and Robin Hood Barn by instinct, trusting always that the money would arrive to keep the roof over our heads and the wolf from the door. Early on it was a tough struggle at times, but it had always worked out in the end. If this also fell into place, our trust in the universe to support our journey would be confirmed. In truth, we didn't do any sums or look objectively at it all in anyway. Chris Wright was probably the only person in Alvin's life he would have talked to about this and he was relaxing in Bali.

Perry had arranged for us to return to the property for lunch on Thursday. Now we were looking with different eyes. Geoffrey Marks took us out to the bungalow to meet Anne and Harold Bishop, the housekeeper and one of the gardeners. There was a moment of hesitation when I realised we were taking on the responsibility for their home and lives. I shrugged it off, figuring it would be ok. If it came together, we would be able to manage everything.

At lunch, Geoffrey Marks peppered our contributions to the conversation with the phrase, "Oh! Super, super, super!" The contrast with Granny's open-hearted welcome and twinkling unpretentiousness at Robin Hood Barn was total. We sat in the light oak-panelled dining room, with a fine wood carving of fruit and leaves above the open fireplace. We were told it was by Grinling Gibbons, a famous wood carver whose work was highly valued. Along another wall were leaded windows and doors that led out to the paved garden, swimming pool, sauna, tennis court and barn. The sun shone, the flowers bloomed, the birds rejoiced and sang. It was a perfect picture of perfect Englishness of which dreams are made.

After another lovely drive through the Oxfordshire and Berkshire countryside, Alvin chased up calls with his accountant and was assured it would be possible to take on a larger mortgage. The money was there. Did we tell anyone at this point? I've no memory that we did. We were probably waiting to see what happened first. We didn't have long to wait. We woke up on Friday morning May 12, to another sunny day and a phone call from Perry.

The developers were happy to buy The Barn for £225,000. It was actually the land they wanted. Mr "Super, Super, Super" Marks was happy to take £250,000 for his property. Taking off the £15,000 mortgage on The Barn, we would have £210,000 from the sale. A £40,000 mortgage would complete the sale. Did we want to go ahead? We were looking at a £210,000 tax-free profit, in 1972. The 2018 equivalent, according to the inflation calculator from the Bank of England, was just over £2.5 million. We abandoned ourselves to the hand of fate.

"Yes," Alvin told Perry on the phone. "Sell The Barn and buy Hook End Manor."

We opened the front door and ran several circuits around the gravel drive, hooting and hollering and hugging. We had just won the lottery. The rest of the day is a blur, but those moments of elation running around the drive are etched on my memory like an Oscar win. The sadness we had felt about the fate of Robin Hood Barn had turned into an unforeseen miracle.

We called our parents, who were all incredulous. It really was too much for them to take in. My mother must have been delighted; after all, this was the life she had dreamed for me: the lady of an English country manor house, though she hadn't pictured Alvin as the squire. Sam and Doris were more cautious though obviously delighted. Various very close friends were gobsmacked. I don't remember what was said by the band when they returned from their holidays, but Chelle told me many decades later that Chris had exclaimed, "Bloody hell, that Alvin always lands on his feet."

The move was in the future. Nothing happens quickly when properties are bought and sold in the UK. It was early May, the garden was in bloom, there were summer gigs and recording to get on with. Also, we were happy that the wonderful garden at Robin Hood Barn was ours to enjoy for one more summer. It seemed horrendous that this magical house would be bulldozed. From time to time I had disquiet about it, especially because Granny and her family were such lovely people. Part of me felt like maybe there was some bad karma attached to this but I couldn't see an alternative. Staying in the middle of a housing development would have been hard, but an industrial development impossible. We had moved to the country for peace, an undisturbed life. Hook End was precisely that. Perhaps that was the point.

Alvin's income, though increasing, had not suddenly leapt up to support this huge house and the staff we would need to run it. Having always moved slightly ahead of what we could afford, we didn't take stock or ask realistic questions. We trusted the gods had our best interests at heart. Was it hubris or a terrible naivety? Into the already souring mix of increasing fame, fate had added a huge dollop of unearned, tax-free fortune.

In the summer of 1972 they were back at Olympic, with Chris Kimsey in the producer's chair, to record *Rock & Roll Music To The World*. Two tracks, 'Convention Prevention' and 'You Can't Win Them All' had already been recorded at Cap Ferrat in February. Alvin had written 18 new songs at Robin Hood Barn in his attic studio for this and *A Space In Time*. Some were autobiographical, or imagined being in someone else's shoes. The more melodic side of his musical palette had time to emerge, with lyrics considered for both albums more progressive and mature. *A Space in Time* was a gold record, eventually certified platinum. I can hear Robin Hood Barn, *Star Trek*, and the influence of the countryside on that album.

Chrysalis transposed Alvin's lyrics for the publishing. I went through them with a girl from Chrysalis but interpretations with a sexual edge were their choice. It was pretty hilarious. We had a good laugh when I hung up the phone and I wish I had written some of them down. I knew his voice and accent well and to me what he was singing never seemed obscure.

Prior to recording, TYA would rehearse new numbers for recording or for shows. No wives or girlfriends ever went to week-long rehearsals, just the band, Andy J and John H. Alvin would take in cassette demos of songs he had written and from those choices were made and arrangements of songs put together. Occasionally Alvin would come back in a bad mood, generally the result of a conflict with Leo.

Chris Wright has suggested that Alvin and Leo were in such conflict on stage, they would turn each other's amps down, and that towards the end in 1974 they actually fought on stage. I never saw anything like that in all the years. It has crossed my mind that this may have helped Chris get the band out of the Columbia contract, but that's conjecture. Recently asking Leo in an email about this he confirmed they had never fought etc. on stage. Leo would curse and swear and was always aggressive in his playing but only towards his bass. He physically attacked it while playing and would cut his fingers, especially at the start of a tour when they'd softened up after a break. He discovered that urine hardens the finger ends. Sometimes he bound them with tape until they were calloused again.

On August 13, 1972, Ten Years After headlined the 11th Reading Festival, their first UK festival since the IOW two years earlier. The band played great, the audience brought them out for three encores but the press was pretty dismissive. The British press had never been very supportive of the band, criticising Alvin for being super-fast, and calling him 'Captain Speedfingers'. Oddly, in classical music, dexterous technique is seen as something to admire.

A half dozen great dates in Germany lifted their spirits immensely. In October *Rock & Roll Music To The World* was released while they were on a short tour of Canada and the US, opening in Toronto and ending in Florida. Meanwhile, rather sadly, I was moving house again, leaving Alvin to tour on his own for the first time since spring 1969.

During the summer we had suggested to my younger brother Harold and his girlfriend Barbara that they might come to live at Hook End, in the self-contained staff flat. Harold was very musically talented and I was sure he could help Alvin build a studio and use modern technology. My brother was intelligent, resourceful and we had always been close. I thought it would work out all round. Barbara had been working as an assistant to a photographer and was willing to take on the admin that Hook End would generate. We all got on well enough and agreed wages for them both.

Sam and Doris came down to the Barn in September to help me with packing up and unpacking at the other end. At least that was the plan. In the morning when both sales were to be completed, everything had been packed into two large removal lorries that sat in the circular drive. The phone rang. I don't remember who was on the line but I was told that completion of The Barn had been delayed by two weeks and Geoffrey Marks at Hook End was happy to wait. I went straight out to Sam and Doris who were standing by their car and swore. "Fuck, fuck!" I yelled.

Sam looked very shocked. "I've never ever heard you swear before," he exclaimed.

Once I told him what had happened, he was sympathetic. What to do? I still had a home but all of its contents were in the removal vans. Was I going to have them unloaded? Maybe just a bed and some essentials and camp out in The Barn for two weeks? I had a suitcase with a few clothes and essentials. I made a quick decision. Take away everything and put it in storage. Sam and Doris would go back to Nottingham. I would put my suitcase in the boot of the car and spend two weeks visiting friends and having a rest. It had been very stressful packing up the house. Alvin was thousands of miles away on a rock'n'roll tour. I didn't have the energy to join him for two weeks.

Sam and Doris left. The removals vans left. I got the TR3A from the garage and loaded up the boot. Once more around the house, quietly checking the rooms and cupboards, looking out over the glorious back garden clothed in autumn hues. So many sweet memories came back to me going from room to room, window to window, and the attic where Alvin wrote. Now a new adventure was looming.

As I left and locked up the front door I noticed a big black bug on the doormat and bent down to look at it. It raised its tail up over its head like a scorpion. Later, when my *Book of the British Countryside* was unpacked, I looked it up. It was a Devil's Coach Horse beetle. In medieval times it was seen as a curse if it raised its tail and sprayed you with a stinky liquid from two tail glands. I noticed no smell and thankfully was not sprayed.

I drove up to London to Johnnie and Judy's flat on Ladbrooke Grove with their three black and white cats. We three would go up to Wales for a few days. I visited my parents and Sam and Doris for a weekend, also Kris and Woody, and Harold and Barbara in London. With no responsibilities or schedules to follow it was very relaxing. I spoke with Alvin on the phone and explained what had happened. We missed one another but knew it wasn't for long. He knew I was being well supported by our friends. It was my personal space in time.

Two weeks later I moved into Hook End with the help of Sam and Doris. The removal vans unloaded everything into the big central hall, such a lot of stuff. October evenings come in early and we discovered that every single light bulb had been removed from the house. When we had moved into The Barn, Granny had left the bulbs, some curtains, and grates in the fireplaces. It never occurred to me that the previous owners would take so much money yet remove everything that wasn't screwed down. I should have known better when we were sent an inventory of items they wanted us to buy from them. Among some prints and the like were the strip lights in the stables outside, £5 each. I couldn't believe they would remove them but they did, along with all the light bulbs.

A day or so later the phone rang one morning. It was Geoffrey Marks.

"Hello, how are you settling in?"

"Fine, thank you Geoffrey. What can I do for you?" I asked. It was unlikely he was calling just to wish me well.

"I was wondering if it would be ok for me to bring Nelson (his horse) and leave him in the orchard for a while?"

"Sorry, really can't do that Geoffrey, no chance at all. Goodbye."
I was astonished at his cheek.

I told Alvin about the lack of lightbulbs and about my exchange over Nelson with Geoffrey Marks. He thought it was hilarious. We had come from such different backgrounds and in a way Hook End amplified that. I was not impressed by the Marks. These were the kinds of people whose children I had grown up among at my nice young ladies' private school. I had been to their posh houses and knew them as real people, warts and all. My mother held status in high regard but it didn't impress me. Kind and caring were the qualities I valued. The light bulbs told me everything I needed to know about Geoffrey Marks.

After two dates in Canada and 17 in the US, mainly on the east coast, Alvin and I had a magical lovers' reunion at Hook End. We spent a few days exploring this huge house in disbelief. As a hands-on maker, I was excited at the prospect of transforming this quintessential but rather stuffy English country house into a warm, welcoming, colourful home, a larger version of Robin Hood Barn.

It had four attic bedrooms, but the attic had no bathroom, just a sink. A few months later when I was up there alone, painting and decorating, I needed to pee and decided the sink would do. I managed to dislodge it from the wall, which meant telling Sam a repair job was needed. I announced it at dinner to give everyone a laugh. This house needed a joker to keep the energy light. I added another hat to my pile.

On the first floor was the big master bedroom, with adjoining his and hers dressing rooms, and a bathroom with a large bath and his and hers sinks. The bathroom, made by Royal Doulton, was a glorious blue, custom hand-made porcelain 1920s affair, wallpapered with a floral design. To make it less fussy, I stripped down the wallpapers in there and the dressing rooms, and painted them plain purple and blue. My own dressing room I painted over one night when I was completely alone in the house. It was a full moon and I was captivated by the light and shadows in the gardens down below as I worked.

Nearby were two more ensuite bedrooms, one of which I chose for a sewing room. There were many curtains to make or alter. In our room another platform was built but Alvin had decided against a water bed for himself though I still loved them. What to do? A regular mattress one side and a water bed the other worked out ok. I made dark blue curtains with stars by Peter Max from bed sheets, and hung fabulous Afghan rugs either side. Small low tables completed a hippie bedroom. The promo video for 'Time And Space' from Alvin's 1975 album *Pump Iron* was filmed at Hook End and opens with him in that bed. I never saw it or heard the song until the arrival of YouTube.

Down a long landing with a window that looked out onto the swimming pool were two more bedrooms and a 1930s bathroom, with green and black tiles and angular sinks, very art deco. The corner bedroom was cosy with an open fire, perfect for a brass double bed. The larger bedroom had an astonishing barrel ceiling and deco door frames. I'd bought their large French wardrobe from the Marks inventory, an armoire.

A door on this landing accessed the entrance to the self-contained flat with a lounge, kitchen, bedroom and bathroom. Overlooking the gardens, it would offer Harold and Barbara a degree of privacy. On the ground floor was a cloakroom and an entrance hall with galleried staircase. The main hall, where all our stuff had been delivered, opened out to two large sitting rooms on one side, one all white that became our listening room. With our HiFi system installed, shag pile carpet like The Barn and the Russian and Chinese red bean bags in place, we had a chill-out room.

Next door was an oak-panelled room, where I added a secondhand green velvet three-piece suite from the Furniture Cave, and the altered curtains from the dining room at The Barn. Both rooms had French windows out into the gardens. A dozen prints of Alice in Wonderland by Arthur Rackham fit into the panels on one wall. On the mantelpiece stood a small plaque, a three-dimensional cast of a portrait of Beethoven, another Sagittarian composer. I thought he would bring Alvin inspiration.

Back across the main hall through a curved stone archway was a short hall, with a French door that led out to the garden. On this side was a small oak-panelled office room. Across the little hall was another small oak-panelled lounge, where the TV was installed along with a sofa and two easy chairs. This became the main daily lounge. The oak-panelled rooms and hall had fabulous polished oak floorboards, as did the dining room with its beautiful fireplace and Grinling Gibbons carving. Here sat the snooker-cum-dining table, pinball machine and a pianola. In New York we'd found an Aeolian shop that sold the piano rolls that fed into it. One sunny afternoon Keith Emerson sat and played something classical on it. I would rediscover my piano playing delights.

Walking out from the back door, crossing the stable yard was the large old oak-timbered barn, the swimming pool and the dairy, now a tennis court, then bull pens, greenhouses, orchard, more farm buildings and the weighbridge. Hook End Manor had been Hook End Farm when Geoffrey Marks moved in and upgraded the name. We spent days exploring in a bit of a daze, realising the enormity of what we had taken on. There was a house to make livable and a studio to design and build in the barn.

One evening at sunset, Alvin and I walked out into the garden from the TV room corridor through the glass door, out past the walled rose garden and down the lawned slope, past the huge monkey puzzle tree to the hedge where we turned to look back up to the house we had bought. The lights were on in many of the rooms. The evening was fair and still. Alvin was silent for a while, staring at Hook End Manor.

"That's a big pile of bricks," he said with a smile.

"We don't have to stay here if it doesn't work out," I quietly replied.

chapter 40
Hook End, Space Studio

The last three gigs of the October 1972 US tour were in Florida, which is where Alvin might have caught another STD. What is the incubation period? It was well over a week before he noticed symptoms. We made another trip to Harley Street to visit Dr Davis for penicillin shots. A few weeks later we returned to be checked. It seemed it was an NSU. I was clear but Alvin was not. To this day I don't know if what happened next was real or a con. We never found out.

Dr Davis would tell Alvin every month that he was still not clear, give him some treatment and warn him not to have full sex. This was a huge challenge for me at 25, and Alvin at 27. We had always enjoyed our bedtime activities, a big bond between us. We thought the situation would resolve itself after a month or two but, sadly, it did not, and this was the background to all that happened for me at Hook End during 1973.

Sex and drugs and rock'n'roll. I have read quite a few memoirs of those who enjoyed hedonistic lives. I don't remember reading much about STDs in them, but it's obvious promiscuous sex will create problems alongside pleasure. Alvin talked openly about how Ivan Jay had impressed him when girls ran after him down the Nottingham streets in 1960. Touring alone he befriended the nearest, and probably most pushy, girl in the queue that formed nightly. Most men faced with a queue of women wanting sex under these circumstances would have happily done the same.

Those were different times. It was pre-AIDS, which I understood had a dampening effect on his activities, as I'm sure it did for many. It was a time of experimentation in all areas, particularly sex, with birth control pills and the knowledge that a shot of penicillin would cure any problems. It was also a time when men were brought up to believe themselves superior to women, without anyone really questioning that position. Alvin's generation were chauvinists through ignorance of cultural history. It was the mid-seventies before the women's liberation movement challenged the patriarchy of modern times.

At Hook End there was much to focus on day-to-day and no time to ponder these issues. Did I scream and shout and make demands for faithfulness? No, that had never been my style. I didn't do that when Alvin returned from the first US tour with the clap, and it was too late to start now. Occupational hazard was probably my assessment. He was always contrite and full of apologies. I didn't want to tell him how to behave. I was not his parent. He was a talented and intelligent person and that was what I valued most about him. I truly loved his music and supporting him to feel free in himself. Are performers who have high libidos seen as being sexually attractive because of that?

We now had a paid staff of five: my brother Harold and his girlfriend Barbara; Ann Bishop, who cleaned the house and polished the oak floors and paneling; and Harold Bishop, Ann's husband, who along with Henry Crump were full-time gardeners. Harold Bishop complained to me on Mondays that he hadn't won the football pools and said that when he did he would have a house like Hook End. In his younger days, Harold had worked for Sir Charles Clore, a multi-millionaire and previous owner of Hook End. A set of servants' bells over the old kitchen doors included Mr Clore and Mrs Clore's bedrooms. They no longer worked.

Harold Bishop told me that Clore was a keen marksman, but not a very good shot and they would tie birds' feet to the branches of trees so he could shoot them easily. I think he was quite put out that exotic young people like Alvin and me could afford Hook End. When I went out to the garden on a sunny day with bare feet, he'd tell me I should wear shoes or I might get a chill. In November we had a small fireworks party, as we had at The Barn, and Harold arrived with a pail of water, standing silently by, ready for fireworks that misbehaved. We hadn't ask him to do this but it summed up how he must have felt – that we were young and irresponsible and he needed to protect Hook End from us.

Ann Bishop was fully focused on her work, interested to know when we would be away so she could polish the wooden floors and walls. Henry Crump, the second gardener, was short and bow-legged. His passion was riding the motor mower over the many lawns.

My brother Harold and I were blessed with the ability to immerse ourselves in projects to the exclusion of all else. He was happy to work on building the studio but girlfriend Barbara found it oppressive and uncomfortable in a large house in the country. I spent many hours playing cards with her, which seemed to help her to get through the days.

As long as I had been with Alvin, the evening meal was for everyone in the house. Each morning a large box of vegetables and fruits from the greenhouses was left inside the back porch. I'd prepare dinner for whoever was there to eat. Barbara and I got into making jam, as there was so much soft fruit, far more than we could eat.

We were away with TYA on an 11-date UK tour in October and early November followed by four weeks across the USA, mainly in sports halls and stadiums. It included a return to Bill Graham's Winterland in early December, a welcome return to a smaller crowd. The tour had given Ann the chance to polish Hook End's oak floors and panelling.

Our first Christmas at Hook End was looming and back in the UK I delighted in cutting boughs from the large fir trees to decorate the main oak hall by hanging them over all the doors. A suitably large Christmas tree was decorated and plans for our first Christmas included Sam and Doris, Harold and Barbara and Andy Jaworski, who brought a quarter bottle of his dad's specially prepared fruit vodka. After a lovely lunch and exchange of presents we non-drinkers enjoyed a small glass of the vodka. Adjourning to the chill-out room Alvin put on an album and we all fell asleep for a few hours. It was a magical few days. Alvin loved Christmas time.

By New Year Hook End was feeling more like home. It was certainly an advantage to have Harold and Barbara as residents when we went to gigs, or were away on tour. Not needing to close everything down was a great help. Post *Woodstock*, Alvin was clearly not enjoying touring with Ten Years After as he had a few years before. The venues were too big and from the moment they arrived on stage there was an energy verging on hysteria, the potential for a riot, and endless shouts for 'I'm Going Home'. The audience had taken over the show. It was rare to find a gig where he could comfortably get high and really fly into transcendent guitar playing.

Hook End had changed Alvin's perspective. He would soon have his own professional standard recording studio and we discussed hiring it out to other musicians. My brother was especially keen on that idea, seeing himself as an engineer who could be part of a commercial enterprise. Barbara did the paperwork and we applied to the local council for change of use for the barn, to a private recording studio, which was granted.

Though Alvin's income had not increased to the extent that he could leave the band, especially with all our new overheads, it seemed like a possibility on the horizon. We knew we had a large capital sum invested in Hook End, and if necessary we could borrow against that. Without the recording studio and Hook End as a financial asset, he would have been dependent on keeping TYA together. It was an extreme twist of fate on so many levels. Nothing was the same as it had been.

There was plenty of hard work for everyone during the next six months. There was a recording studio to build and the part demolition and rebuilding of an enlarged kitchen undertaken by Sam and me. More TYA tours were already booked. More interviews than ever took place at Hook End, and word was out that Alvin was unhappy with TYA. His interviews were again littered with two phrases in particular, that the band had become "a musical jukebox" and his concern for "musical integrity". Hook End was both an attraction and a mystery to most journalists, and it would have given Alvin more status in their eyes, though that never crossed my mind at the time. Dr Davis was still "treating" Alvin's incurable NSU and still advising him to not have full sex, a major connection and source of relaxation for us both.

Much of my frustration was taken out by rebuilding the kitchen. Partition walls with windows were demolished, the two old kitchen ranges were dismantled and removed. They were packed with insulation made from crushed sea shells. A small four-door, bright red, oil fired Aga was installed on one side with a seating area built up against the back of it where the other range had been. There had been an Aga at The Barn and I had grown used to cooking on it.

Plaster was stripped to reveal red brick archways and Sam built more small archways in red brick either side, not for structure but looks. The old painted, extremely useful, built-in kitchen cabinets were attacked with Nitromors, toxic paint stripper, metal tools and elbow grease. On the cupboard doors, which were plywood, I found a collage home for postcards. The floors were covered in linoleum which when removed revealed an old red quarry tiled floor. The whole area was covered in black tar to create a smooth surface.

I hired a sanding machine and sanded off the dried tar. I tackled patches that were left on my hands and knees with a small sanding machine. I was becoming kind of manic. Dressed in my paint stained clothes and wool hat to keep my hair clean, I remember Alvin one day mistaking me for my brother Harold. My work efforts were relentless and my cannabis relaxation was disappearing, but the finished kitchen was fabulous. I had about £1,000 in my bank account when we moved in – my budget for the whole transformation of the house.

The studio too was coming to completion. Its heart, the Helios desk, was installed in the control room that had been built above the main performance area. There was a glass partition to see down into the transformed barn, and the main studio area had a separate vocal booth. There was tremendous pressure to complete the studio to record an album with Mylon Le Fevre that he and Alvin had spasmodically been working towards. In the last two weeks of the build project Harold developed a badly inflamed knee, they call it housemaid's knee. He had to stay in bed, there was nothing else for him to do and it really freaked him out. He had put his heart and soul into the project and for him it felt like he had failed at the final hurdle, though none of us thought so.[1*]

Time was spent reassuring and tending to Harold whilst Sam, Andy and Alvin had some help with putting up the last few sound proofing panels from musicians already arriving for the first project. The studio was completed in July 1973 and ready to immediately start recording the album *On The Road to Freedom*, with Alvin, Mylon and a host of guest musicians and contributors. By then Harold had happily recovered, he and Andy worked as engineers with Alvin producing and mixing. A momentous achievement by everyone involved.

[1*] Technical details of the Hook End studio can be found at the back on the book.

chapter 41
Tales of Dogs, Cats, Mylon and a Beatle

We had all put in so much hard work, Barbara running the accounts and paperwork for the studio build and doing the wages, Harold and Sam, Andy Jaworski, John Hembrow, and Alvin when not on tour with TYA. Between late January and late March 1973, there were short tours in France, Germany and Sweden, then ten gigs around the UK in April, and a mid-April to mid-May tour of America followed by a week-long second Japanese tour. Hook End had taken me over so much that I came back to the UK at the end of the US tour and Alvin went to Japan alone. I knew that because he was under doctor's celibacy rules he wasn't going to do any serious philandering. One strong memory from that last US tour was how some people came up to me claiming we were friends, that we had spent time together, yet I simply did not remember them at all.

Early on I decided that living in Hook End, this big country house, called for dogs, mainly for security, to bark and let us know when people arrived, and to look like they might give intruders a nip. Having only ever owned cats before, I didn't want a guard dog or a large dog. Alvin had Buddy, his little terrier, when I met him, so I guess he had more experience. I did my research, reading a book on dogs, poring over the pictures and descriptions.

Doris and I both loved all things Egyptian so a Pharaoh hound would be perfect. Elegant and beautiful, like a small greyhound, with pointed pricked-up ears and a long tail that curved high over their backs, they were believed to be descendants of the god Anubis, and with their pointed muzzles they looked like they had a good set of teeth for deterring those who needed to be deterred. A breeder was found and we brought home a girl dog who, after a few days' observation, I called Loopy, a perfect name for her. She spent her nights in the kitchen, enjoying the warmth of the Aga, but it soon seemed unfair for her to be on her own.

The choice for her companion was a black and white Cocker spaniel, the runt of the breeder's litter, a reject with no black fur patches on her eyes. Unlike Loopy, who was a little nervy and reticent to make friends, her new pal was relaxed, the friendliest of dogs, which was good for Loopy. Since she was a Cocker, I decided to call her Joe. Loopy and Joe became great friends. Out in the orchards and fields where I took them for walks, little Joe would stay still and huddle down while Loopy would run great, galloping, figure-of-eight circles around her. Non-dog owners would be astonished at how fast you fall in love with them. They say owners become like their dogs, but I think my choice of these two dogs reflects how unstable I was becoming. Was I the frightened, elegant Loopy or the loving, down-to-earth Joe?

One evening when we were eating, we heard a cat meowing in the small paved garden area. We couldn't see it in the dark and when we went out it became silent. This went on for a couple of nights until we went out with a torch and after searching in the bushes came across an all-black, fluffy kitten. We lured it into the house with saucer of milk and a little dog food and made up a cat bed with a box and blanket. In the morning I hoped to find its owner.

A half hour or so later I went back to the kitchen to check on the kitten. It was foaming at the mouth, obviously terrified to be indoors and left alone. There was a comfy old armchair by the Aga. I got a pillow and a blanket and slept there with this little purring kitten snuggled into my shoulder all night. The next day I set off down the road to the nearest neighbour, knocked on her door and asked if this was her lost kitten. She told me that there was a litter of young feral kittens in her barn. This was one of them and I was welcome to keep him.

What could I say? I stayed by the Aga for a second night and again he slept snuggled into my shoulder. After that he was fine in the house as long as he stayed in the kitchen, but when he found his way to anywhere with soft furnishing he would be so overcome with pleasure he would shit himself. On account of his fluffy neck I named him Ruffles. He grew into a beautiful black cat.

I'm sure that by now you'll think I was acquiring baby substitutes and I probably was. The Jamaican ladies' admonishments had left an impression on me and the last time we had visited John and Eva Fowlie in Copenhagen their baby son was a few months old. Much of my time there was spent nicely stoned, enraptured by this new baby. Alvin didn't seem to notice him, or notice my involvement, but he was really taken with Ann and Mylon LeFevre's daughter Summer, a toddler, when we first met her in Atlanta. One day in an airport he'd given me one of two tiny Steiff teddy bears he bought, the other he gave to Summer. We both still had them in 2020.

Since my early teens, I had never been interested in children, never even really noticed them. It was as if they didn't exist, especially babies. I had enjoyed being around smaller children when I was a child but when pre-teenage hormones kicked in they simply disappeared. My focus then moved to taking appropriate steps to ensure I didn't get pregnant. Little Summer Le Fevre was the first child I remember in those rock'n'roll years. Perhaps a Tchelitchew painting *Hide And Seek* I'd seen at MOMA, with its astonishing, slightly surreal, images of babies and small children, had charmed me. But I had plenty to deal with right now and the idea of adding a baby to the mix was a fleeting fancy for the future.

Mylon's arrival brought plenty of energy into the household. Unknown to me at the time, he was a mess, with serious drug issues he kept hidden from everyone. Had I known, he would certainly have been challenged. Cocaine was becoming common in the music business, and I knew that unlike cannabis it was very toxic. After the passing of Janis, Jimi and Jim, keeping toxic drugs out of the house became important to me.

Mylon was very extrovert and knew that this opportunity for him to record in this new studio, for free, was a dream come true. In fact, that was the phrase he used to describe what was happening. His talent for finding musicians, and inviting them down to write a song and record it, was his forte, and it amused Alvin and me. He would tell stories about this band and that band that he had hung out with. Innocently unaware of anyone's real motives, we still believed that if you were young with long hair and smoked with us, then you were cool. The album they made together at Space Studio, as it became known, was a genuine musical adventure for Alvin. Titled *On The Road To Freedom,* the songs written and co-written by and with a variety of musicians. It was probably the most collaborative project he ever worked on.

Mylon could prize reclusive Alvin out of the house and one night early on in this process, they went to a pub by the river in Henley-on-Thames. Now I never knew Alvin to go into a pub, so Mylon had already taken him out of his comfort zone. Who should be sitting in the pub but George Harrison, whom we knew lived in grand style at Friar Park on the outskirts of the town. Mylon quietly told Alvin, "Hey man, go and say hello to George."

Well there was no way Alvin would have made an approach even if he wanted to, and probably no way that George would have approached Alvin; two English musicians, no. So Mylon got up and went over to George.

"Hi, my name's Mylon LeFevre. I'm from Atlanta, Georgia. I'd like for you to come on over and meet my friend Alvin Lee."

The offer was such that George was unable to tactfully refuse.

George from Liverpool and Alvin from Nottingham had more in common than simply playing guitar. They made an instant connection which lasted for the remainder of George's life. Somewhere in the conversation Mylon no doubt asked George if he would like to write a song or perform on the album that he and Alvin were producing.

So the first time I met George Harrison, he arrived unannounced at our glass kitchen door and rang the bell. Loopy barked. I went to the door, recognised him, opened it and said, "Hello, come in." I stood holding the door open but rather than walk straight in, he stopped in front of me, looked me up and down, smiled and in his warm Liverpool drawl said, "It's very nice here."

I was taken aback. Never in all my time with Alvin, during which I'd met hundreds of musicians, had any of them made a calculated come on like this. Jimmy Page might have threatened to "piss in my fur hat" but all I'd received from everyone else was friendliness and respect. Then again, none of them were ex-Beatles.

We went to Friar Park and met Pattie, George's beautiful wife, who also came to Hook End, maybe to have a swim. They showed us around Friar Park, an extraordinary mansion, pointing out renovations they had made. Its over-the-top grandeur put Hook End into a lesser perspective. George's recording console was housed in carved oak, in keeping with the house. It was magnificent but where was the heart of this house? Well, in a very large kitchen, of course.

In one of the smaller lounges we wound up watching *The Producers*, the brilliant Mel Brookes, Gene Wilder and Zero Mostel version. The movie and most of its script had been memorised by the residents of Friar Park, and was endlessly quoted by them all. Among them was Terry Doran, Pattie and George's PA, a friend who had known The Beatles in Liverpool, and Legs Larry Smith and others who played with the Bonzo Dog Doo Dah Band. With this crew "hanging out" at Friar Park, it struck me that Pattie had little privacy in her home. The bigger the house, the more people it accommodates. It was, of course, very entertaining and I liked Pattie but there was so much going on at Hook End with Mylon that there was no time to cultivate friendships.

Before the main recordings were underway we had a visit from George, without Pattie, that lasted a few days. We hardly knew them and had no idea that their relationship was going through hard times. My dear friend Kris and her husband Woody were also visiting. Everyone stayed overnight. We were far from London and it made perfect sense with so many bedrooms. At the end of the evening I wasn't sure why George didn't return home, but no one was about to ask him if things were ok there. Kris and I had a good catch-up while the boys were out in the studio and she told me that things were not going so great with her and Woody, but this was not new. Their relationship had always struggled. Woody lived as if his life was a perpetual party, while Kris was a homemaker who wanted that type of relationship, at least some of the time.

The next day Woody said he had to get back to London. He needed to work on his own album, *I've got My Own Album to Do*, in his home studio at the Wick in Richmond. He took some jars of my homemade blackcurrant jam with him, and distributed them amongst his musical friends. Next time I saw him he told me that Mick Jagger had really loved my jam. Meanwhile, to my delight, Kris stayed on. George stayed on too, even though Friar Park was only 10 miles away. He hung out in the studio with Alvin and Mylon. Everyone came in for supper, and as Kris and I had always done we smoked something nice and talked endlessly.

In the morning I made a cooked breakfast, set it up in the kitchen and called for Alvin, Mylon, George and Kris. Kris didn't come down but George sat at the head of the table, took his plate and proceeded to cut up white powder on it. It was the first time I had seen or been around cocaine. Alvin and Mylon sat facing him in the Aga seating alcove and he proceeded to talk, talk and talk about Krishna and his spiritual beliefs. I had already called Ann Bishop and prudently suggested she take the day off. It was becoming obvious to me that while George was in some ways just another musician, Alvin and Mylon were in awe of him. He carried on snorting the cocaine he had chopped up. I knew that Alvin and I wouldn't take any and neither did Mylon. Those guys knew I wouldn't have put up with it, regardless of the company they were keeping.

The breakfast feast that I had lovingly prepared was going cold and I was getting pissed off. Watching those two hanging on George's every high utterance was irritating the life out of me. Eventually George stopped talking and disappeared back into the house. I walked out into the garden with

Alvin, across the lawn and down to the gate into the field. We talked and he said he had felt closer to having a religious experience than ever before. I was incredulous, my hunger and spoiled breakfast meant I had somehow missed that revelatory experience.

As the day went on Mylon, Alvin and George hung out. I talked with Kris and learnt she had spent the night with George. We walked the dogs around the orchard and she suggested we try chanting "Hare Krishna, Hare Krishna, Hare Rama, Hare Rama", the Krishna chant. I joined in with as much enthusiasm as I could muster, but frankly I wasn't happy. George seemed to have taken over the house. Everything was now about him and he was calling the shots. Also, the gap between his spiritual beliefs and his fondness for sex, drugs and rock'n'roll was confusing to say the least. I was starting to feel like the housekeeper in a Fellini movie; and remember, the celibacy imposed on me by Alvin's NSU was not making my life easier.

That evening, as I was getting ready for bed in our Royal Doulton bathroom, there was a knock on the hallway door. It was Kris. George wanted to know if I would like to take a bath with them. Alvin heard the knock, came into the bathroom and took in what she said. I told her no thank you. Someone had to say no to George, I thought. Alvin and I didn't discuss this incident, we simply went to sleep. The next morning, I was struggling emotionally with all that was happening in the house, my sexual energies running around in all directions. George had been a teenage fantasy for me in 1962, all the way back to my bedroom in Nottingham. He was the Beatle I fancied all those years ago and here he was suggesting I join him in the bath. In the kitchen I made some tea and bowls of muesli and put them on a tray. As I started out the door, Alvin asked me where I was going. "To take some breakfast to Kris and George," I said.

I walked with a purpose out of the kitchen up the various staircases and knocked on the attic bedroom door. Alvin did not follow me. Kris asked who was knocking and opened the door to let me in. George grinned. There was a little light conversation about my prolonged celibacy. George twinkled and invited me under the covers. It was very erotic and all reason flew out of the attic window. Soon there was another knock on the door. It was Alvin but Kris wouldn't let him in. In hindsight it might have been better if she had as there wasn't much to see. There hadn't been time for anything much to happen. Alvin and Kris persisted with their tug-of-war over the door. Eventually he gave up and went back downstairs. The erotic energy followed my reason out of the window. Did George say "I think you should go"? Probably, after all he had taken over the house.

When I reached our bedroom, I found Alvin prostate and crying. I understood, I sympathized. But a part of me was overjoyed that I had broken the spell that George had cast on the house. Time passed until there was a knock on the door. Mylon came in to ask what was going on.

George was now in the lounge below us. We could hear him playing guitar and singing 'Jealous Guy', the John Lennon song.

Alvin told Mylon he had "found me in bed with George".

"Hell man, I'd fuck a Beatle!" was his honest response

chapter 42
A Roof Falls, On The Road To Freedom

Was that the day when George suggested his Ayurvedic doctor might cure Alvin's NSU with his own urine? He sent over a lovely cut glass decanter for Alvin to fill and send back. Perhaps it was a peace offering from George. Either way, Alvin was desperate and happy to try anything.

It was some time before the potion arrived and in the meantime Kris and George went off on a month's holiday together. In her memoir *Wonderful Tonight*, Pattie wrote that in 1973 George was using cocaine and at his most sexually promiscuous. "In India George had become fascinated by the god Krishna, who was always surrounded by young maidens," she wrote, "and came back wanting to be some kind of Krishna figure, a spiritual being with lots of concubines. He actually said so. And no woman was out of bounds."

When Kris returned to Friar Park from Portugal she invited me over to share her holiday stories. We left George and had a wander in the gardens. It was obvious to me she was very confused by all that had happened. Another couple had been with them, and Kris had gone into the nearby town with them, leaving George to meditate and chant. All meals at the house were vegetarian and this couple had pounced on hamburgers once they reached the town. Having not smoked around George, they eagerly bought cigarettes. Kris was an honest, open-hearted lady and this disturbed her. She felt there was a fantasy around George because of his celebrity, and she was not happy with it. She thought Woody was having an affair with Pattie and the whole saga was turning sour.

Alvin was away that night and I stayed over with Kris and George. We all ended up in bed together, a blue, flute-playing Krishna painting watching over us. After months living like a nun, I was like a sexual pressure cooker. How ironic it was to break my sex fast at Friar Park. Having been disturbed in our little frolic at Hook End, I lay into George like a devouring Hindu goddess while Kris waited her turn. After I was finished with George, I wrapped myself in a blanket and sat at the window, gazing out over the amazing moonlit gardens to a soundtrack of their ecstasy mingling with gentle Indian music. On the window was a beautiful peacock butterfly. I had woken it from its evening sleep and it was trying to get out. I undid the catch and opened the window, allowing the butterfly to escape, and I watched it as it disappeared into the night. It felt highly symbolic.

In the morning I showered in the most extraordinary bath I have ever seen, an old Victorian water closet. It had a structure at one end, with overhead showers and vertical jets of water. George encouraged us both to join him for yoga exercises. After breakfast I left for Hook End. I truly hoped that Kris would realise that life with George would always involve other women and that she needed to look elsewhere for the faithful lover she deserved. This is not to say that my jaunt had been entirely altruistic, it was pure sexual lust. I hoped it might relax me.

As I left that morning, George took my hand and gave me five small uncut rubies, which he carried and handed out to friends. Pattie wrote that the head of the Hare Krishna chapter, who lived for a while at Friar Park, had brought George a sack of ruby chips from India. He gave some lovely larger pieces and other jewelry to Pattie which she intended to make into necklaces for relatives. "He couldn't think what to do with the rest, so he scattered them amongst the gravel on the path to the swimming pool."

George's genuine dedication to his spiritual life and Krishna was even more remarkable since he was by nature and background a randy Northerner. Growing up in the Midlands, I had known plenty of similar randy men, Alvin amongst them. That male culture was quite normal, not exceptional. Since his death there's been a tendency for George to be painted as a saint, but this diminishes the all too human frailties he was fighting to achieve his spiritual goals. He was wrestling some heavy demons and it makes me respect his dedication more.

When I first saw Monty Python's movie *Life of Brian,* which George heroically financed after the Delfonts pulled out, one line stood out to me. When Brian has fled to his mum's house and she opens the window to address his horde of rabid followers who are calling for "the messiah", she screams, "He's not the messiah, he's a very naughty boy!" That seemed a nod to George. He called his record label Dark Horse, also the title of his album from this period.

I did like George. He always travelled with a small guitar and happily sat and played Beatle songs. He told me they all referred to each other with the prefix "Beatle", as in Beatle John, Beatle Paul, Beatle Ringo. Together they had been on a journey of celebrity like no other, and when it ended they had to carry that weight, as Paul wrote. That was in 1970, only three years earlier. It was messy for him and his confusion can't have been helped by Friar Park. Big houses are shit to live in, especially for a couple wanting a close relationship. How dreadful for Pattie, who really loved George, to be put through the craziness of 1973, and no surprise that she thought Eric Clapton would be an escape to happiness.

If two people live in a house with over 30 rooms, it is very possible they will lose one another. When Alvin and I lived in one room at Warwick Square we discovered ourselves and each other, we played and had fun. Hook End was not turning into a cosy home, despite all my best attempts. In fact, we had forgotten why we moved to the country in the first place. During Ten Years After's hectic schedule we opened the door to musicians and strangers at Gloucester Place Mews, calling it party central. That was behind the decision to move to the country and have a proper private home, a balance to recording, endless touring and living out of a suitcase. Now we seemed to have fallen back into the same rock'n'roll trap, with a huge house, empty bedrooms and a recording studio. Nature abhors a vacuum and vacant beds were soon filled, in our case with rock musicians, not good for privacy or a settled home.

Before the first recordings in the new Space Studio, Andy, my brother Harold, and Alvin did plenty of work as they learned to use the Helios desk. One late evening in early April 1973 Mylon and Alvin went over to see George at Friar Park, while Harold and Andy continued their experiments. One of them suggested trying out the echo in the tennis court, since it was lined with tiles and was previously a dairy. They took the two Neumann U87 microphones on stands and a Fender Twin Reverb amplifier down to the tennis court and ran wiring back, through the pool room up to the desk. They could put sound through the Fender at one end and pick up the ambient echo through the microphones at the other. As they listened in the control room to the echo from the tennis court, they were puzzled by a crackling noise. Harold decided to go and investigate.

"So, I went down there and when I entered the room there were patches of white plaster dust on the floor," he told me. "As the tennis court floor was black asphalt this was really obvious. I got alongside the first mic to waggle the cables to see if the noise returned and the entire roof dropped about four inches with a 'whump', followed by the spookiest silence I've ever experienced. Andy was still in the control room listening to the mics and he heard me say, 'The roof is coming down, help me get the gear out.' He ran in, maybe 20 seconds later, saw me at the far end, picking up the amplifier, and said, 'I'll get the mics out.' He reached the pool room a bare yard ahead of me. Then this huge roar and a pressure wave blew us both off our feet, we flew across the room and smashed into the glass-panelled outer doors."

When they came around, thankfully unharmed, they saw the dust settling on a huge pile of debris, and realised the entire roof had collapsed. They'd been seconds away from certain death. The pool room, which had a shower and dressing room, was a later addition with joint access to the barn and the tennis court. This probably saved their lives since the roofs were not built together, and the pool room stayed intact.

Later, as they sat by the pool having a calming smoke and a brandy, Harold said, "We both agreed that we should have ignored the noises from the room, rolled the tape machine and done a mix with a spectacular noise halfway through."

Alvin and Mylon arrived back after midnight. I had been sound asleep in our bedroom on the far side of the house and wasn't woken by the crash. It was only later in the night that Alvin told me what had happened. At daylight Alvin went out with his camera and took many photos of the remaining rubble. I wonder where they are.

Over the years the fall of the roof became a rock'n'roll story that many would claim to have witnessed, even Alvin in one interview. For me it was traumatic. I almost my lost my lovely younger brother and Andy Jaworski, a dear and important friend. Andy was almost 25 and Harold not yet 23. He was only there that night because I had involved him in my crazy world and, had he died, I would have been burdened for the rest of my life by guilt and grief.

It turned out to be another legacy of Mr "Super Super Super" Marks. He had turned the old tile-lined, dairy-cum-milking parlour into a tennis court. The problem was that although it was big enough, it wasn't high enough. So, he had removed some of the lower steel girders that held the large flat roof in place. With raised edges and some skylights, it became a large basin which held water when it rained. Unbeknownst to us, Henry Crump would go up there and sweep off the water. There had been a huge storm that day, starting in the early hours and enough water settled on the roof for the weight to bring it down.

Only a few months earlier we had been in the tennis court with Mike Patto, Ollie Halsall, Tim Hinkley, Boz Burrell, Ian Wallace, playing an impromptu stoned game of hilarious balloon tennis. I hadn't seen Alvin relaxed and having so much fun all year. It was a joy. After the roof fell in, it was sobering for everyone to see the huge pile of bricks, glass, tiles and rubble. No one said so it but it was a dark symbol.

Meanwhile, Mylon and Alvin were laying down tracks and ideas. Mylon was the first musician with whom Alvin co-wrote and it was great to see. *On The Road To Freedom* would have 12 songs, four by Alvin, three by Mylon, four co-written, and the remaining two by George and Woody. Mylon sang all the lead vocals bar two sung by Alvin. This was very generous of Alvin, a real gift to Mylon. It was a melodic album and strikingly different from any Ten Years After albums. It holds up very well as time goes by, though it wasn't a big seller and the music press were confused by what the new Alvin was all about.

Space Studio was a great success, the Helios desk and the acoustics of the soundproofed barn was applauded. The studio was where it was at, leaving us with no home life at all and still no satisfactory sex life. What I didn't discover, or even suspect, was that Mylon had been luring Alvin into cocaine. Its effects brought on the kind of intensity that amphetamine had in the early sixties. Alvin was a naturally speedy person, with a very active mind, more suited to cannabis that brought relaxation and focus. Bearing in mind how fast he played when he was stoned, he didn't need any additional help.

The last time that I spoke to Alvin, in December 2012, we talked a lot about what had gone wrong at Hook End. I asked him if he had been taking cocaine at that time. I already knew he had taken it later in the seventies. He once told me he had spent "£30,000 on cocaine". He was adamant that he had never taken it during the time we were together, and it wasn't until after his death that I reconnected with musicians from those sessions and finally asked about cocaine. I was gently laughed at. Everyone had been taking it in the studio. Mylon was heavily into cocaine. When I watched George taking it at the breakfast table, it must have been tough for Alvin and Mylon to simply sit there. They both knew how I felt.

In the house at Hook End, I was getting more and more lost, cooking for more and more guests. Ironically, I was losing weight. After preparing and cooking large amounts of food I had no appetite myself. Cooking for as many as 12-14 a night was becoming a drudge. Was it even appreciated? They always wanted to get back to recording. The control room was not very big and I didn't spend time there, which was also a drag, as I loved to hear music really loud through playback speakers.

Most evenings I would spend in the house, in the kitchen making tea for whoever came out for a cup and sitting talking to whoever was taking a break. One night I was still up at about 2am when George come in to find me stirring big saucepans of bubbling jam. "What are you doing?" he asked.

"Making jam," I replied.

"Oh!" George smiled and went back to the studio. Towards the end of the album, we started to note the credits and learned that for contract reasons George needed a pseudonym. A few of us, including George, sat in the small lounge, coming up with ideas. Suddenly I said, "Hari Georgeson." It just popped into my head because Kris and I had been chanting the Hari Krishna mantra and, of course, it stuck.

Sometimes, in the privacy of our bedroom, I tried to talk to Alvin about how lost and unhappy I was feeling. His responses were short. "Why can't you be like Andy, he's always happy?" he said one time. "Maybe you should have a baby?" was another response. That was the furthest from my mind, bringing up a baby out in the middle of the countryside while he was away touring. When I complained about the amount of cooking I was doing he suggested I "have a night off, get fish and chips for everyone". This meant driving into Reading, getting them, bringing them back and serving them up, hardly a night off. His responses were so cold, and quite unlike the man I knew and loved, who would have been kinder and more loving. Had I known then that he was already involved in cocaine, I might have understood his coldness. What would I have done?

Alvin, Mylon, Steve Winwood, Jim Capaldi, Rebop Kwaku Baah, Ronnie Wood, George Harrison, Mike Patto, Bob Black and Andy Stein all contributed to the recording. Ian Wallace, Boz Burrell and Tim Hinkley, the rhythm core for the tracks, wound up living at Hook End. There was no way for them to drive the 45 miles to where they lived in London every night and return in the morning. I liked them all, but it was getting overcrowded and their habits started to irritate. One morning in the kitchen, as I walked past one of them, who shall be nameless, there was a terrible smell of rancid feet. Something needed saying and I tried to be funny and silly rather than heavy.

"Goodness, can I smell cat shit? Oh (nameless musician), it's your feet that stink! I thought I smelt cat shit. Can't you take a bath?"

After all, there were three full bathrooms available, with hot running water and fresh towels. I made sure there were clean towels and beds changed. Yes, I was also the laundry maid. Later that morning Barbara challenged me. "How dare you speak to him like that, you were so rude!"

I was amazed. "This is my home, it's not ok for someone to stay here and stink."

No hierarchical lines had been drawn in this house. I had assumed that everyone would work together but also respect the fact that this was our home. It seemed that Alvin was seen as the one to indulge. He was paying their wages. What is that dynamic? For ten years Alvin had been my life, he had my dedication and now it seemed there were unspoken agendas and I was being elbowed out. It was becoming very claustrophobic.

Ever since our sex life had been curtailed, and before the attic nonsense with George, Alvin has made some odd accusations about my behaviour. One winter night I had walked Perry Press out to his car. When I got back to the house Alvin accused me of getting up to something with Perry. The reason? My nipples were erect when I came in. It was a cold night for chrissakes! Perry never had a girlfriend and I always thought he was gay. One morning when I went food shopping and took a longer drive to explore some little country roads, Alvin asked if I was having an affair with the butcher!

Another time, before the recording started and we were relatively alone at the house, I used the sauna and took a naked dip in the adjacent swimming pool. Alvin saw the guy who had serviced our boilers for three years standing at the landing window watching me. He was cross with the guy and later really annoyed with me. Where the hell was my life and my freedom in this set up? Who was I? Would it have been different if we had married? I don't think so. We were having a crisis but there was no time or privacy for a crisis.

On August 3, 1973, Ten Years After played at Alexandra Palace as part of the London Music Festival series. It was a great night. The music was loud and rockin' and I enjoyed seeing everyone. Being a London gig, some friends came, including Johnnie and Judy who had brought along Rod Duncombe, my jive partner from early sixties Nottingham. We found that neither of us had forgotten our moves and had a great dancing reunion. Rod had moved to London some years back and was working in the music business himself. Small world.

At Hook End, Kris came down with Woody, who this time went back to London and left her with Mylon. I had no idea she knew Mylon. She told me they had met in Paris, when she was trying to get backstage at a Who gig. He was already sweet with security and spotted Kris, shouting to the security guard, "Hey man, that's my wife, let her in!" Needless to say, that had impressed her. During the last few months, her life had become even more complicated than mine. She was still desperately in love with Woody but had no idea how he felt about her anymore. Her time with George had only confused her further.

Jim Capaldi was also a good friend of Kris and he came into the house that evening and sat down for a cup of tea and a chat with us. Jim was an interesting man, and we three had a good long talk about many things. He mentioned he had a small cottage in Wales and that if we ever wanted an escape from rock'n'roll, we were welcome to go there. It was near the Black Mountains and sounded wonderful. It was only a passing comment but it had lodged in my mind.

By now I was definitely losing the plot. I didn't keep a diary but in a notebook I scrawled two very anxious pages: "Have to get away to cottage in Wales for a month... with Kris, Joe, Loopy. Aim to get Krissy together Hare Krishna, to get Joe and Loopy together and incidentals like Fan Club magazine. Reason, present state of mind is very self-destructive to everyone around. Dogs are becoming a hassle due to lack of attention. I feel lack of energy etc. etc. need to recharge and review situation from afar."

It showed my confused state. Where did I start and end? The reference to Krishna was my hope to help get Kris over George, with whom she was still emotionally involved.

In my mind, getting away from Hook End seemed to be a way to get clear about what my problems actually were. We had been non-stop since we moved in and a holiday seemed a good idea. However, I had no money. My account had been drained by the renovations and I felt that if I asked Alvin for money for a holiday, it would have caused further complications. He was clearly completely engaged with the album, the studio, the musicians and keeping it all together.

I was so confused, which is actually the time when you should do nothing. It would have been better to have gone to bed for a couple of days, something I had never done. I did have more conversations with Jim and suggested that maybe Kris and I would take a break at his cottage. We had been discussing it as a bit of fun, a little adventure for both of us. Kris and I agreed that we would go away together soon and I would call her to arrange that.

A promotional gig was arranged for the album on a Sunday at The Rainbow rooms, a small club at the top of the BIBA store in Kensington High Street. It was being filmed for a TV special to be shown in the USA later in the year. I decided that the following day, the Monday, would be the best day for Kris and I to head for the hills. I would tell Alvin that morning.

He had loads of promo set up in London with Mylon, the musicians would have all left, and it would have caused the least disruption. During the week rehearsals took place in the studio for the few numbers they would play.

Steve Winwood and Tim Hinckley were on keyboards, Ian Wallace on drums, Mike Patto and Jim Capaldi on backing vocals and two lovely young black ladies on backing vocals. Alvin and Mylon sang lead vocals and played acoustic guitars. Photos were needed for the album sleeve and advertising. The morning of the shoot there was a knock on my bathroom door and there stood Mylon, like an apparition, dressed from head-to-toe in a fancy matching white cotton outfit, completely over the top. It had frills and lace on the shirt and flared pants, something between a Spanish flamenco dancer and a Mexican mariachi musician.

Alvin appeared, took one look, and said, "No way man, you're not wearing that."

Mylon was crestfallen. "Gee Alvin, I had this made specially."

"Well you ain't wearing it. Just put your denims on."

"What was that all about?" he said when Mylon had gone.

"Ridiculous, what was he thinking?" I replied. What indeed.

They went out with cameras, tripod and Andy Jaworski to the small lane through some lovely woods and shot the images used for *On The Road to Freedom*'s cover. The sun was shining and the trees were magnificent, but Alvin does not look happy. Mylon, however, looks like it is a dream come true, despite the denims.

chapter 43
Crazy Time. Pirate Poet

Friday morning arrived, the *Midnight Special* TV recording was two days away, and Mylon and Alvin spent most of the day out in the studio. I called Kris in the afternoon to check with her that we were still on for our little break from Monday. She was sorry but something was happening and she wouldn't be able to come. I can't remember what she said, only feeling so unhappy when she said she was sorry. Well, I shouldn't have been surprised as we had never taken off on a trip together but I was really feeling desperate. No one else was as close to me as Kris. The only women friends I had were Chelle and Ruthann. The way things were with Ten Years After at the time, being with either of them would only have added to the strain I was feeling. Johnnie and Judy? Sam and Doris? No, they were all too close to Alvin and wouldn't have welcomed me bringing my problems to them.
My mother? No chance.

My plan for a break was not designed to upset Alvin, just to clear my head, get a perspective, something, just something, just somewhere else. My brother Harold was in the kitchen and I asked his advice. I'm sure he had no idea how desperate I felt. Everyone was far too occupied with the upcoming show. "Well you don't want to be like mum and stay in a situation where you are unhappy, do you?" he said, referencing the time when mum could have left dad for her boyfriend but chose not to. I had no boyfriend, there was no choice like that to be made. I thought I was going crazy. I was quite manic.

I went to Barbara in her little office and tried to explain my problem, but it was so nebulous. The point was I wanted to get away, to be able to clear my head. Did she really understand me? We had been living in the house together for a year but we hadn't grown close. She was with Harold whenever possible but I had mentioned to her that Kris and I had planned a stay in Jim Capaldi's Welsh cottage. Like everyone else, she knew about how Alvin's NSU led to our lack of sex.

Out of the blue Barbara said, "Have you noticed that Jim really fancies you? Haven't you noticed that he always dresses up when he comes here and likes to talk to you?"

This was not advice to make me less confused, more like someone throwing a hand grenade into the room.

"Really? No, I've never noticed," I replied.

I left the room even more confused than before and thought about Jim. I had enjoyed our talks. He did listen to me but it never crossed my mind there was anything else. My physical frustrations had become overwhelming, not only the lack of sex, but the lack of closeness Alvin and I had always enjoyed. So, I did something crazy, something completely out of character, something only a deep level of desperation could arouse.

I called Jim. Somehow, I was completely calm, totally other. It was like an out-of-body experience, though I could feel my heart beating very fast. I explained that Kris couldn't come with me next Monday but I wanted to go to his cottage and would he like to come with me? Unbelievable. Well, he was delighted with my offer. Yes, he'd love to go to Wales with me.

Tomorrow was Saturday. Alvin and Mylon would be out that evening. So, we arranged to meet in the evening. In my madness, a little voice was telling me, "You have never even kissed this man." I suggested we met at Friar Park. Why there? I have no idea. Why not at Jim's? Did I think it was a secret location? Now you know how nuts I was.

All I remember of the Saturday evening at Friar Park was that I was operating on a different waveband. I was the devouring goddess again. George was there and so was Terry Doran, in the big kitchen. Maybe there were others? I didn't care. I took over the sofa in the main galleried hall with Jim. We kissed and talked and kissed and talked, entwined but never undressed; highly erotic, intense. Several times Terry came out and asked if we would prefer one of the bedrooms. "No, we are fine here," I told him. I was secretly delighted to have made George feel uncomfortable, to have taken over his home, as he had taken over mine. Quite nuts.

My loyalty to Alvin was still intact. I had no intention of leaving him the night before the *Midnight Special* recordings. I knew it would freak him out and might have wrecked the show. I arranged to go to Jim's on the Monday, when Alvin was off to London with Mylon. On Sunday my thoughts were a blur. What is the sex hormone that floods the body and brain and removes sanity? Ever since this time I have sympathized with those who go off the rails and have crazy, uncontrollable, erotic sex; sex that puts their stable lives and relationships at risk. It is inexplicable.

The gig at the Rainbow Rooms was good fun but not incredible. Mylon seemed unsure of himself alongside Alvin performing live. Jim and Patto were among the back-up singers, doing spins and hamming it up, but it seemed ok in the spirit of the night. George and party were there but I don't remember speaking to them. Was I embarrassed about the Saturday night? No. I think I felt like I was lit up like a Christmas tree. As usual I took a space to the side to dance, clap and sing along. I remember one of the girl singers spotting me and beckoning to me to go and sing with them. Well, that would have been too much for Alvin, Mylon and the musicians. That I knew. I wasn't totally crazy.

There are black and white photos from that evening and on one close-up I look so thin, gaunt and stressed. I was down to about seven stone. There is one of Patto and Jim with a huge wine goblet and one of me and Jim lighting cigarettes and looking rather furtive. A small colour photo shows me singing, clapping, looking so high. A woman is watching me with a smile. I don't look like I was about to jump off a cliff.

Monday morning Alvin and Mylon were getting ready to go to London for interviews and, on an impulse, I went to Mylon's room, sat down very seriously with him and told him that I was leaving that day and that I wanted him to know so that Alvin wouldn't be worried when he got back and I wasn't there. What was I thinking, so he wouldn't be worried? I don't think I mentioned Jim. They set off to town. I packed a little suitcase and set off to Jim's house in Marlow. Did I say any goodbyes? No memory. I wanted to get away, get away, it was all too much. Did anyone try to stop me? No, no one.

If I had known that cocaine was involved, it would have changed things completely. I hadn't stopped loving Alvin, we hadn't had a blazing row, our story was not finished. We had lost each other in a mansion. In AA apparently, they call it doing a geographic when people run away from an unmanageable life.

I had never been to Jim's house in Marlow. It wouldn't have mattered what it was like. I was on the run to a man not a house. I had directions, it was in the town, an old vicarage. It was very old, Jim opened the door and I entered a whole new world and a new life. We went to bed, what need was there to talk, and Jim was very passionate. I stayed in his bed until the next morning. In the evening Steve and his lady, Penny, came to visit and I stayed in bed. Jim asked if I wanted to come downstairs but I couldn't deal with it. I slept.

Was it the next day or the day after that, I drove back to Hook End? Barbara or Harold were in the kitchen, the dogs were ecstatic. I asked them to tell Alvin I was in the bedroom and I walked up the back stairs, through my dressing room and waited for him on the bed. After a while he came in and sat with me and I tried to explain that I was in love with Jim, and I was leaving. It clearly wasn't true, I was in lust with Jim but I was still in love with Alvin and cross with him for neglecting me. He didn't shout or ask me not to leave. It felt as though some invisible force was in charge of us both that we could not resist. We sat and wept together. It was so sad, there were no more words.

Alvin left the room and I sat for a while and composed myself. I went back downstairs and quickly left. It was autumn, early evening. It had been a sunny day and as I started to drive through the woods, an autumn mist started to come down. Approaching Henley and the Thames it had turned into a heavy fog, making it really hard to navigate the winding road by the river. The road ahead was far from clear. Why didn't I recognise this sign from the universe and turn around whilst there was still time? In my rearview mirror there was no knight on a white horse galloping after me to stop me and take me back to our castle. I had made my bed and now I would have to lie in it.

For almost ten years Alvin and I had lived so easily together. I had met him so young, at 16 years old, and I thought all my relationships would be this easy, that somehow I was magically able to have good relationships, despite the fact that I knew people who struggled with theirs. Never having lived with anyone else, it was so ridiculously naive. It was pure lust that had so distorted my vision and not that I had fancied Jim for weeks, not at all. It wasn't until we started snogging on George's sofa that I had found he was a turn on at all. We are at the mercy of our hormones in our teens and twenties. So, what did I find once I climbed out of my new bed in the home of my new bedmate?

Jim Capaldi was so different, such an extrovert, such a man's man. He had a best friend, Noggy, who lived with him at Marlow. Jim was working on his second solo album, *Whalemeat Again,* that year and on the back cover was a picture of him and Noggy. They were on the banks of the Colorado river at the base of the Grand Canyon, where they had been rafting down the rapids. Standing there with their two native American guides, they looked amazing. He told me Chris Blackwell, his manager and head of Island Records, had flown in by helicopter to join them for a couple of nights. Jim lived an adventurous life in the world outside of music.

Jim and Noggy had been doing renovation work at Marlow, changing the bathroom, kitchen, the usual stuff. Well not quite. In the bathroom they had put in a metal tub shaped like the quarter of a circular pie. They had spent months covering it with tiny, tiled mosaic and it was now finished, so we wanted to try it out, since it was big enough for two. We set the hot water running and after a while, when this big tub only had about six inches in it, the water ran cold. There would never be enough hot water for this tub from the hot water system in the house. It was dismantled and removed and we went to London and bought a shaped double bath, with a pillow, to lie down in. It cost about £400 all fitted in and was practical and luxurious.

Jim's bedroom was on the front overlooking the road, quite bland, but next door was a smaller room totally different. It was in the oldest part of the house with rich dark oak panelling. The leaded windows overlooked the walled garden, and it was like a nest, somewhere to hide. Just what I needed. We bought a lovely brass bed, another £400 on a trip to London. I liked to sleep in there and found it restful but Jim found it claustrophobic. Soon we would mov back into the big front bedroom again.

The kitchen had been altered and a modern eye level oven had been installed. I decided to cook a roast chicken lunch for us all, only to find that the gas would not stay lit. It was the oven control, which kept popping out. I completed the roast by jamming a piece of wood between it and a cupboard to keep it lit. Jim and Noggy were lovely guys and good fun and kind to me. At lunchtime we would walk down the street to the local pub by the Thames. I took to drinking a half-pint glass of Mackeson, black stout, like Guinness but sweeter. Jim and Noggy smoked cannabis but not regularly and I was happy enough to cut down. Giving up anything never seemed a problem.

The other resident at Marlow was a great Dane, white with black patches, sort of like a Dalmatian. He was called Saracen and spent most of his time in the garden. He was huge and thanks to Jim and Noggy, didn't really have a routine. Jim told me he bought him on a whim as a puppy, in the pet department of Harrods. There was a garage where he slept but sometimes in the night, he would take to barking. I can still hear Jim shouting to him from the bedroom window. "Saracen! SARacen! SARAcen! SARACEN!" starting in a normal voice, then louder and louder until he would eventually stop barking. I found it hilarious. I dare say most of the neighbours were awake by then. Noggy, Jim and I all took him for walks along the Thames footpath near the house, but he just lacked routine, as did we.

A few times Saracen got out of the garden and he usually headed for the butcher's shop on Marlow High Street. Once there he would lay himself across the main entrance, barring it to customers. The butcher would lure him to one side with a bit of something and call the house. His number was on his name tag and Noggy would go off to fetch him back. One time, Saracen disappeared for the whole day and in the early evening the phone rang.

"Hello," said a rather proper, elderly English, female voice. "Are you missing a large dog?"

"Oh, yes, it's Saracen", I said. "Where are you? We'll come and pick him up."

"Oh no, no need to do that, I'll drive him over to you."

"Thank you, if you're sure."

"Yes, no trouble."

I told Jim who thought it was great and hoped she would cope. A while later the doorbell rang and out we went. A small, plump, grey haired lady stood there and parked outside was her Mini, with Saracen on the back seat. Jim was astonished she had coaxed him into the little car, but very pleased that everything was ok. Saracen lumbered out into the house and we asked if she wanted to come in for a cup of tea. No, she had to get off, things to do.

On reflection, Jim, Noggy, Saracen and a never-ending troupe of friends, family and musicians with their antics, humour and great music helped me to get through the following months. Music aside, the passions in Jim's life were concern for the environment and unfairness in the world. Nixon's politics, unnecessary killing of whales and ugly concrete buildings were his special concerns and they were all issues that concerned me. He had a great phrase about bad ugly architecture. "If there's no love in the buildings, they'll be no love in the people."

We went off on trips around the UK, and the classic city of Bath was a favourite. We would take a camera and take pictures of ugly buildings. I would pose, pointing to the offending structure. We took pictures of each other, and selfies with the timer. They tell quite a story. I often look quite lost and I remember Jim's mum telling me years later that I always looked very miserable. Well, my love for Alvin didn't stop, it hadn't petered out as some loves do. We hadn't grown apart. It was the first crisis we had ever had and we both failed to deal with it. Some relationships are highly strung, people fight, quarrel, break up, make up and take it all as part of their love. That wasn't my temperament, nor Alvin's. The cannabis probably helped.

I wasn't in love with Jim when I ran away. We hadn't had an affair, just pure lustful madness. If we could have sneaked an affair for a few months that might have been what I needed. I believed in being faithful as I knew that just having sex was never just having sex. Although Alvin was unfaithful when on tour alone, I didn't blame him. When I saw those young women it would have taken a saint to resist. He wasn't a saint.

I've never understood people who actually get a kick out of cheating on their partners, though I know some do and good luck to them. However, I had put Jim and me onto a very intense footing by running away from my home and moving in, without Jim having much say. After a couple of weeks, he said he wanted to marry me and we would go away at Christmas and be married then. Another day he asked me if I would have left Alvin with or without him, and I said yes. What else could I say? He said he was worried because he knew he could blow hot and cold. You see the confusion.

I did grow fonder of Jim and cared for him. He brought a big energy into any room. He was full of rhythm and music and loved to get a jam happening when a few musicians were about. First and foremost, he was a natural drummer. I'd loved his drumming on the early Traffic albums. He wasn't a heavy rock drummer, he seemed to have a light touch and bring interesting original breaks and fills to his drumming. I was intrigued back at Warwick Square, years earlier when I saw an article in *Melody Maker* about him not playing drums with Traffic any more so as to concentrate on singing. Pleased to have the chance, I asked Jim about it. He said he suffered anxiety on stage when drumming, and would get paranoid that he might have a heart attack.

That really surprised me, but then as time went on he would have anxious days. Nowadays we know all about anxiety and panic attacks. At that time, it wasn't understood. How could I help? We found playing backgammon was an excellent focus for calming his mind when he felt out of control. We played for hours, and I enjoyed it. We were well matched and the games would be closely fought. His background was Italian and he had been brought up a Catholic. Years before in my teens, I'd already formed opinions on most of the world's religions. The Catholics were brilliant at instilling guilt and anxiety in young children and generally messing up their heads. So, I wasn't surprised he struggled and I was sympathetic.

The biggest and best surprise was discovering that Jim was the lyricist for Traffic and had written the words to all the extraordinary songs they played, 'Dear Mr Fantasy', 'No Face No Name No Number', 'Evening Blue', '40,000

Headmen' and many more. 'Low Spark Of High Heeled Boys', seemed to be Jim's personal favourite, he often quoted from it:

> *"And the man in the suit has just bought a new car,*
> *From the profit he's made on your dreams.*
> *But tonight they just said that the man was shot dead,*
> *By a gun that didn't make any noise.*
> *Well it wasn't the bullet that laid him to rest,*
> *Was the low spark of high-heeled boys."*

Steve Winwood wrote the music and Jim the lyrics. Steve has one of the most exceptional, soulful voices in music and delivered the words from his heart, so most people assumed they were his words. Steve was such a brilliant musician, a complete talent, like Stevie Wonder his black counterpart. Both Taurians, both precocious talents, both predominantly organists, born a day and two years apart: Steve Winwood on May 12, 1948, and Stevie Wonder on May 13, 1950.

Steve Winwood and Jim Capaldi needed each other to produce the brilliant Traffic songs. Look at the Traffic albums and the songwriting credits, Winwood/Capaldi. I don't know why it was rarely talked about, though fortunately it has started to be since Jim died in 2005. A complete set of his lyrics and original drafts has been put together, as a deluxe limited edition. Hopefully one day it will be a paperback.

Traffic was a band of very creative characters. In the late sixties they lived together in a house in the Berkshire countryside, smoking cannabis and taking psychedelics together, jamming and developing their jazz rock-based music. As a result, they were a family, always looking out for each other. Chris Wood who played sax, flutes, was a magical gentle soul on and off stage. Maybe they were the English Grateful Dead. The Dead certainly picked up on them. Jim told me when they first went to the USA, they landed in San Francisco and the Dead were at the airport to meet them. They took them back to The Dead house and offered them all LSD, which they took.

A few times I went with Jim to Steve's house in Gloucester, where work was going on for the album that would be their last, as the original Traffic, *Where The Eagle Flies*. Earlier in 1973 they had released *Low Spark of High Heeled Boys*, another exceptional album. I connected with Penny Massot, Steve's remarkable lady and her lovely box of Burmese kittens, keeping warm in the winter on the top of the kitchen range. Everyone was very welcoming to me, but it seemed so surreal to be around a band, such a familiar environment, with strangers, even lovely friendly ones.

At lunchtime on my 27th birthday November 10, 1973, we were at the pub by the river in Marlow and Barbara arrived with Loopy and Joe, to wish me happy birthday. The dogs were so pleased to see me and it was very difficult. I knew with Saracen at Jim's there was no chance of me trying to have the dogs there. Somewhere amongst my thoughts it seemed kinder for both for them and for Alvin if they stayed at Hook End. Barbara started to tell me things about Alvin that were not very kind. It seemed as if my leaving him meant that I wanted to gossip about his weaknesses, which was far from my mind. I've never enjoyed hearing about the misfortunes of others, it's just not my thing. Years later Jim told me I was the only woman he had known who didn't gossip. I was learning about life, it was as if I had lived in a bubble.

A while later I heard that Alvin had met someone at Keith Emerson's birthday party on November 2, barely six weeks after I had left, again gossip was involved, but it was not my business anymore. It would go on for many years, people telling me this about Alvin, that about his relationship. A favourite seemed to be that Hook End was exactly as I had left it with my shopping notes still pinned up. I hated to be told these things and never asked. In the end it felt like a place stuck in time. I was very relieved when Alvin sold it to David Gilmore in the early eighties.

Ignoring the fact that I was now wearing Jim's clothes – I had yet to get anything from Hook End – the arrival of another women at Hook End prompted me to go and collect my clothes and things to which I felt attached. That included the Arthur Rackham *Alice In Wonderland* prints, some glass bead curtains, and an Afghan carpet, all things I thought would enhance Jim's house. I met Suzanne when Alvin brought her into the small lounge with a large grey great Dane. "This is Suzanne and this is Blue," he said. "I've always wanted a dog called Blue." It was very uncomfortable. I remember hugging her and saying, "Have fun."

You cannot leave a wealthy, successful musician with an empty bed in a mansion. I had left Alvin. She hadn't been involved with any of that so it was not for me to be pissed off. Had I not left, it wouldn't have happened. The responsibility was mine. I had tea chests for my clothes, shoes, books and other stuff. I think there were about ten tea chests. I left the Crown Derby tea set that Dee Anthony had given me, a wonderful coloured glass drops mobile, that Chelle had given me, and a sky viewing telescope that my mum and dad had given us. My mother was very annoyed about that.

I left behind two fantastic photos of Alvin and me, one the Avedon print, from the New York session, the other a large print of us on a roof top in Boston. I left them so he would see them and miss me. How fucked up.

At Christmas Jim and I went to Jamaica for a holiday. Getting married was thankfully never mentioned. I heard that Alvin was also on the Island and I was grateful our paths didn't cross. Jamaica with Jim was intense, crazy and fantastic. We hired a car and covered the whole Island in about seven days. Arriving in Montego Bay we drove the magical North coast, where we stayed the night at the home of Chris Blackwell's mother, Blanche, at Oracabessa. She was an amazing character, living in a house overlooking that beautiful bay and well looked after by Jamaican staff. Jim was in his element with Blanche. He told her great stories of his life on the road and stories about Chris. She told us stories about Ian Fleming, Noel Coward and Errol Flynn, who all had properties in Jamaica.

Noel Coward's house, Firefly, and Ian Fleming's house, Goldeneye, with its own private beach, were equidistant from Blanche around the 12 mile stretch of Oracabessa Bay. The next day she took us to see both. She and Ian Fleming had a long relationship, and the James Bond books were written at Goldeneye. He had taught her to snorkel from the beach there, her lifelong passion. Firefly was on a hillside, the main living room overlooking the bay, and was the inspiration for his classic song 'A Room With A View'.

Reluctantly we left and drove to Kingston and up into the Blue Mountains to Strawberry Hill, Chris Blackwell's home at 2,000 feet. With Chris absent, the house was being looked after by Dickie Jobson and included Countryman, a beautiful young Rasta, who was hiding out because of a problem involving gangsters and his wife. He asked Jim if we could take him to Negril on the south east coast to meet up with his wife and their young son, named Shookup, after the Elvis song, 'All Shook Up'. Early next morning we took Countryman to his home on Hellshire Beach, close to Kingston.

Countryman told us that when he first lived out there, no road went through the 14 miles of crocodile swamp that he would travel through on foot. With a crocodile tooth necklace, I didn't doubt it was true. Chris Blackwell referred to him as "Country". He was unique, so centred and calm, living in a basic home on the beach and wearing only shorts and his crocodile teeth necklace. I watched in wonder as he played a game of head butting with a young goat. Having smoked some fine ganja, it looked like a slow-motion dance. I could see the mental connection between them as they read each other's movements. There was no aggression from his goat or from Country, it was dreamlike.

From Hellshire Beach we three set off for Negril on Christmas Day 1973, Jim driving, me in the passenger seat and Country in the back rolling nice fat spliffs we all shared. Jim often stopped for hitchhikers in the UK. He would play them the latest Traffic material and ask their opinions. So he pulled up a few times to offer rides. I got out and moved my seat forward, so they could get into the back. When they saw Country on the back seat, they would smile and decline the ride. Jim and I looked at one another confused. Country explained that he was the reason that they didn't want to ride with us. They would have been happy to get into a car with two white English strangers, but not a Rasta.

We stopped in a village. Country went off and came back with coconuts cut for us to drink the fresh coconut milk, which he said was excellent and medicinal. Later we stopped on a secluded road to take a pee in the bushes. When we had finished, Country, without a word, ran off at a rapid pace back down the road and over a hill. After 10 minutes he reappeared still running, having released his energy, I guess. Everywhere there were donkeys, and elegant white birds on their backs. It seemed spiritual, a true Christmas Day.

We covered much of the island, including four-miles of overgrown Bamboo Walk on the south coast. Countryman sat cross-legged, like a guru, on the back seat. When I looked round he was smiling and he held my gaze with his soft brown eyes. On we went to Negril, an unspoiled small community of houses by the ocean, where we left Countryman with his wife and little Shookup, a child whose energy was as chilled out and free as his father. We stayed for a couple of days at a small hotel in Negril and then drove back to Montego Bay.

In 1982 Dickie Jobson released his film *Countryman,* it is seen as a cult classic. Country, the legendary, Rasta fisherman, is the main character of this action, adventure movie. It really shows the Jamaican Rasta culture. Dee Anthony plays Mr Porter a rich New Yorker.

From Montego Bay we flew to Nassau, where water skiing was among the attractions, to join Chris Blackwell and his wife Marilyn. It was a culture shock after Jamaica and Countryman. I was still high and wandered over the soft white sand beach collecting twinkling, tiny perfect shells of all shapes and sizes. One surreal afternoon with Jim was spent at Frank Barsalona's house in the same development as Blackwells. He was unfazed to see me with Jim, not Alvin. That's rock'n'roll. He showed us an art book with a photo of a Picasso oil painting that was like one that he owned. He said it was kept in a bank vault.

Back in Marlow in the New Year, it was obvious to me that we weren't settling down. I added my glass bead curtains and the Afghan rug and Alice prints. I discovered that the painted fire place in the front lounge was marble underneath and stripped off the paint. I was trying to contribute by adding something to this lovely house. Sometimes we would sit together in the Inglenook fireplace, in the magical main galleried hall, the oldest part of the house. The walk-in fireplace had built-in seats and was the inspiration for 'Evening Blue'.

"Sitting all alone in the firelight,
Listen to the wind in the chimney top.
Haven't slept for days and I'm still wide eyed.
Trying not to think but my brain won't stop.
If I had a lover whose heart was true,
I wouldn't be alone in this Evening Blue."

I understood.

We would go into London where Jim introduced me to friends of his, all lovely people. He was trying but I wasn't emotionally available, though I didn't know that at the time. One day at Basing Street, Island Records' centre of operations, we were in the office of Denise Mills, Chris Blackwell's PA. A young woman came in, walked up to Jim and kissed him, very passionately and he responded likewise. I recognised her from photos. It was Anna, his previously "old lady". It was clear there was unfinished business between them, as I knew there was with me and Alvin.

Anna had a daughter from a previously relationship, called Eve and he had written and recorded a lovely song for her on the 1974 album *Oh How We Danced*. Eve was a hit for Jim. He also told me he wrote 'Light Up Or Leave Me Alone' on the 1971 Traffic album *Low Spark of High-heeled Boys* for Anna.

It was an intense, honest lyric. It was too much for me to deal with. I needed to be somewhere calm and quiet. I needed help to sort out my brain. It wasn't coping well at all.

chapter 44
Confusion, Death, New Direction

Despite the spring my mood didn't lift. Jim was off at Steve's recording *Where The Eagle Flies* while at Marlow a gentle couple, Mick and Sue Balch, had moved in. I was happy not to be alone, though I spent a lot of time on my own deliberately, which was fine by them. One day I wanted to ask them something and went to their room, knocked and opened the door.
I found Sue meditating. It was the first time I'd seen anyone just sitting with closed eyes, quiet and calm. I was fascinated, but quickly apologised and left. I felt like an intruder. They showed me how to cook brown rice and stir-fry vegetables, which would one day become a staple part of my diet.

A friend of Jim's called Martian came and painted a big mural of Bo Diddley on the wall of a small studio Jim was building. I watched for days as he worked from a small black and white photo, creating a strong image with a tin of black house paint and brushes. I was frustrated without somewhere to sew, though I wasn't particularly inspired. I drew a self-portrait on an A3 size pad. It captures how lost I felt.

When Traffic went on a European tour, I went up to Nottingham to visit my parents, whom I had not seen since I left Alvin. It was tense at first but my dad took a night off and we went on a tour of all the pubs in which we had lived. At The Rose of England we persuaded the landlord to take us up to the living accommodation, to the bedroom where I was born. Standing there with both my parents was memorable and heartwarming.

We went on to The Albany and had a drink in the music hall room. I had a wonderful Alice in Wonderland moment gazing at the pillars where we had played maypole dancing. We went upstairs to the bar that my mother had called the Rainbow Room. The next day dad insisted we drive out to visit his childhood homes and back past the grocer's shop on Grassington Road. It was very special to be with them and revisit the past. It was nine years since I had left Nottingham as a teenager. After all that I had been through it felt more like we were now meeting as adults. We stood and hugged for a while before I left and he smiled at me. I felt really close to him.

Traffic were on the road in Italy and Jim wanted me to come out and join him. Percussionist Rebop's face lit up like sunshine when I walked into the dressing room. He ran over and hugged me so hard and exclaimed, "Loraine, Loraine, where have you been?" laughing. Rebop Kwaku Baah was a great conga player. I would watch him in wonder as his hands bounced and danced from drum to drum.

On April 4 we travelled by bus into Naples, through tiny roads teeming with life, arriving at the sea-front hotel where we were staying. It was late afternoon and in the bedroom I spotted a big black bug on the white pillowcase on the bed. Jim took it and shook it out of the window. It made me shudder. We freshened up and went down for dinner. Half way through the meal a waiter come over and said there was a telephone call for me.

Who knew I was there? Who could it be? I was confused. The phone was on the restaurant desk. It was Barbara.

"I'm so sorry Loraine," she said. "Your father has died."

It seemed he had a massive brain aneurysm and had died early evening the day before. It was two weeks since I had visited him in Nottingham. He had been his usual self, with no sign of any problems. He was 64 years old, eight weeks shy of 65. He had told me that he wasn't looking forward to becoming a pensioner. He didn't want a free bus pass.

I was so glad of my visit; it felt like some unseen force had a hand in guiding me there. Apparently, the urge to revisit childhood homes is quite common in people close to death. It had been at least a year before that when I had last seen him. It felt as if everything was as it was meant to be and I was at peace with his passing.

Going back to the table and my half-eaten dinner, Jim looked up and asked me who it had been. When I told him, he was kind and gentle with me. He would organise a flight back to England for me the next day. We went back to our room and he went to the bathroom and came back with a pill, a Valium and suggested I took it. It was a revelation that it was a part of his life, for his anxiety obviously. Not wanting to be alone at the hotel I went and watched Traffic play, from the side of the stage.

According to the Internet there was trouble at the concert in Naples. The show was cut short to 45 minutes only. I don't remember anything of that evening or the flight home or the car that took me up to Nottingham. When I arrived, the pub was open and busy, with all the regular customers sitting in their regular places, drinking their regular drinks. I remember thinking no one is indispensable. For 27 years they never took a holiday because dad thought the pub couldn't run without him. It seemed ridiculous, a lesson for me to remember.

Me, mum and two of my brothers went to see him in the funeral parlour, the first corpse I ever saw. He looked peaceful and we were surprised. We said he looked like was about to tell us a joke. In the back of the hearse we had a group hug and a cry together. It felt natural and right, a simple connection. The funeral was held in a church, which was packed. He was popular in the community. He had been anti-church all his life, and no one, none of his football fan pals, none of my brothers, rose to speak about him. The vicar never met him, and said nothing of any real meaning to commemorate this larger-than-life character. It was typical of those times. I wish I'd known it was to have been like that. I wish I'd been asked to speak. It made me angry.

After the service we stood outside. People filed past and shook our hands. When his close pals came up to me several started to cry as they spoke to me. He had been working as usual the night before and for him to leave in a day, puffed out, like a candle flame, was a trauma for his community of customers.

I stayed on with mum and with my brothers. We helped out with the pub for a few days. It carried on running relentlessly as it always had. Mum asked them all if they wanted to take over the license and run it with her. It was very profitable, but none of them did. Dad had left £50,000 in a current bank account and £10,000 in a deposit account. Mum gave each of us £400, about £2,000 today. We were not in his will, everything was left for mum.

I stayed on until Jim got back from the Traffic tour. He drove up to Nottingham and stayed overnight. We even shared a bed, a first for me in my mother's house. He was charming with mum and I worried about leaving her but my own problems soon took over. The £400 was enough for me to try to do what I had wanted to do the previous year, when I ran away from Alvin.

When we got back to Marlow, I told Jim that I felt our relationship was not really working out. He seemed to agree with me. In fact, it would be a couple of years before it was completely over. He would call me regularly, wherever I was staying in London. Usually he'd call on a Friday and invite me down to Marlow, where we would have a passionate night. Saturday he would go out and not come back, just calling in to see how I was every few hours and encouraging me to stay.

One weekend a lovely Jamaican, Esther, was visiting and we had a fine weekend together, talking about my favourite island. I was never sure whether to leave or not, and that weekend Esther encouraged me to stay on, but on Sunday evening I headed back to London. It was good to have a break from my little room there, to walk by the Thames, but it was also unsettling. In 1975 Jim met his future wife, Aninha, a vivacious Brazilian. They seemed very well suited. I was really happy to draw a line under our indecision.

Jim and Aninha's marriage weathered the highs and lows of three decades together, no mean feat in the rock'n'roll world. They had two daughters and Jim involved himself, in Brazilian life, its rhythms and musical culture. They had a second home in Rio where they lived off and on, and he and Aninha supported the Jubilee Action Street Children's Charity which works with the poor children in Rio. He was a great inspiration to them through music and his other love, football. When Jim passed in January 2005 after a short battle with stomach cancer, I couldn't help but remember how he had found the barbarities of the world literally too tough to stomach.

In 2011, Genesis published *Mr Fantasy*, the limited-edition book of Jim's lyrics, with facsimiles of his handwritten words, photos and contributions from musician friends. Among the tributes to Jim was one from Tom Petty: "When you read these lyrics, ask yourself if anyone ever wrote better. The pirate poet indeed." Perhaps one day it will have a general release so more can appreciate his lyrical poetry.

In the autumn of 1974, Harold organised a holiday in Jamaica for mum and me. Joining us was another widowed friend of mum's and her daughter and son-in-law. I think it was the most relaxed I had ever seen her. A couple of times Harold encouraged her to drink several more gins and that no doubt helped. She had given up the pub, which was too much for her to deal with alone. She was 56 years of age and lived to be 96, despite believing for the first half of her life that she would probably die in her 40s, as her own mother had done.

In the winter of 1974 I was what is now called "sofa surfing", which is only one step up from being homeless on the streets. I had three different friends whose sofas I would occupy for three to four days, rotating between them so no one got too stressed by me being there.

In Jamaica Harold had brought me an acoustic guitar which I tried to master for the next few years. I really missed hearing a guitar, the background music to my life for a decade. Alvin was right, the F major chord was the hardest to master. I wrote some songs. Unsurprisingly they were quite bleak. Harold, who was still living at Hook End, asked Alvin if it was ok for me to go down there when he was away. I did some recordings at Space Studios.

One track 'Superstar', had a sweet dreamy lyric, so Harold rocked it up and added some outrageous lyrics. I sang it, for fun, with his girlfriend Dee adding backing vocals. I thought it was quite a strong track, but I knew I was way too fragile to have pushed it forward. Also, it was a mean lyric that suggested Alvin was far more unpleasant to me than he actually was. Revenge did not interest me, neither did meanness. I still believed in peace and love, as I do to this day.

At Hook End I discovered that little Joe had disappeared in the woods when the three dogs, Loopy, Joe and Blue, had been wandering out there. Loopy was so happy to see me and I enjoyed a wonderful reunion with her. The next morning, before I woke up, there was a fight between Loopy and Blue. Harold the gardener told me that Blue had torn Loopy's throat out. He had buried that lovely sweet dog in the garden. He was very distressed by what happened, as we all were. It was a bloody end to a story that had begun so innocently. I have never had another dog and still feel guilty for having them, for leaving them, for not handling that responsibility properly.

In July 1974 Alvin phoned to ask me if I would sell him the TR3A. My emotions were still all over the place, but later in the year I drove to Hook End and sold it to him for £1,000. We left Suzanne in the house, went for a walk, sat on the hay bales in a barn and talked for some time. I wept uncontrollably. My brother Harold gave me his car, a Morris Traveller, which I would drive for more than a decade.

Jim had introduced me to friends of his in London and it was really helpful that he had, as I knew very few people. One couple who lived in a garden flat at Earl's Court had a spare room they were happy to rent to me. I stayed there from early 1975 until 1979. They were a very kind, sociable couple and in respect to them I have left their identities from this memoir. I was more lost, confused and unhappy during this period than at any time in my life and if it had not been for their support, openness and hospitality, my story might have become a tragedy.

Without a shadow of doubt I was suffering a huge identity crisis, though at the time I wouldn't have been able to describe it so clearly. I had no idea who I was, or how to relate to people in everyday circumstances. I was often profoundly anxious in the company of strangers. Having spent ten years living as Alvin's other half, supporting his life and dreams, my own sense of self was indistinct. Apart from the loss of security, both financial and emotional, I was still smoking dope on a daily basis and this doubtless increased my confusion. Much as I loved to smoke I knew that in the wrong setting a smoke might increase my introspection, making me silent company.

My host had an incredible personality, relaxed but energetic and his very gregarious partner had all the sophisticated confidence of a life-long London lady. There were frequent parties and gatherings in their spacious mansion flat. Often I would hide in my little room at the far end of the corridor, but if I was down there for more than a couple of evenings he would come and knock on my door. "Hey Lori, what's happening? Are you sick? Come on out and join the fun."

I recall sitting around their large table in the kitchen with my friend and a small group of her girlfriends. At some point Japan became a topic of conversation. "What an interesting culture, how different, wouldn't it be great to go there." Having been there four years before, I should have been able to add to, or at least, enjoy this exchange. Instead my palms were sweating, my heart raced and I felt increasingly uncomfortable, unable to tell anyone I'd been there, as it would mean speaking about Alvin. I didn't want to appear flashy or reveal myself as Alvin Lee's now ex-girlfriend. It was much too raw, too personal. Being the partner and support to an extraordinary man can be difficult, but being the ex-girlfriend was proving way more problematic, especially as it was becoming clear to me how much I loved him and missed him.

During 1975 and 1976 my life took a strange detour. On April 24, 1975, I had been with friends for supper, with my best friend Krissie. She and Woody had continued to be my good friends. Afterwards Kris and I had gone to the Split Coconut, a small club in Earls Court, where we were still catching up.

Kris was one of very few people I felt comfortable around because she knew me so well with Alvin. Physically beautiful, she had a wonderfully beguiling nature, very loving, open-hearted and trusting in an almost childlike way. She was not a gossip. I don't remember her ever talking negatively about anyone. She liked to find the good in people. When we first saw *Rowan & Martin's Laugh-In*, we all thought Goldie Hawn was Kris's soul sister. The men in her life were everything to her. She had no idea or desire for a life of her own. She loved naively and totally and that was her Achilles heel. Having been together since their mid-teens, Kris and Woody had married in 1971, but his increasing fame and money had brought pressures to their relationship. Both of our circumstances had changed so much and for six months she had been living with Led Zeppelin guitarist, Jimmy Page, at Plumpton Place, his Grade II Elizabethan Manor House in its own grounds near Lewes in East Sussex. She was estranged from Woody, and we had spent much less time together.

It was about 2 am when we stood on the pavement, outside the Split Coconut, saying goodnight and knowing there was still plenty more to talk about. "Do you want to come back to The Wick?" she asked. "There's no one there, and I would like to go and check out my things. Woody's been there on his own with various women, groupies, and I'm concerned that my clothes and stuff don't go missing."

My time was my own, my life was fluid, and The Wick, the beautiful house on top of Richmond Hill overlooking the river Thames, seemed an infinitely more appealing place to wake up the next morning than my little room in Earls Court. Little did I know where this decision would lead both of us, for the bad and the good.

chapter 45
Full Moon Madness

Kris and I hailed a cab to Richmond Hill. I knew The Wick very well having visited quite a lot with Alvin, in the first few years after Kris and Woody had first bought it. Back then Woody and Alvin would talk or play music together and Kris and I would talk, laugh, make tea, roll joints, cook dinner, breakfast, snacks, and keep the boys fueled up. Kris and Woody had bought The Wick from Sir John Mills, the renowned English actor, whose wife was the writer Mary Hayley Bell. In a gypsy caravan in the garden she wrote books and plays, including *Whistle Down The Wind,* a sweetly profound story of three children who, on discovering a tramp-like fugitive, keep him hidden, as they believe him to be Jesus. In 1961 producer Bryan Forbes made it into an acclaimed film, starring John Mill's 15-year-old daughter Hayley. No doubt the inspirational atmosphere of The Wick's garden and its setting overlooking the Thames contributed to this magical film.

Alvin and I had thought it was a magnificent house and would sometimes stay overnight rather than drive back out to the country in the small hours. So Kris and I had lovely memories of time spent together in The Wick, when things had been happier and less confused for us all. I knew that all was not well with her and Jimmy Page, even though she would speak about him as if she was closer to him than she'd been in her relationship with Woody. She told me she had gone to Plumpton Place with Woody and when it became obvious there was an attraction between her and Jimmy, Woody was happy to leave without her. Having seen a similar situation between them involving George Harrison and Mylon at Hook End Manor, I believed it was true.

The Wick is a glorious Georgian house built over four main floors, designed in 1775 by architect Robert Mylne for Lady St Aubyn, whose ghost haunts its corridors. From 1772, for the last 20 years of his life, Sir Joshua

Reynolds, the famed English portrait painter, lived next door at Wick House and is reputed to have painted from The Wick's balcony. It has three large oval rooms sitting one above the other like stacked chocolate boxes, all with spectacular river views. One is a dining room at basement level, opening onto the enclosed walled garden fashioned in terraces down the hillside. The next, on the ground floor, is the main lounge overlooking the garden, and is the room shown on the cover of Woody's first solo record, *I've Got My Own Album To Do*. The photo shows the Georgian mouldings, fireplace, chandelier and French windows leading out to the balcony, along with the eclectic kilims and more exotic furnishings of its inhabitants. The last is the main oval bedroom on the first floor, which certainly had the most glorious views. This was where our drama began.

The Wick was in darkness when we arrived. Kris let us in and turned off the burglar alarm. The house was empty. It was about 2:30 am. Quite tired by now, we went down to the basement kitchen to make cups of hot milk and honey, very rock'n'roll. This was a favourite bedtime drink with Kris and me from when we had all lived together at Gloucester Place Mews in 1969. Woody had a recording studio in the basement and we wandered from room to room talking, sipping hot milk, as she checked that all was well. It was obvious that there had been many people there. There were wine glasses, mugs and a general disarray from music-making and hanging-out. Kris had a wonderful German cleaner, Leisl Schiffer, who was unfazed by rock'n'roll partying and would come in and clean once a week. She was very protective of Kris, always looking out for her interests, but it seemed she hadn't been in to tidy up for a few weeks.

During that time Woody had been there recording with Mick Jagger, Keith Richards and other musicians. He was in transit from The Faces to The Rolling Stones, a move that disturbed Kris. The sixties English pop group, The Small Faces, which comprised Ronnie Lane, Ian McLagan aka Mac, and Kenney Jones had split with their front man, Steve Marriott, in 1969, the same year that Rod Stewart and Woody had split with The Jeff Beck Group. They joined Woody, Mac and Kenney to become The Faces, a band with unusual musical equality. Their individual songwriting contributions and musical inputs was encouraged, recognized and respected. The Faces made energetic, up-tempo, feel-good music together, which seemed effortless, their gigs were loose and felt like a party, the band and the audience having a real good time.

In the seventies Woody was at the height of his creative powers and I have always wondered if joining the "biggest rock'n'roll band in the world" was the best place for his prodigious output. After Brian Jones' unexpected death, Mick and Keith seemed like vampires bringing in fresh blood, first Mick Taylor then Woody, using them to inject new energy and creativity into the band but not honouring their contributions. Mick Taylor has spoken openly of his lack of songwriting credits and the financial consequences, which contributed to him leaving the band. I once asked Woody directly about his lack of songwriting credits, on tracks I could hear his hand in. "That will all come later," he told me innocently.

Having been a Rolling Stones fan from his teens, he was in thrall to Mick and Keith, and consciously or unconsciously they took advantage of that. It wasn't until the Stones' 1980 album, *Emotional Rescue,* that he would be attributed as a songwriter on one track, yet as far back as the Jeff Beck Group's 1969 album, *Beck-Ola,* Woody's name is on more than half the tracks, a contribution that continued on all of the Faces' albums. I had always seen the music "business", the percentage merchants, the managers, promoters, record companies, as the ones who might rip you off, not fellow musicians.

On the ground floor of The Wick we checked the lounge and the music room and set off up the grand main staircase, going through the oval bedroom and into the dressing room, all the while chatting and catching up with our stories. Kris looked through the rails of clothes, fabulous velvet, lace, multicolored patchworks. She was very stylish in her own unique way, putting together vintage garments alongside classic staples, like Levis, and denim dungarees. Kris was one of the originators of the look we now refer to as 'rock chic', but with a soft, sensual femininity, never obviously sexy and with effortlessly, funky elegance.

Having come straight from dinner with friends and a club, I had no clothes with me, but we were best friends and sharing clothes and toiletries was no problem to us. It must be difficult for men to understand how women can be comfortable with one another in very intimate circumstances. From my teens in Nottingham, in dance hall toilets, the girls would go into cubicles together, mainly so conversations, usually about some bloke, didn't have to stop. The male pre-occupation with sex and their genitals, and heterosexual men's general distrust of homosexuals' intentions, seems to create a barrier to the sort of intimacy that girls and women take for granted. We talk way more than men, while doing all the mundane stuff, dancing, walking, getting dressed, undressed, putting on make-up, taking it off, in the bath, on the loo, sitting drinking tea, wine, eating, shopping, trying on clothes, all these activities that we undertake with our girlfriends never seriously interrupt our dialogue.

Had Woody been home I would have slept in Hayley's Room at the front of The Wick. The plaque was still on the door from when Hayley Mills had lived there as a child. Tonight, though, we got in the big, king-sized, brass bed in the main oval bedroom. In her dressing room, Kris had picked out a hospital nightie, the kind with a frumpy front that opens down the back. She thought it was funny and put this on over her knickers while telling me about how she had come by it on a trip to hospital in Los Angeles. Stripping down to my knickers, I joined Kris in the bed.

The oval bedroom has floor to ceiling windows with an incredible view of the terraced garden and on down Nightingale Lane, across the riverside meadow all the way to a big bend in the Thames. There sits a small eyot, Glovers Island, with houseboats of all shapes and sizes moored around it, with more moored down the centre and banks of the river. That night the sky was clear and a huge full-moon lit up the idyllic landscape. The gothic towers of the Petersham Hotel were silhouetted beyond the garden's terraces. It was stunning, an electric night, the brilliant, glittering moonlight reflected off of the wide, calm surface of the ancient river.

I remember the beauty of the view sparking the following wishful exchange.

"Wouldn't it be nice to have a smoke. It's a shame I don't have any with me, that view is so lovely tonight."

"Yes, that would be great, but there isn't anything here."

We carried on talking for a while. Kris talked about Woody and I talked about Alvin, happily reminded of him in this house, and eventually our conversation petered out as we drifted off to our private dream worlds.

I don't remember exactly what woke us, a noise or a voice, but very alarmingly, at about 6.30 am, we were suddenly aware of four men in dark suits standing around the large bed. In the first few seconds neither of us had any idea who these people were or what they were doing there or whether we were in any danger. It was terrifying and bizarre. From the bathroom there was a loud crash, which turned out to be the dressing room door being kicked in. It was not locked.

We were told by their leader and main spokesman that they were the drug squad. He held aloft a piece of paper which he said was a warrant to search the house. He quickly put it back in his pocket without offering it to us to read. We sat up in the bed, adrenaline pumping, the covers pulled up, hearing people moving around and talking in the rooms above and below us. In all there were at the least a dozen plain clothes drug squad officers and uniformed police in the house. They also had a sniffer dog and its handler.

They asked us if there were any others in the house. Their initial, rather over-excited, manner became more subdued when they realized that we were the only occupants. We were not the big fish they had hoped to catch. How to deal with two pretty young women, startled from sleep like a pair of fairy-tale princesses, would prove to be quite taxing for their inventiveness. They sent out for a policewoman. All the men left while she supervised us getting out of the bed, washed and dressed. At no time did any of the men see what we had been wearing in the bed. We held the covers up around us. It was left to their imaginations.

For what seemed hours they crawled all over The Wick, room by room checking everywhere for drugs. For the entire time we remained in the oval bedroom, sitting on the bed. Their leader, red-haired and florid faced, who had been so upbeat announcing their purpose, was Detective-Sergeant Edward Ellison. He sat with Kris and me, talking and asking questions. Though he would deny it in court, he asked Kris about Keith Richards and Anita Pallenberg, whether they still lived in Cheyne Walk. The elephant in the room was that we all knew they had come looking for Keith, Mick, Woody and anyone else who might enhance their career promotion, but they had to carry on with this overstaffed affair as if we warranted the tax payers' expense. Which quite obviously we did not.

I was quite happy to talk to him, just small talk although I was still quite shocked. I knew we hadn't even had a smoke in the house the night before. We were totally straight. What could they do to us, even though we were so outnumbered? In my total naivety I thought the law was also straight, not corrupt, and as we were innocent of anything connected with drugs in this place, at this time. I thought we had nothing to fear.

Of course, I had heard that drugs were planted on people, but with so many of them here, and us, I couldn't see how that would happen. Kris was much quieter, possibly nervous that Woody and his musical mates might have left something behind when they had left to go on tour. Sensing her mood and feeling protective towards her, I chatted to Ellison about nothing in particular to try to keep his attention from Kris, to take some pressure off of her. A couple of times Kris answered Ellison's questions with "I take full responsibility", which he tried to get her to elaborate, but I knew that she was saying this to protect me from anything that might be found.
She was saying, this is my house and my friend here is an innocent visitor. It's at times like these you discover the depth in your friends and their loyalty

From the basement studio we could hear someone playing on the drum-kit and music from the jukebox. It was starting to feel more like a 'gawping at the rock star's house and lifestyle tour' than a serious police operation. In the bedroom there were endless little curios, bits of paper, envelopes, correspondence, photos, creative debris on the mantelpiece and cabinets. Everything was looked at, looked in, shaken or squeezed like a bizarre archeological dig, a treasure hunt.

It started to become pretty obvious that they were getting desperate when they went so far as to unscrew the large brass knobs from the bed on which we were sitting. This revealed large quantities of white powder, which excited their forensic curiosity. Several did the classic finger to tongue test, before bagging it up in a large plastic bag. Had it been a class A substance it would have been very valuable and no doubt worth a long prison term. It turned out to be nothing more sinister than French chalk.

Around 10.00 am Ellison asked us if we would mind going to Richmond Police Station to give our details and sign for the items they were taking from the house. Apart from the four brass knobs and the white powder in them, we had no idea what they were taking. We had not seen anything else or been asked about anything else. There was no classic caution, "We want you to a accompany us to the station and we must warn you anything you might say will be taken down and could be used in evidence…" There was no suggestion we were being arrested and because this was my first such encounter, I had no idea what they intended. I believed what they said. They wanted us to go to the station to give our details and sign for items taken from the house.

"No problem," I told Kris who at this point was reluctant to leave.

"I think I should call my solicitor," she said to me.

"But they just want us to go to sign for the stuff they've taken," I naively said, pushing against her wiser instincts.

As we emerged from the front of The Wick and were gestured towards the open, back doors of a Black Maria police van – in the US they call it a Paddy-wagon – my misplaced confidence in their honesty evaporated. This certainly looked like an arrest.

At the station we had our fingerprints taken as well as our personal details.

"Name?"

"Christine Alice Marcella Wood."

"Name?"

"Audrey Loraine Burgon."

Kris looked surprised. "Your name's not Audrey," she said emphatically, with wide-eyed innocence.

Sergeant Ellison looked confused.

I turned to look at Kris. "Yes, it is" I said firmly and calmly, as my mind raced. This was in danger of becoming a farce.

Sgt. Ellison asked me how many O-levels I had, and when I told him "five" he said, "Same as me," looking very pleased with himself, strange. It was the only time in my life I have ever been asked. Both of us signed a document which listed items taken from The Wick. I didn't read through it. I was feeling utterly confused and it would have meant little to me. Were we arrested or were we not? Nothing was made clear. Then we were told we could leave.

I don't remember how we returned to The Wick, probably the police took us, but we may have been collected by Frank, who worked for Kris and Woody. He was certainly with us back at the house. Obviously, the whole morning had thrown us into mental chaos and the story was told and re-told to Frank, who made us tea and offered sympathy. Frank was a very down-to-earth, good-natured, practical young guy with an abundance of the most essential quality for his job, a sense of humour. He lifted our spirits and we decided that a thorough check through the house was called for, in case the crazy gang came back for an encore.

For all their sniffing and searching, several small paper packets with tiny morsels of cocaine were found. On the mantelpiece in Kris's dressing room was a small, innocuous pile of pink powder, sitting openly for all to see. The drug squad had searched past it that morning, including the dog. It turned out to be more cocaine. How had it become dyed pink? Perhaps it had been wrapped in pink tissue or a red napkin and dumped onto the shelf, quite a disguise. Frank and Kris decided to destroy the evidence up their noses. The ineptitude of the search took on a Monty Python tone, the pompous Ellison coming in for some well-deserved ridicule, which modulated the morning's trauma.

Two young women, lying peacefully asleep in bed in a private residence, causing absolutely no harm to anyone else, had been subjected to a nasty ordeal by a dozen paid establishment lackeys, hoping to show the English tax-payer how well their money was spent fighting the war on drugs. Their agenda, as it had been since the early sixties in the UK, was to bust some rock star and earn instant promotion. Meanwhile real crimes of violence, abuse and theft were being committed in and around the area, that could have benefited from the man hours so pointlessly wasted. No doubt this picture has been played out millions of times in the decades since the sixties, with a similar waste of time and money, in a vain attempt to stop people from living their lives in ways that no successive governments have dared to sanction.

Why did I say it was Frank and Kris who destroyed the evidence, was I trying to elevate my innocence? This was my personal irony that weird morning in 1975. I had never ever taken cocaine. I had smoked plenty of marijuana, hashish, even opium once, taken LSD, mescaline, angel dust and as a teenager some amphetamines, but I had never taken cocaine. It had been around me but it was something I had my own personal strong views about. Observing how it affected people made me feel it was not for me.

So, it was horribly ironic that a few months later I would find myself, along with Kris, charged with possession of a minute amount of cocaine, 15 milligrams between us, described in court as the equivalent of a 277th part of one sugar cube, which had been gathered from eight different surfaces around The Wick that morning. Enough to show up as a cloudy trace on a small plastic bag. Lucky they never found the pink stuff. Kris was also charged with a tiny amount of cannabis, found in one of her handbags, equivalent to a 70th part of one sugar cube, so small it wouldn't even have made a decent smoke the previous night to enhance the full-moon view.

We were probably lucky that the drug squad had been so confident, convinced that they would find large quantities of drugs, that they didn't bring their own to plant on us, just in case. One of our lawyers told us that someone had been spotted by customs at Heathrow airport, London, with a large quantity of drugs. Instead of being arrested, they were followed to The Wick some weeks before the bust. The drug squad had set up surveillance in The Petersham Hotel, in a tower overlooking The Wick garden, where they had spied Woody, Keith, Mick and others. Thinking this was a golden opportunity, they put in a request for a search warrant. Good idea, terrible timing. The house had been empty for at least a week before they sprung their masterplan. It was totally accidental that Kris and I were there.

I wasn't going to hand any kind of a victory to people who had treated us with little respect. When we heard music and the drums being played downstairs, we had queried what was going on. "We can get heavy with you," said Ellison. What was that supposed to suggest? Legalized thugs, threatened violence was not the only tactic they could use. Around their breakfast table in the police station canteen on April 25, 1975, still smarting from their failed bid for glory, they concocted verbal evidence, salacious images and lies in the hope of redeeming the morning's fiasco. All was written into one small, black, flip-open police notebook. It's called verbalising.

Something very wonderful was to happen as a result of the bust. Kris and Woody met to discuss what had happened. Kris needed his support. It re-kindled their feelings and gradually they got back together. They were pretty happy again and it was great to be with them, as I was a number of times. Woody had his own form of diverting therapy for us. He would put on Marx Brothers movies, his favourites, and we would soon all be laughing. It helped a lot. The lawyer, J Cheever Loophole's antics in *At The Circus*, played by Groucho, was especially heartening. Kris had always complained that Woody was not someone with whom you could sit down and have a proper conversation. It was true, but laughter is great medicine and shared humour good communication.

The Rolling Stones were just about to embark on their first tour with Woody, and I met them all at the Stones office one day. They are not people who make a stranger feel welcome. The Faces were such relaxed, open people, unpretentious, easy vibes, so it didn't seem that the Stones were going to be such an easy camaraderie for Woody. I knew all the Faces and always felt relaxed around them. Kris was trying her best to bring her gentle, carefree friendliness to this meeting but only Charlie Watts seemed able to be open and friendly. The bust was not mentioned and I found the whole experience uncomfortable.

Kris and I had agreed we were going to fight this trumped up charge. One night, when I was visiting her at The Wick, we were sitting on the same big brass bed, when she told me some startling news. She had heard from the Stones office. It seemed Mick and Keith were saying, "Why are these girls being so silly, why don't they just plead guilty and not make such a fuss?" I was incredulous, not only were we fighting the establishment but also the rebels, the very people whose carelessness had put us in this position. My head spun. Anger gave me calm clarity.

"Do you realize that if you plead guilty it will have dire consequences for you travelling with Woody?" I said to Kris. "You will have a criminal record for all time and the USA will not be welcoming you with open arms. Why would you do that for these people? We are not guilty and that is how I will be pleading whatever you choose to do." I spoke gently but firmly. This was not a game.

We spent the next half hour going over this again and again, as you do when trying to come to peace with yourself about such a major decision. For me it was clear-cut, there was only myself and my own reputation to consider. I was the outsider. Fate had dealt me a weird hand and being charged as Miss Audrey Burgon was a glimmer of light. Only close friends would link me with Alvin. It was neither to his advantage nor mine that the police or the courts found out about my rock'n'roll past. Kris' situation was far more complicated. As unsure as she was about Woody joining the Stones, he was very happy about it and didn't want anything rocking the boat.

Kris loved to travel, enjoyed America and valued being able to visit there. Maybe deep down she also knew that despite being newly reunited with her great love he might not always be with her, especially if she had a visa ban and had to stay home. Whatever it was that weighed the most in her thinking, she resolved to plead not guilty.

Chapter 46
In Court With Alice
In Wonderland

During the late summer and autumn of 1975, Krissie and I attended the local Magistrates Court several times. On one occasion the police didn't turn up at all. Mind games were starting. In the UK on this charge, you are seen first in the Magistrates Court, where you can plead guilty and be given a fine, a jail term or a suspended sentence. If you pleaded not guilty, in 1975, you could ask for a jury trial, which we were advised would give us a better chance of proving our innocence. I never asked what the sentence could be if we were found guilty but a jail sentence was a possibility. Holloway women's prison in London had a fearsome reputation.

The day before our arraignment in Richmond Magistrates Court, I met with my solicitor, Gibson Grenfell, in Earls Court. I was still unemployed and living off the £400 I had been given by my mother when my father died and the £1,000 that Alvin had given me to buy back the Triumph TR3A. I was just starting to find my feet from my reversal of circumstances and eking the funds out to give me breathing space. In the UK we had legal aid for those who are charged with a crime but don't have the resources to afford legal defence. Gibson Grenfell had been allotted to me by that system and he turned out to be an intelligent, calm advisor.

In his anonymous looking office that day he spelt out, very directly, the next mind-game the drug squad were employing.

"I have had a message from the police. If you don't plead guilty tomorrow, they will say you are lesbians. It will be all over the newspapers."

I couldn't believe what I was hearing. "We aren't lesbians. That's ridiculous. How can they say that?"

"They found you in bed together."

"It was a huge bed. We are good friends. Women sleep together for company." This was becoming a farce but a dangerous one. I was being threatened and cajoled on all sides.

"They will make it very unpleasant for you. Are you sure you want to plead not guilty?"

This latest threat made my resolve stronger.

"We are not guilty. We are not lesbians. We will not give in to threats, it's ludicrous."

I hoped that if Kris was being given the same message she would view it in the same way.

The next day was a sunny one. Kris had been told of the police threats and it had the same effect of making her resolve deeper. The proceedings were quick. All we had to do was confirm our names and, after the charges had been read out, state whether we were guilty or not.

"Not guilty," we both replied calmly and with grave dignity.

We would now be embarking on an unknown journey.

Our solicitors told us there were reporters outside the front of the court building and that we could exit from the back. We got into a car that drove us around the Richmond one-way system and brought us to the front of the court. On the pavement outside stood Det. Sgt. Edward Ellison, relaxed in the sunshine in the midst of a group of reporters, talking animatedly. We knew he was feeding lies and innuendoes to the tabloid sharks. I was sure that if we had pleaded guilty, he would have done the same thing. A guilty plea would have given him even more to crow about as his bungled raid would have been justified.

My life was in turmoil. It wasn't exactly normal before the bust but now I had this grey cloud hanging over me. In the police station on the morning of the arrest, after Kris was surprised to learn my name was Audrey, we were asked our occupations. Kris, being a married women at that time, was not expected to have a job. I was single and unemployed, but knowing this was temporary, I blurted out the first thing that entered my head, songwriter. Well it was an aspiration, and I had written and made demos of a few songs that year, but it wasn't the best answer given the circumstances. I was a dressmaker and always had ongoing jobs altering clothes making them for family and friends, including Kris. I charged a little pin money for this but had never considered it a job. It was just something I loved to do.

I was living in my small rented room in Earl's Court, a single bed, a small cupboard, a table and a chair. It was like a small cell in a jail or a monastery, yet it became a secure nest, a refuge. When I moved in it had check wallpaper, small squares, dark blue and white, which made it feel even smaller. After a smoke the check pattern would become unstable, a visual nightmare. I produced some very stark drawings in that room, including a harrowing self-portrait in dark blue felt-tip pen. In note books my rambling stoned confusion runs endlessly around the same theme of love and loss. Who am I? Why am I so intense? What do I want from life? And Alvin, feeling sad then happy, lucky then cursed.

Thankfully I was not living totally alone. My hosts enjoyed a lively lifestyle, laughter and conversation, and there was always wonderful music playing, often an album or a track played over and over. It was comforting to go to sleep hearing The Isley Brother's 'Summer Breeze' and wake up to it wafting down the corridor. The Meters' *Rejuvenation,* with great tracks like 'Just Kissed My Baby' and 'Hey Pocky A-Way' embodying excellent funky taste. I was allowed to hide for a few days before a knock on the door and an invitation to join the party. It was helpful therapy from a very special, kind and wise host.

One evening in the front room I was introduced to a new visitor, a tall, striking red-haired Californian. Greg Hodal born in Hollywood, worked for Ryan O'Neal, and connected strongly to that crazy world. Greg turned out to be an angel, relaxed, intelligent and hilarious, his quick mind picking up on the absurd connections in life and recycling them to surreal effect. I had spent weeks in the USA on rock'n'roll tours with Alvin, and American attitudes and irreverent humour were very familiar to me, just what the doctor ordered, a sunny breath of fresh air. Greg had been in Ireland with Ryan who was working on Stanley Kubrick's *Barry Lyndon.* When a replacement actor was needed, Greg had suggested John Bindon, and Kubrick flew him out. Greg spent days schooling him for the part of a recruiting soldier, a great role for John. Now back in London, Greg was staying at Bindon's Belgravia mews flat.

We spent that evening telling each other our life stories. It seemed easy for me to open up about Alvin and the court case, especially as he was a fellow Scorpio. Astrology, how it annoys some people, yet the links have always been strong in my life, certain signs, even particular dates, turning up time and again. After Greg left that night it was not surprising that the phone rang a little while later. He asked me out the following evening.

Pretty soon we were together night and day, making the most of our Scorpio passions, enjoying a smoke, talking about life, the arts, and making love. It was all very easy and a great relief for my tormented mind. I didn't want to know if this was a serious relationship, if it had a future. Sometimes things are perfect in the moment. I would stay with Greg at John Bindon's, sleeping on the couch-bed in the living room. Sometimes we were there for days without ever going out. He nicknamed it "the siege flat", which I thought hilarious. It was the time of the Balcombe Street siege, a stand-off between the IRA and the London Metropolitan police, which kept the British glued to their TVs during the same six days we were in court.

Greg was a fantastic story teller and one of my favourites had him living in North Beach, San Francisco at the height of Flower Power. Greg wasn't a hippie but he was certainly a hipster and a tripster. He kept snakes, red-tailed South American Boas, and fed them on rats. One sunny day, out of stoned curiosity, he and a friend took a dead rat and put it on the street below their window, covertly watching the reactions of passers-by. People stopped and looked. The rat was moved onto a patch of earth under a tree. Finally, a sweet, young hippie guy came along, dug a hole, buried the rat and after looking about found two small sticks, fashioned them into a cross, which he stuck over the grave of the snake's dinner while performing a short ceremony. Wonderful times.

John Bindon, actor, and, some say, gangster, has had books written, and TV documentaries, about him which cite his supposed relationships with criminals and two well-known women, Princess Margaret, younger sister of Queen Elizabeth II, and Vicki Hodge, the daughter of a Baronet, Sir John Rowland Hodge, 2nd Baronet of Chipstead, Kent. Sir John was married four times, which suggests he was a wild character and not the best role model for matrimonial fidelity. Though Vicki was married, John was her lover, and they were together as often as Vicki could manage. Their antics were high energy, like a pantomime. They would encourage each other's outrageous behaviour, which was very entertaining and often unnerving. John was infamous for having a very large penis. Vicki egged him on to expose this asset. I soon got used to his pub party trick – how many beer glasses he could hang on it. It was impressive, but after spending time with John and Vicki it became ridiculous.

Vicki was the most crazy and extrovert. One night, at Dana Gillespie's, she and Dana and Angie Bowie engaged in a threesome of cuddles and suggestive dialogue on a carpeted play area in the centre of a room. All were fully dressed but in ways that left little to the imagination for the other half dozen visitors. I felt totally provincial that night, even after my dozen years in rock'n'roll. I wasn't ready for this exposure to swinging London and knew I was out of my depth. Naturally John and Greg found it very entertaining and were in full flow with ribald banter, which made me laugh and helped me relax, but I knew that whatever my scene was, this was not it. How do you find out who you are? Sometimes by discovering who you are not.

Greg was a fine collage artist, cutting out pictures from magazines and juxtaposing them to create surreal images. He was also a wannabe guitarist, with a sunburst Fender Telecaster and little travel amp, and he would play blues riffs and get lost in sweet sounding music. It was lovely to hear a guitar being played again but it was the least of his attractions to me. I wasn't looking for another guitar playing boyfriend. John also had an acoustic guitar in his bedroom and would often come in late evening and sit and play and sing the blues, with his door shut, too shy or too considerate to perform in front of us. Even for such a confident extrovert, maybe it was just too personal for him. It sounded as if he was pouring his heart out to the universe.

There was an etch-a-sketch that John would spend hours on making incredibly details surreal drawings. He and Greg played stoned Scrabble together for hours. Both would regularly find good seven letter words, an extra 50 points. They were high-scoring games, competitive, in a very good humoured way. While all these creative pursuits went on around me I doodled small black and white ink drawings, psychedelic pop-art style. Without Vicki, we were a relaxed trio and I felt very safe and much happier than I had for a long time. They were both straightforward, easy company.

Greg and John shared a common life experience, which was a gift to me in 1975. They had both served time in prison. Aged 21, Greg had done two years in the USA for smuggling Mexican weed across the border, and John for something for which he felt he'd been "stitched up". When I told him I came from Nottingham he told me he'd been in the Borstal at Lowdham Grange, the same village where my grandfather had run a pub called the Magna Carta and my mother had first met my father. Small world.

"I was only 15 years old and in court for living off of immoral earnings," he told me. His girlfriend was a prostitute, she paid the rent and bought the food. "The judge asked me to hold up my hands for the jury to see." John was broad and stocky and his knuckles were exceptionally wide. "Why did he do that? I felt like I was deformed, like a kind of beast. What did my hands have to do with the charges?" He was genuinely aggrieved to be profiled so negatively, so young, purely as a result of the body he'd been born with. I remember thinking that day how, like a lottery, the appearance of our bodies can influence and decide our paths in this world.

So here I was, facing a Crown Court trial and fate had provided me with two lifestyle gurus, who were more than willing, and able, to guide and coach me through this unknown territory. What a gift and what a sweet mystery life is. John was rightfully alarmed when I said, "Well, I am innocent so I don't have anything to worry about."

He laughed at me. "Great stuff. You're too much of a hippie. You're crazy if you think this will be straight forward and above board."

"But I'll be telling the truth. We didn't take anything in The Wick that night."

"Oh dear, peace and love your honour. It's all just a big mistake," quipped Greg.

I hate being told what to do but as I sat there between these two intelligent men, who had my best interests at heart, their good-natured teasing woke me up to a reality I had not really faced. Two pretty, long-haired blondes, with rock'n'roll links, caught in bed together, with the remnants of drugs around them. We would look guilty by default. So, what about Miss Audrey Burgon, who was she? By sheer good fortune my mother had given us all two Christian names and then always called us by the second one, in my case Loraine. Audrey was unknown to my friends and family. She was a blank slate I could develop into a straight, law-abiding young lady, someone the judge and jury could not easily stereotype.

I wasn't about to cut off my hair but I could tuck it out of the way into a hat, and I could dress in a more demure style, neat little skirts and jackets, and leave my Afghan in the wardrobe. Kris was stuck with a public persona but, as Mick Jagger would later describe me in a biography, I was "the anonymous girl in bed with Krissy". Vicki had a tight-fitting little hat that I wore for the entire time in court, my hair tucked into it. Gradually my songwriter persona shifted to dressmaker, without much fuss. Perhaps honesty is not always the best policy. Did I feel that it was dishonest? No, I felt I was caught up in a game of other people's making, written by persons with strong agendas, like a bit part actor cast in a drama. A victim? No. Life was beginning to seem like a series of challenges and this was the biggest yet.

The week before the trial I had a postcard from my mother. I hadn't told her about the court appearance. Her address in Nottingham was Windsor Court and mine was Earls Court. "I've just noticed we both have the word Court in our address," she wrote as a postscript, apropos to nothing. The psychic links between mothers and children are very strong.

The night before the trial Greg and I went to stay with Kris at The Wick, so we could all travel together to Kingston Crown Court early the following morning. We had only been together for about a month but Greg had never tried to back out of this impending public farce. It was fantastic to have someone so solidly by my side. Officially a tax exile, Woody was not in the UK. In truth, it was helpful he wasn't there. Perhaps the press would be less interested without his face to photograph. It was tough for Kris not to have his support. She had her mum and dad staying with her and her younger brother Brian. Coincidentally, Kris and I had been the third child, and only daughter, in a family of four and closest to our younger brothers, Brian and Harold. They were with us throughout the trial and, though both were only in their early twenties, they had much to contend with when we walked out of The Wick on the morning of Wednesday, December 3, 1975.

Celebrities being jostled by paparazzi is a common sight, but nothing can prepare you for being on the receiving end. Kris had organized a Daimler limo, with a large back door, for us to travel in. We needed that as the flash lights popped in the rugby scrum that awaited us. Being the centre of attention in a paparazzi attack gives way to blind panic, not too strong a word. You are under attack and completely dehumanized. All you represent to these people is a wage packet, the best picture takes the prize.

They don't stand still. They push and shove each other to get the best angle, the memorable image, all the while shouting, "Hey, look this way! Hey Kris! Come on girls! Give us a smile!" I had Greg and Harold either side of me, and went ahead of Kris in the hope it would take some of the pressure off of her. I think the anonymous women in a brown hat confused them on the first day. Greg and Harold were fantastic. Even though they were hopelessly outnumbered they held off the crush and pushed enough to keep our tight-path clear. As we scrambled into the car, Kris was behind me, protected by Brian and also Ray, a roadie working for Jimmy Page. The Stones' office had evidently washed their hands of "those silly girls".

This routine of running the gauntlet carried on all week. Photographers often stood in the open doorway of the car, barring the way, but they were easily pushed aside by Greg or Brian or Harold who no doubt enjoyed the opportunity to vent their anger. I have a lot of sympathy for celebrities who grab cameras and thump photographers who overstep the line.

Kingston Crown Court, circa 1975, was a very grand, imposing building. In contrast, Richmond Magistrates Court was more like a fusty old school hall set up for a play about a court case. The Crown Court was purpose built and its purpose was to intimidate.

The defendant, in British law, is innocent until proven guilty. You have to keep reminding yourself of your innocence as you are led into the court room and put in the dock. It's surreal, an overused word, but it's an apt description of UK court proceedings: the judge and counselors in black robes and arcane wigs, the judge's big leather VIP chair behind his elevated bench, the raised sections for the jury, and the enclosed dock where the "innocent" defendants sit, facing the judge, flanked by police officers. The raised witness box where the cast of those present on the day of the crime, swear on the Bible and solemnly profess to tell the truth, the whole truth and nothing but the truth, so help them God. How bizarre it all becomes as you, the accused, sit and watch policemen, policewomen, and Detective Inspectors stand in the witness box, on oath, and openly lie about things they and you know never ever took place, because on that day you were all there together. It is a mind-numbing experience, like a bad dream, only it really is happening.

The judge, Frederick Gibbens, was elderly and prudish looking, completely out of his depth trying to understand everyday life in the rock'n'roll mansion on the hill, the comings and goings of musicians, their crew and hangers on. He could have been hearing a script by Samuel Beckett as he stage managed the proceedings, trying to make sense of it all.

The prosecuting counsel, Mr Alistair Hill, short and rotund in a wide black robe and a tiny wig perched on his round head, was soon nicknamed by us "the pig in the wig", not very original but it relieved the tension. Kris's solicitor, Jeremy Horsefall, was a jolly and upbeat fellow who, when we were out of court, loved to tell us stories about clients he had defended accused of weird sexual peccadilloes. One chap, that stuck in my mind, was apparently turned on by bicycle tubing. Jeremy recommended that Kris hire a heavyweight barrister, Sir Peter Rawlinson, Conservative Member of Parliament for Epsom & Ewell and a former Attorney General. He was tall, handsome and, with presence and gravitas, he outranked everyone else in the court. Like the judge, he also had little idea about the rock'n'roll world and even less, it seemed, about cocaine. We would educate him so well that when Keith Richards was busted later that year, it was to Sir Peter that he turned, for his defence. "Oh, those silly girls."

The main evidence on which the drug squad's case hinged was verbal, what we were supposed to have said in that couple of hours in the bedroom at The Wick as they ransacked the house around us. The only statement they presented that was true was Kris saying, "I take full responsibility," which I knew and they knew was her way of saying, this is my house and whatever you have found here had nothing to do with anyone else. It was never an admission of guilt, just a statement made out of decency to protect a close friend, the honourable way to behave.

However, they then claimed that Kris went on to say: "I thought nobody was unduly worried about what we did in private. I don't use much coke. Just a small amount to have a pleasant time." A complete fabrication, of course.

As was a statement attributed to me. "Now you know why we didn't hear you getting in. We've had a great evening." Another complete fabrication.

No one seemed to realise that cocaine is a stimulant. We were sound asleep, which meant this "statement" of mine would have been preposterous. This would come in handy later.

Ellison read out a second statement I was supposed to have made: "I have committed the terrible crime of enjoying myself in private. I thought society had progressed beyond that."

So here we were: two little air-heads in a big bed saying, "Oops, fair cop guv, we done it." How they had managed to persuade the Crown Prosecution Service to agree to this trial on the basis of these "statements", and a miniscule amount of cocaine dust scrapped from eight different surfaces over three floors of a large house will always be a mystery to me.

We were both women with no previous police records of any kind and the case was so slight, the evidence so flimsy, that their only hope was to besmirch our reputations. So it was that WPC Eleanor McGowan stated falsely on day one that we were naked together in bed, and that when she examined Kris's arms for needle marks, she "didn't tell her to take her clothes off. Both women were naked when they got out of bed... I think."

The tabloids now had a story to titillate their readers. A week of front-page headlines began.

"What Yard saw in Sleeping Beauties' bedroom."

"Girls lay 'almost naked' in giant bed."

"Pop star's wife and a daylight drug raid on two sleeping beauties."

"What the police found in a pop girl's boudoir."

"Pop girl's bedmate."

"'Rude awakening' for the pop girls when drug squad called."

"Sleeping beauties held in drug raid at The Wick."

The fact we were both in our late twenties and therefore 'women' lacked the sexy ring of 'pop girls' but reality was disappearing before our very eyes. Many hours were spent in court discussing our supposed nakedness, in a classic brass bed that started out large, became bigger than king-sized, possibly emperor sized and eventually circular. What was the charge again? Oh yes, possession of 15 milligrams of cocaine between us, which 12 drug squad officers and police had scraped from eight surfaces on three floors of a house. Nonetheless, whether or not we were wearing flimsy panties became far more important than their flimsy evidence, and generated more ludicrous headlines and photo captions.

"We were not naked in bed, says Krissie."

"I was wearing a nightie when drug police burst in."

Audrey Burgon... "She was wearing panties in bed."

"The girl in my bed... by a pop wife.

After the prosecution had laid out their case, which hinged on the police's evidence of our supposed statements, Sir Peter began to whittle away at their evidence by cross examination. Ellison admitted they had expected to find more people there, though he would not say who. He eventually said the names Keith and Anita meant something to him. After Sir Peter pulled some theatrics with a sugar cube, describing the amount as a 277th part of one cube, Ellison admitted that the amount of cocaine was very tiny, only a trace. Detective Sergeant Rodney Pearson told the court they had "been looking for a large quantity of cocaine, which we did not find".

Alistair Hill bullied and badgered Kris for four hours in the witness box. Realizing she was vulnerable and overwhelmed by what was taking place, he tried over and over to trip her up on her evidence. Even though in her frustration to convince him that guilt lay elsewhere, her description of the loose comings and goings of life at The Wick sometimes seemed exaggerated. She brilliantly walked a tight rope to protect Woody and establish her own defence. The house locks had been changed "perhaps a half dozen times, because keys fell into the wrong hands". We had been in bed together because she was nervous of being alone. The bed was "bigger than king-sized, the size of a small room". After four hours he gave up. He had misjudged Kris's inner strength and was left looking like a bully.

Hill spent much less time with me. I described with calm resolve the details of the bust and the "arrest", the way the police behaved during the raid, the fact we were not cautioned, and that their verbal evidence was untruthful. Kris and I were in marked contrast under cross examination. Hill saw no weaknesses in me that day and soon realized my clarity was unhelpful to the prosecution's case. Watching Kris being terrorized by him made me angry and clear-headed.

The headline makers struggled.

"Sleeping Beauty tells of four men around bed."

"My rude awakening at The Wick."

"It's all lies, says Krissie's bedmate. I wore only panties, she says."

"Krissie Wood... she was wearing a nightgown."

Kris' brother, Brian, and Leisal Schiffer, her German cleaner, both supported her assertion that The Wick was a very loose household and no one could be sure who was there at any time or what their motives were. Leisal graphically described how she cleaned the house thoroughly when Mr and Mrs Wood were away "Zen, ze next time I vud go zair the bed vud have been slept in, ashtrays vere full and ze bathrooms were feelthy, feelthy!" It was an unintentional moment of light relief.

"Krissie and the hangers-on. The show-biz spongers."

"Drugs Court told that locks were changed six times."

In his summation, the "pig in the wig" referred to Kris as being like Alice in Wonderland and to me as Stonewall Jackson. If he wrote that in his notes for future reference he would live to regret it, as events further unfolded. He claimed we were found by the drug squad in an emperor-sized bed, with traces of drugs around us, and Krissie reacted like Alice. "It's very rude of him to come and spoil our fun."

"'Fairy-tale' of the Sleeping Beauties."

"Drug raid Krissie 'was like Alice in Wonderland'."

In his summing up, Sir Peter described the trial as, "Sad and sickening. Sad because two women of perfectly good character have been pilloried, and because of the small amounts of drugs that were found. Sickening because of slurs and innuendoes, which had no right to be introduced. What was the point in mentioning the alleged nakedness of the two girls, or describing the bed as emperor sized."

The trial lasted for six days, excluding the weekend. On the last day the jury were sent out with the direction from Judge Frederick Gibbens, that either we were both lying or the police were all lying. "If the police are lying then they should all lose their jobs," he directed them. This was of no use in helping them to make an objective decision, knowing that four or five police officers could forfeit their livelihoods and reputations. Judge Gibbens was frustrated. Someone had been taking drugs at The Wick. Someone was responsible. The law had been broken. The jury had listened for six days to a whole lot of supposed statements and innuendo but very little actual evidence. I didn't envy them their job and I wondered how long they would take to unpick fact from fiction.

Sir Peter told us that the longer the jury was out, the greater the chance that we would be found not guilty. There was plenty of analysing of what had been said and how it looked to Sir Peter and my solicitor, Gibson Grenfell, who had taken a secondary role at the side of his more senior colleague. However, they were increasingly optimistic as the hours ticked by.

After about three hours we were called back into court and the jury was recalled and asked if they had come to a verdict. They had not. Judge Gibbens seemed very tense. He must have thought things were going our way, and it seemed obvious to me that he wanted us to be found guilty. Someone must be held responsible. He sent the jury back out and told them he would accept a majority verdict. I wondered what the split was. There were 11 men and one women. They had been introduced to a world that must have seemed like total fiction, then asked to decide who was telling the truth. That was the crux of this case.

Less than an hour later Judge Gibbens had had enough. He recalled the jury. They had reached a verdict on the cannabis in the handbag. Krissie was not guilty of that, but they were still undecided about the cocaine. To the utter astonishment of Sir Peter and all of us, he dismissed the jury and ordered a re-trial. Sir Peter confronted him. "This has been before the court for six days, and you appreciate the strain on these two women. Would your honour ask the jury to reach a verdict to see if this can be disposed of, so we can know the result by the end of the day?"

It was clear to me that Judge Gibbens did not want a 'not guilty' verdict. We were young and pretty and seemed to be having fun. Given his age and position in life, fun was not something of which he had much experience, let alone approved of. Why should we leave his courtroom scot free? What were things coming to? Young people living in mansions, once the reserve of the upper classes, and leading lives of excess. What did it matter who was responsible? We had been there on the day.

He still had the power to turn this around. He could wash his hands of it, send us to another judge, make life uncomfortable for us. He told Sir Peter, "If they have not reached a verdict by now I do not think they will. In those circumstances I discharge the jury. It is the proper course." This was an outcome that had never been discussed.

"'Two in a bed' girls face drug retrial."

"Krissie retrial agony."

"New trial for the Sleeping Beauties."

Christmas was just two weeks away. It would be nearly Easter before we would be in court again, a whole year since the bust.

chapter 47
Old Macdonald's Snorting Habits

The Crown Prosecution Service decides whether or not to pursue a case to a retrial. If they feel that the expense to the public outweighs the benefits, they can choose to offer no evidence and we could have been cleared. With the reputations of half a dozen members of the elite of the British Drug Squad at stake, that consideration was no doubt substantially more important than the financial aspects. We would be going back to court again, the cost so far to the British taxpayer was the original surveillance and the raid of The Wick, the three visits to Richmond Magistrates Court, six days in Kingston Crown Court and all the attendant expenses and fees.

For the next four months, I lived day to day in a kind of stupefied limbo. I needed to get a job, but having not been in regular employment since January 1968, when I was a house model at Laura Lee Frocks, my CV was sparse. How I was going to include five years as company secretary to Alvin Lee Ltd., an honorary tax position, I had not even considered. Also, in a job interview I could hardly mention that I needed a week off in April 1976 to defend myself in a notorious tabloid headline-grabbing court case involving a Class A drug and my alleged lesbian lover.

Greg was still in the UK and a great support and diversion, so it was not all doom and gloom, but I couldn't seem to do any forward planning. I was happy to get high, surrender myself to Greg and enjoy my days. It was winter in the UK, the days were short and often cold and wet, a shock to his Californian metabolism. We were in hibernation, mostly in the "siege flat", waiting for the odd sunny day when Greg and gang could throw frisbees in Hyde Park. This involved a high level of skill. Gently throwing a frisbee disc around a group, thirty feet at a time, doesn't scratch the surface of its potential. Frisbee ballet, on the other hand, means knowing what strength to use to throw long distances and heights, coupled with the agility needed to run and catch impossible throws. It wasn't a competitive, gladiatorial sport for glory and trophies – it was stoned camaraderie, joyful, exhilarating fun. I was mostly a spectator.

Somedays we would go back to my flat for music and wine, and a visitor might arrive with a little smoke or cocaine. I was a cocaine virgin. No one pressed me and not partaking left more for everyone else. My host had only one strict rule: no heroin in the house. One night, musing on the ridiculousness of going back to court to answer for something I still had not even tried, I decided to try coke and find out what it did. The knowledge would prove invaluable in court.

In a social environment, cocaine is chopped up with a small razor blade, and spread into narrow lines. Using a short plastic straw (cut from a long one) or more often, a rolled-up banknote held under a nostril, it is inhaled like a hoover moving along the line. Once snorted, it is absorbed by the blood stream. The first, fast physical effect is that the nose, and the upper gums go numb. There is a chemical smell and taste to coke and because it has gone up the nose, some of it will find its way into your throat. Since cocaine is usually taken with alcohol, which reduces your sense of smell and taste, it's not as physically distasteful as it sounds.

Sometimes, in wealthy settings, coke may be presented already chopped, in a small phial and offered as a treat from a tiny, elegantly designed silver spoon, or even a specially grown fingernail. An affectation of the day was to grow a very long nail on the pinky finger which, loaded with coke, could be balanced under the nostril. Much more intimate than passing around a mirror, man to woman, this could be part of seductive foreplay, involving physical closeness and eye contact.

I was unimpressed by coke. It reminded me most of amphetamine, accelerated heartbeat and speeding brain, but it didn't make me giggle or feel euphoric in the way that a good smoke would. Whereas alcohol or a smoke would make you appear stoned to someone else, coke is undetectable in that way. It also made it possible to drink a great deal more and not appear drunk. In fact, the two drugs seemed to go hand in hand. It certainly gave people more confidence, increasing the volume of conversation and the general energy in a room.

Far from making me confident, coke made me withdraw when people spoke to me. Black & white ink drawings I did on cocaine are very tight and intense. Luckily for me I had very little money otherwise I might have wound up getting more involved in a drug habit. Cocaine is certainly delusional. My situation in life was pretty miserable but sometimes I felt it was a very glamorous life I was sharing with a cast of musicians and movie stars. Alvin had no taste for parties but I was curious about the glitzy London life. It was by chance not design that I had fallen in with this crowd. I met people I liked and would have liked to get to know better, but that is not how it was. Everything was fleeting, superficial, distracting, fun yes, but like the sun glittering on the surface of the pool we were floating together without diving into the depths.

Perhaps it was the unresolved cloud of the bust that kept me more down-to-earth. Certain events over the winter of 1975 would alter the tone of the second court case, scheduled for April 1976. On January 7, Finn, Kris' father, died suddenly from a heart attack. Kris was close to her parents Pat and Finn, and he involved himself with the first trial, making observations and suggestions. It was more than an emotional loss for Kris who felt the trial had contributed to his death. Nevertheless, she was totally reconciled with Woody and to everyone's delight she discovered she was pregnant not long before the trial. Those events, the death of her father, the reconciliation with Woody and her pregnancy gave Kris more strength and determination than she had previously shown.

My mother had been a disapproving voice in my life since my early teens and a favourite line of derision had been, "You'll end up in *The News Of The World*", a comment she first made about my mature dress when I was 13 or 14 years old. She was a great worrier and when the bust happened I hadn't told her about it or about the trial. I must have been hoping we wouldn't become tabloid fodder. After the barrage of press outside The Wick on day one, my brother Harold realized it would be highly visible in the papers and decided to call her with the news. She took a train to London and, when I left the court that evening, there she was. I wasn't pleased but realised she needed to be told before she saw the headlines. After all, her name was Audrey Burgon and, even though no one thought she was the "pop girl's bedmate", her neighbours might spot that she shared the same name. Kris and my mothers were now both widowed. They stayed together in the Richmond Hill Hotel for the duration of the second trial, and proved a great support to each other.

At the first trial, the case was heard in Kingston Crown Court's smaller secondary courtroom, but for the second trial we found ourselves in the main room. This really was even more intimidating, with plenty of highly polished woodwork and pseudo grandeur. I vividly remember looking around at the judge, the clerks, the barristers and the police and thinking that without us, the hapless defendants, these people, some very highly paid, would have been without a job. How bizarre to create these situations that allow some to prosper at the cost of others. At no time did I feel like a criminal on any level. The events that had led me to this place seemed as arbitrary, as the throw of a dice.

Apart from a different judge, all of the same characters were back. Facing us now was Roger Titheridge QC, much younger than the previous judge, with an intelligent, open face. I instantly felt we would receive a less biased hearing. Having already been through this whole case once, I felt calm and clear-headed and able to look more objectively at the prosecution's case. I had trusted that Kris's highly respected counsel, Sir Peter Rawlinson and my young, bright barrister, Gibson Grenfell, were clever and wise defenders, but I was not over impressed with the defense they produced.

It seemed that none of them, the judge, barristers or indeed the drug squad, had much idea about the effects of cocaine. However, my recent first-hand experience revealed gaping holes in the prosecution's case. It was accepted by the police, from our previous trial, that we had not arrived at The Wick until 2.30 am. Their case rested on the notion that we had used coke in eight different places around the house and studio, from where they had managed to scrape 15 milligrams of residue. As I now knew, coke is a stimulant and after snorting our way all around The Wick for a few hours it was highly unlikely we'd have been sleeping at 6.30 when the raid took place. It simply did not add up.

From my position in the dock, I could watch the back of the witness box as the parade of drug squad officers followed each other to give their evidence. I saw that each one leaving passed a small, black flip-over notebook to the next one going on the stand and that all of them were reading from the same notebook. At the next break I mentioned the notebook to Sir Peter and he questioned the next officer about it. He told the court that it was common practice for them to sit in the canteen after a raid and, together, write a single account of what had taken place, along with the verbal exchanges, which they would then all refer to. The judge looked quite surprised by this revelation and I am sure it also surprised the jury. What sort of evidence is it when you have three people all reading from the same script? Their case had not developed. No new evidence was presented. Effectively it all rested on the verbal statements and the scant trace of powder clinging to the tiny plastic bag.

Even the tabloids were no longer very interested. We were relegated to a few column inches in the inside pages, their headlines bland or even favouring us. This had to be a good sign.

"Pop wife Krissie on trial again."

"Drug raid evidence 'a fiasco'."

The "pig in the wig", Alistair Hill, had revised his notes from the first trial and worked out a strategy. Kris, aka Alice in Wonderland, would have the kid glove treatment. He would hope to trip her up by being gentle with her, ambush her with kindness. Myself, aka Stonewall Jackson, would have the full-frontal barrage this time, all guns blazing, relentlessly wearing down my strong resolve. One way or another he would beat us this time. He would prove this case was not a waste of taxpayer's money.

Poor little piggy. To his astonishment, Kris had become an Amazon. The spirits of her dead father and her unborn child shone through her in the dock. She vehemently denied the verbal evidence. Swearing oath after oath "on my dead father and my unborn child, that I am innocent, I never said those things, the police are lying." Clarity and energy permeated every cell of her being. The piggy snorted and turned redder and redder, just as he had in the kitchen from the cook's pepper in *Alice In Wonderland*. Get her off of the stand, quick as you can, his face said. His case crumbled like dried-out madeira cake.

Ah, but he had one last chance. He could use his increasing anger to lay into me. He was hard, mean, his questions short, staccato, to the point, shot out like a machine gun in rapid bursts, demanding answers to the obvious. We were there, the cocaine was there, someone was guilty of having a good time, a very good time. Well, what did I have to say?

It was at that moment that something happened to me. Perhaps it was an accumulation of all the misery and unhappiness of the last three years. I started to cry. I simply broke down and wept.

"I don't understand why this is happening to me," I cried. "I am not guilty of saying these things, of doing these things. Why am I being persecuted and why are all these lies being told? I don't understand why this is happening to me."

The court was still. All eyes were on me. The "pig in the wig" was dumbstruck. A weeping woman pleading innocence was his worst nightmare, I imagine.

"No more questions."

He thought Kris a pussy cat and me a tiger but we had reversed our roles. Without any discussion or forethought, we had defeated his tactics and left him scrabbling for land, adrift in his murky, lie-infested backwater, drowning in front of the whole court. Walking back to the dock, I was dumbstruck. Why had I cried? I hadn't intended to and it wasn't a charade. I truly had had enough. I had repeated the truth over and over and listened to the police tell lie after lie. I could no longer make any sense of it. The clerk of the court handed me a note from Gibson Grenfell. "Very well done," he had written. "That was brilliant."

"Drug-case pop wife is having a baby. She and Ronnie mend marriage."

"The Legal break-in. Why police kicked down Krissie's door."

"Drugs charge Krissie is expecting a baby."

After giving his evidence on day one, Det. Sgt. Ellison had come to the court every day, sitting very prominently to our right, listening intently, knowing if it went our way he would have a lot of explaining to do. I could see him clearly. Every day his face became more florid. He seemed to be developing boils. He was extremely stressed.

The summing up by the prosecution was almost perfunctory. There were no allusions to Kris's fairy tales this time. Piggy knew his case hung only on police statements, which in turn hung on our characters. Unable to penetrate either of our defenses, nor find proof of our bad characters, Alistair Hill must have known it was a long shot.

I had explained to Sir Peter that cocaine is a stimulant and that if we had been taking it all around the house in the manner their case suggested, we would have been wide awake when they kicked in the doors. He understood this was a valuable piece of the jigsaw and concocted a brilliant scenario in his summing up.

The chorus to 'Old MacDonald Had A Farm' was his blueprint, the climax of his theatrics. Addressing the jury, he asked them to picture the scene that the drug squad were suggesting. Kris and I had arrived late at the Wick, where first, after making a hot milky drink, we had taken a mirror, some straws and put out some cocaine and both taken a sniff. Next, we had gone to the studio where we had produced several mirrors, more straws and taken more sniffs. Moving up to the lounge, we used another mirror and more straws for more sniffs. The music room, mirror, straws, sniffs, the bedroom, mirror, straws, sniff... "with a sniff sniff here and a sniff sniff there, with a sniff sniff here and a sniff sniff there." There was laughter in court.

"Your honour, cocaine is a stimulant. These ladies are supposed to have sniffed their way around eight different places in the house and a couple of hours later, when this raid took place, they were sound asleep." His voice was incredulous. He was brilliant, a tour de force of oratory.

The judge, Roger Titheridge, looked deeply unhappy to have been spending his time, in effect, perpetuating a charade to save face for the drug squad's ineptitude. "Someone has lied to the court," he told the jury. "Either the two women charged were lying or the detectives, who gave evidence against them, were lying. If you believe the defendants' claim, then it follows, as night follows day, the police witnesses are lying."

The jury was out for four hours and 20 minutes. Sir Peter told me, "If any of the jury look at you when they come back in, the verdict will be not guilty."

As they filed in to take their seats, several of them looked at us. One gave me a small smile.

"Not Guilty!"

Mr Titheridge did not award costs to Kris. In effect he was fining whoever had been sloppy in leaving all this paraphernalia around The Wick, £15,000. As I had no money, my costs were met by legal aid.

"Now I just want to go and have a nice baby. Cleared Krissie is hoping for a girl."

"I am so happy, says cleared pop wife Krissie."

"Stone's wife cleared with £15,000 bill."

"Star's wife goes free."

"I am terribly relieved," said Audrey Burgon.

It was true. In fact, I had spoken the truth throughout the whole affair, from the day of the bust to the final day in court. I had never had to tell a lie.

chapter 48
And After All That

I began writing this memoir over Christmas of 2008 in Marfa, Texas,
a very special art town in the Chihuahua desert where I rented a small house
for a month. Primarily I wanted to see Donald Judd's art foundation and
installations. With no television or distractions, I started to write longhand,
in a large notebook, about my childhood, and to map out the chapters and
main events of my life up until the late seventies. More recently I revised
all the chapters written over the proceeding dozen years. The revision was
completed during the Coronavirus lockdown of spring 2021 when, yet
again, I was alone with no television and only minor distractions.

At times, the juxtaposition of writing about the most wonderful
times and events, and experiencing this pandemic, proved emotionally
overwhelming. It was without doubt the most dreadful global event of my
75 years of life. No doubt the intense focus of revision helped me to cope
with the lockdown, and provided the opportunity to complete this work.
There is no way to understand the timing of such things. Now I need to
make some conclusions about the events you have read.

Revisiting my early life brought unexpected revelations and realisations.
As such, I would encourage everyone to consider a similar enterprise after
the age of 50. If you have children, grandchildren, nieces, nephews, for them
to be able to read a first-hand account, not only your life but also the times
through which you lived, do it for them. What a gift such an account from a
grandparent, elder relative, can be – a real lived journey.

Nowadays, my life sits quietly in my heart and mind. The connections
with family, friends, lovers, people and society are understood more
clearly, more calmly. Nevertheless, my relationship and experiences with
Alvin Lee remain at the core and bedrock of my life and understanding
of the world. My mature attitudes, values, beliefs and outlook all stem

from the life we lived together and the times in which we lived. All of it, whether good or bad.

2019 was the 50th Anniversary of Woodstock and I was fortunate to be invited to attend a London cinema screening of the *Woodstock* movie released in 1970. To relive the music, the audience, the locals in upstate New York, on the big screen reminded me of all the truthful energy of those days, when we really believed we would change the world.

Afterwards I stayed on to answer questions from the appreciative audience. It was heartwarming to experience, and to again realise, that the magical power and fascination with the sixties has not gone away.
No era since has progressed tolerance, inclusivity and cultural connection so well. It is now embedded in Western culture. It will not fade away because subsequent generations enjoy the music and the stories. Peace and Love is perennial. There is no better philosophy. I am humbled to have been a small part of those times.

Early research found me reading a number of musical memoirs from people of my sixties' generation, some I knew personally, many I admired. Mostly, it was their psychedelic adventures that attracted my curiosity but, to my regret, they were often absent, brushed over, disavowed. Nevertheless, these were the consciousness expanding experiences that triggered the cultural awakening and musical, creative explorations that became the sixties.

To a large extent, marijuana in the USA and cannabis in the UK and Europe replaced alcohol for a whole generation. The sense of mellow, connected community enjoyed by slowing down to savour music was central. We learned to listen deeply, sharing time together, and musicians responded with incredibly innovative records that explored not only their musical gifts and connections but also the developing studio technologies with a freedom never heard before. Live musical events revealed us to each other, musicians to audiences and vice-a-versa, travelling to higher realms of affinity.

I was indeed fortunate to find myself with Alvin in the midst of this. We embraced it all with wonder and some caution. We were people loving life and wanting to survive and thrive, not wind up as rock'n'roll casualties as many did. This was never discussed but it was understood. We were rock'n'roll adventurers, travelling a path seemingly written for us, discovering threads to follow to weave a tapestry of our own lives. Drugs were a central part of our journey. In 2021 it feels that these truths need bringing into the open, acknowledged and discussed.

Over the years we became very gentle and open with each other. Meeting so young, while still living at home with parents, all the journeys and, especially, the psychedelics helped us to be trusting and vulnerable. Together we grew stronger as people through our shared unfolding life.

The events of the last few years, the increasing fame and all that was demanded of Alvin, was further intensified with the sudden windfall from the sale of Robin Hood Barn. Hook End wasn't desired, though a personal professional studio was a pipedream possibly somewhere down the line. Yet there it was, presented in such a way that it was impossible to refuse. We were holding tightly to the thread, leading us like kite flyers into a hurricane we hadn't seen whirling in the distance. Life had been so good to us. We trusted it would continue.

It was such a heady mix that we had completely forgotten that the goal of a move to the country was to find a peaceful, private home to balance out the extremes of life on the road. All the pieces and players fell neatly into place, as did the seemingly impossible task of building the studio. The stage was set, the house renovated so successfully that people arrived and stayed. Initially the music flowed and laughter, fun, community warmth, celebration followed. Gradually *On The Road to Freedom* evolved from something magical, albeit intense and demanding and fueled with cocaine, the emerging drug of the day. It was the very worst drug for loving connection, creating euphoria, invulnerability, emotional coldness. Though aware it had entered the rock'n'roll world, I instinctively knew it was the wrong drug for Alvin and for musical freedom.

It never occurred to me that with so many musicians visiting it was inevitable that he would be seduced. He kept it hidden from me in the studio, while all my energies were focused on the house renovation and running the household. A peaceful, private home in the countryside became a nightmare I couldn't understand. My role, while indispensable, was indistinct and overwhelmingly over my head. I was scrambling, bobbing on the surface, barely breathing, holding on in a tsunami, trying to stay afloat and find the shore. Finally running away seemed like sanity. Was it an act of total selfishness or drastic survival?

When I came back and sat with Alvin to explain what I was doing, that I was leaving, he told me I was "abandoning a sinking ship". It seemed so far from what was happening with the studio, the house, the staff, the album completed, the publicity machine geared up and already in action. He must also have felt in over his head yet he had seemed clear and focused, dismissing my cries for help. It seemed he abandoned me emotionally and my actions felt impossible to undo. I believe it saved my soul.

The cocaine court case with Krissie forced me to reach into the depths of my being to discover my strength and resilience. For Kris, it was far more difficult since she was publicly known. Despite our innocent verdict, she would carry it as more of a burden. I could abandon my temporary role as Audrey Burgon when the trial ended, resume life as Loraine Burgon and tuck the whole experience away for four decades. Krissie would always be Krissie Wood.

Writing this memoir has shown me how drugs were a central part of my young life. They excited me, transformed me, freed me. No one can say they were peripheral to those times, whatever their views about their use. The sixties wouldn't have produced the cultural shifts, the music, arts, ecological and political movements without those instruments of perception. Yet the role of cocaine, from the seventies, its reshaping of the times, first among the cultural shape shifters and now, 40 years later, fully into western culture, is hardly discussed.

Cocaine is grown and manufactured in South America, specifically Columbia, Peru and Bolivia, where its use is very low. Its global use is in the affluent Western cultures.

Cocaine's use in the West is hidden and respectable. Dinner parties in affluent middle-class homes often end with cocaine offered with coffee. Its use is not restricted to the young club scene. It is used by politicians and city bankers. Like amphetamine, it is a stimulant that doesn't produce outward behaviour changes, unlike alcohol or cannabis. You can work harder for longer, which makes it compelling to ambitious city high flyers.

It releases dopamine in the brain and inhibits its recycling, which causes a build up, hence the euphoria, energy, confidence, feelings of physical strength and talkativeness. The effect is short lived and users quickly want more. Long-term use is damaging to the dopamine balance in the brain, with a downside for mental health. Can we blame the last banking crisis, and the reckless behaviour that led to sub-prime mortgages and other financial disasters, on cocaine use in the city?

Obviously, I am not against drug use. I have always felt it is a personal decision. However, drugs that can lead to reckless behaviour by those in charge of global finance and politics. How would we control this? If people go to work stoned on cannabis or drunk on alcohol, it would be noticeable and dealt with. A drug that gives you more confidence and makes you work harder sounds like an ideal drug for any boss or institution to ignore or even encourage.

In my research for these chapters I Googled certain legal figures. The most surprising discovery was Det. Sgt. Ellison who, after retiring from the drug squad but, more surprisingly, while he was still working, spoke out in favour of legalizing drugs. This was not because he wanted to advocate drug use – he was still opposed to that – but for well-evaluated reasons based on his many years of experience. He was primarily concerned about how the international drug trade was controlled by gangsters who are motivated by profit and indifferent to the quality of drugs they sell, mostly to young people. Articles and a WiKi page can be found under the name Eddie Ellison that include the quote below on the subject of drug policy, made while he held the position of Detective Chief Inspector in operational command of the Drug Squad. There is also a link to his website. Eddie Ellison died from cancer in January 2007, and was a vocal International campaigner for the legalisation, research and control of all drugs until his passing.

"Each and every police officer has their own ranking of the relative seriousness of all criminal offences that is often based on their background experiences. However hard they try, their attitudes and behaviour are often affected by that assessment. I have never, and can never, see the drug user as a 'criminal'. I see them as, among other descriptions, a rebellious youth, a risk-taking idiot, a seeker of relief, a lobbyist for independent thought and freedom, someone in need of guidance and help or a very real exasperation to parents and friends. But in as much as the drug use is concerned, not a criminal and therefore the criminal law cannot be the appropriate weapon to counter or deter a choice of use."

The USA and the UK top the list for global cocaine use. The illegal cocaine trade is worth over $150 billion annually. It is the highest grossing Class A drug. With a sense of irony, I am closing this memoir with a list from Detective Inspector Eddie Ellison's own writings, the guarantees that he stated would occur with the continued prohibition of drugs. Like him, I would never advocate drug use. It's a very personal choice and decision. Also like him, however, I advocate legalisation, sane debate and an attempt to understand all aspects of drug use both legal and illegal. Phenomenal amounts of tax money are used in the war on drugs that would be better spent in education, research and mental health.

Edward Ellison. These are the **guarantees** of continued prohibition.

Guaranteed to maintain a high crime rate for the rest of society.

Guaranteed to present a supply monopoly to the criminal organisations with high levels of illegal profits.

Guaranteed to ensure that users of the more minor drugs continue to maintain contact with that criminal supply chain and the accompanying ease of moving to more dangerous drugs.

Guaranteed to ensure that users will continue to overdose and sometimes die because of a lack of testing or legal, clean supply.

Guaranteed to prevent honest, open debate and education.

Guaranteed to criminalise individuals who choose to commit acts in private at no threat to others, with a loss of their future individual contribution to society.

Guaranteed to bring other laws into disrepute through the illogicality and mass distain of drug prohibition.

Guaranteed to alienate youth from the policing service.

Guaranteed to waste enormous sums of public monies that could be much better utilised in health support and education.

APPENDIX
Specifications of Space Studio, Hook End Manor

Here is my brother Harold Burgon's account of the technical specifications and building of Space Studios at Hook End Manor.

"After Alvin had bought Hook End Manor, from the sale of The Barn, he decided to put a professional recording studio in the large cattle-barn adjacent to the main house. The barn was double gabled with a raised hayloft at the end nearest the house, the far end was the tradesmen's entrance drive-in.

"So a plan was hatched to use the raised hay loft as the control room, looking down on the main barn-floor which would become the main studio recording space. Under the raised control room we added a vocal booth and tape store. At the time TYA's live sound engineer, Andy Jaworski, had a 16 channel live mixer and so the decision was reached to get a recording mixer with at least that number of microphone channels. Up to this point TYA had recorded most of their recent albums at Olympic Studios in Barnes, which had a mixing console designed and built by Dick Swettenham.

"So we went to his company, Helios Electronics, to discuss the project and Dick came up with a design for a wrap-around mixing desk with 8 group busses, a 16 track monitor mixer and 18 microphone/line inputs. We had figured that we needed 16 mic channels and Dick suggested adding two more mic channels so we could use live sounds during 16 track mix-down. The console also had 2 stereo echo returns, two stereo headphone sends and a 4-band parametric EQ with switchable high-pass filters on all channels.

"Hook End is close to Reading where an associate of Dick's, Mike Bevell, had his own custom electronics company, Audio Design And Recording Ltd., specialising in professional audio interfaces. We bought 4 compressor limiter/ expander units and two 'Vocal Stresser' channel-strips, all of which Helios mounted into the console.

"The master tape recorders were Studer A80 MkII 2 inch 16 track and 1/4 inch stereo machines bought from the importers Bauch Ltd in Borehamwood. There we met Werner Wal, their chief technician who helped us with maintenance and recording expertise including providing Studer remote transport control panels, which were mounted into the console.

"Alvin already had 2 Revox A77 1/4 inch tape machines from his Robin Hood Barn home-studio set-up, so we used these for tape copying and by adding vari-speed, for tape echo and delay. We also bought a 3rd. Revox A77 with a specially modified capstan motor that could record at 70 inches per second for ADT and flanging effect. All three machines had remote transport controllers and vari-speed pots built into the Helios console. We also fitted the Studer tape machines with Dolby noise-reduction via a Dolby M16 and two Dolby A channels for the stereo machine.

"Hook End has several large wood-panelled rooms and the main hallway, so we decided to fit a remote microphone panel in the centre of the house and also brought the line-out signals from the domestic hifi's and TV sets in the house back to the console's patchbay. Dick designed a remote box that had a PPM meter, gain pot and fader that could balance a microphone's gain directly to the tape machine's inputs, alongside a Studer A80 remote transport controller and tape counter. In this way, one person could record or dub either in the studio or any part of the house, without the need of any assistance.

"For main monitoring we had a pair of Tannoy 15" 'Reds' in Lockwood cabinets and a pair of JBL 4320's with a 15" driver, a 'fish fryer' mid-range horn and 075 tweeter in each. The Tannoys were powered by a Crown DC300 stereo amplifier and the JBLs had a Harmon-Kardon 'Citation' power amplifier. The JBLs and their amp Alvin bought in New York at the end of a tour and shipped back with the stage-gear. Nearfield monitors were a pair of AKG Cubes powered by a Quad 303 power amp.

"From Bauch we bought 2 Neumann U87's and two U47 microphones. We got a further 6 AKG 451's and two AKG D12 microphones. We also bought an EMT 140 stereo reverb plate, which we housed in the store-room behind the control room. There were also several Shure and Sennheiser mics that were part of Andy's PA system. Headphones were AKG K141's and Beyer DT100's powered by Quad 303 amplifiers. We also had a Technics SL1210 record deck and Nakamichi 3 head cassette recorder in the control room.

"Stanley Brinsmead of Brinsmead Pianos in Camden, London restored an 1880's Steinway 7 foot grand piano for the studio. Alvin also bought a Hammond B3 Organ and Leslie 144 valve rotary speaker with an auxiliary guitar-line input. Other keyboards included a Wurlitzer electric piano, a Fender Rhodes suitcase 88 piano, a Hohner Clavinet D6 and an ARP 2600 synth."

ACKNOWLEDGEMENTS

This memoir, which I began writing in 2009,
took 14 years to complete. There were no ghostwriters,
except for the ghosts of memories that live within me.
I am grateful to everyone I have written about,
whose paths I crossed, which made the tapestry we
wove together into a story. Thank you all.

This text grew to 200,000 words until 2022 when
Chris Charlesworth became part of the story. An expert
editor, with over 40 years of experience in music journalism,
Chris wrestled the text down to less than 150,000 words
and helped it flow to a fine rhythm.

Special thanks to my friend Richard Evans, whom I knew
in my teens in Nottingham, who reconnected with me
a decade ago on Facebook, and connected me to
Chris Charlesworth his Facebook friend.

Ingram Content Group UK Ltd.
Milton Keynes UK
UKHW050829170723
425264UK00003B/5